Emotionally Healthy Spirituality

Day by Day

Emotionally Healthy Spirituality

Day by Day

A 40-DAY JOURNEY *with the* DAILY OFFICE

Previously published as *The Daily Office*

Peter Scazzero

ZONDERVAN®

ZONDERVAN

Emotionally Healthy Spirituality Day by Day

Previously published as *The Daily Office*

Requests for information should be addressed to:
Zondervan, *3900 Sparks Dr. SE, Grand Rapids, Michigan 49546*

Zondervan titles may be purchased in bulk for educational, business, fundraising, or sales promotional use. For information, please email SpecialMarkets@Zondervan.com.

ISBN 978-0-310-35166-5 (softcover)
ISBN 978-0-310-34108-6 (ebook)

Author is represented by The Christopher Ferebee Agency, www.christopherferebee.com.

Cover design: AbneyRanville
Cover image: ©jgroup / iStockphoto®
Interior design: Katherine Lloyd, The DESK
Interior illustration: © iconeer / iStock®

Printed in the United States of America

21 PC/LSCH 21

Contents

Acknowledgments

I want to thank Geri, my wife, my best friend, and my favorite companion in "The Journey." She has spent countless hours prayerfully pondering and experimenting with these Daily Offices in a variety of contexts. Her work crafting thoughtful questions is meant to touch the soul and lead us to a personal experience of God. What a gift!

Thank you.

An Invitation to Loving Union

Most Christians today are struggling spiritually, especially when it comes to spending time with God. You may be one of them. If so, it might help you to know that the struggle is real, and that you are far from alone.

Throughout more than thirty years of being a pastor, I've encountered this struggle in virtually every person and in every corner of the church—from people in our own international congregation in Queens, New York, to Christian leaders in a variety of settings and denominations throughout the world. If you asked me to summarize what I've observed about the spiritual condition of believers today, here is what I'd say. We are ...

- feeling stuck in our spiritual journey with Christ;
- living off of other people's spirituality;
- scattered, fragmented, and uncentered;
- tired—physically, spiritually, and emotionally;
- existing with only a one-inch-deep spirituality;
- praying and communing with God very little;
- busy and not very intentional in pursuing Jesus;
- struggling to stop our "life on the run."

The bottom line? Too many of us have a relationship with Jesus that is seriously underdeveloped. We talk *to* God, or even perhaps *at* God, but don't actually listen to him very much. And that is nothing less than a global spiritual crisis—especially when we consider that God intends for his love to reach the world through us!

The outlook may seem bleak. But what if I told you that, while the problem is real and pervasive, it is far from a lost cause? There *is* a way to live a relaxed, unhurried, contented life in Jesus amidst the pressures and difficulties of life. There *is* a way to mature into spiritual adulthood anchored in the love of God. There *is* a way to remain thoughtful when triggered in conversations and listen for God's voice. There *is* a way to surrender to God's love and will consistently—even when it is difficult. There *is* a way to give our lives in service to others without becoming chronically exhausted.

How? The answer lies in intentionally rearranging our days to integrate the Christian practice of being still and silent in God's presence.

AN ANCIENT AND REVOLUTIONARY SPIRITUAL DISCIPLINE

The purpose of this book is to introduce you to this spiritual discipline that is both ancient and revolutionary. It's called the "Daily Office."[1] The Daily Office provides a structured way of spending time with God each day, but it differs from what we tend to think of as "quiet time" or "devotions." Quiet time and devotions normally take place once a day, usually in the morning, and focus on "getting filled up" for the day or on interceding for the needs of others. The Daily Office takes place at least twice a day, and it is not so much about turning to God to *get* something as it is turning to God to simply *be with* him.

The goal of the Daily Office is to pay attention to God throughout the entire day and in the midst of our activities. This is the great challenge for all of us. The enormous pressure of the world and our own stubborn self-will make it extraordinarily difficult to sustain any consistent awareness of God's presence. But it is far from impossible.

So why is it called the "Daily Office"? The word *office* comes from the Latin word *opus*, or "work." For the early church, the Daily Office—praying at fixed times throughout the day—was always the first "work of God" to be done. Nothing was to interfere with that priority.

But this practice of fixed-hour prayer is one that actually long predates the early church. Three thousand years ago, King David practiced set times of prayer seven times a day (Psalm 119:164). The prophet Daniel prayed three times a day (Daniel 6:10). Devout Jews in Jesus' time prayed at morning, afternoon, and evening. Such set times of prayer were one of the Israelites' great spiritual and cultural treasures, a practical way to keep their lives centered on loving God at all times. Even after the resurrection, Jesus' disciples continued to pray at certain hours of the day (Acts 3:1; 10:2–23).

It was about AD 525 when a monk named Benedict created a formal structure for these prayer times that he anchored in eight Daily Offices (including one for monks in the middle of the night). Prayer was the framework for the day, and everything else in their lives was ordered around it. Benedict wrote: "On hearing the signal for an hour of the divine office, the monk will immediately set aside what he has in hand and go with utmost speed. Indeed, nothing is to be preferred to the Work of God [the Daily Office]."[2]

All of these people—from the ancient Israelites to first-century disciples and early Christian leaders like Benedict—realized that stopping to be with God, by means of the Daily Office, was the key to creating a continual and easy familiarity with God's presence. And having practiced the Daily Office for over fourteen years, I can affirm it has done that for me. Routinely setting aside small units of time for morning, midday, and evening prayer infuses the activities of my day with a deep awareness of the sacred—of God. In those moments, I remember that all time is God's time. There is no division between the sacred and the secular.

HOW TO USE THIS BOOK

Emotionally Healthy Spirituality Day by Day provides a flexible structure for your time with God. My hope is that you will adapt it to the unique needs and demands of this season in your life. God has built each of us differently. What works for one person will not necessarily work for another, and what worked for you at one time in the past may no longer work for you now. Allow grace—not legalism—to be the foundation for your practice.

The book includes material to guide you through a forty-day journey of praying the Daily Office. I've collected the days into eight weekly themes, with each theme based on a chapter from *The Emotionally Healthy Spirituality* book and *The Emotionally Healthy Spirituality Course* (which also includes a DVD and workbook) and provide a means to stay deeply connected to Jesus, who reminds us: "Apart from me you can do nothing" (John 15:56). On the last page of the devotional you will find a checklist to keep you on track as you move through the course. Fill it out along the way and, when completed, go to emotionallyhealthy.org to receive your certificate of completion.

There are two Offices per day—one for morning or midday, and the other for midday or evening. You may, for example, do one in the morning and the other at midday, or one at midday and the other in the evening before you go to bed. You choose the length of time for your Offices. The key, however, is to keep your focus on attending to God, not the number of minutes you spend with God. Pausing to be with God might last anywhere from two to twenty to forty-five minutes. My wife, Geri, and I choose to have longer times with God in the mornings and then shorter ones at midday and in the evenings. It is up to you.

Each Office contains five elements: Silence and Stillness, Scripture, a Devotional Reading, a Question to Consider, and Prayer.

1. Silence and Stillness. This is the foundation of a Daily Office. We stop our activity and turn our attention to the Living God. We heed the words of the psalmist to, "Be still before the LORD and wait patiently for him" (Psalm 37:7), to "Be still, and know that I am God" (Psalm 46:10). We choose to enter into awareness of God's presence and to rest there in his love. That choice alone is no small feat. There are occasions when I pause for my midday prayer and find that I spend the entire time—be it five or twenty minutes—centering my thoughts so I can let go of tensions and distractions and begin resting in the love of God.

Each Office begins and ends with two minutes of silence and stillness. Many religions have some practice of silence, so there is nothing particularly Christian about the silence itself. What makes silence unique for us as followers of Christ is that we are still and silent in the context of our relationship with the living God. In a posture of attentiveness and surrender, we allow him and his will access to the innermost parts of our lives. This is the very core of what it means to be in loving union with him.[3]

This may be difficult for you, especially at first. Our internal and external worlds are filled with noise and distractions. For this reason, spending time alone with God in silence is perhaps the most challenging and least experienced spiritual practice among Christians today. However, that doesn't justify taking a pass. If we fail to learn how to be quiet in God's presence—to stop talking long enough and routinely enough to listen—how will we mature into Christian adults? How will our relationship with God develop any depth?

There are a number of ways to approach this. The following are a few guidelines to help you begin entering into silence and stillness:[4]

- Settle into a comfortable and quiet place. Take a few deep breaths, allowing yourself to inhale and exhale slowly. (For additional guidance on a practice called the "breath prayer," see Appendix B, pages 177–78).
- Begin with a simple prayer—often just one word—that expresses your openness to God and your desire to spend time with him. You might use your favorite name for God, such as *Abba*, *Father*, or *Jesus.* Or you could use a phrase such as, *Here I am, Lord.* (My wife, Geri, often doesn't use any words, preferring to spend time with Jesus as two lovers might, content to simply be together in a quiet corner. In those moments she imagines God wrapping his arms of love around her).
- When distractions come—and they most certainly will come—entrust them to God's care and use your simple prayer phrase to turn your thoughts back to God.

Give yourself lots of grace here, especially at the beginning. Remember, this is a revolutionary and countercultural practice, not a walk in the park. When you choose to sit in silence and stillness, you are choosing to allow God to be the center of your life. That means you are choosing, even if just for a few moments, to let go of control and your own agenda.

That is no small thing.

But if you persevere through the awkwardness at the beginning—if you truly stop to surrender your will to God's will—you will begin to experience a gradual transformation. And slowly, you will find that silence will become a normal and regular part of each day. You will find yourself briefly pausing for silence, for example, before turning on the car, writing a difficult email, or starting a meeting at work.

2. Scripture. The important thing to remember here is the adage that "less is more." The Scripture selections are intentionally brief. Read slowly—possibly aloud—chewing on any words or phrases that stand out to you. If God leads you to linger over a verse, do so. Be attentive to what God is doing inside of you. There is no need to finish all that is provided for each office! Allow the Holy Spirit to guide you.

3. Devotional Reading. Readings are drawn from a wide variety of sources—ancient spiritual writers, poets, monks, rabbis, and contemporary writers, as well as some of my own writings. As with Scripture, these selections are meant to be read slowly and prayerfully. There are times when I come to the midday or evening office with so much on my mind that I actually choose to begin my time of silence with the devotional reading as a means of redirecting my thoughts to God. Sometimes the readings will speak powerfully to where you are. At other times, you may find yourself wanting to skim or skip them. Once again, it's important to remember that the purpose of the Daily Office is to commune with God, not to get though all the reading!

4. Question to Consider. Each office ends with a brief but probing question. You may find it helpful to write out your answers in the form of a prayer to God. Or, if you don't find the questions helpful, feel free to skip them. If you use this guide repeatedly over time, don't be surprised if God leads you along very different paths as you reflect on the questions each time.

5. Prayer. For a large part of my Christian life, I avoided written prayers. In recent years, however, I have found them to be a rich supplement to my devotional life. You may want to pray the words as written, or simply use them as inspiration and a starting point for your own prayers. Note that The Lord's Prayer is included in Appendix A as an additional resource for your time with God. Because of its depth and simplicity, I often pray it as part of my Daily Offices each day. Again, use these prayers only if you find them helpful.

In Appendix D, I have also included instructions about compline (pronounced "comp-line" or "comp-lin"), which is a going-to-sleep prayer of trust. Although it is prayed at the end of the day, I find that it also helps me to pay attention to God during all my waking hours.

CLOSING THOUGHTS

As you begin your journey with the Daily Office, I encourage you to allow a lot of time and practice to make progress in this. Few of us have life-giving rhythms, so rearranging our days to stop and be with Jesus is a major shift. Add to this the reality that little silence exists in the culture, our families of origin, even in our churches and the challenge can feel overwhelming. But I can assure you that if you will persevere and ask the Holy Spirit for help, you will find that God has been waiting for you. You will get to know him in ways that can happen only in silence (Psalm 46:10). Your listening-to-God "muscles" may develop slowly, but they will develop. By God's grace, your capacity to be with Jesus will enlarge and expand. But most importantly, you will discover, as millions of others have across the ages, that his love really is better than life (Psalm 63:3).

USING THE DAILY OFFICE WITH GROUPS

The Daily Offices are written for individuals, but they can be easily adapted for groups meeting for morning, midday, or evening prayer. Here are a few guidelines:

- Appoint a facilitator to pace the time.
- Read the Scripture selections aloud together.
- Appoint one person to read aloud the Devotional Reading and the Question to Consider.
- Pause briefly—five to ten seconds—between each section of the Office.
- Option: When our staff at New Life meets for midday prayer, rather than read the closing prayer aloud together at the end, we break up into groups of two or three for intercession and close with a worship song. Be flexible for what works best in your context.

The Problem of Emotionally Unhealthy Spirituality

1

DAILY OFFICES

Week One

Emotionally unhealthy spirituality wreaks havoc in our personal lives and our churches. When, for example, we deny the past's impact on the present, judge other people's spiritual journeys, or spiritualize away conflict, we hurt both ourselves and those around us. An emotionally unhealthy spirituality also hinders us from breaking deeply rooted, unhealthy relationship patterns and maturing in Christ.

The problem is twofold: First, we neglect to pay attention to what is going on inside us. And second, we are too busy to stop, slow down, and be with God. As a result, we run the high risk of remaining stuck as spiritual infants, failing to grow into spiritual/emotional adults in Christ.

Spending time with God each week through the Daily Office helps us give Jesus access to what is deeply beneath the surface of our lives and cultivate a deep, personal relationship with him. Learning to spend time with Jesus is God's way to transform us into free, mature disciples who can serve as gifts to the world.

ADDITIONAL RESOURCES

The Daily Offices throughout this book were written to be used as companions to *The Emotionally Healthy (EH) Spirituality Course*. Each week, the corresponding session from the course and DVD are listed as additional resources.

- *Emotionally Healthy Spirituality: Updated Edition*, chapter 1
- *The Emotionally Healthy Spirituality Workbook Updated Edition*, Session 1
- *The Emotionally Healthy Spirituality DVD: Updated Edition*, Session 1

DAY 1: MORNING/MIDDAY OFFICE

Silence and Stillness before God (2 minutes)

Scripture Reading: Mark 11:15 – 17

On reaching Jerusalem, Jesus entered the temple courts and began driving out those who were buying and selling there. He overturned the tables of the money changers and the benches of those selling doves, and would not allow anyone to carry merchandise through the temple courts. And as he taught them, he said, "Is it not written: 'My house will be called a house of prayer for all nations'? But you have made it 'a den of robbers.' "

Devotional

Jesus' intense anger and overturning of the tables in the temple courts ought to make us gasp. He knows that if we don't get to God, invaluable treasures will be lost or obscured. We lose the space where we experience God's unfailing love and amazing forgiveness. We lose an eternal perspective on what is important and what is not. We lose compassion. We gain the world but lose our souls (Mark 8:36 – 37).

Be Free for God

I have a need
of such clearance
as the Savior effected in the temple of Jerusalem
a riddance of clutter
of what is secondary
that blocks the way

to the all-important central emptiness
which is filled
with the presence of God alone.
—Jean Danielou[5]

Question to Consider

How would you describe "what is secondary" in your life, the thing that might be "blocking the way" to experiencing God?

Prayer

Lord, help me to see how much I lose when I lose you. My perspective on my life and all of life gets distorted when I don't make space for you, obscuring your love for me. Your love is better than life, and truly I long for more tastes of that love. In Jesus' name, amen.

Conclude with Silence (2 minutes)

DAY 1: MIDDAY/EVENING OFFICE

Silence and Stillness before God (2 minutes)

Scripture Reading: 1 Samuel 15:22–23

But Samuel replied:

"Does the LORD delight in burnt offerings and sacrifices
as much as in obeying the LORD?
To obey is better than sacrifice,
and to heed is better than the fat of rams.
For rebellion is like the sin of divination,
and arrogance like the evil of idolatry.
Because you have rejected the word of the LORD,
he has rejected you as king."

Devotional

Saul, the first king of Israel, did not know much about silence or listening to God. Like David, he was a gifted, anointed, successful military/political leader. Yet unlike David, we never see him seeking to be with God. In this passage, Samuel the prophet reprimands Saul for doing many religious acts (i.e., offering burnt offerings and sacrifices) but not quieting himself enough to listen, or "to heed" God (v. 22).

> We all must take the time to be silent and to contemplate, especially those who live in big cities like London and New York, where everything moves so fast.... I always begin my prayer in silence, for it is in the silence of the heart that God speaks. God is the friend of silence — we need to listen to God because it's not what we say but what He says to us and through us that matters. Prayer feeds the soul — as blood is to the body, prayer is to the soul — and it brings you closer to God. It also gives you a clean and pure heart. A clean heart can see God, can speak to God, and can see the love of God in others.
>
> — Mother Teresa[6]

Question to Consider

How could you make more room in your life for silence in order to listen to God?

Prayer

Unclutter my heart, O God, until I am quiet enough to hear you speak out of the silence. Help me in these few moments to stop, to listen, to wait, to be still, and to allow your presence to envelop me. In Jesus' name, amen.

Conclude with Silence (2 minutes)

DAY 2: MORNING/MIDDAY OFFICE

Silence and Stillness before God (2 minutes)

Scripture Reading: Jonah 1:1 – 4

The word of the LORD came to Jonah son of Amittai: "Go to the great city of Nineveh and preach against it, because its wickedness has come up before me."

But Jonah ran away from the LORD and headed for Tarshish. He went down to Joppa, where he found a ship bound for that port. After paying the fare, he went aboard and sailed for Tarshish to flee from the LORD.

Then the LORD sent a great wind on the sea, and such a violent storm arose that the ship threatened to break up.

Devotional

Jonah is an example of a prophet with a case of emotionally unhealthy spirituality. He hears and serves God but refuses to listen to God's call to love and show mercy to Nineveh, a world power of that day known for its violent, barbaric behavior. Jonah flees 2,400 miles in the opposite direction, to Tarshish, in present-day Spain.

> And why Tarshish? For one thing, it is a lot more exciting than Nineveh. Nineveh was an ancient site with layer after layer of ruined and unhappy history. Going to Nineveh to preach was not a coveted assignment for a Hebrew prophet with good references. But Tarshish was something else. Tarshish was exotic. Tarshish was adventure.... Tarshish in the biblical references was a "far off and sometimes idealized port." It is reported in 1 Kings 10:22 that Solomon's fleet of Tarshish fetched gold,

> silver, ivory, monkeys and peacocks.... In Tarshish we can have a religious career without having to deal with God.
>
> — Eugene Peterson[7]

As Jonah runs, however, God sends a great storm. Jonah loses control of his life and destiny. He is thrown overboard and swallowed by a great fish. It is from the belly of the fish that Jonah begins to wrestle with God in prayer.

Question to Consider

What internal or external storm might God be sending into your life as a sign that something is not right spiritually?

Prayer

> *Lord, may your will, not my will, be done in my life. You know how easy it is to call myself a Christian but then become busy, forgetting about your will and desires. Forgive me for this sin. Help me listen to you, and grant me the courage to faithfully surrender to you. In Jesus' name, amen.*

Conclude with Silence (2 minutes)

DAY 2: MIDDAY/EVENING OFFICE

Silence and Stillness before God (2 minutes)

Scripture Reading: 1 John 2:15 – 17

> Do not love the world or anything in the world. If anyone loves the world, love for the Father is not in them. For everything in the world — the lust of the flesh, the lust of the eyes, and the pride of life — comes not from the Father but from the world. The world and its desires pass away, but whoever does the will of God lives forever.

Devotional

At the end of the third century in the deserts of Egypt, an extraordinary phenomenon occurred. Christian men and women began to flee the cities and villages to see God in the desert. They discerned how easy it was to lose one's soul in the entanglements and manipulations found in society, so they pursued God in a radical way by moving to the desert. They became known as the "Desert Fathers."

> Society ... was regarded by them as a shipwreck from which each single individual man had to swim for his life.... These were men who believed that to let oneself drift along, passively accepting the tenets and values of what they knew as society, was purely and simply a disaster.... They knew they were helpless to do any good for others as long as they floundered about in the wreckage. But once they got a foothold on solid ground, things were different. Then they had not only the power but even the obligation to pull the whole world to safety after them.
>
> — Thomas Merton[8]

Question to Consider

How do you hear the words of the apostle John today: "Do not love the world or anything in the world" (1 John 2:15)?

Prayer

Lord, in order to be with you, I need you to show me how to "create a desert" in the midst of my full, active life. Cleanse me from the pressures, illusions, and pretenses that confront me today so that my life may serve as a gift to those around me.

Conclude with Silence (2 minutes)

DAY 3: MORNING/MIDDAY OFFICE

Silence and Stillness before God (2 minutes)

Scripture Reading: Genesis 32:22 – 26, 30

That night Jacob got up and took his two wives, his two female servants and his eleven sons and crossed the ford of the Jabbok. After he had sent them across the stream, he sent over all his possessions. So Jacob was left alone, and a man wrestled with him till daybreak. When the man saw that he could not overpower him, he touched the socket of Jacob's hip so that his hip was wrenched as he wrestled with the man. Then the man said, "Let me go, for it is daybreak." But Jacob replied, "I will not let you go unless you bless me."

So Jacob called the place Peniel, saying, "It is because I saw God face to face, and yet my life was spared."

Devotional

Jacob's name can mean "cheat" or "grabber," and he lived up to his name. He was manipulative, deceptive, and aggressive — not someone you'd likely nominate for a leadership position in your church. Jacob was a seriously flawed person growing up in a dysfunctional family. He seemed to be either getting into trouble, just getting out of it, or about to make some more.[9]

Jacob's story is so universal because it is so personal. Throughout his life, Jacob was stubborn and unwilling to trust anyone — even God. It was at the Jabbok brook that Jacob was finally broken by God and radically transformed. He was given a new name and a new freedom to live as God originally intended. This came, however, at the price of a permanent limp that rendered him helpless and desperate to cling to God. And it is out of this weak place of dependence that Jacob became a nation (Israel) that would bless the world.

In the same way, God sometimes wounds us in our journey with him in order to move us out of an unhealthy, "tip of the iceberg" spirituality to one that truly transforms us from the inside out. When these wounds come, we can deny them, cover them, get angry with God, blame others, or like Jacob we can cling desperately to God.

Question to Consider

In what way(s) has God put your life or plans "out of joint" so that you might depend on him?

Prayer

Father, I relate to Jacob in striving, manipulating, scheming, denying, and spinning half- truths to those around me in order to get my way. At times, I too find myself serving you in order to get something from you. Lord, I invite you to teach me to live in dependence on you. Help me to rest and be still in your love alone. In Jesus' name, amen.

Conclude with Silence (2 minutes)

DAY 3: MIDDAY/EVENING OFFICE

Silence and Stillness before God (2 minutes)

Scripture Reading: Matthew 16:21 – 23

From that time on Jesus began to explain to his disciples that he must go to Jerusalem and suffer many things at the hands of the elders, the chief priests and the teachers of the law, and that he must be killed and on the third day be raised to life.

Peter took him aside and began to rebuke him. "Never, Lord!" he said. "This shall never happen to you!"

Jesus turned and said to Peter, "Get behind me, Satan! You are a stumbling block to me; you do not have in mind the concerns of God, but merely human concerns."

Devotional

The apostle Peter had a passionate heart for Jesus, but he was also rash, proud, immature, and inconsistent. His impulsiveness and stubbornness are evident throughout the gospels.

Yet Jesus patiently led Peter to a crucifixion of his self-will, in order that he might experience genuine resurrection life and power.

> When I am still, compulsion (the busyness that Hilary of Tours called "a blasphemous anxiety to do God's work for him") gives way to compunction (being pricked or punctured). That is, God can break through the many layers with which I protect myself, so that I can hear his Word and be poised to listen. . . .
>
> In perpetual motion I can mistake the flow of my adrenaline for the moving of the Holy Spirit; I can live in the illusion that I am ultimately in control of my destiny and my daily affairs. . . .
>
> French philosopher and mathematician Blaise Pascal observed that most of our human problems come because we don't know how to sit still in our room for an hour.
>
> —Leighton Ford[10]

Question to Consider

What might be one way your busyness blocks you from listening and communing intimately with the living God?

Prayer

Lord, forgive me for running my life without you today. I offer my anxieties to you now — as best I can. Help me to be still, to surrender to your will, and to rest in your loving arms. In the name of the Father, the Son, and the Holy Spirit, amen.

Conclude with Silence (2 minutes)

DAY 4: MORNING/MIDDAY OFFICE

Silence and Stillness before God (2 minutes)

Scripture Reading: Luke 10:38 – 42

As Jesus and his disciples were on their way, he came to a village where a woman named Martha opened her home to him. She had a sister called Mary, who sat at the Lord's feet listening to what he said. But Martha was distracted by all the preparations that had to be made. She came to him and asked, "Lord, don't you care that my sister has left me to do the work by myself? Tell her to help me!"

"Martha, Martha," the Lord answered, "you are worried and upset about many things, but few things are needed — or indeed only one. Mary has chosen what is better, and it will not be taken away from her."

Devotional

Mary and Martha represent two approaches to the Christian life.

Martha is actively serving Jesus, but she is also missing Jesus. She is busy in the "doing" of life. Her life is pressured and filled with distractions. Her duties have become disconnected from her love for Jesus. Martha's problems, however, go beyond her busyness. I suspect that if Martha were to sit at the feet of Jesus, she would still be distracted by everything on her mind. Her inner person is touchy, irritable, and anxious.

Mary, on the other hand, is sitting at the feet of Jesus, listening to him. She is "being" with Jesus, enjoying intimacy with him, loving him, and taking pleasure in his presence. Her life has one center of gravity — Jesus. I suspect that if Mary were to help with the many household chores, she would not be worried or upset. Why? Her inner person has slowed down enough to focus on Jesus and to center her life on him.

Our goal is to love God with our whole being, to be consistently conscious of God through our daily life — whether we are stopped like Mary, sitting at the feet of Jesus, or active like Martha, taking care of the tasks of life.[11]

Question to Consider

What things are worrying or upsetting you today?

Prayer

Help me, O Lord, to be still and wait patiently for you (Psalm 37:7). I offer to you each of my anxieties and worries this day. Teach me to be prayerfully attentive and to rest in you as I enter into the many activities of this day. In Jesus' name, amen.

Conclude with Silence (2 minutes)

DAY 4: MIDDAY/EVENING OFFICE

Silence and Stillness before God (2 minutes)

Scripture Reading: Psalm 62:5 – 8

Find rest, O my soul, in God alone;
 my hope comes from him.

He alone is my rock and my salvation;
he is my fortress, I will not be shaken.
My salvation and my honor depend on God;
he is my mighty rock, my refuge.
Trust in him at all times, O people;
pour out your hearts to him,
for God is our refuge. (NIV 1984)

Devotional

David, a man after God's own heart, beautifully models the seamless integration of a full emotional life with a profound contemplative life with God. He trusts in the Lord, pouring out his struggles, fears, and anguish over the lies being said about him.

In *The Cry of the Soul*, Dan Allender and Tremper Longman summarize why awareness of our feelings is so important to our relationship with God:

> Ignoring our emotions is turning our back on reality; listening to our emotions ushers us into reality. And reality is where we meet God.... Emotions are the language of the soul. They are the cry that gives the heart a voice.... However, we often turn a deaf ear — through emotional denial, distortion, or disengagement. We strain out anything disturbing in order to gain tenuous control of our inner world. We are frightened and ashamed of what leaks into our consciousness. In neglecting our intense emotions, we are false to ourselves and lose a wonderful opportunity to know God. We forget that change comes through brutal honesty and vulnerability before God.[12]

Question to Consider

What are you angry about today? Sad about? Afraid of? Pour out your response before God, trusting in him as David did.

Prayer

Lord, like David I often feel like a leaning wall, a tottering fence that is about to be knocked down! So many forces and circumstances seem to be coming against me. Help me, Lord, to find rest in you and to take shelter in you as my fortress. In Jesus' name, amen.

Conclude with Silence (2 minutes)

DAY 5: MORNING/MIDDAY OFFICE

Silence and Stillness before God (2 minutes)

Scripture Reading: John 7:2 – 8

But when the Jewish Festival of Tabernacles was near, Jesus' brothers said to him, "Leave Galilee and go to Judea, so that your disciples there may see the works you do. No one who wants to become a public figure acts in secret. Since you are doing these things, show yourself to the world." For even his own brothers did not believe in him.

Therefore Jesus told them, "My time is not yet here; for you any time will do. The world cannot hate you, but it hates me because I testify that its works are evil. You go to the festival. I am not yet going up to this festival, because my time has not yet fully come."

Devotional

Jesus moved slowly, not striving or rushing. He patiently waited through his adolescent and young adult years to reveal himself as the Messiah. Even then, he did not rush to be recognized. He waited patiently for his Father's timing during his short ministry.

Why is it then that we hate "slow" when God appears to delight in it? Eugene Peterson offers us at least two reasons:

> *I am busy because I am vain.* I want to appear important. Significant. What better way than to be busy? The incredible hours, the crowded schedule, and the heavy demands of my time are proof to myself—and to all who will notice—that I am important. If I go into a doctor's office and find there's no one waiting, and I see through a half-open door the doctor reading a book, I wonder if he's any good....
>
> Such experiences affect me. I live in a society in which crowded schedules and harassed conditions are evidence of importance, so I develop a crowded schedule and harassed conditions. When others notice, they acknowledge my significance, and my vanity is fed.
>
> *I am busy because I am lazy.* I indolently let others decide what I will do instead of resolutely deciding myself. It was a favorite theme of C. S. Lewis that only lazy people work hard. By lazily abdicating the essential work of deciding and directing, establishing values and setting goals, other people do it for us.[13]

Question to Consider

What is one step you can take today to slow down and live more attentively to the voice of Jesus?

Prayer

> *Lord, grant me the grace to do one thing at a time today, without rushing or hurrying. Help me to savor the sacred in all I do, be it large or small. By the Holy Spirit within me, empower me to pause today as I move from one activity to the next. In Jesus' name, amen.*

Conclude with Silence (2 minutes)

DAY 5: MIDDAY/EVENING OFFICE

Silence and Stillness before God (2 minutes)

Scripture Reading: 2 Corinthians 12:7 – 10

Therefore, in order to keep me from becoming conceited, I was given a thorn in my flesh, a messenger of Satan, to torment me. Three times I pleaded with the Lord to take it away from me. But he said to me, "My grace is sufficient for you, for my power is made perfect in weakness." Therefore I will boast all the more gladly about my weaknesses, so that Christ's power may rest on me. That is why, for Christ's sake, I delight in weaknesses, in insults, in hardships, in persecutions, in difficulties. For when I am weak, then I am strong.

Devotional

The Bible does not spin the flaws and weaknesses of its heroes. Abraham lied. Hosea's wife was a prostitute. Peter rebuked God! Noah got drunk. Jonah was a racist. Jacob lied. John Mark deserted Paul. Elijah burned out. Jeremiah was depressed and suicidal. Thomas doubted. Moses had a temper. Timothy had ulcers. Even David, one of God's beloved friends, committed adultery with Bathsheba and murdered her husband. Yet all these people teach us the same message: that every human being on earth, regardless of their gifts and strengths, is weak, vulnerable, and dependent on God and others.[14]

The pressure to present an image of ourselves as strong and spiritually "together" hovers over most of us. We feel guilty for not measuring up, for not making the grade. We forget that all of us are human and frail.

The apostle Paul struggled with God not answering his prayers and removing his "thorn in the flesh." Nevertheless, he thanked God for his brokenness, knowing that without it, he would have been an arrogant, "conceited" apostle. He learned, as we all must, that Christ's power is made perfect only when we are weak.

Question to Consider

How might brokenness or weakness in your life today present an opportunity for God's power to be demonstrated?

Prayer

> *Father, the notion of admitting to myself and to others my weaknesses and failures is very difficult. Lord, I am weak. I am dependent on you. You are God, and I am not. Help me to embrace your work in me. And may I be able to say, like Paul, "when I am weak (broken), then I am strong." In Jesus' name, amen.*

Conclude with Silence (2 minutes)

Know Yourself That You May Know God

2

DAILY OFFICES

Week Two

Awareness of ourselves and our relationship with God are closely related. In fact, the challenge of Scripture to shed our old "false" self in order to live authentically in our new "true self" in Christ is the very core of discipleship.

In AD 500, Augustine wrote: "How can you draw close to God when you are far from your own self?" In 1530, John Calvin wrote: "Our wisdom . . . consists almost entirely of two parts: knowledge of God and of ourselves." And Teresa of Avila wisely wrote: "Almost all problems in the spiritual life stem from a lack of self-knowledge."

Powerful spiritual breakthroughs take place deep below the surface of our lives when we slow down to spend time with God in stillness and Scripture. This provides space for his purifying love to burn away all that is false within us and set us free to live authentically in Jesus.

ADDITIONAL RESOURCES

- *Emotionally Healthy Spirituality: Updated Edition*, chapter 2
- *The Emotionally Healthy Spirituality Workbook Updated Edition*, Session 2
- *The Emotionally Healthy Spirituality DVD: Updated Edition*, Session 2

DAY 1: MORNING/MIDDAY OFFICE

Silence and Stillness before God (2 minutes)

Scripture Reading: Mark 1:33 – 38

The whole town gathered at the door, and Jesus healed many who had various diseases. He also drove out many demons, but he would not let the demons speak because they knew who he was.

Very early in the morning, while it was still dark, Jesus got up, left the house and went off to a solitary place, where he prayed. Simon and his companions went to look for him, and when they found him, they exclaimed: "Everyone is looking for you!"

Jesus replied, "Let us go somewhere else — to the nearby villages — so I can preach there also. That is why I have come."

Devotional

The challenge to shed our "old false" self in order to live authentically in our "new true" self strikes at the very core of true spirituality. We see this authenticity in the life of Jesus.

In the midst of a mini-revival in the town of Capernaum, Jesus was able to withstand the pressure of everyone looking for him, and to move on to another place. He also knew his Father, who loved him and had a work for him to complete. In living faithfully to his true self, however, Jesus disappointed a lot of people. For example:

- He disappointed his family to the point where his mother and siblings wondered if he was out of his mind (Mark 3:21).
- He disappointed the people he grew up with in Nazareth. When Jesus declared who he really was — the Messiah — they tried to push him off a cliff (Luke 4:28 – 29).

- He disappointed his closest friends, the twelve disciples. They projected onto Jesus their own picture of the kind of Messiah they expected him to be. When he failed to meet their expectations, they quit on him.
- He disappointed the crowds. They wanted an earthly Messiah who would feed them, fix all their problems, overthrow the Roman oppressors, work miracles, and give inspiring sermons. They walked away from him.
- He disappointed the religious leaders. They did not appreciate the disruption his presence brought to their day-to-day lives or to their theology. They finally attributed his power to demons and had him crucified.[15]

Question to Consider

What might be one specific way that you give in to the expectations of others rather than being faithful to what Jesus has for you?

Prayer

Jesus, I am so grateful that you understand what it is like to feel pressure from the expectations of others. It can feel crushing at times. Lord, help me to love others well while at the same time remaining faithful to you. In Jesus' name, amen.

Conclude with Silence (2 minutes)

DAY 1: MIDDAY/EVENING OFFICE

Silence and Stillness before God (2 minutes)

Scripture Reading: 1 Samuel 17:38 – 40, 45

Then Saul dressed David in his own tunic. He put a coat of armor on him and a bronze helmet on his head. David fastened

> on his sword over the tunic and tried walking around, because he was not used to them.
>
> "I cannot go in these," he said to Saul, "because I am not used to them." So he took them off. Then he took his staff in his hand, chose five smooth stones from the stream, put them in the pouch of his shepherd's bag and, with his sling in his hand, approached the Philistine.
>
> David said to the Philistine, "You come against me with sword and spear and javelin, but I come against you in the name of the LORD Almighty, the God of the armies of Israel, whom you have defied."

Devotional

Even as a young man, David knew both himself and God. Having taken off Saul's armor, he went up against the nine-foot Goliath with only his slingshot and a few smooth stones, confident in the living God.

Unlike David, however, the vast majority of us go to our graves without ever really knowing who we are. We unconsciously live someone else's life, or at least someone else's expectations for us.

We are so unaccustomed to being our true self that it can seem impossible to know where to begin. Thomas Merton describes what we so often do:

> I use up my life in the desire for pleasures . . . power, honor, knowledge and love, to clothe this false self. . . . And I wind experiences around myself and cover myself with pleasures and glory like bandages in order to make myself perceptible to myself and to the world, as if I were an invisible body that could only become visible when something visible covered its surface. But there is no substance under the things with which I am clothed. I am hollow, and my structure of pleasures and

> ambitions has no foundation. . . . And when they are gone there will be nothing left of me but my own nakedness and emptiness and hollowness.[16]

The path we must walk to remove the layers of our false self is initially very hard. Powerful forces around and inside us can smother the process. At the same time, the God of the universe has made his home in us (John 14:23), and the very glory God gave Jesus has also been given to us (John 17:21 – 23).

Question to Consider

What might be one false layer or bandage God is inviting you to remove today?

Prayer

> *Lord, grant me the courage of David to resist the temptation to live a life that is not the one you have given to me. Deliver me from the "Goliaths" in front of me, and from the negative voices I hear so often. Help me to listen and obey your voice today. In Jesus' name, amen.*

Conclude with Silence (2 minutes)

DAY 2: MORNING/MIDDAY OFFICE

Silence and Stillness before God (2 minutes)

Scripture Reading: Psalm 139:13 – 16

For you created my inmost being;
    you knit me together in my mother's womb.
I praise you because I am fearfully and wonderfully made;

your works are wonderful,
I know that full well.
My frame was not hidden from you
when I was made in the secret place,
when I was woven together in the depths of the earth.
Your eyes saw my unformed body;
all the days ordained for me were written in your book
before one of them came to be.

Devotional

David seems to have maintained the tension of two complementary truths taught in Scripture. We are sinners who desperately need forgiveness and a Savior. At the same time, God created us in his image, knit each of us together in our mother's womb with enormous care, and chose us for a special purpose on earth. Parker Palmer captured well the wonder of Psalm 139:

> Vocation does not come from a voice "out there" calling me to become something I am not. It comes from a voice "in here" calling me to be the person I was born to be, to fulfill the original selfhood given me at birth by God.
>
> It is a strange gift, this birthright of self. Accepting it turns out to be even more demanding than attempting to become someone else! I have sometimes responded to that demand by ignoring the gift, or hiding it, or fleeing from it, or squandering it — and I think I am not alone. There is a Hasidic tale that reveals, with amazing brevity, both the universal tendency to want to be someone else and the ultimate importance of becoming one's self. Rabbi Zusya, when he was an old man, said, "In the coming world, they will not ask me: 'Why were you not Moses?' They will ask me: 'Why were you not Zusya?' "[17]

Question to Consider

What do you think might be one of your "birthright" gifts from God that you have ignored in your life?

Prayer

Lord, I come this day inviting you to cut those deeply entrenched chains that keep me from being faithful to my true self in Christ. In doing so, may my life be a blessing to many. In Jesus' name, amen.

Conclude with Silence (2 minutes)

DAY 2: MIDDAY/EVENING OFFICE

Silence and Stillness before God (2 minutes)

Scripture Reading: Ephesians 3:14 – 19

For this reason I kneel before the Father, from whom every family in heaven and on earth derives its name. I pray that out of his glorious riches he may strengthen you with power through his Spirit in your inner being, so that Christ may dwell in your hearts through faith. And I pray that you, being rooted and established in love, may have power, together with all the Lord's holy people, to grasp how wide and long and high and deep is the love of Christ, and to know this love that surpasses knowledge — that you may be filled to the measure of all the fullness of God.

Devotional

Bernard of Clairvaux (AD 1090 – 1153), the abbot of a Cistercian monastery in France, was perhaps the greatest Christian leader and writer of his day. In his great work entitled *Loving God*, Bernard describes four degrees of love:

1. Loving ourselves for our own sake
2. Loving God for his gifts and blessings
3. Loving God for himself alone
4. Loving ourselves for the sake of God

The highest degree of love, for Bernard, was simply that we love ourselves as God loves us — in the same degree, in the same manner, and with the very same love. We love the self that God loves, the essential image and likeness of God in us that has been damaged by sin.[18]

Question to Consider

Where do you see yourself on Bernard's list of the four degrees of love?

Prayer

Lord, strengthen me with your power that I might grasp how wide and long and high and deep is the love of Christ that surpasses human knowledge. May I love you for you alone, and not your gifts or blessings. And may I live in the deep experience of your tender love this day. In Jesus' name, amen.

Conclude with Silence (2 minutes)

DAY 3: MORNING/MIDDAY OFFICE

Silence and Stillness before God (2 minutes)

Scripture Reading: Mark 10:26 – 31

The disciples were even more amazed, and said to each other, "Who then can be saved?" Jesus looked at them and said, "With man this is impossible, but not with God; all things are possible with God." Then Peter spoke up, "We have left everything to follow you!"

"Truly I tell you," Jesus replied, "no one who has left home or brothers or sisters or mother or father or children or fields for me and the gospel will fail to receive a hundred times as much in this present age: homes, brothers, sisters, mothers, children and fields — along with persecutions — and in the age to come eternal life. But many who are first will be last, and the last first."

Devotional

Anthony (AD 251 – 356) grew up in a wealthy family in Egypt, receiving an excellent education and upbringing from his Christian parents. One Sunday, Anthony heard the words: "Go sell all you have and give it to the poor, and you shall have treasure in heaven," and he felt God speaking directly to his heart. Unlike the rich young ruler, he responded to Jesus in faith.

Selling his possessions, Anthony went off into the solitude of the Egyptian desert, not just for a few days or weeks, but for twenty years! He renounced all possessions to learn detachment; he renounced speech in order to learn compassion; and he renounced activity in order to learn prayer. In the desert, Anthony both discovered God and did intense battle with the devil.

When Anthony emerged from his solitude after twenty years, people recognized in him the qualities of an authentic "healthy" man — whole in body, mind, and soul. God soon catapulted him into one of the most remarkable ministries of that day. He preached the gospel among the rich and the poor, performed many healings, expelled demons, and more. Emperor Constantine Augustus sought out Anthony's counsel. He served tirelessly in prisons and among the poor.[19]

In his old age, Anthony retired to an even deeper solitude to be totally absorbed in direct communion with God. He died in the year 356 at the age of 106 years old.[20]

Question to Consider

What impresses you most about the story of Anthony's life?

Prayer

Lord, it is clear that layers of Anthony's false, superficial self were shed during his time with you. Crack the hard shell over my heart that obscures and buries my true self in Christ. Transform me into the kind of person you desire me to be. In Jesus' name, amen.

Conclude with Silence (2 minutes)

DAY 3: MIDDAY/EVENING OFFICE

Silence and Stillness before God (2 minutes)

Scripture Reading: Matthew 4:1 – 3, 8 – 11

Then Jesus was led by the Spirit into the desert to be tempted by the devil. After fasting forty days and forty nights, he was hungry. The tempter came to him and said, "If you are the Son of God, tell these stones to become bread."

Again, the devil took him to a very high mountain and showed him all the kingdoms of the world and their splendor. "All this I will give you," he said, "if you will bow down and worship me."

Jesus said to him, "Away from me, Satan! For it is written: 'Worship the Lord your God, and serve him only.' " Then the devil left him, and angels came and attended him.

Devotional

Solitude is the furnace of transformation. Without solitude we remain victims of our society and continue to be entangled in the illusions of the false self. Jesus himself entered into this furnace. There he was tempted with the three compulsions of the world: to be relevant ("turn stones into loaves"), to be spectacular ("throw yourself down"), and to be powerful ("I will give you all these kingdoms"). There he affirmed God as the only source of his identity ("You must worship the Lord your God and serve him alone"). Solitude is the place of the great struggle and the great encounter — the struggle against the compulsions of the false self, and the encounter with the loving God who offers himself as the substance of the new self....

In solitude I get rid of my scaffolding: no friends to talk with, no telephone calls to make.... The task is to persevere in my solitude, to stay in my cell until all my seductive visitors get tired of pounding on my door and leave me alone.

— Henri Nouwen[21]

Question to Consider

What temptations or trials do you find yourself in today that God might be using as a furnace to help develop your interior life?

Prayer

Lord, help me to turn down the volume of the voices that tell me I have little worth unless I am wealthy, influential, and popular. Grant me the grace today to experience your voice, which tells me: You are "my [child], whom I love; with [you] I am well pleased" (Matthew 3:16). In Jesus' name, amen.

Conclude with Silence (2 minutes)

DAY 4: MORNING/MIDDAY OFFICE

Silence and Stillness before God (2 minutes)

Scripture Reading: 1 Kings 19:1 – 5

Now Ahab told Jezebel everything Elijah had done and how he had killed all the prophets with the sword. So Jezebel sent a messenger to Elijah to say, "May the gods deal with me, be it ever so severely, if by this time tomorrow I do not make your life like that of one of them."

Elijah was afraid and ran for his life. When he came to Beersheba in Judah, he left his servant there, while he himself went a day's journey into the wilderness. He came to a broom bush, sat down under it and prayed that he might die. "I have had enough, Lord," he said. "Take my life; I am no better than my ancestors." Then he lay down under the bush and fell asleep.

All at once an angel touched him and said, "Get up and eat."

Devotional

After Elijah's great victory over 850 false prophets at Mount Carmel, he had to run for his life. During that process, he became both exhausted and depressed — to the point of wanting to die. For reasons not given in this text, we find Elijah alone under a broom bush and asking for death. He is, as we call it today, "burned out."

> When I give something I do not possess, I give a false and dangerous gift, a gift that looks like love but is, in reality, loveless — a gift given more from my need to prove myself than from the other's need to be cared for....
>
> One sign that I am violating my own nature in the name of nobility is a condition called burnout. Though usually

regarded as the result of trying to give too much, burnout in my experience results from trying to give what I do not possess — the ultimate in giving too little! Burnout is a state of emptiness, to be sure, but it does not result from giving all I have; it merely reveals the nothingness from which I was trying to give in the first place.

— Parker Palmer[22]

Question to Consider

What would it look like for you to respect yourself in light of your God-given human limits?

Prayer

Jesus, you know my tendency to say yes to more commitments than I can possibly keep. Help me to embrace the gift of my limits physically, emotionally, and spiritually. And may you, Lord Jesus, be glorified in and through me today. In your name, amen.

Conclude with Silence (2 minutes)

DAY 4: MIDDAY/EVENING OFFICE

Silence and Stillness before God (2 minutes)

Scripture Reading: Exodus 3:1 – 5

Now Moses was tending the flock of Jethro his father-in-law, the priest of Midian, and he led the flock to the far side of the wilderness and came to Horeb, the mountain of God. There the angel of the LORD appeared to him in flames of fire from within a bush. Moses saw that though the bush was on fire it did not burn up. So Moses thought, "I will go over and see this strange sight — why the bush does not burn up."

When the LORD saw that he had gone over to look, God called to him from within the bush, "Moses! Moses!"

And Moses said, "Here I am."

"Do not come any closer," God said. "Take off your sandals, for the place where you are standing is holy ground."

Devotional

God's presence in us is like the fire in the Burning Bush. It gradually takes us over, so that although we remain fully ourselves, we are being made over into our true selves, the way God originally intended us to be. He is Light, and we are filled with His light — maybe even literally, as some saints were said to visibly glow. The term for this transformation is fairly scandalizing: *theosis*, which means being transformed into God, divinized or deified. Of course we do not become little mini-gods with our own universes. We never lose our identity, but we are filled with God like a sponge is filled with water.

— Frederica Mathewes-Green[23]

Question to Consider

What is one area of your inner person that the fire of God's presence might want to burn away (e.g., selfishness, greed, bitterness, impatience)?

Prayer

Jesus, I believe that you came to save me from the penalty of my sins — death — and for eternal life. At the same time, you came to save me from the poison that flows in my veins, from that which keeps me from your Light. Come invade me with your burning fire that I might become the person you have created me to be in you. In your name, amen.

Conclude with Silence (2 minutes)

DAY 5: MORNING/MIDDAY OFFICE

Silence and Stillness before God (2 minutes)

Scripture Reading: Romans 8:35 – 39

Who shall separate us from the love of Christ? Shall trouble or hardship or persecution or famine or nakedness or danger or sword? As it is written:

"For your sake we face death all day long;
we are considered as sheep to be slaughtered."

No, in all these things we are more than conquerors through him who loved us. For I am convinced that neither death nor life, neither angels nor demons, neither the present nor the future, nor any powers, neither height nor depth, nor anything else in all creation, will be able to separate us from the love of God that is in Christ Jesus our Lord.

Devotional

Most of us place a higher premium on what other people think than we realize. As can be seen in Galatians, the apostle Paul understood this struggle intimately.

M. Scott Peck illustrates the point through a story of meeting a high school classmate at the age of fifteen. Here are his reflections after a conversation with his friend:

> I suddenly realized that for the entire ten-minute period from when I had first seen my acquaintance until that very moment, I had been totally self-preoccupied. For the two or three minutes before we met, all I was thinking about was the clever things I might say that would impress him. During our five minutes together, I was listening to what he had to say only so that I might turn it into a clever rejoinder. I watched him only

> so that I might see what effect my remarks were having upon him. And for the two or three minutes after we separated, my sole thought was of those things I could have said that might have impressed him even more.
>
> I had not cared a whit for my classmate.[24]

What is most startling in reading this detailed explanation of what was going on beneath the surface of this fifteen-year-old boy, is the recognition that the same dynamics continue for most of us into our twenties, thirties, fifties, seventies, and nineties! We remain trapped in living a pretend life — always seeking the approval of others.

True freedom comes when we no longer need to be special in other people's eyes because we know we are loveable and good enough in Christ.

Question to Consider

How might it change your day today if you were to cease looking for human approval and begin seeking only the approval of God?

Prayer

> *Grant me courage, Lord, to do today what you have given me to do, to say what you have given me to say, and to become who you have called me to become. In Jesus' name, amen.*

Conclude with Silence (2 minutes)

DAY 5: MIDDAY/EVENING OFFICE

Silence and Stillness before God (2 minutes)

Scripture Reading: Isaiah 40:28 – 31

Do you not know?
    Have you not heard?

The Lord is the everlasting God,
the Creator of the ends of the earth.
He will not grow tired or weary,
and his understanding no one can fathom.
He gives strength to the weary
and increases the power of the weak.
Even youths grow tired and weary,
and young men stumble and fall;
but those who hope in the Lord
will renew their strength.
They will soar on wings like eagles;
they will run and not grow weary,
they will walk and not be faint.

Devotional

In his book *The Song of the Bird*, Tony de Mello tells the following story:

> A man found an eagle's egg and put it in a nest of a barnyard hen. The eaglet hatched with the brood of chicks and grew up with them.
>
> All his life the eagle did what the barnyard chicks did, thinking he was a barnyard chick. He scratched the earth for worms and insects, he clucked and cackled. And he would thrash his wings and fly a few feet into the air.
>
> Years passed and the eagle grew very old. One day he saw a magnificent bird above him in the cloudless sky. It glided in graceful majesty among the powerful wind currents, with scarcely a beat of its strong golden wings. The eagle looked up in awe. "Who's that?" he asked.
>
> "That's the eagle, the king of the birds," said his neighbor. "He belongs to the sky. We belong to the earth — we are chickens."

So the eagle lived and died a chicken, for that's what he thought he was.[25]

Question to Consider

In what area of your life might you be living as a chicken when God, in reality, has made you an eagle?

Prayer

Father, you have made me a golden eagle — able to fly. In so many ways, however, I still live as a chicken, unaware of the heights and the richness to which you have called me. Fill me, Holy Spirit. Set me free to be the unique person the Lord Jesus has created me to be. In Jesus' name, amen.

Conclude with Silence (2 minutes)

Going Back in Order to Go Forward

3

DAILY OFFICES

Week Three

The very heart of spirituality and discipleship in the family of God is breaking free from the destructive, sinful patterns of our pasts in order to live the unique lives God intends for us. Yet few of us have reflected honestly on the impact of our family of origin and our culture. The result is that we carry baggage and excess weight that hinders us from loving God, ourselves, and others.

This is difficult work and requires courage, but the power to go forward originates not with us but in communion with Jesus. He is the one who anchors us in the Father's love and empowers us with the Holy Spirit. He is the one who enables us to surrender all the broken parts of our histories to God so he can transform them into gifts for those around us.

ADDITIONAL RESOURCES

- *Emotionally Healthy Spirituality: Updated Edition*, chapter 3
- *The Emotionally Healthy Spirituality Workbook Updated Edition*, Session 3
- *The Emotionally Healthy Spirituality DVD: Updated Edition*, Session 3

DAY 1: MORNING/MIDDAY OFFICE

Silence and Stillness before God (2 minutes)

Scripture Reading: Hebrews 11:24 – 27

> By faith Moses, when he had grown up, refused to be known as the son of Pharaoh's daughter. He chose to be mistreated along with the people of God rather than to enjoy the fleeting pleasures of sin. He regarded disgrace for the sake of Christ as of greater value than the treasures of Egypt, because he was looking ahead to his reward. By faith he left Egypt, not fearing the king's anger; he persevered because he saw him who is invisible.

Devotional

Even the worst and most painful family experiences become part of our total identity. God had a plan in placing us in our particular families and cultures. And the more we know about our families, the more we know about ourselves — and the more freedom we have to make decisions about how we want to live.

If we ignore the truth out of fear, we will end up like Miss Havisham from Charles Dickens's novel *Great Expectations*. The daughter of a wealthy man, she received a letter at 8:40 a.m. on her wedding day, saying that her husband-to-be was not coming. She stopped all clocks in the house at the precise time the letter arrived and spent the rest of her life in her bridal dress (which eventually turned yellow), and wearing only one shoe (since she had not yet put on the other one at the time of the disaster). Even as an old lady she remained crippled by the weight of that crushing blow. It was as if "everything in the room and house had stopped." She decided to live in her past, not her present or future.[26]

Moses' life had more than its share of pain and failure. After being raised in a wealthy, privileged home, he murdered a man, lost everything, and spent the next forty years of his life in obscurity in the desert. Yet, by faith he "sees him who is invisible" and hears God's invitation to do something that will be a blessing to many.

Question to Consider

What invitation might God be offering to you out of the failures and pain of your past?

Prayer

Lord Jesus, set me free to be the person you have destined me to be. Help me to pause to hear your voice today, and to leave behind the "baggage" I am carrying as I seek to follow you. Help me to discern your hand at work in and through my life, both in the past and the future. In Jesus' name, amen.

Conclude with Silence (2 minutes)

DAY 1: MIDDAY/EVENING OFFICE

Silence and Stillness before God (2 minutes)

Scripture Reading: Luke 9:59 – 62

[Jesus] said to another man, "Follow me."

But he replied, "Lord, first let me go and bury my father."

Jesus said to him, "Let the dead bury their own dead, but you go and proclaim the kingdom of God."

Still another said, "I will follow you, Lord; but first let me go back and say goodbye to my family."

Jesus replied, "No one who puts a hand to the plow and looks back is fit for service in the kingdom of God."

Devotional

> There's an old story about a boy who, having grown up at the edge of a wide, turbulent river, spent his childhood learning to build rafts. When the boy reached manhood, he felled some trees, lashed them together, and riding his raft, he crossed to the far side of the river. Because he had spent so long working on the raft, he couldn't see leaving it behind when he reached dry land, so he lashed it to his shoulders and carried it with him, though all he came upon in his journeys were a few easily fordable streams and puddles. He rarely thought about the things he was missing out on because he was carrying the bulky raft — the trees he couldn't climb, vistas he couldn't see, people he couldn't get close to and races he couldn't run. He didn't even realize how heavy the raft was, because he had never known what it was like to be free of it.
>
> — Lori Gordon[27]

While all of us are affected by powerful external events and circumstances throughout our earthly lives, our families of origin are the most influential group to which we will ever belong. Even those who leave home as young adults, determined to "break" from their family history, soon find their family's way of "doing life" follows them wherever they go.

Family patterns from the past are played out in our present relationships — often without us necessarily being aware of it. The price we pay for this is high. Our family history lives inside of all of us, even in those who attempt to bury it.

Only the truth sets us free. What was learned can be unlearned. And by God's grace and power, we can learn new ways of "doing life," making change and freedom possible.

Question to Consider

What heavy "raft" might you be carrying as you seek to climb the mountains God has placed before you?

Prayer

Lord, I too prefer to not look at or remember the painful past. Show me, O Father, the heavy weights and rafts I am carrying due to my past. Help me to learn what it means to honestly face my past, lift it up to you, and allow you to use it as a means to my maturing and growing in Christ. In Jesus' name, amen.

Conclude with Silence (2 minutes)

DAY 2: MORNING/MIDDAY OFFICE

Silence and Stillness before God (2 minutes)

Scripture Reading: Mark 3:31 – 35

Then Jesus' mother and brothers arrived. Standing outside, they sent someone in to call him. A crowd was sitting around him, and they told him, "Your mother and brothers are outside looking for you."

"Who are my mother and my brothers?" he asked.

Then he looked at those seated in a circle around him and said, "Here are my mother and my brothers! Whoever does God's will is my brother and sister and mother."

Devotional

When we become Christians we are adopted into the family of Jesus. Jesus was clear and direct in calling people to have a first loyalty to him. Discipleship, he made clear, is putting off the sinful patterns of unbelief so that we might put on the choices of faith, being transformed to live as members of Jesus' family.

As we go back to go forward, we find that it is a never-ending process. We go back, breaking some destructive power of the past. Then later, on a deeper level, God has us return to the same issue on a more profound level.

Thomas Keating compares God's work in us to a Middle Eastern "tell," or archeological site, where one civilization is built on another in the same place. Archeologists excavate, level by level, culture by culture, down through history. The Holy Spirit, he says, is like a Divine Archeologist digging through the layers of our lives.

> The Spirit intends to investigate our whole life history, layer by layer, throwing out the junk and preserving the values that were appropriate to each stage of our human development.... Eventually, the Spirit begins to dig into the bedrock of our earliest emotional life.... Hence, as we progress toward the center where God actually is waiting for us, we are naturally going to feel that we are getting worse. This warns us that the spiritual journey is not a success story or a career move. It is rather a series of humiliations of the false self.[28]

Question to Consider

What false self are you struggling with that Christ wants you to die to so that you can truly live?

Prayer

Holy Spirit, I invite you to dig through the layers of my being that hinder my relationships and communion with others. Grant me perseverance to allow you to dig deeply, excavating out of me all that is not of Christ so that I may be filled with your presence. In Jesus' name, amen.

Conclude with Silence (2 minutes)

DAY 2: MIDDAY/EVENING OFFICE

Silence and Stillness before God (2 minutes)

Scripture Reading: Hebrews 12:1 – 3

> Therefore, since we are surrounded by such a great cloud of witnesses, let us throw off everything that hinders and the sin that so easily entangles. And let us run with perseverance the race marked out for us, fixing our eyes on Jesus, the pioneer and perfecter of faith. For the joy set before him he endured the cross, scorning its shame, and sat down at the right hand of the throne of God. Consider him who endured such opposition from sinners, so that you will not grow weary and lose heart.

Devotional

Francis of Assisi, one of the most influential Christians in the past two thousand years, broke with his family in a very dramatic way. As Francis grew more passionate about his relationship with Christ and less interested in his father's lucrative business, their tension grew. This climaxed in the following scene:

> The father [dragged] the son before the local bishop in the hopes that the town's religious authority could talk some sense into the young man. But the plan backfired. There in front of God and everybody, Francis stripped off his clothing and handed it to his father. Standing there naked as the day he was born, Francis said, "Until now I called you father, but from now

> on I can say without reserve, 'Our father who art in heaven.' "
>
> Francis's father carried his son's clothes back to a large house that was now strangely quiet. Francis, on the other hand, went on his way rejoicing, suddenly freed from the encumbrances of wealth, family, and social esteem....
>
> But one final barrier was left to cross before he could serve God with his whole heart. One day as he was walking down the road and saw a leper approaching him, he knew his opportunity was at hand.... Francis reached out and kissed him.[29]

Francis of Assisi represents one of the "great cloud of witnesses" mentioned in Hebrews 12. He literally "threw off everything that hindered him" and was launched by God into an extraordinary life and destiny. His life continues to speak to us today.

Questions to Consider

What most impacts you in this story about Francis? How is God speaking to you through it?

Prayer

> *Lord, there is none like you. I want to know you as my ultimate Father, the one whose unfathomable, unconditional love sets me free to live for you — far above all other loyalties and expectations. In Jesus' name, amen.*

Conclude with Silence (2 minutes)

DAY 3: MORNING/MIDDAY OFFICE

Silence and Stillness before God (2 minutes)

Scripture Reading: Genesis 50:15, 19 – 21

> When Joseph's brothers saw that their father was dead, they said, "What if Joseph holds a grudge against us and pays us back for all the wrongs we did to him?"
>
> His brothers then came and threw themselves down before him. "We are your slaves," they said.
>
> But Joseph said to them, "Don't be afraid. Am I in the place of God? You intended to harm me, but God intended it for good to accomplish what is now being done, the saving of many lives. So then, don't be afraid. I will provide for you and your children." And he reassured them and spoke kindly to them.

Devotional

Joseph was born into a family characterized by great brokenness and sadness. Lying, jealousy, secrecy, and betrayal visited upon Joseph's young life, and he spent ten to thirteen years in prison, completely cut off from his family.

Nonetheless, Joseph was able to observe the large, loving hand of God through all his setbacks and disappointments. In doing so, he affirmed that God mysteriously leads us into his purposes through darkness and obscurity. God is the Lord God Almighty who has all history in his grip, working in ways that are mostly hidden to us on earth. Joseph understood that in all things God is at work — in spite of, through, and against all human effort — orchestrating his purposes.[30]

God never discards any of our past for his future when we surrender ourselves to him. He is the Lord! Every mistake, sin, and detour we take in the journey of life is taken by God and becomes his gift for a future of blessing when we surrender ourselves to him.

Why did God allow Joseph to go through such pain and loss?

We see traces of the good that came out of it in Genesis 37 – 50, but much remains a mystery. Most important for us to recognize today is that Joseph did not deny his past but trusted in God's goodness and love, even when circumstances went from bad to worse.[31]

Question to Consider

What would it look like for you to surrender the pains of your past (mistakes, sins, setbacks, and disappointments) to God today?

Prayer

Father, I affirm with Joseph that you sovereignly placed me into my family, my culture, and my present circumstances. I cannot see all that you see, but I ask you to show me how, like Joseph, I can rest in your love and power — even when I can't see any good that you might be doing. In Jesus' name, amen.

Conclude with Silence (2 minutes)

DAY 3: MIDDAY/EVENING OFFICE

Silence and Stillness before God (2 minutes)

Scripture Reading: Genesis 45:4 – 7

Then Joseph said to his brothers, "Come close to me." When they had done so, he said, "I am your brother Joseph, the one you sold into Egypt! And now, do not be distressed and do not be angry with yourselves for selling me here, because it was to save lives that God sent me ahead of you. For two years now there has been famine in the land, and for the next five years there will not be plowing and reaping. But God sent me ahead of you to preserve for you a remnant on earth and to save your lives by a great deliverance."

Devotional

Most of us resist remembering and feeling the hurt and pain of our past. It can feel like an abyss that might swallow us up. We can wonder if we are only getting worse. Yet Joseph wept repeatedly when he reunited with his family. In fact, Scripture relates that he wept so loudly that the Egyptians heard him (Genesis 45:2).

Joseph did not minimize or rationalize the painful years of his life. He could have destroyed his brothers in anger. Instead, out of the honest grieving of his pain, he genuinely forgave the brothers who had betrayed him, and was able to bless them. Joseph was able to discern that God had sent him ahead to Egypt to save his brothers' lives by a great deliverance (Genesis 45:7).

The question is, "How did he do it?"

Joseph clearly developed a secret history over a long period of time in his relationship with God. His whole life was structured around following the Lord God of Israel. Then, when the moment came for him to make a critical decision, he was ready. He took leadership of his family — and continued to the end of his days — providing for them financially, emotionally, and spiritually.

Question to Consider

What pains in your life are waiting to be acknowledged and grieved?

Prayer

Lord, lead me through the process of grieving and healing that I might offer genuine kindness and forgiveness to those who have not been kind to me. Help me, like Joseph, to join with you to become a blessing to many other people. In Jesus' name, amen.

Conclude with Silence (2 minutes)

DAY 4: MORNING/MIDDAY OFFICE

Silence and Stillness before God (2 minutes)

Scripture Reading: Acts 9:1 – 6, 15 – 16

Meanwhile, Saul was still breathing out murderous threats against the Lord's disciples. He went to the high priest and asked him for letters to the synagogues in Damascus, so that if he found any there who belonged to the Way, whether men or women, he might take them as prisoners to Jerusalem. As he neared Damascus on his journey, suddenly a light from heaven flashed around him. He fell to the ground and heard a voice say to him, "Saul, Saul, why do you persecute me?"

"Who are you, Lord?" Saul asked.

"I am Jesus, whom you are persecuting," he replied. "Now get up and go into the city, and you will be told what you must do."

But the Lord said to Ananias, "Go! This man is my chosen instrument to proclaim my name to the Gentiles and their kings and to the people of Israel. I will show him how much he must suffer for my name."

Devotional

Saul's great conversion and life as an apostle can only be understood by looking at his entire life and training leading up to this famous passage in Acts 9.

Søren Kierkegaard once observed that life is lived forward, but only understood backward. This was certainly Aleksandr Solzhenitsyn's experience.

Solzhenitsyn is considered by many to be the greatest Russian writer of the twentieth century, but his sense of calling was not always clear. His purpose grew in his experiences of the Gulag, the Soviet concentration camps — a place where he experienced a deadly struggle to write, a miracle of a cure from cancer, a conversion through a Jewish follower of Jesus, and a deepening burden to put "the dying wish of millions" on record. He wrote:

> The one worrying thing was that I might not be given time to carry out the whole scheme. I felt as though I was about to fill a space in the world that was meant for me and had long awaited me, a mold, as it were, made for me alone, but discerned by me only this very moment. I was a molten substance, impatient, unendurably impatient, to pour into my mold, to fill it full, without air bubbles or cracks, before I cooled and stiffened. . . .
>
> Later, the true significance of what happened would inevitably become clear to me, and I would be numb with surprise.[32]

Question to Consider

What space in the world (for which your past has prepared you) is waiting to be filled by you?

Prayer

> *Lord, you are good, and your love endures forever. Help me to trust you — with the good as well as the difficult, the successes and the failures, the joys and the sorrows of my past. I surrender to your voice that whispers to me, "All is well, and all will be well." In Jesus' name, amen.*

Conclude with Silence (2 minutes)

DAY 4: MIDDAY/EVENING OFFICE

Silence and Stillness before God (2 minutes)

Scripture Reading: 1 Samuel 16:6 – 7

When they arrived, Samuel saw Eliab and thought, "Surely the Lord's anointed stands here before the LORD."

But the LORD said to Samuel, "Do not consider his appearance or his height, for I have rejected him. The LORD does not look at the things people look at. People look at the outward appearance, but the LORD looks at the heart."

Devotional

Chaim Potok, in his novel *The Chosen*, tells the story of a friendship between two boys growing up in Brooklyn, New York. Danny is a strict Hasidic Jew, and Reuven is a conservative Jew. Danny's father is the leader of a Hasidic community and raises his son in silence. He never speaks to him directly.

Danny is hurt and confused. He cannot understand why his father is so distant and afflicts him with so much pain. At the end of the novel, Danny's father explains that he did it for him as an act of love.

Danny later reflects on the painful experience: "My father never talked to me, except when we studied together. He taught me with silence. He taught me to look into myself, to find my own strength, to walk inside myself in company with my soul."

In the book, Danny discovers that the suffering he experienced had a good outcome. "One learns of the pain of others by suffering one's own pain, by turning inside oneself, by finding one's own soul. And it is important to know of pain. It destroys our self-pride, our arrogance, and our indifference toward others. It makes us aware of how frail and tiny we are and of how much we must depend upon the Master of the Universe."[33]

In reading 1 Samuel 16, one has to wonder what life was like for David as the youngest of seven sons. What did he learn from being considered invisible, not only by his brothers, but his father as well? How might this experience have helped to shape his character so that he is later called "a man after God's own heart"?

Question to Consider

Can you name some of the ways in which you have learned the pain of others by suffering your own pain?

Prayer

Father, may the pains I experience in life kill the things that need to die in me — arrogance, pride, and indifference to others. Help me, daily, to see my frailty and how dependent I am on you, the Master of the Universe. In Jesus' name, amen.

Conclude with Silence (2 minutes)

DAY 5: MORNING/MIDDAY OFFICE

Silence and Stillness before God (2 minutes)

Scripture Reading: Exodus 14:10, 13 – 16

As Pharaoh approached, the Israelites looked up, and there were the Egyptians, marching after them. They were terrified and cried out to the LORD.

Moses answered the people, "Do not be afraid. Stand firm and you will see the deliverance the LORD will bring you today. The Egyptians you see today you will never see again.

The LORD will fight for you; you need only to be still."

Then the LORD said to Moses, "Why are you crying out to me? Tell the Israelites to move on. Raise your staff and stretch out your hand over the sea to divide the water so that the Israelites can go through the sea on dry ground."

Devotional

Moses demonstrated godly leadership as Egypt's army was overtaking the Israelites at the Red Sea. However, in their anxiety, the Israelites distorted the past and refused to move forward. They preferred their miserable past to an unknown future with God.

Moses courageously stands alone and calls them to "be still" and to "move on." He picks up his staff and takes deliberate steps to move ahead. By remembering the Lord (being still), Moses courageously does what is best (moving on), despite the Israelites' lack of support. He models the delicate balance of being still while at the same time moving on. In doing so, he transforms not only his own life, but the life of all those around him.

> Everyone who draws breath "takes the lead" many times a day. We lead with actions that range from a smile to a frown; with words that range from blessing to curse; with decisions that range from faithful to fearful.... When I resist thinking of myself as a leader, it is neither because of modesty nor a clear-eyed look at the reality of my life.... I am responsible for my impact on the world whether I acknowledge it or not.
>
> So, what does it take to qualify as a leader? Being human and being here. As long as I am here, doing whatever I am doing, I am leading, for better or for worse. And, if I may say so, so are you.
>
> — Parker Palmer[34]

Question to Consider

How might the words from Exodus 14:14 – 15 — "The Lord will fight for you, you need only to be still" and "move on" — apply to you today?

Prayer

Lord, I can relate to the Israelites in the desert and their desire to return to what is predictable — even if it is miserable. Change is hard. Grant me the courage of Moses to walk the delicate balance of being still and moving on to the new life in Christ that you have for me. In Jesus' name, amen.

Conclude with Silence (2 minutes)

DAY 5: MIDDAY/EVENING OFFICE

Silence and Stillness before God (2 minutes)

Scripture Reading: Psalm 131

My heart is not proud, LORD,
    my eyes are not haughty;
I do not concern myself with great matters
    or things too wonderful for me.
But I have calmed and quieted myself,
    I am like a weaned child with its mother;
    like a weaned child I am content.
Israel, put your hope in the LORD
    both now and forevermore.

Devotional

We often forget our humanity, our limits, and our inability to change others. Considering that David was one of the more powerful people in his day, it is striking how he reminds himself in this psalm to not think too highly of himself.

The following quotation is from an anonymous Hasidic rabbi on his deathbed. These words have served me well over the years; they keep me focused on Christ changing me:

> When I was young, I set out to change the world. When I grew a little older, I perceived that this was too ambitious, so I set out to change my state. This too, I realized as I grew older, was too ambitious, so I set out to change my town. When I realized I could not even do this, I tried to change my family. Now as an old man, I know that I should have started by changing myself. If I had started with myself, maybe then I would have succeeded in changing my family, the town, or even the state — and who knows, maybe even the world![35]

Question to Consider

In Psalm 131:1 David prays: "I do not concern myself with great matters or things too wonderful for me." How do you hear these words?

Prayer

Lord Jesus, give my heart eyes to see and ears to hear the ways I need to change. May I be more deeply, radically, and powerfully transformed for your name's sake. Amen.

Conclude with Silence (2 minutes)

Journey through the Wall

4

DAILY OFFICES

Week Four

A mature spirituality requires that you go through the pain of the Wall—or, as the ancients called it, "the dark night of the soul." Just as a physical wall stops us from moving ahead, God sometimes stops us in our spiritual journey through a spiritual Wall in order to radically transform our character. Often, we are brought to the Wall by circumstances and crises beyond our control.

Regardless of how we get there, every follower of Jesus at some point will confront the Wall. Failure to understand and surrender to God's working in us at the Wall often results in great long-term pain, ongoing immaturity, and confusion. Receiving the gift of God in the Wall, however, transforms our lives forever.

ADDITIONAL RESOURCES

- *Emotionally Healthy Spirituality: Updated Edition*, chapter 4
- *The Emotionally Healthy Spirituality Workbook Updated Edition*, Session 4
- *The Emotionally Healthy Spirituality DVD: Updated Edition*, Session 4

DAY 1: MORNING/MIDDAY OFFICE

Silence and Stillness before God (2 minutes)

Scripture Reading: Genesis 12:1 – 3

The LORD had said to Abram, "Go from your country, your people and your father's household to the land I will show you.

"I will make you into a great nation,
 and I will bless you;
I will make your name great,
 and you will be a blessing.
I will bless those who bless you,
 and whoever curses you I will curse;
and all peoples on earth
 will be blessed through you."

Devotional

Like few other metaphors, the image of the Christian life as a journey captures our experience of following Christ. Journeys involve movement, action, stops and starts, detours, delays, and trips into the unknown.

God called Abraham to leave his comfortable life in Ur at the age of seventy-five and to embark on a long, slow journey — a journey with God that would require much patient trust.

Patient Trust

Above all, trust in the slow work of God. We are quite naturally impatient in everything to reach the end without delay. We should like to skip the intermediate stages. We are impatient of being on the way to something unknown, something new. And yet it is the law of all progress that it is made by passing through some stages of instability — and that it may take a very long time.

And so I think it is with you; your ideas mature gradually — let them grow, let them shape themselves, without undue haste. Don't try to force them on, as though you could be today what time (that is to say, grace and circumstances acting on your own good will) will make of you tomorrow.

Only God could say what this new spirit gradually forming within you will be. Give our Lord the benefit of believing that his hand is leading you. And accept the anxiety of feeling yourself in suspense and incomplete.

— Pierre Teilhard de Chardin[36]

Question to Consider

What does it mean for you to trust in the slow work of God today?

Prayer

Grant me courage, Father, to embark on the unique journey you have crafted for me. By faith, I surrender my need and desire to be in control of every event, circumstance, and person I will meet today. In Jesus' name, amen.

Conclude with Silence (2 minutes)

DAY 1: MIDDAY/EVENING OFFICE

Silence and Stillness before God (2 minutes)

Scripture Reading: Song of Songs 1:2, 3:1 – 3

Let him kiss me with the kisses of his mouth —
for your love is more delightful than wine. . . .

All night long on my bed
I looked for the one my heart loves;
I looked for him but did not find him.
I will get up now and go about the city,
through its streets and squares;
I will search for the one my heart loves.
So I looked for him but did not find him.
The watchmen found me
as they made their rounds in the city.
"Have you seen the one my heart loves?"

Devotional

Christians primarily read the Song of Songs on two levels: as the marital love of a man and woman, and as a description of our love relationship with the Lord Jesus — our Bridegroom. Song of Songs 3:1 – 3 describes, in particular, the experience of Mother Teresa of Calcutta. Regarding her painful struggle with God's absence throughout her fifty-year service among the poor, she wrote:

> When I try to raise my thoughts to Heaven — there is such convicting emptiness that those very thoughts return like sharp knives and hurt my very soul. Love — the word — it brings nothing. I am told God loves me — and yet the reality of darkness and coldness and emptiness is so great that nothing touches my soul. . . .
>
> In spite of all — this darkness and emptiness is not as painful as the longing for God. . . .
>
> Before I could spend hours before Our Lord — loving Him — talking to Him — and now — not even meditation goes properly. . . . Yet deep down somewhere in my heart that longing for God keeps breaking through the darkness. . . .
>
> My soul is just like [an] ice block — I have nothing to say.[37]

Mother Teresa came to realize that her darkness was the spiritual side of her work, a sharing in Christ's suffering, a treasure for her and her unique work. She eventually wrote: "I have come to love the darkness. For I believe that it is a part, a very small part, of Jesus' darkness and pain on earth."[38]

Question to Consider

What treasures might there be in the darkness or difficulties in your own life today?

Prayer

> *Father, teach me to trust you even when I feel like I am alone and that you are asleep in the boat with storms raging all around me. Awaken me to the treasures that can only be found in darkness. Grant me the grace to follow you into the next place you have for me in this journey called life. In Jesus' name, amen.*

Conclude with Silence (2 minutes)

DAY 2: MORNING/MIDDAY OFFICE

Silence and Stillness before God (2 minutes)

Scripture Reading: Hebrews 12:7 – 11

> Endure hardship as discipline; God is treating you as his children. For what children are not disciplined by their father? If you are not disciplined — and everyone undergoes discipline — then you are not legitimate, not true sons and daughters at all. Moreover, we have all had human fathers who disciplined us and we respected them for it. How much more

> should we submit to the Father of our spirits and live! They disciplined us for a little while as they thought best; but God disciplines us for our good, in order that we may share in his holiness. No discipline seems pleasant at the time, but painful. Later on, however, it produces a harvest of righteousness and peace for those who have been trained by it.

Devotional

The best way to understand the dynamics of suffering is to examine the classic work of St. John of the Cross entitled *Dark Night of the Soul*, written over five hundred years ago. St. John describes the spiritual journey in three phases: beginners, progressives, and perfect. To move out of the beginning stage, he argues, requires receiving God's gift of the dark night, or the wall. This is the ordinary way we grow in Christ.

The wall is God's way of rewiring and "purging our affections and passions" so that we might delight in his love and enter into a richer, fuller communion with him. God works to free us from unhealthy worldly attachments and idolatries. He wants to communicate his true sweetness and love to us. He longs for us to know his true peace and rest.

For this reason, John of the Cross wrote that God sends us "the dark night of loving fire" to free us from such deadly spiritual imperfections as pride (being judgmental and impatient with the faults of others), avarice (suffering discontentment), luxury (taking more pleasure in our spiritual blessings than in God himself), wrath (becoming easily irritated or impatient), spiritual gluttony (resisting the cross), spiritual envy (always comparing ourselves to others), and sloth (running from what is hard).[39]

Question to Consider

What are some unhealthy attachments or idols God wants to remove from your life in order to lead you to a deeper, richer communion with him?

Prayer

Lord, I invite you this day to cut any unhealthy attachments or idols out of me. You promise in Psalm 32 to teach me the way to go. Help me not to be stubborn like a mule, but rather to be cooperative as you seek to lead me to freedom. Lead me to a place of communion with you, where true peace and rest is found. In Jesus' name, amen.

Conclude with Silence (2 minutes)

DAY 2: MIDDAY/EVENING OFFICE

Silence and Stillness before God (2 minutes)

Scripture Reading: Genesis 22:9 – 12

When they reached the place God had told him about, Abraham built an altar there and arranged the wood on it. He bound his son Isaac and laid him on the altar, on top of the wood. Then he reached out his hand and took the knife to slay his son. But the angel of the LORD called out to him from heaven, "Abraham! Abraham!"

"Here I am," he replied.

"Do not lay a hand on the boy," he said. "Do not do anything to him. Now I know that you fear God, because you have not withheld from me your son, your only son."

Devotional

We encounter the wall when a crisis turns our world upside down. These walls are not simply one-time events that we pass through and get beyond. They are issues we return to as a part of our ongoing relationship with God.

We see this in Abraham, waiting at the wall of infertility for twenty-five years before the birth of his first child with his wife, Sarah. Ten to thirteen years later, God led him to another wall—the separation from Ishmael, his eldest son (conceived with Sarah's maidservant, Hagar). Abraham encountered a third wall a few years later, when God commanded him to sacrifice his long-awaited, beloved son Isaac on the altar.

Abraham appears to have gone through the wall numerous times in his journey with God. Why? Thomas Merton explains, "Unintentionally and unknowingly we fall back into imperfections. Bad habits are like living roots that return. These roots must be dug away and cleared from the garden of our soul.... This requires the direct intervention of God."[40]

Question to Consider

What things or people are you rooting your identity in that God may want to dig up so that your identity might be replanted in him?

Prayer

Abba Father, I open my clenched fists to surrender everything you have given to me. Reestablish my identity in you—not in my family, my work, my accomplishments, or what others think of me. Cleanse the things in me that are not conformed to your will. By faith I unite my will to yours so that the likeness of Jesus Christ may be formed in me. In his name, amen.

Conclude with Silence (2 minutes)

DAY 3: MORNING/MIDDAY OFFICE

Silence and Stillness before God (2 minutes)

Scripture Reading: Romans 11:33 – 36

Oh, the depth of the riches of the wisdom and knowledge of God!
How unsearchable his judgments,
and his paths beyond tracing out!
"Who has known the mind of the Lord?
Or who has been his counselor?"
"Who has ever given to God,
that God should repay them?"
For from him and through him and for him are all things.
To him be the glory forever! Amen.

Devotional

Our experience at the wall can be fruitful in providing a greater appreciation for what I call "holy unknowing" or mystery. This expands our capacity to wait on God when everything inside us is saying, "Do something!"

There is an old story about a wise man living on one of China's vast frontiers. One day, for no apparent reason, his son's horse ran away and was taken by nomads across the border. Everyone tried to offer consolation for the man's bad fortune, but his father, a wise man, said, "What makes you so sure this is not a blessing?"

Months later, the horse returned, bringing with her a magnificent stallion. This time everyone was full of congratulations for the son's good fortune. But now his father said, "What makes you so sure this isn't a disaster?"

Their household was made richer by this fine horse the son loved to ride, but one day he fell off his horse and broke his hip.

Once again, everyone offered their consolation for his bad luck, but his father said, "What makes you so sure this is not a blessing?"

A year later, nomads invaded, and every able-bodied man was required to take up his bow and go into battle. The Chinese families living on the border lost nine out of every ten men who went to fight. Only because the son was lame did the father and son survive to take care of each other.

Often, what appears to be success or a blessing is actually a terrible thing; what appears to be a terrible event can turn out to be a rich blessing.[41]

Question to Consider

Have you ever experienced a terrible circumstance that (in time) actually turned out to be a rich blessing?

Prayer

Forgive me, Father, for at times treating you as if you were my personal assistant or secretary. Your ways are unsearchable and beyond understanding. Help me to put my trust in you and not in my circumstances. In your presence, I am silenced. In Jesus' name, amen.

Conclude with Silence (2 minutes)

DAY 3: MIDDAY/EVENING OFFICE

Silence and Stillness before God (2 minutes)

Scripture Reading: Job 42:1 – 6

Then Job replied to the LORD:

"I know that you can do all things;
no plan of yours can be thwarted.

> You asked, 'Who is this that obscures my counsel without knowledge?'
> Surely I spoke of things I did not understand,
> things too wonderful for me to know.
> You said, 'Listen now, and I will speak;
> I will question you,
> and you shall answer me.'
> My ears had heard of you
> but now my eyes have seen you.
> Therefore I despise myself
> and repent in dust and ashes." (NIV 1984)

Devotional

Job was faithful and blameless, a man of integrity. Yet he experienced the cataclysmic loss of his family, wealth, and health, and found himself at a wall like few others in all of Scripture. From this place of deep wrestling with his faith and God, he experiences God's love and grace. He is transformed.

> Now, believe it or not, we are threatened by such a free God because it takes away all of our ability to control or engineer the process. It leaves us powerless, and changes the language from any language of performance or achievement to that of surrender, trust and vulnerability.... That is the so-called "wildness" of God. We cannot control God by any means whatsoever, not even by our good behavior, which tends to be our first and natural instinct.... That utter and absolute freedom of God is fortunately used totally in our favor, even though we are still afraid of it. It is called providence, forgiveness, free election or mercy.... But to us, it feels like wildness — precisely because

we cannot control it, manipulate it, direct it, earn it or lose it. Anyone into controlling God by his or her actions will feel very useless, impotent and ineffective.

— Richard Rohr[42]

Questions to Consider

What words or phrases from the Richard Rohr quote most speak to you? Why?

Prayer

Father, when I read even part of the story of Job, I too am overwhelmed by your "wildness." Your ways and timing are beyond me. Job moved from hearing about you to having "seen you." Lead me, Lord, on a pathway so that I too can pray as Job prayed: "My ears had heard of you, but now my eyes have seen you" (Job 42:5). In Jesus' name, amen.

Conclude with Silence (2 minutes)

DAY 4: MORNING/MIDDAY OFFICE

Silence and Stillness before God (2 minutes)

Scripture Reading: Psalm 69:1 – 3, 15 – 16

Save me, O God,
  for the waters have come up to my neck.
I sink in the miry depths,
  where there is no foothold.
I have come into the deep waters;
  the floods engulf me.
I am worn out calling for help;
  my throat is parched.

My eyes fail,
    looking for my God.
Do not let the floodwaters engulf me
    or the depths swallow me up
    or the pit close its mouth over me.
Answer me, LORD, out of the goodness of your love;
    in your great mercy turn to me.

Devotional

The Bible presents David as a man after God's own heart, yet the preceding Scripture reading shows us that David's emotional world was very human and broken. He bares his soul in these heart-wrenching poems — as prayers back to God. While he often struggles with his circumstances, David affirms that God is good, and that his love endures forever. David knows that God's ways are higher and deeper than our ways (Isaiah 55:9 – 10).

In *Paradise Lost*, John Milton compares the evil of history to a compost pile — a mixture of decaying substances such as animal excrement, potato skins, egg shells, dead leaves, and banana peels. If you cover it with dirt, after some time it smells wonderful. The soil has become a rich, natural fertilizer and is tremendously well suited for growing fruits and vegetables — but you have to be willing to wait — years, in some cases.

Milton's point is that the worst events of human history — those that we cannot understand — even hell itself — are compost in God's wonderful eternal plan. Out of the greatest evil, the death of Jesus, came the greatest good.

The fact that God exists does not lessen the awfulness of the evil in the world; nevertheless, we can rest in him, placing our hope in a God who is so great and sovereign that he ultimately transforms all evil into good.[43]

We can trust God at the Wall.

Question to Consider

How is God inviting you to wait on him today?

Prayer

Lord, fill me with the simple trust that even out of the most awful evil around me, you are able to bring great good — for me, for others, and for your great glory. In Jesus' name, amen.

Conclude with Silence (2 minutes)

DAY 4: MIDDAY/EVENING OFFICE

Silence and Stillness before God (2 minutes)

Scripture Reading: John 21:17 – 19

The third time he said to him, "Simon son of John, do you love me?"

Peter was hurt because Jesus asked him the third time, "Do you love me?" He said, "Lord, you know all things; you know that I love you."

Jesus said, "Feed my sheep. Very truly I tell you, when you were younger you dressed yourself and went where you wanted; but when you are old you will stretch out your hands, and someone else will dress you and lead you where you do not want to go." Jesus said this to indicate the kind of death by which Peter would glorify God. Then he said to him, "Follow me!"

Devotional

Jesus had this different vision of maturity: It is the ability and willingness to be led where you would rather not go. Immediately after Jesus commissions Peter to be a leader of his sheep, Jesus confronts Peter with the hard truth that the servant-leader is the leader who is being led to unknown, undesirable, and painful places. Henri Nouwen expressed it well:

> The way of the Christian leader is not the way of upward mobility in which our world has invested so much, but the way of downward mobility ending on the cross.... Powerlessness and humility in the spiritual life do not refer to people who have no spine and who let everyone make decisions for them. They refer to people who are so deeply in love with Jesus that they are ready to follow him wherever he guides them, always trusting that, with him, they will find life and find it abundantly.[44]

Question to Consider

In your own words, speak to God about your willingness to go where he leads you. What joys and/or fears accompany your willingness?

Prayer

> *Father, to you I acknowledge that I don't want to go the way of powerlessness and humility. Like Peter, I want to know what you are doing with those around me. I love you. Help me to trust you with this day, with tomorrow, and with my whole life. In Jesus' name, amen.*

Conclude with Silence (2 minutes)

DAY 5: MORNING/MIDDAY OFFICE

Silence and Stillness before God (2 minutes)

Scripture Reading: James 1:2 – 5

Consider it pure joy, my brothers and sisters, whenever you face trials of many kinds, because you know that the testing of your faith produces perseverance. Let perseverance finish its work so that you may be mature and complete, not lacking anything. If any of you lacks wisdom, you should ask God, who gives generously to all without finding fault, and it will be given to you.

Devotional

If there were never any storms or clouds in our lives, we would have no faith. "His way is in the whirlwind and the storm, and clouds are the dust of his feet" (Nahum 1:3b). Clouds are a sign that God is there. What a revelation to know that sorrow, bereavement, and suffering are actually the clouds that come along with God!

> It is not true to say that God wants to teach us something in our trials. Through every cloud He brings our way, He wants us to unlearn something. His purpose in using the cloud is to simplify our beliefs until our relationship with Him is exactly like that of a child — a relationship simply between God and our own souls, and where other people are but shadows. Until other people become shadows to us, clouds and darkness will be ours every once in a while. Is our relationship with God becoming more simple than it has ever been?... Until we come face to face with the deepest, darkest fact of life without damaging our view of God's character, we do not yet know Him.
>
> — Oswald Chambers[45]

Question to Consider

What is one thing God might want you to unlearn today?

Prayer

Father, I confess that when difficulties and trials come into my life, large or small, I mostly grumble and complain. I realize the trials James talks about are not necessarily "walls," but they are difficult to bear nonetheless. Fill me with such a vision of a transformed life, O God, that I might actually consider it "pure joy" when you bring trials my way. I believe, Lord. Help my unbelief. In Jesus' name, amen.

Conclude with Silence (2 minutes)

DAY 5: MIDDAY/EVENING OFFICE

Silence and Stillness before God (2 minutes)

Scripture Reading: Matthew 26:50b – 53

Then the men stepped forward, seized Jesus and arrested him. With that, one of Jesus' companions reached for his sword, drew it out and struck the servant of the high priest, cutting off his ear.

"Put your sword back in its place," Jesus said to him, "for all who draw the sword will die by the sword. Do you think I cannot call on my Father, and he will at once put at my disposal more than twelve legions of angels?"

Devotional

Walls are sometimes God's way of saying no. The Gospel of John tells us it was the apostle Peter who drew his sword to defend Jesus by force. Peter found it very difficult to accept Jesus' no to his plan for a life and future without a crucifixion. In contrast, we observe David accepting God's no to his desire to build the Temple (2 Samuel 7). Additionally, we read of Jesus submitting to his Father's no — that the cup of the cross be taken from him (Matthew 26:37 – 44).

You may want to use the following prayer found on an unknown soldier in Gettysburg to help you embrace God's response when he says yes or no in your journey with him:

> I asked God for strength that I might achieve,
> I was made weak that I might learn to obey.
> I asked for health that I might do great things.
> I was given infirmity that I might do better things.
> I asked for riches that I might be happy;
> I was given poverty that I might be wise.
> I asked for power when I was young that I might
>   have the praise of men;
> I was given weakness that I might feel the need for God.
> I asked for all things that I might enjoy life;
> I was given life that I might enjoy all things.
> Almost despite myself, my unspoken prayers were answered.
> I am, among all people, most richly blessed.

Questions to Consider

Which words speak to you the most from the above prayer? Why?

Prayer

Lord, I relate to Peter's headstrong nature, and to his struggle to understand what you were telling him. It is difficult for me to understand how you are running the universe and my place in it. Transform my stubborn will, O Lord. Teach me to wait on you. Help me to trust you. In Jesus' name, amen.

Conclude with Silence (2 minutes)

Enlarge Your Soul through Grief and Loss

5

DAILY OFFICES

Week Five

Loss is a place where self-knowledge and powerful transformation can happen. Paying attention to our losses enlarges our souls—when we pour them out before the Lord (see Psalm 62:8) and participate in what God wants to do in us.

We all face many "deaths" within our lives. Our culture routinely interprets these losses and griefs as alien invasions and interruptions to our "normal" lives. The choice is whether these deaths will be terminal (crushing our spirit and life) or will open us up to new possibilities and depths of transformation in Christ. Staying with Jesus during these challenging times—remaining, abiding, communing with him—makes all the difference.

ADDITIONAL RESOURCES

- *Emotionally Healthy Spirituality: Updated Edition*, chapter 5
- *The Emotionally Healthy Spirituality Workbook Updated Edition*, Session 5
- *The Emotionally Healthy Spirituality DVD: Updated Edition*, Session 5

DAY 1: MORNING/MIDDAY OFFICE

Silence and Stillness before God (2 minutes)

Scripture Reading: Matthew 26:36 – 39

Then Jesus went with his disciples to a place called Gethsemane, and he said to them, "Sit here while I go over there and pray." He took Peter and the two sons of Zebedee along with him, and he began to be sorrowful and troubled. Then he said to them, "My soul is overwhelmed with sorrow to the point of death. Stay here and keep watch with me."

Going a little farther, he fell with his face to the ground and prayed, "My Father, if it is possible, may this cup be taken from me. Yet not as I will, but as you will."

Devotional

In the garden of Gethsemane, we see Jesus troubled and overwhelmed with sorrow — to the point of death. We see him falling with his face to the ground and praying three times. We also see the Father say no to Jesus' request that the cup be taken away from him.

We want to follow Jesus into the abundant life of resurrection, but we are less than enthusiastic about following him into the garden of Gethsemane.

Lament for a Son, by Nicholas Wolterstorff, is a record of the author's reflections and struggles following the death of his twenty-five-year-old son, Eric, in an Austrian mountain-climbing accident. Wolterstorff doesn't have any explanations or answers for why God would have allowed such a tragedy. Who does? At one point, however, he comes upon a profound insight:

Through the prism of my tears I have seen a suffering God.

It is said of God that no one can behold his face and live. I always thought this meant that no one can see his splendor and live. A friend said perhaps this meant that no one could see his sorrow and live. Or perhaps his sorrow is splendor.[46]

Question to Consider

What does it mean for you to pray, "Yet not as I will, but as you will"?

Prayer

Lord, everything in me resists following you into the garden of Gethsemane to fall on my face to the ground before you. Grant me the courage to follow you all the way to the cross, whatever that might mean for my life. And then, by your grace, lead me to resurrection life and power. In Jesus' name, amen.

Conclude with Silence (2 minutes)

DAY 1: MIDDAY/EVENING OFFICE

Silence and Stillness before God (2 minutes)

Scripture Reading: Job 2:7 – 10

So Satan went out from the presence of the LORD and afflicted Job with painful sores from the soles of his feet to the crown of his head. Then Job took a piece of broken pottery and scraped himself with it as he sat among the ashes.

His wife said to him, "Are you still maintaining your integrity? Curse God and die!"

He replied, "You are talking like a foolish woman. Shall we accept good from God, and not trouble?"

In all this, Job did not sin in what he said.

Devotional

Jonathan Edwards, in a famous sermon on the book of Job, noted that the story of Job is the story of us all. Job lost everything in one day: his family, his wealth, and his health. Most of us experience our losses more slowly — over the span of a lifetime — until we find ourselves on the door of death, leaving everything behind.[47]

> Catastrophic loss by definition precludes recovery. It will transform us or destroy us, but it will never leave us the same. There is no going back to the past. . . .
>
> It is not therefore true that we become less through loss — unless we allow the loss to make us less, grinding our soul down until there is nothing left. . . . Loss can also make us more. . . .
>
> I did not get over the loss of my loved ones; rather, I absorbed the loss into my life, until it became part of who I am. Sorrow took up permanent residence in my soul and enlarged it. . . .
>
> One learns the pain of others by suffering one's own pain, by turning inside oneself, by finding one's own soul. . . .
>
> However painful, sorrow is good for the soul. . . .
>
> The soul is elastic, like a balloon. It can grow larger through suffering.
>
> — Jerry Sittser[48]

Question to Consider

How can you see God enlarging your soul through your losses?

Prayer

Father, when I think about my losses, it can feel like I have no skin to protect me. I feel raw, scraped to the bone. Looking at Job and Jesus helps, but I must admit that I struggle to see something new being birthed out of the old. Enlarge my soul through the trials and losses of my life. In Jesus' name, amen.

Conclude with Silence (2 minutes)

DAY 2: MORNING/MIDDAY OFFICE

Silence and Stillness before God (2 minutes)

Scripture Reading: 2 Corinthians 4:7 – 11

> But we have this treasure in jars of clay to show that this all-surpassing power is from God and not from us. We are hard pressed on every side, but not crushed; perplexed, but not in despair; persecuted, but not abandoned; struck down, but not destroyed. We always carry around in our body the death of Jesus, so that the life of Jesus may also be revealed in our body. For we who are alive are always being given over to death for Jesus' sake, so that his life may also be revealed in our mortal body.

Devotional

Joni Eareckson Tada has been paralyzed from the neck down for over thirty years. As a result, she has experienced both the death of Jesus and the life of Jesus. She says:

> The cross is the center of our relationship with Jesus. The cross is where we die. We go there daily. It isn't easy.
>
> Normally, we will follow Christ anywhere — to a party, as it were, where he changes water into wine, to a sunlit beach where he preaches from a boat. But to the cross? We dig in our heels. The invitation is so frighteningly individual. It's an invitation to go alone.
>
> Suffering reduces us to nothing and as Soren Kierkegaard noted, "God creates everything out of nothing. And everything which God is to use, he first reduces to nothing." To be reduced to nothing is to be dragged to the foot of the cross. It's a severe mercy.

When suffering forces us to our knees at the foot of Calvary, we die to self. We cannot kneel there for long without releasing our pride and anger, unclasping our dreams and desires.... In exchange, God imparts power and implants new and lasting hope.[49]

Question to Consider

How is God bringing you to your knees before him through difficulties and setbacks in your life?

Prayer

Lord, everything in me kicks against going to the foot of the cross where you will root out of me all that is not of you. Help me not to fear the "deaths" it will take for me to be transformed into a free person who loves you and others well. Have mercy on me, O Lord. In Jesus' name, amen.

Conclude with Silence (2 minutes)

DAY 2: MIDDAY/EVENING OFFICE

Silence and Stillness before God (2 minutes)

Scripture Reading: Psalm 22:1 – 5

My God, my God, why have you forsaken me?
    Why are you so far from saving me,
    so far from my cries of anguish?
My God, I cry out by day, but you do not answer,
    by night, but I find no rest.
Yet you are enthroned as the Holy One;
    you are the one Israel praises.

In you our ancestors put their trust;
they trusted and you delivered them.
To you they cried out and were saved;
in you they trusted and were not put to shame.

Devotional

In the 1870s Horatio Spafford was a successful Chicago lawyer and a close friend of evangelist Dwight L. Moody. Spafford had invested heavily in real estate, but the Chicago fire of 1871 wiped out his holdings. His son had died shortly before the disaster. Spafford and his family desperately needed a rest, so in 1873 he planned a trip to Europe with his wife, Anna, and their four daughters. Yet just before they set sail, a last-minute business development forced Horatio to return to work. Not wanting to ruin the family holiday, Spafford persuaded his family to go as planned, and intended to catch up with them later.

With this decided, Spafford returned to Chicago, and Anna and the four daughters sailed to Europe. Unfortunately, their ship collided with an English vessel and sank in only twelve minutes. The accident claimed the lives of 226 people. Anna Spafford had stood bravely on the deck, with her daughters (Annie, Maggie, Bessie, and Tanetta) desperately clinging to her. Her last memory of the disaster is that of her baby being violently torn from her arms by the force of the waters. Just nine days later, Spafford received a telegram from his wife in Wales. It read: "Saved alone." When Horatio Spafford made the ocean crossing to meet his grieving wife, he sailed near the place where his four daughters had sunk to the ocean's depths. There, in the midst of his sorrow, he wrote "It Is Well with My Soul." The words of Staffords's hymn have brought comfort to so many in grief:

When peace, like a river, attendeth my way,
When sorrows like sea-billows roll,
Whatever my lot, Thou hast taught me to say,
It is well, it is well, with my soul.

Though Satan should buffet, though trials should come,
Let this blessed assurance control,
That Christ hath regarded my helpless estate,
And hath shed His own blood for my soul.[50]

Question to Consider

What about Spafford and his relationship with Christ moves you the most?

Prayer

Father, I can only bow to you before such unimaginable loss and suffering. I join with Spafford and pray to you: "Whatever my lot, Thou has taught me to say, It is well, it is well, with my soul." In your Son's name, amen.

Conclude with Silence (2 minutes)

DAY 3: MORNING/MIDDAY OFFICE

Silence and Stillness before God (2 minutes)

Scripture Reading: Ecclesiastes 3:1 – 8

There is a time for everything,
    and a season for every activity under the heavens:

a time to be born and a time to die,
    a time to plant and a time to uproot,
a time to kill and a time to heal,

a time to tear down and a time to build,
a time to weep and a time to laugh,
a time to mourn and a time to dance,
a time to scatter stones and a time to gather them,
a time to embrace and a time to refrain from embracing,
a time to search and a time to give up,
a time to keep and a time to throw away,
a time to tear and a time to mend,
a time to be silent and a time to speak,
a time to love and a time to hate,
a time for war and a time for peace.

Devotional

We don't control the seasons; they happen to us. Winter, spring, summer, and fall come to us whether we like it or not. Their rhythms teach us about our spiritual lives and the ways of God. Consider the following description of the paradox of death and rebirth in nature and in our lives:

> Autumn is a season of great beauty, but it is also a season of decline: the days grow shorter, the light is suffused, and summer's abundance decays toward winter's death.... In my own experience of autumn, I am rarely aware that seeds are being planted.... But as I explore autumn's paradox of dying and seeding, I feel the power of metaphor. In the autumnal events of my own experience, I am easily fixated on surface appearances—on the decline of meaning, the decay of relationships, the death of a work. And yet if I look more deeply, I may see the myriad possibilities being planted to bear fruit in some season yet to come.
>
> In retrospect, I can see in my own life what I could not see at the time—how the job I lost helped me find work I needed

to do, how the "road closed" sign turned me toward terrain I needed to travel, how losses that felt irredeemable forced me to discern meanings I needed to know. On the surface it seemed that life was lessening, but silently and lavishly the seeds of new life were always being sown.

— Parker Palmer[51]

Question to Consider

What "road closed" sign is before you today that may be God's way of redirecting you to something new?

Prayer

Lord, grant me wisdom and prudence to see the larger picture, to wait, and to discern the seasons in my life with you. Forgive me for fighting the "deaths" you send into my life in order to plant something new. In Jesus' name, amen.

Conclude with Silence (2 minutes)

DAY 3: MIDDAY/EVENING OFFICE

Silence and Stillness before God (2 minutes)

Scripture Reading: John 3:26 – 30

They came to John and said to him, "Rabbi, that man who was with you on the other side of the Jordan — the one you testified about — look, he is baptizing, and everyone is going to him."

To this John replied, "A person can receive only what is given them from heaven. You yourselves can testify that I said, 'I am not the Messiah but am sent ahead of him.' The bride

> belongs to the bridegroom. The friend who attends the bridegroom waits and listens for him, and is full of joy when he hears the bridegroom's voice. That joy is mine, and it is now complete. He must become greater; I must become less."

Devotional

Experiencing loss makes us confront our humanity and our limits. We quickly realize we are not in control of our lives; God is. We are simply creatures, not the Creator.

Consider the example of John the Baptist. Crowds that formerly followed John for baptism switched their allegiances once Jesus began his ministry. They began leaving John to follow Jesus. Some of John's followers were upset about this dramatic turn of events. They complained to him, "Everyone is going to him" (John 3:26).

John understood limits and replied, "A person can receive only what is given them from heaven" (John 3:27). He was able to accept his limits, his humanity, and his declining popularity and say, "He must become greater; I must become less" (John 3:30).

Getting off of our thrones and joining the rest of humanity is a must if we are to develop spiritual maturity. We are not the center of the universe. The universe does not revolve around us.

Yet a part of us hates limits. We won't accept them. This is one of the primary reasons that biblically grieving our losses is such an indispensable part of spiritual maturity.

Embracing our limits humbles us like little else.[52]

Question to Consider

Name one or two limits God has recently placed in your life as a gift.

Prayer

Lord, forgive me for the arrogance that sees interruptions to my plans as alien invasions. Forgive me for constantly trying to do more than you intend with my life. Help me to be like John the Baptist, embracing my losses and respecting my limits. In Jesus' name, amen.

Conclude with Silence (2 minutes)

DAY 4: MORNING/MIDDAY OFFICE

Silence and Stillness before God (2 minutes)

Scripture Reading: 2 Samuel 1:17–20, 24–25 (NIV 1984)

David took up this lament concerning Saul and his son Jonathan, and ordered that the men of Judah be taught this lament of the bow (it is written in the Book of Jashar):

"Your glory, O Israel, lies slain on your heights.
How the mighty have fallen!
"Tell it not in Gath,
proclaim it not in the streets of Ashkelon,
lest the daughters of the Philistines be glad,
lest the daughters of the uncircumcised rejoice.
"Daughters of Israel,
weep for Saul,
who clothed you in scarlet and finery,
who adorned your garments with ornaments of gold.
"How the mighty have fallen in battle!
Jonathan lies slain on your heights."

Devotional

David not only sang this lamentation, but he also ordered the people to learn it, memorize it, and inhabit it as their experience.

> Pain isn't the worst thing. Being hated isn't the worst thing. Being separated from the one you love isn't the worst thing. Death isn't the worst thing. The worst thing is failing to deal with reality and becoming disconnected from what is actual. The worst thing is trivializing the honorable, desecrating the sacred. What I do with my grief affects the way you handle your grief; together we form a community that deals with death and other loss in the context of God's sovereignty, which is expressed finally in resurrection....
>
> We don't become mature human beings by getting lucky or cleverly circumventing loss, and certainly not by avoidance and distraction. Learn to lament. Learn this lamentation. We're mortals, after all. We and everyone around are scheduled for death (mortis). Get used to it. Take up your cross. It prepares us and those around us for resurrection.
>
> — Eugene Peterson[53]

Question to Consider

What might it mean for you to mature by entering the painful reality of your losses rather than avoiding them?

Prayer

> *Lord, I have spent much of my life running from pain and loss, medicating my pain and quickly moving on to the next project — the new urgent demand. I ask for the grace to embrace all of life — the joys and the sorrows, the deaths and the births, the old and the new. In Jesus' name, amen.*

Conclude with Silence (2 minutes)

DAY 4: MIDDAY/EVENING OFFICE

Silence and Stillness before God (2 minutes)

Scripture Reading: Luke 19:41 – 44

As he approached Jerusalem and saw the city, he wept over it and said, "If you, even you, had only known on this day what would bring you peace — but now it is hidden from your eyes. The days will come upon you when your enemies will build an embankment against you and encircle you and hem you in on every side. They will dash you to the ground, you and the children within your walls. They will not leave one stone on another, because you did not recognize the time of God's coming to you."

Devotional

The Greek word used to describe Jesus weeping over Jerusalem is that of a person wailing or sobbing. Imagine the scene!

Sadly, many of us, unlike our Lord, feel guilty expressing raw feelings such as sadness and anger. The problem is that when we deny our pain, losses, and feelings year after year, we transform slowly into empty shells with smiley faces painted on them. But when we begin to allow ourselves to feel a wider range of emotions (including sadness, depression, fear, and anger), a profound change takes place in our relationship with God. As Ken Gire wrote:

> C. S. Lewis said that "we should bring to God what is in us, not what ought to be in us." The "oughts" will keep us from telling the truth. They will also keep us from feeling the truth. Especially the truth about our pain....
>
> When Jesus realized the nearness of His own death, He went to a quiet place and prayed.... We are told that He agonized

with "loud crying and tears" (Heb. 5:7). We are also told that He fell to the ground, where He prayed fervently and sweated profusely (Luke 22:44).

This was no Renaissance painting. This was a real portrait, a portrait of how we pray when the earth beneath our feet begins to quake. We pray however we can, with whatever words we can. We pray with our sweat, with our tears. And with whatever friends we have who will sit with us in the darkness.[54]

Question to Consider

How would it change your prayer life to bring to God what is actually in you and not what you think ought to be in you?

Prayer

Abba Father, I admit that I am often afraid and embarrassed to openly tell you all that is going on inside me — even though I know you know it all anyway. Teach me what boldness in prayer looks like as I draw near your throne of grace. In Jesus' name, amen.

Conclude with Silence (2 minutes)

DAY 5: MORNING/MIDDAY OFFICE

Silence and Stillness before God (2 minutes)

Scripture Reading: Hebrews 5:7 – 8

During the days of Jesus' life on earth, he offered up prayers and petitions with fervent cries and tears to the one who could save him from death, and he was heard because of his reverent submission. Son though he was, he learned obedience from what he suffered.

Devotional

The capacity to grieve is almost lost in our culture. People use work, TV, drugs, alcohol, shopping, food binges, busyness, sexual escapades, unhealthy relationships, and even serving others at church — anything — to medicate the pain of life. Year after year we deny and avoid the difficulties and losses of life, the rejections and frustrations. When a loss enters our life we become angry at God and treat it as an alien invasion from outer space.

This is unbiblical and a denial of our common humanity. Consider the following examples: The ancient Hebrews physically expressed their laments by tearing their clothes and utilizing sackcloth and ashes. Jesus himself offered up "prayer and petitions with fervent cries and tears." During Noah's generation, God was grieved about the state of humanity (Genesis 6). Jeremiah wrote six confessions or laments in which he protested to God about his circumstances. Then, after the fall of Jerusalem, he wrote an entire book called Lamentations.

The God-like response to loss is neither spin nor a cover-up. Scripture teaches us to deal honestly and prayerfully with our losses and disappointments (big and small), and all their accompanying confusing emotions. Why? Losses are indispensable if we are going to change and grow into the men and women God has called us to be.[55]

Question to Consider

In what ways are you tempted to spin or cover over your losses and miss God's deeper work in you?

Prayer

Lord, I acknowledge that I prefer to ignore and deny my pain and loss. I struggle with seeing how resurrection life can come out of death. Grant me the courage to pay attention to what you are doing, and to wait on you — even when everything in me wants to run away. In Jesus' name, amen.

Conclude with Silence (2 minutes)

DAY 5: MIDDAY/EVENING OFFICE

Silence and Stillness before God (2 minutes)

Scripture Reading: Job 42:12 – 17

The LORD blessed the latter part of Job's life more than the former part. He had fourteen thousand sheep, six thousand camels, a thousand yoke of oxen and a thousand donkeys. And he also had seven sons and three daughters. The first daughter he named Jemimah, the second Keziah and the third Keren-Happuch. Nowhere in all the land were there found women as beautiful as Job's daughters, and their father granted them an inheritance along with their brothers.

After this, Job lived a hundred and forty years; he saw his children and their children to the fourth generation. And so Job died, an old man and full of years.

Devotional

Good grieving is not just letting go, but also letting the loss bless us. Job did just that.

The old life for Job was truly over. That door remained closed. That is the source of the great grief that arises from our losses. There is finality. We can't get what we've lost back. Yet if we follow Job's path, we will be blessed. That is one of the major lessons of Job. He followed the difficult path of allowing his losses to enlarge his soul for God, and God blessed him superabundantly. Not only was Job spiritually transformed, but the Lord blessed him with new prosperity. His wealth was doubled, God gave him ten children once again, and he lived to a ripe old age.

This account is meant to encourage us to trust the living God with the many mini-deaths that we experience in our lives. The central message of Christ is that suffering and death bring resurrection and transformation. Jesus himself said, "I tell you the truth, unless a kernel of wheat falls to the ground and dies, it remains only a single seed. But if it dies, it produces many seeds" (John 12:24 NIV 1984).

But remember, resurrection only comes out of death — real death. Our losses are real, and so is our God — the living God.[56]

Question to Consider

How is God coming to you through the "mini-deaths" in your life now?

Prayer

Lord, after his loss, you gave Job prosperity, blessing him with twice as much as he had before, but that has not always felt like my experience. Grant me patience. Help me to trust and wait on you, especially in those areas of my life where I have no idea what you are doing, when my hardship will end, or where you are taking me. In Jesus' name, amen.

Conclude with Silence (2 minutes)

Discover the Rhythms of the Daily Office and Sabbath

6

DAILY OFFICES

Week Six

Many of us are eager to develop our relationship with God. But we are busy, very busy. And if we aren't busy, we feel guilty that we are wasting time and not being productive. We struggle to stop long enough to be with Jesus to cultivate our own direct experience of God.

But God is offering us a way to deeply root our lives in him. This can be found in two ancient disciplines going back thousands of years—the Daily Office and Sabbath. When placed inside present-day Christianity, the Daily Office and Sabbath are groundbreaking, countercultural acts that go against the grain of our fast-paced Western culture. They offer a rhythm to be with God in our chaotic world, enabling us to stay attuned to God's presence throughout our days and weeks.

ADDITIONAL RESOURCES

- *Emotionally Healthy Spirituality: Updated Edition*, chapter 6
- *The Emotionally Healthy Spirituality Workbook Updated Edition*, Session 6
- *The Emotionally Healthy Spirituality DVD: Updated Edition*, Session 6

DAY 1: MORNING/MIDDAY OFFICE

Silence and Stillness before God (2 minutes)

Scripture Reading: Luke 8:11 – 15

"This is the meaning of the parable: The seed is the word of God. Those along the path are the ones who hear, and then the devil comes and takes away the word from their hearts, so that they may not believe and be saved. Those on the rocky ground are the ones who receive the word with joy when they hear it, but they have no root. They believe for a while, but in the time of testing they fall away. The seed that fell among thorns stands for those who hear, but as they go on their way they are choked by life's worries, riches and pleasures, and they do not mature. But the seed on good soil stands for those with a noble and good heart, who hear the word, retain it, and by persevering produce a crop."

Devotional

Awareness of the love of God — and responding to it — is at the heart of our lives.

Every moment and every event of every man's life on earth plants something in his soul. For just as the wind carries thousands of winged seeds, so each moment brings with it germs of spiritual vitality that come to rest imperceptibly in the minds and wills of men. Most of these unnumbered seeds perish and are lost, because men are not prepared to receive them: for such seeds as these cannot spring up anywhere except in the good soil of freedom, spontaneity and love.

This is no new idea. Christ in the parable of the sower

> long ago told us that "The seed is the word of God." We often think this applies only to the word of the Gospel as formally preached in churches on Sundays.... But every expression of the will of God is in some sense a "word" of God and therefore a "seed" of new life. The ever-changing reality in the midst of which we live should awaken us to the possibility of an uninterrupted dialogue with God....
>
> We must learn to realize that the love of God seeks us in every situation, and seeks our good.
>
> — Thomas Merton[57]

Question to Consider

Pause and consider your day. What seeds from God might be coming to you that you don't want to miss?

Prayer

Lord, I praise you because your love seeks my good in any and every situation. Forgive me for the seeds that I have squandered. Soften my heart to surrender to your will in and through me. In Jesus' name, amen.

Conclude with Silence (2 minutes)

DAY 1: MIDDAY/EVENING OFFICE

Silence and Stillness before God (2 minutes)

Scripture Reading: Genesis 2:9b, 15 – 17

> In the middle of the garden were the tree of life and the tree of the knowledge of good and evil.
>
> The LORD God took the man and put him in the Garden

> of Eden to work it and take care of it. And the LORD God commanded the man, "You are free to eat from any tree in the garden; but you must not eat from the tree of the knowledge of good and evil, for when you eat from it you will certainly die."

Devotional

At the heart of the Daily Office and Sabbath disciplines is stopping to surrender to God in trust. Lack of trust is the very essence of the sin in the garden of Eden. Adam and Eve legitimately worked and enjoyed their achievements in the garden. However, they were called to embrace their limits and not eat from the tree of the knowledge of good and evil. They were not meant to see and know that which belongs to Almighty God.

As theologian Robert Barron has argued, the heart of the original sin is the refusal to accept God's rhythm for us. The essence of being created in God's image is our ability, like God, to stop. We imitate God by stopping our work and resting. If we can stop for one day a week, or for a mini-Sabbath each day (a Daily Office), we touch something deep within us as image bearers of God. Our brains, bodies, spirits, and emotions are all wired by God for the rhythm of working and resting in him.

Stopping for a Daily Office or the Sabbath is not meant to add another obligation to our already busy schedules. It is an entirely new way of being in the world, resetting all of our days toward a new destination — God.[58]

Question to Consider

How do you hear the invitation to "stop and surrender to God in trust" today?

Prayer

Lord, help me to grab hold of you today. I need you. Set me free to begin reorienting my life around you, and you alone. Help me to pay attention to and honor how you have uniquely made me. Thank you for the gift of rest. In Jesus' name, amen.

Conclude with Silence (2 minutes)

DAY 2: MORNING/MIDDAY OFFICE

Silence and Stillness before God (2 minutes)

Scripture Reading: 1 Kings 19:11 – 12

The LORD said, "Go out and stand on the mountain in the presence of the LORD, for the LORD is about to pass by."

Then a great and powerful wind tore the mountains apart and shattered the rocks before the LORD, but the LORD was not in the wind. After the wind there was an earthquake, but the LORD was not in the earthquake. After the earthquake came a fire, but the LORD was not in the fire. And after the fire came a gentle whisper.

Devotional

When God appeared to Elijah (after his flight from Jezebel and during his suicidal depression), he told him to stand and wait for the presence of the Lord to pass by. God did not appear in ways he had showed up in the past. God was not in the wind (as with Job), an earthquake (as when he gave the Ten Commandments on Mount Sinai), or fire (like the burning bush Moses saw). God revealed himself to Elijah in "a gentle whisper," which can also be translated as "a sound of sheer silence." The common translation of this passage does not fully capture the original Hebrew, but what could the translators do? How do you hear silence?

The silence after the chaos, for Elijah and for us, is full of the presence of God. God spoke to Elijah out of the silence.[59]

God invites you to stand and to wait like Elijah. Why? God also wants to speak to you out of the "sound of sheer silence."

Question to Consider

When can you set aside some time for extended, uninterrupted silence to hear God?

Prayer

Lord, you know how difficult it is for me to be in silence before you. At times it feels almost impossible, given the demands, distractions, and noise all around me. I invite you to lead me to a quiet, silent place before you — to a place where I can hear you as Elijah did. In Jesus' name, amen.

Conclude with Silence (2 minutes)

DAY 2: MIDDAY/EVENING OFFICE

Silence and Stillness before God (2 minutes)

Scripture Reading: John 15:4 – 6

"Remain in me, as I also remain in you. No branch can bear fruit by itself; it must remain in the vine. Neither can you bear fruit unless you remain in me.

"I am the vine; you are the branches. If you remain in me and I in you, you will bear much fruit; apart from me you can do nothing. If you do not remain in me, you are like a branch that is thrown away and withers; such branches are picked up, thrown into the fire and burned."

Devotional

When we are busier than God requires us to be, we do violence to ourselves. Thomas Merton understood this and wrote:

> There is a pervasive form of contemporary violence ... activism and overwork. The rush and pressure of modern life are a form, perhaps the most common form, of its innate violence. To allow oneself to be carried away by a multitude of conflicting concerns, to surrender to too many demands. To commit oneself to too many projects, to want to help everyone in everything, is to succumb to violence. The frenzy ... kills the root of inner wisdom which makes work fruitful.[60]

And when we do this violence to ourselves, we are unable to love others in and through the love of Christ.

Question to Consider

In what ways are you busier than God requires?

Prayer

Father, I know how often I am carried away by too many concerns and demands and projects. I have felt the violence to my soul. Deliver me from this whirlwind around me and in me. Heal my tired and weary spirit, allowing the wisdom that comes from rest in you to flow deep within me. In Jesus' name, amen.

Conclude with Silence (2 minutes)

DAY 3: MORNING/MIDDAY OFFICE

Silence and Stillness before God (2 minutes)

Scripture Reading: Psalm 46:1 – 3, 10

God is our refuge and strength,
an ever-present help in trouble.

Therefore we will not fear, though the earth give way
 and the mountains fall into the heart of the sea,
though its waters roar and foam
 and the mountains quake with their surging.
He says, "Be still, and know that I am God;
 I will be exalted among the nations,
 I will be exalted in the earth."

Devotional

Many are avidly seeking but they alone find who remain in continual silence.... Every man who delights in a multitude of words, even though he says admirable things, is empty within. If you love truth, be a lover of silence. Silence like the sunlight will illuminate you in God and will deliver you from the phantoms of ignorance. Silence will unite you to God himself....

More than all things love silence: it brings you a fruit that tongue cannot describe. In the beginning we have to force ourselves to be silent. But then there is born something that draws us to silence. May God give you an experience of this "something" that is born of silence. If only you practice this, untold light will dawn on you in consequence ... after a while a certain sweetness is born in the heart of this exercise and the body is drawn almost by force to remain in silence.

— Isaac of Nineveh[61]

Question to Consider

What keeps you from silence?

Prayer

Lord, help me to be still and to wait patiently for you in silence. In Jesus' name, amen.

Conclude with Silence (2 minutes)

DAY 3: MIDDAY/EVENING OFFICE

Silence and Stillness before God (2 minutes)

Scripture Reading: Matthew 13:31 – 33

He told them another parable: "The kingdom of heaven is like a mustard seed, which a man took and planted in his field. Though it is the smallest of all seeds, yet when it grows, it is the largest of garden plants and becomes a tree, so that the birds come and perch in its branches."

He told them still another parable: "The kingdom of heaven is like yeast that a woman took and mixed into about sixty pounds of flour until it worked all through the dough."

Devotional

In these two parables describing the kingdom of God, we hear Jesus calling us to slow down and take a longer view of our lives.

> We can work without stopping, faster and faster, electric lights making artificial day so the whole machine can labor without ceasing. But remember: No living thing lives like this. There are greater rhythms that govern how life grows: seasons and sunsets and great movements of seas and stars.... We are part of the creation story, subject to all its laws and rhythms.
>
> To surrender to the rhythms of seasons and flowerings and dormancies is to savor the secret of life itself.
>
> Many scientists believe we are "hard-wired" like this, to live in rhythmic awareness, to be in and then step out, to be engrossed and then detached, to work and then to rest. It follows then that the commandment to remember the Sabbath is not a burdensome requirement from some law-giving deity — "You ought, you'd better, you must" — but rather a remem-

brance of a law that is firmly embedded in the fabric of nature. It is a reminder of how things really are, the rhythmic dance to which we unavoidably belong.

— Wayne Muller[62]

Question to Consider

How do the rhythms you see in nature (e.g., spring, summer, fall, winter, day, night) speak to you and point to the kind of rhythms you desire for your own life?

Prayer

Lord, I thank you that you are working even when I am sleeping. Teach me to respect the built-in rhythms of life, and to live from a place of deep rest in you. In Jesus' name, amen.

Conclude with Silence (2 minutes)

DAY 4: MORNING/MIDDAY OFFICE

Silence and Stillness before God (2 minutes)

Scripture Reading: Mark 2:23 – 28

One Sabbath Jesus was going through the grainfields, and as his disciples walked along, they began to pick some heads of grain. The Pharisees said to him, "Look, why are they doing what is unlawful on the Sabbath?"

He answered, "Have you never read what David did when he and his companions were hungry and in need? In the days of Abiathar the high priest, he entered the house of God and ate the consecrated bread, which is lawful only for priests to eat. And he also gave some to his companions."

Then he said to them, "The Sabbath was made for man,

not man for the Sabbath. So the Son of Man is Lord even of the Sabbath."

Devotional

Sabbath is not dependent upon our readiness to stop. We do not stop when we are finished. We do not stop when we complete our phone calls, finish our project, get through this stack of messages, or get out this report that is due tomorrow. We stop because it is time to stop.

Sabbath requires surrender. If we only stop when we are finished with all our work, we will never stop — because our work is never completely done. With every accomplishment there arises a new responsibility.... If we refuse rest until we are finished, we will never rest until we die. Sabbath dissolves the artificial urgency of our days, because it liberates us from the need to be finished....

We stop because there are forces larger than we that take care of the universe, and while our efforts are important, necessary, and useful, they are not (nor are we) indispensable. The galaxy will somehow manage without us for this hour, this day, and so we are invited — nay, commanded — to relax, and enjoy our relative unimportance, our humble place at the table in a very large world....

Do not be anxious about tomorrow, Jesus said again and again. Let the work of this day be sufficient....

Sabbath says, Be still. Stop. There is no rush to get to the end, because we are never finished.

— Wayne Muller[63]

Question to Consider

What is your greatest fear in stopping for a twenty-four-hour period each week?

Prayer

Keeping the Sabbath, Lord, will require a lot of changes in the way I am living life. Teach me, Lord, how to take the next step with this in a way that fits my unique personality and situation. Help me to trust you with all that will remain unfinished and to enjoy my humble place in your very large world. In Jesus' name, amen.

Conclude with Silence (2 minutes)

DAY 4: MIDDAY/EVENING OFFICE

Silence and Stillness before God (2 minutes)

Scripture Reading: Psalm 92:1 – 6

It is good to praise the LORD
    and make music to your name, O Most High,
proclaiming your love in the morning
    and your faithfulness at night,
to the music of the ten-stringed lyre
    and the melody of the harp.

For you make me glad by your deeds, LORD;
    I sing for joy at what your hands have done.
How great are your works, LORD,
    how profound your thoughts!
Senseless people do not know,
    fools do not understand.

Devotional

Psalm 92 is a song that was intended for the Sabbath. It stands as an indictment against today's culture of exhaustion and destruction. It also presents us with a positive vision of observing the Sabbath that takes us far beyond a mere reprieve from six days of frantic exertion. Sabbath is the focus and culmination of a life that is daily and practically devoted to honoring God.

> Abraham Joshua Heschel once observed, "Unless one learns how to relish the taste of Sabbath while still in this world, unless one is initiated in the appreciation of eternal life, one will be unable to enjoy the taste of eternity in the world to come." We are simply naïve if we think that having wasted or squandered the many good gifts of this creation, we will not do the same with the gifts of heaven. Sabbath practice, on this view, is a sort of training ground for the life of eternity, a preparation for the full reception and welcome of the presence of God.
>
> — Norman Wirzba[64]

Question to Consider

How might Sabbath keeping (for an entire twenty-four-hour period) or practicing the Daily Office (a mini-Sabbath for a few minutes) provide you with a taste of eternity?

Prayer

> *Lord, show me how to welcome your presence, not only one day a week, but every day. Train me for eternity. Grant me a taste of heaven through the experience of true Sabbath rest. In Jesus' name, amen.*

Conclude with Silence (2 minutes)

DAY 5: MORNING/MIDDAY OFFICE

Silence and Stillness before God (2 minutes)

Scripture Reading: Psalm 23:1 – 3

The LORD is my shepherd, I lack nothing.
He makes me lie down in green pastures,
he leads me beside quiet waters,
he refreshes my soul.
He guides me along the right paths
for his name's sake.

Devotional

The Sabbath teaches us grace because it connects us experientially to the basic truth that nothing we do will earn God's love. As long as we are working hard, using our gifts to serve others, experiencing joy in our work along with the toil, we are always in danger of believing that our actions trigger God's love for us. Only in stopping, really stopping, do we teach our hearts and souls that we are loved apart from what we do.

During a day of rest, we have the chance to take a deep breath and look at our lives. God is at work every minute of our days, yet we seldom notice. Noticing requires intentional stopping, and the Sabbath provides that opportunity. On the Sabbath we can take a moment to see the beauty of a maple leaf, created with great care by our loving Creator. . . .

Without time to stop, we cannot notice God's hand in our lives, practice thankfulness, step outside our culture's values or explore our deepest longings. Without time to rest, we will seriously undermine our ability to experience God's unconditional love and acceptance. The Sabbath is a gift whose blessings cannot be found anywhere else.

— Lynne Baab[65]

Question to Consider

How will you allow God to lead you to the "quiet waters" of rest this week so that you experience his unconditional love and acceptance?

Prayer

Lord, I now take a deep breath and stop. So often I miss your hand and gifts in my life because I am preoccupied and anxious. Grant me the power to pause each day and each week to simply rest in your arms of love. In Jesus' name, amen.

Conclude with Silence (2 minutes)

DAY 5: MIDDAY/EVENING OFFICE

Silence and Stillness before God (2 minutes)

Scripture Reading: Deuteronomy 5:12 – 15

"Observe the Sabbath day by keeping it holy, as the LORD your God has commanded you. Six days you shall labor and do all your work, but the seventh day is a sabbath to the LORD your God. On it you shall not do any work, neither you, nor your son or daughter, nor your male or female servant, nor your ox, your donkey or any of your animals, nor any foreigner residing in your towns, so that your male or female servants may rest, as you do. Remember that you were slaves in Egypt and that the LORD your God brought you out of there with a mighty hand and an outstretched arm. Therefore the LORD your God has commanded you to observe the Sabbath day."

Devotional

Sabbath was intended to shape our lives as a liberated people. The fourth commandment calls for a day of rest — even for people who had been enslaved.

The Deuteronomy reason for Sabbath-keeping is that our ancestors in Egypt went for four hundred years without a vaca-

> tion (Deuteronomy 5:15). Never a day off. The consequence: they were no longer considered persons but slaves. Hands. Work units. Not persons created in the image of God but equipment for making brick and building pyramids. Humanity was defaced.
>
> — Eugene Peterson[66]

Keeping the Sabbaths is meant to be an experience of the truth that you are not a "doing machine," but a deeply loved son or daughter of God. He is not interested in simply using you to get work done; God delights in you. He provides free time once a week so that you might relish your release from all forms of oppression and slavery.

Question to Consider

How might the truth that God doesn't want to use you, but to enjoy you, give you a vision for celebrating the Sabbath?

Prayer

Lord, Sabbath rest is truly an unbelievable gift! Thank you that there is nothing I can do to earn your love; it comes without any strings attached. As I close my eyes for these few minutes before you, all I can say is, thank you! In Jesus' name, amen.

Conclude with Silence (2 minutes)

Grow into an Emotionally Mature Adult

7

DAILY OFFICES

Week Seven

To become an emotionally mature Christian adult is to recognize that loving well is the essence of true spirituality. Out of our connection with God, and with ourselves, we learn a simple but powerful truth from Jesus—that loving God and loving people exist in an unbreakable union (Matthew 22:37–40).

But to become emotionally mature requires learning, practicing, and integrating such skills as speaking respectfully, listening with empathy, negotiating conflict fairly, and uncovering the hidden expectations we have of others . . . just to name a few.

It also requires ongoing renewal and transformation, something the Daily Office helps us to do by routinely placing ourselves in God's presence. When we linger in God's presence, he softens us to become more generous. And most importantly, we receive God's love in such a way that we are able to give it away to those around us.

ADDITIONAL RESOURCES

- *Emotionally Healthy Spirituality: Updated Edition*, chapter 7
- *The Emotionally Healthy Spirituality Workbook Updated Edition*, Session 7
- *The Emotionally Healthy Spirituality DVD: Updated Edition*, Session 7

DAY 1: MORNING/MIDDAY OFFICE

Silence and Stillness before God (2 minutes)

Scripture Reading: Luke 9:49 – 55

"Master," said John, "we saw someone driving out demons in your name and we tried to stop him, because he is not one of us."

"Do not stop him," Jesus said, "for whoever is not against you is for you."

As the time approached for him to be taken up to heaven, Jesus resolutely set out for Jerusalem. And he sent messengers on ahead, who went into a Samaritan village to get things ready for him; but the people there did not welcome him, because he was heading for Jerusalem. When the disciples James and John saw this, they asked, "Lord, do you want us to call fire down from heaven to destroy them?" But Jesus turned and rebuked them.

Devotional

We often forget that the people Jesus chose to form the leadership of his church were neither spiritually nor emotionally mature. Like us, they had a great deal to learn.

Peter, the point leader, had a big problem with his mouth and was a bundle of contradictions. Andrew, his brother, was quiet and remained behind the scenes. James and John were called "sons of thunder" because they were aggressive, hotheaded, ambitious, and intolerant. Philip was skeptical and negative. He had limited vision. "We can't do that," summed up his lack of faith when confronted by the problem of feeding the five thousand. Nathanael Bartholomew was prejudiced and opinionated. Matthew was the most hated person in Capernaum, working in a profession that abused innocent people. Thomas was melancholy, mildly depressive, and pessimistic. James, son of Alphaeus, and Judas, son of James, were nobodies. The Bible says nothing about them. Simon the Zealot was a freedom fighter and a terrorist in his day. Judas, the treasurer, was a thief and a loner. He pretended to be loyal to Jesus and then betrayed him.

Most of them, however, did have one great quality. They were willing. That is all God asks of us.[67]

Question to Consider

What is one step you can take to place yourself (with all your flaws) in the hands of Jesus, inviting him to mold you into a spiritually and emotionally mature disciple?

Prayer

Lord Jesus, I can relate to the disciples who wanted to call down fire from heaven on the Samaritans and who fought over which of them was the greatest. Forgive my arrogance.

Cleanse me and fill me with your power so that I might love well today for your name's sake. Amen.

Conclude with Silence (2 minutes)

DAY 1: MIDDAY/EVENING OFFICE

Silence and Stillness before God (2 minutes)

Scripture Reading: Mark 5:30 – 34

At once Jesus realized that power had gone out from him. He turned around in the crowd and asked, "Who touched my clothes?"

"You see the people crowding against you," his disciples answered, "and yet you can ask, 'Who touched me?' "

> But Jesus kept looking around to see who had done it. Then the woman, knowing what had happened to her, came and fell at his feet and, trembling with fear, told him the whole truth. He said to her, "Daughter, your faith has healed you. Go in peace and be freed from your suffering."

Devotional

As emotionally mature Christian adults, we recognize that loving well is the essence of true spirituality. This requires that we experience connection with God, with ourselves, and with other people. God invites us to practice his presence in our daily lives. At the same time, he invites us to "practice the presence of people," within an awareness of his presence, in our daily relationships. Sadly, the two are rarely brought together.

Jesus' profound, contemplative prayer life with his Father resulted in a contemplative presence with people. Love is "to reveal the beauty of another person to themselves," wrote Jean Vanier. Jesus did that with each person he met. We see this in his interaction with the woman suffering from a twelve-year bleeding problem (Mark 5).

This ability to really listen and pay attention to people was at the very heart of Jesus' mission, and it could not help but move him to compassion. In the same way, out of our contemplative time with God, we too are invited to be prayerfully present to people, revealing their beauty to them.

Unfortunately, the religious leaders of Jesus' day, the "church leaders" of that time, never made that connection.[68]

Question to Consider

How can you "practice the presence of people" within an awareness of God's presence today?

Prayer

Lord, I have unhealthy ways of relating to others that are deeply imbedded in me. Please change me. Make me a vessel to spread mature, steady, and reliable love so that those I come in contact with will sense your tenderness and kindness through me. In Jesus' name, amen.

Conclude with Silence (2 minutes)

DAY 2: MORNING/MIDDAY OFFICE

Silence and Stillness before God (2 minutes)

Scripture Reading: Luke 15:20b – 24

"But while he was still a long way off, his father saw him and was filled with compassion for him; he ran to his son, threw his arms around him and kissed him.

"The son said to him, 'Father, I have sinned against heaven and against you. I am no longer worthy to be called your son.'

"But the father said to his servants, 'Quick! Bring the best robe and put it on him. Put a ring on his finger and sandals on his feet. Bring the fattened calf and kill it. Let's have a feast and celebrate. For this son of mine was dead and is alive again; he was lost and is found.' So they began to celebrate."

Devotional

In the famous parable of the prodigal son, Jesus' description of the father gives us a glimpse of what it looks like for us to be emotionally mature adults.

The church is full of "younger sons" who wander from the love of God every time he does not meet their expectations. It is also full of "elder brothers" who are angry, bitter, and grumpy. I know them both well. I relate to both.

Yet people are desperately looking for fathers and mothers in the faith who are able to embrace, love, empathize, be present, and forgive freely. It is a love without conditions, something the world knows very little about. To become this kind of person does not come naturally. As Henri Nouwen has written:

> I have to kneel before the Father, put my ear against his chest and listen, without interruption, to the heartbeat of God. Then, and only then, can I say carefully and very gently what I hear. I know now that I have to speak from eternity into time, from the lasting joy into the passing realities of our short existence in this world, from the house of love into the houses of fear, from God's abode into the dwellings of human beings.[69]

Question to Consider

Which words from Nouwen's quotation about the prodigal son speak to you?

Prayer

Father, help me to be still and listen to you, feel your embrace, and rest in your love — and then to speak to others from that place. In Jesus' name, amen.

Conclude with Silence (2 minutes)

DAY 2: MIDDAY/EVENING OFFICE

Silence and Stillness before God (2 minutes)

Scripture Reading: Psalm 130

Out of the depths I cry to you, O LORD;
O Lord, hear my voice.
Let your ears be attentive
to my cry for mercy.
If you, O LORD, kept a record of sins,
O Lord, who could stand?
But with you there is forgiveness;
therefore you are feared.
I wait for the LORD, my soul waits,
and in his word I put my hope.
My soul waits for the Lord
more than watchmen wait for the morning
more than watchmen wait for the morning.
O Israel, put your hope in the LORD,
for with the LORD is unfailing love
and with him is full redemption.
He himself will redeem Israel
from all their sins. (NIV 1984)

Devotional

I am able to "wait for the Lord" for something — a new opportunity, blessings for my children, the healing of a friendship, or a safe trip out of town. It is much more difficult for me to "wait for the Lord" for nothing, but to simply be still before him. Yet this is one of the keys to loving others well.

> Although I often try to pull it off, I know that I cannot really be present for another person when my inner world is filled with preoccupations and distractions. This is one of the biggest challenges I face in being present for others — being still within my own soul. Stillness is the precondition of presence. I must first be still to myself if I am to be still with another. And,

of course, I must learn to be still before God if I am to learn to be still in myself. Presence begins with a still place within one's self. If I have no such still inner place, I cannot really be present for others.

— David Benner[70]

Question to Consider

What is the biggest challenge you face in being still before the Lord?

Prayer

Lord, I confess to you that I am not sure what it looks like to still and quiet my soul before you. Lead me on a journey to discover that still place within myself, and I will follow wherever and however you lead me. In Jesus' name, amen.

Conclude with Silence (2 minutes)

DAY 3: MORNING/MIDDAY OFFICE

Silence and Stillness before God (2 minutes)

Scripture Reading: Matthew 25:34 – 36, 40

"Then the King will say to those on his right, 'Come, you who are blessed by my Father; take your inheritance, the kingdom prepared for you since the creation of the world. For I was hungry and you gave me something to eat, I was thirsty and you gave me something to drink, I was a stranger and you invited me in, I needed clothes and you clothed me, I was sick and you looked after me, I was in prison and you came to visit me.'

"The King will reply, 'Truly I tell you, whatever you did for one of the least of these brothers and sisters of mine, you did for me.'"

Devotional

In 1952 Mother Teresa began picking up the dying in the streets of Calcutta, India. By 1980 she and over three thousand members of her order, the Missionaries of Charity, were working in fifty-two countries. Her teachings and life give us profound insight into what it means to follow Jesus as emotional and spiritual adults in our world. She wrote:

> I never look at the masses as my responsibility. I look only at the individual. I can love only one person at a time. I can feed only one person at a time. Just one, one, one. You get closer to Christ by coming closer to each other. As Jesus said, "Whatever you do to the least of my brethren, you do it to me." So you begin ... I begin. I picked up one person.... The whole work is only a drop in the ocean. But if we don't put the drop in, the ocean would be one drop less. Same thing for you. Same thing in your family. Same thing in the church where you go. Just begin ... one, one, one! At the end of our lives, we will not be judged by how many diplomas we have received, how much money we have made or how many great things we have done. We will be judged by "I was hungry and you gave me to eat. I was naked and you clothed me. I was homeless and you took me in."[71]

Question to Consider

How can you begin to see Jesus Christ in the people you meet this week?

Prayer

> *Lord, I am often overwhelmed by the needs of the world around me. Thank you that you are responsible for the world, and I am*

not. Help me to see the individual today — the "one, one, one" — so that the words and actions that flow from my life might reflect your life. In Jesus' name, amen.

Conclude with Silence (2 minutes)

DAY 3: MIDDAY/EVENING OFFICE

Silence and Stillness before God (2 minutes)

Scripture Reading: Luke 10:30 – 37

In reply Jesus said: "A man was going down from Jerusalem to Jericho, when he was attacked by robbers. They stripped him of his clothes, beat him and went away, leaving him half dead. A priest happened to be going down the same road, and when he saw the man, he passed by on the other side. So too, a Levite, when he came to the place and saw him, passed by on the other side. But a Samaritan, as he traveled, came where the man was; and when he saw him, he took pity on him. He went to him and bandaged his wounds, pouring on oil and wine. Then he put the man on his own donkey, brought him to an inn and took care of him. The next day he took out two denarii and gave them to the innkeeper. 'Look after him,' he said, 'and when I return, I will reimburse you for any extra expense you may have.'

"Which of these three do you think was a neighbor to the man who fell into the hands of robbers?"

The expert in the law replied, "The one who had mercy on him."

Jesus told him, "Go and do likewise."

Devotional

The great Jewish theologian Martin Buber described the healthiest or maturest relationship possible between two human beings as an "I-Thou" relationship. In such a relationship, I recognize that I am made in the image of God, and so is every other person. This makes them a "Thou" to me. They have dignity and worth, and are to be treated with respect. I affirm them as being a unique and separate human being apart from me.

In most of our human relationships, however, we treat people as objects — as an "it." In an "I-It" relationship, I treat you as a means to an end — as I might a toothbrush or a car. I talk to people in order to get something off my chest, not to be with them as separate individuals. I talk about people — authority figures, people in the news, and so on — as if they were subhuman. I get frustrated when people don't conform to my plans or see things the way I do.

The priest and the Levite did not make the connection that emotional maturity (loving well) and loving God are inseparable. They missed the "Thou" lying on the side of the road and simply passed him by.[72]

Question to Consider

Take a few moments to consider the people you will encounter today. What might it look like for you to slow down and treat each one as a "thou" rather than an "it"?

Prayer

Lord Jesus Christ, Son of God, have mercy on me. I am aware, Lord, of how often I treat people like an "it." Help me to view each person I meet with the eyes and heart of Christ. In Jesus' name, amen.

Conclude with Silence (2 minutes)

DAY 4: MORNING/MIDDAY OFFICE

Silence and Stillness before God (2 minutes)

Scripture Reading: Luke 7:36 – 39

When one of the Pharisees invited Jesus to have dinner with him, he went to the Pharisee's house and reclined at the table. A woman in that town who lived a sinful life learned that Jesus was eating at the Pharisee's house, so she came there with an alabaster jar of perfume. As she stood behind him at his feet weeping, she began to wet his feet with her tears. Then she wiped them with her hair, kissed them and poured perfume on them.

When the Pharisee who had invited him saw this, he said to himself, "If this man were a prophet, he would know who is touching him and what kind of woman she is — that she is a sinner."

Devotional

The Pharisee did not see the sinful woman as a human being loved by God. He saw a sinner, an interruption, and a person without the right to be at the dinner table. Jesus saw her very differently.

Love springs from awareness. It is only inasmuch as you see someone as he or she really is here and now and not as they are in your memory or your desire or in your imagination or projection that you can truly love them, otherwise it is not the person that you love but the idea that you have formed of this person, or this person as the object of your desire not as he or she is in themselves.

Therefore the first act of love is to see this person or this object, this reality as it truly is. And this involves the enormous discipline of dropping your desires, your prejudices, your memories, your projections, your selective way of looking, a discipline so great that most people would rather plunge headlong into good actions and service than submit to the burning fire of this asceticism.... So the first ingredient of love is to really see the other.

The second ingredient is equally important to see yourself, to ruthlessly flash the light of awareness on your motives, your emotions, your needs, your dishonesty, your self-seeking, your tendency to control and manipulate.

— Anthony De Mello[73]

Question to Consider

What sometimes distracts you from seeing the people you are with as they really are?

Prayer

Lord, I have been forgiven for much more than I will ever realize. Yet I can relate to the Pharisee in this parable. Help me to slow down and be present with you and others so that I might truly see people as you do. In Jesus' name, amen.

Conclude with Silence (2 minutes)

DAY 4: MIDDAY/EVENING OFFICE

Silence and Stillness before God (2 minutes)

Scripture Reading: Mark 10:41 – 44

When the ten heard about this, they became indignant with James and John. Jesus called them together and said, "You

> know that those who are regarded as rulers of the Gentiles lord it over them, and their high officials exercise authority over them. Not so with you. Instead, whoever wants to become great among you must be your servant, and whoever wants to be first must be slave of all."

Devotional

Jesus taught that the kingdom of God is an upside-down kingdom. The disciples kept thinking of the worldly model of power over people rather than Jesus' model of power under — to serve.

> It seems easier to be God than to love God, easier to control people than to love people, easier to own life than to love life.
>
> Jesus asks, "Do you love me?" We ask, "Can we sit at your right hand and your left hand in your kingdom?" (Matthew 20:21). Ever since the snake said, "The day you eat of this tree your eyes will be open and you will be like gods, knowing good from evil" (Genesis 3:5), we have been tempted to replace love with power.
>
> Jesus lived that temptation in the most agonizing way from the desert to the cross. The long painful history of the Church is the history of people ever and again tempted to choose power over love, control over the cross, being a leader over being led.
>
> — Henri Nouwen[74]

Question to Consider

What might be one way you can let go of power and control and, in love, choose to serve someone today?

Prayer

Father, you know how much I struggle with trying to love some of the difficult people in my life. I find it easier, like the disciples, to exercise control and have power over people. Fill me with your power so that I can choose to serve, in love, the people I encounter this day. In Jesus' name, amen.

Conclude with Silence (2 minutes)

DAY 5: MORNING/MIDDAY OFFICE

Silence and Stillness before God (2 minutes)

Scripture Reading: Matthew 7:1 – 5

"Do not judge, or you too will be judged. For in the same way you judge others, you will be judged, and with the measure you use, it will be measured to you.

"Why do you look at the speck of sawdust in your brother's eye and pay no attention to the plank in your own eye? How can you say to your brother, 'Let me take the speck out of your eye,' when all the time there is a plank in your own eye? You hypocrite, first take the plank out of your own eye, and then you will see clearly to remove the speck from your brother's eye."

Devotional

From the third to the fifth century, the Desert Fathers left a rich deposit of wisdom about how a genuine life with God must lead to a mature, non-judgmental love toward others.

> The monk must die to his neighbor and never judge him at all in any way whatever.
>
> If you are occupied with your own faults, you have no time to see those of your neighbor.[75]

Many of us have no trouble at all dispensing advice or pointing out the wrongdoings of others. We don't tend to allow others to be themselves before God or move at their own pace. Instead, we project onto them our own discomfort with their choice to live life differently than we do. The result is that we end up eliminating them in our minds, either trying to make them like us, or falling into a "who cares?" indifference.

Unless I first take the log out of my own eye, knowing that I have huge blind spots, I am dangerous. I must see the extensive damage sin has done to every part of who I am — emotion, intellect, body, will, and spirit — before I can attempt to remove the speck from my brother's eye.

Questions to Consider

Is there someone God is calling you to stop judging? What might it look like to bless and extend mercy to them?

Prayer

Abba Father, forgive me for having so many opinions about so many people and judging them. Wipe my slate clean and give me grace to see my own logs instead of rushing to judge others. In Jesus' name, amen.

Conclude with Silence (2 minutes)

DAY 5: MIDDAY/EVENING OFFICE

Silence and Stillness before God (2 minutes)

Scripture Reading: Matthew 10:28, 34 – 36

"Do not be afraid of those who kill the body but cannot kill the soul. Rather, be afraid of the One who can destroy both soul and body in hell.

"Do not suppose that I have come to bring peace to the earth. I did not come to bring peace, but a sword. For I have come to turn

'a man against his father,
a daughter against her mother,
a daughter-in-law against her mother-in-law—
a man's enemies will be the members of his own household.'"

Devotional

Unresolved conflicts are one of the greatest tensions in the lives of Christians today. Most of us hate them. We don't know what to do with them. We prefer to ignore the difficult issues and settle for a false peace, hoping against hope that the issues will somehow go away. They don't, and as a result we end up:

- saying one thing to people's faces and another behind their back.
- making promises we have no intention of keeping, blaming, or becoming sarcastic.
- giving in because we are afraid of not being liked.
- "leaking" out our anger through subtle criticism.
- telling only half of the truth because we can't bear to hurt a friend's feelings.
- saying yes when we mean no.
- avoiding people and giving them the silent treatment.

However, conflict and trouble were central to the mission of Jesus. He disrupted the false peace of his disciples, the crowds, the religious leaders, the Romans, those buying and selling in the Temple, and even in families.

Jesus understood that we cannot build his kingdom on lies and pretense. Only the truth will do.[76]

Question to Consider

Where are you experiencing tension in relationships that you are afraid to disrupt?

Prayer

> *Lord, you know that everything in me wants to run away from tension and conflict, or at least to spin the truth in my favor! Transform my ways of relating to others. Help me to speak the truth with great love and tenderness, and may you be honored and glorified in my relationships. In Jesus' name, amen.*

Conclude with Silence (2 minutes)

The Next Step: Develop a "Rule of Life"

8

DAILY OFFICES

Week Eight

One of the main reasons people turn away from Christianity is because of the many so-called rules that exist. Many of these rules lead to legalism and squeeze the joy of Jesus out of us. So, associating Christian faith with rules seems counterintuitive. But there is an ancient spiritual formation practice called "a Rule of Life" within the Christian faith that is *not* meant to constrain but to liberate us.

A Rule of Life is not a *rule* in the same sense that word is commonly used today. The root of the word *rule* traces back to the ancient Greek word for *trellis*. It referred to a structure, such as those designed to help grapevines grow upward, to help it become more fruitful and productive. A Rule of Life has a similar function and objective. It is a support structure that helps us to grow in Christ. It is an intentional plan centered around spiritual practices that enable us to pay attention to God and remain in Jesus—regardless of the powerful forces that seek to pull us away from him.

ADDITIONAL RESOURCES

- *Emotionally Healthy Spirituality: Updated Edition*, chapter 8
- *The Emotionally Healthy Spirituality Workbook Updated Edition*, Session 8
- *The Emotionally Healthy Spirituality DVD: Updated Edition*, Session 8

DAY 1: MORNING/MIDDAY OFFICE

Silence and Stillness before God (2 minutes)

Scripture Reading: Daniel 1:3–5, 8

Then the king ordered Ashpenaz, chief of his court officials, to bring into the king's service some of the Israelites from the royal family and the nobility — young men without any physical defect, handsome, showing aptitude for every kind of learning, well informed, quick to understand, and qualified to serve in the king's palace. He was to teach them the language and literature of the Babylonians. The king assigned them a daily amount of food and wine from the king's table. They were to be trained for three years, and after that they were to enter the king's service.

But Daniel resolved not to defile himself with the royal food and wine, and he asked the chief official for permission not to defile himself this way.

Devotional

King Nebuchadnezzar and his Babylonian armies conquered Jerusalem and carried off most of the city's inhabitants as slaves. One of those taken was a young teenager named Daniel. Babylon had one simple goal: to eliminate Daniel's distinctiveness as a follower of God and absorb him into the values of their culture — and their gods.

How did Daniel resist the enormous power of Babylon? He was not a cloistered monk living behind walls. He had heavy job responsibilities and many people giving him orders. He had a minimal support system and, I imagine, a very long to-do list each day.

Daniel also had a plan, a "Rule of Life." He did not leave the development of his interior life to chance. He knew what he was up against. While we know little of the specifics, it is clear that he oriented his entire life around loving God. He renounced certain activities, such as eating the king's food (Daniel 1), and engaged in others, such as the Daily Office (Daniel 6). Daniel somehow managed to feed himself spiritually, and he blossomed into an extraordinary man of God — despite his hostile environment.[77]

Question to Consider

What is your plan, in the midst of your busy day, for not leaving the nurturing of your interior life with God to chance?

Prayer

Lord, I just need to be with you — for a long time. I can see that there are a lot of things in me that need to change. Show me one small step I can take today to begin to build a life around you. Lord, help me to develop an effective plan in my life for paying attention to you whether I am working, resting, studying, or praying. In Jesus' name, amen.

Conclude with Silence (2 minutes)

DAY 1: MIDDAY/EVENING OFFICE

Silence and Stillness before God (2 minutes)

Scripture Reading: Psalm 73:12 – 17, 25

This is what the wicked are like —
 always carefree, they increase in wealth.
Surely in vain have I kept my heart pure;
 in vain have I washed my hands in innocence.

All day long I have been plagued;
  I have been punished every morning.
If I had said, "I will speak thus,"
  I would have betrayed this generation to your children.
When I tried to understand all this,
  it was oppressive to me
till I entered the sanctuary of God;
  then I understood their final destiny.
Whom have I in heaven but you?
  And being with you, I desire nothing on earth. (NIV 1984)

Devotional

Christianity is not a set of intellectual beliefs, but a love relationship with God. We need to do what the psalmist did in Psalm 73—go into the sanctuary of God and be alone with him. This especially applies when we are in the midst of suffering and darkness.

The sayings of the Desert Fathers come from men and women who fled to the desert as a sanctuary to seek God with their whole heart. Eventually, they formed communities around a "Rule of Life." The following are a few of the teachings they left behind. Read them slowly and prayerfully. (A "cell" was an ancient term for a quiet, private place to be with God.)

Abba Anthony said.... "just as fish die if they stay too long out of water, so the monks who loiter outside their cells or pass their time with men of the world lose the intensity of inner peace. So like a fish going towards the sea, we must hurry to reach our cell, for fear that if we delay outside we will lose our interior watchfulness."[78]

Abbot Pastor said: "Any trial whatever that comes to you can be conquered by silence."[79]

A certain brother went to Abbot Moses in Scete, and asked him for a good word. And the elder said to him: "Go, sit in your cell, and your cell will teach you everything."[80]

Question to Consider

How and why do you think finding time alone with God in silence might "teach you everything"?

Prayer

Lord, you know how easily and quickly I lose my interior sense of you. Grant me grace for the rest of today to silence the exterior noises around me so that I would hear the warmth of your voice. In the name of the Father, the Son, and the Holy Spirit, amen.

Conclude with Silence (2 minutes)

DAY 2: MORNING/MIDDAY OFFICE

Silence and Stillness before God (2 minutes)

Scripture Reading: Acts 2:42 – 47

They devoted themselves to the apostles' teaching and to the fellowship, to the breaking of bread and to prayer. Everyone was filled with awe at the many wonders and signs performed by the apostles. All the believers were together and had everything in common. They sold property and possessions to give to anyone who had need. Every day they continued to meet together in the temple courts. They broke bread in their homes and ate together with glad and sincere hearts, praising God and enjoying the favor of all the people. And the Lord added to their number daily those who were being saved.

Devotional

My central claim is that we can become like Christ by doing one thing — by following him in the overall style of life he chose for himself. If we have faith in Christ, we must believe that he knew how to live. We can, through faith and grace, become like Christ by practicing the types of activities he engaged in, by arranging our whole lives around the activities he himself practiced in order to remain constantly at home in the fellowship of his Father.

What activities did Jesus practice? Such things as solitude and silence, prayer, simple and sacrificial living, intense study and meditation upon God's Word and God's ways, and service to others. Some of these will certainly be even more necessary to us than they were to him, because of our greater or different need....

... So, if we wish to follow Christ — and to walk in the easy yoke with him — we will have to accept his overall way of life as our way of life totally. Then, and only then, we may reasonably expect to know by experience how easy is the yoke and how light the burden.

— Dallas Willard[81]

Question to Consider

What spoke to you when you read about the lifestyle of the early Christians in Acts and the way they sought to follow the life of Jesus?

Prayer

Lord, you say your yoke is easy and your burden is light (Matthew 11:30), yet the life I live often feels hard and heavy to me. Show me the activities, decisions, priorities, and relationships that are not what you want for me today. I submit my life to your lordship and ways this day. In your name, amen.

Conclude with Silence (2 minutes)

DAY 2: MIDDAY/EVENING OFFICE

Silence and Stillness before God (2 minutes)

Scripture Reading: Psalm 63:1 – 5

You, God, are my God,
earnestly I seek you;
I thirst for you,
my whole being longs for you,
in a dry and parched land
where there is no water.
I have seen you in the sanctuary
and beheld your power and your glory.
Because your love is better than life,
my lips will glorify you.
I will praise you as long as I live,
and in your name I will lift up my hands.
I will be fully satisfied as with the richest of foods;
with singing lips my mouth will praise you.

Devotional

Gregory of Nyssa, the great bishop and theologian of the fourth century, argued that there exists in us a ceaseless yearning for God's infinite beauty and splendor. He wrote: "We are led to God by desire. We are drawn upwards towards Him as if by a rope." When the soul glimpses the beauty of God, it yearns to see more. His writings are filled with images describing our longing for God: a lover asking for another kiss, a person tasting a sweetness that can only be satisfied by another taste, the dizziness one experiences standing at the edge of a precipice as one peers into a vast space.

Gregory compares the contemplation of God to a person looking at a spring that bubbles up from the earth:

> As you came near the spring you would marvel, seeing that the water was endless, as it constantly gushed up and poured forth. Yet you could never say that you had seen all the water. How could you see what was still hidden in the bosom of the earth? Hence no matter how long you might stay at the spring, you would always be beginning to see the water. . . . It is the same with one who fixes his gaze on the infinite beauty of God. It is constantly being discovered anew, and it is always seen as something new and strange in comparison with what the mind has already understood. And as God continues to reveal himself, man continues to wonder; and he never exhausts his desire to see more, since what he is waiting for is always more magnificent, more divine, than all that he has already seen.[82]

Question to Consider

Where can you find the time in your week to "gaze on the infinite beauty of God"?

Prayer

Lord, grant me an even richer glimpse of your infinite beauty and loveliness this day. In Jesus' name, amen.

Conclude with Silence (2 minutes)

DAY 3: MORNING/MIDDAY OFFICE

Silence and Stillness before God (2 minutes)

Scripture Reading: 1 Thessalonians 5:16 – 22

Be joyful always; pray continually; give thanks in all circumstances, for this is God's will for you in Christ Jesus.

Do not put out the Spirit's fire; do not treat prophecies with contempt. Test everything. Hold on to the good. Avoid every kind of evil. (NIV 1984)

Devotional

Fire

What makes a fire burn
is space between the logs,
a breathing space.
Too much of a good thing,
too many logs
packed in too tight
can douse the flames
almost as surely
as a pail of water would.

So building fires
requires attention
to the spaces in between,
as much as to the wood.

When we are able to build
open spaces
in the same way
we have learned
to pile on the logs,
then we can come to see how
it is fuel, and absence of the fuel
together, that make fire possible.[83]

Question to Consider

What difference might it make if you were to practice "building open spaces" into your life?

Prayer

Lord, I need breathing space. I have too much going on in my life, too many logs on the fire. Show me the way to create space in my life, and may the fire of your presence burn in and through me. In Jesus' name, amen.

Conclude with Silence (2 minutes)

DAY 3: MIDDAY/EVENING OFFICE

Silence and Stillness before God (2 minutes)

Scripture Reading: Psalm 27:3 – 4

Though an army besiege me,
  my heart will not fear;
though war break out against me,
  even then I will be confident.
One thing I ask from the LORD,
  this only do I seek:
that I may dwell in the house of the LORD
  all the days of my life,
to gaze on the beauty of the LORD
  and to seek him in his temple.

Devotional

The most striking thing about this psalm is what David does when he finds himself besieged by armies and enemies eager to kill both him and his family. He does not ask for victory or wisdom or changed circumstances. Instead, David gets quiet to seek God, to dwell with him, and to reflect upon his beauty.

> Each of us needs an opportunity to be alone and silent, or even, indeed, to find space in the day or in the week, just to reflect and to listen to the voice of God that speaks deep within us.... In fact, our search for God is only our response to his search for us. He knocks at our door, but for many people, their lives are too preoccupied for them to be able to hear.
>
> — Cardinal Basil Hume[84]

Question to Consider

In what ways might God be searching for you today — knocking at the door of your life?

Prayer

> *Lord, a part of me so longs to be alone with you. Another part of me wants to run and avoid time with you at all costs. Thank you for this opportunity today to stop and listen to you. Thank you for continuing to knock at my door — especially when I am too anxious or distant to hear you. Grant to me, I pray, a heart like David's — one that genuinely longs for you above all else in this life. In Jesus' name, amen.*

Conclude with Silence (2 minutes)

DAY 4: MORNING/MIDDAY OFFICE

Silence and Stillness before God (2 minutes)

Scripture Reading: Psalm 119:27 – 32

Cause me to understand the way of your precepts,
  that I may meditate on your wonderful deeds.
My soul is weary with sorrow;
  strengthen me according to your word.

Keep me from deceitful ways;
be gracious to me and teach me your law.
I have chosen the way of faithfulness;
I have set my heart on your laws.
I hold fast to your statutes, LORD;
do not let me be put to shame.
I run in the path of your commands,
for you have broadened my understanding.

Devotional

The most famous "Rule of Life" in the Western world is the Rule of St. Benedict, written in the sixth century. In a nonstop, distracted world like ours, a "Rule of Life" brings balance and simplicity, inviting us to a life which seeks everything in proper measure: work, prayer, solitude, and relationships.

Benedict begins his Rule with a call to listen and an invitation to surrender to God:

> Listen carefully, my son, to the master's instructions, and attend to them with the ear of your heart. This is advice from a father who loves you; welcome it, and faithfully put it into practice. The labor of obedience will bring you back to him from whom you had drifted through the sloth of disobedience. This message of mine is for you, then, if you are ready to give up your own will, once and for all, and armed with the strong and noble weapons of obedience to do battle for the true King, Christ the Lord....
>
> Therefore we intend to establish a school for the Lord's service.... Do not be daunted immediately by fear and run away from the road that leads to salvation. It is bound to be narrow at the outset. But as we progress in this way of life and in faith, we shall run on the path of God's commandments, our hearts overflowing with the inexpressible delight of love.[85]

Question to Consider

What would it look like for you to "run on the path of God's commandments"?

Prayer

Lord, you know my world can be nonstop and complex. Help me to balance the demands coming at me today, remembering you while I work, and keeping you at the center of all I do. In Jesus' name, amen.

Conclude with Silence (2 minutes)

DAY 4: MIDDAY/EVENING OFFICE

Silence and Stillness before God (2 minutes)

Scripture Reading: Psalm 139:1 – 6

You have searched me, Lord,
  and you know me.
You know when I sit and when I rise;
  you perceive my thoughts from afar.
You discern my going out and my lying down;
  you are familiar with all my ways.
Before a word is on my tongue
  you, Lord, know it completely.
You hem me in behind and before,
  and you lay your hand upon me.
Such knowledge is too wonderful for me,
  too lofty for me to attain.

Devotional

St. Patrick (AD 389 – 461), originally from Britain and raised a Christian, was sold into slavery in Ireland for six years. Upon his escape, he become an ordained bishop and returned to Ireland, traveling widely, evangelizing tirelessly, and organizing churches and monasteries. His mission to Ireland marked an important turning point in the history of missions in the Roman Empire.[86]

Prayer of Saint Patrick

I arise today
Through God's strength to pilot me;
God's might to uphold me,
God's wisdom to guide me,
God's eye to look before me,
God's ear to hear me,
God's word to speak for me,
God's hand to guard me,
God's way to lie before me,
God's shield to protect me,
God's hosts to save me
From snares of the devil,
From temptations of vices,
From every one who desires me ill,
Afar and anear,
Alone or in a multitude....

Christ with me, Christ before me, Christ behind me,
Christ in me, Christ beneath me, Christ above me,
Christ on my right, Christ on my left,
Christ when I lie down, Christ when I sit down,
Christ in the heart of every man who thinks of me,
Christ in the mouth of every man who speaks of me,
Christ in the eye that sees me,
Christ in the ear that hears me.

I arise today
Through a mighty strength, the invocation of the Trinity,
Through a belief in the Threeness,
Through a confession of the Oneness
Of the Creator of creation.[87]

Question to Consider

Which lines from Patrick's prayer speak to you? Carry them in your heart today.

Prayer

Lord, thank you for your reassuring presence that surrounds me. This is almost too wonderful for me to take in! By the Holy Spirit, enlarge my capacity to remain aware of your presence throughout the remainder of this day. In Jesus' name, amen.

Conclude with Silence (2 minutes)

DAY 5: MORNING/MIDDAY OFFICE

Silence and Stillness before God (2 minutes)

Scripture Reading: Romans 8:14 – 17

For those who are led by the Spirit of God are children of God. The Spirit you received does not make you slaves, so that you live in fear again; rather, the Spirit you received brought about your adoption to sonship. And by him we cry, "Abba, Father." The Spirit himself testifies with our spirit that we are God's children. Now if we are children, then we are heirs — heirs of God and co-heirs with Christ, if indeed we share in his sufferings in order that we may also share in his glory.

Devotional

Jesus constantly addressed the Almighty, eternal, infinite Yahweh as "Abba," an intimate, warm, familiar word a child would use — not unlike "Daddy." The heart of the gospel is that Jesus gives his disciples the authority to address God as Father. Through Jesus, we too are Abba's child.

> Contemplative spirituality moves us along toward a more mature relationship with God. We progress from the "give me, give me, give me" attitude of a small child to a more mature way of relating with God in which we delight in being with him as our "Abba Father." The progression of this movement can be broken down as follows:
>
> - Talking at God: This is simply parroting what our parents or authorities told us to pray. For example, "Bless me, Lord, for these thy gifts, which we are about to receive through Christ our Lord, amen."
> - Talking to God: We become more comfortable finding our own words to speak to God, rather than using the ready-made prayers of our childhoods. For example, "Give me, give me, give me more, O God."
> - Listening to God: At this point we begin to listen to God, and we begin to enjoy a two-way relationship with him.
> - Being with God: Finally, we simply enjoy being in the presence of God — who loves us. This is far more important than any particular activity we might do with him. His presence makes all of life fulfilling.[88]

Question to Consider

What fears are you carrying that you can release to your Abba Father today?

Prayer

Lord, I believe that living a life in your presence is what makes all of life fulfilling. I am just not sure how to get to that point in my spiritual walk. I want to grow beyond a "give me, give me" relationship with you. Fill me with the Holy Spirit so that I might learn to enjoy being with you and stop simply going to you for your gifts and blessings. In Jesus' name, amen.

Conclude with Silence (2 minutes)

DAY 5: MIDDAY/EVENING OFFICE

Silence and Stillness before God (2 minutes)

Scripture Reading: 1 John 4:7 – 12

Dear friends, let us love one another, for love comes from God. Everyone who loves has been born of God and knows God. Whoever does not love does not know God, because God is love. This is how God showed his love among us: He sent his one and only Son into the world that we might live through him. This is love: not that we loved God, but that he loved us and sent his Son as an atoning sacrifice for our sins. Dear friends, since God so loved us, we also ought to love one another. No one has ever seen God; but if we love one another, God lives in us and his love is made complete in us.

Devotional

God has a different path for each of us. My closing prayer for you is that you would be faithful to your own path. It is a tragedy to live someone else's life. I know; I did it for years.

I would like to end our time together with a story about Carlo

Carletto. He lived among Muslims in North Africa for ten years with the Little Brothers of Jesus community. He wrote about how, one day, he was traveling by camel in the Sahara desert and came upon about fifty men laboring in the hot sun, trying to repair a road. When Carlo offered them water, to his surprise, he saw his friend Paul, another member of his Christian community.

Paul had been an engineer in Paris — working on the atomic bomb for France. God had called him to leave everything and become a Little Brother in North Africa. At one point, Paul's mother came to Carlo and asked for help understanding her son's life.

"I have made him an engineer," she said. "Why can't he work as an intellectual in the church? Wouldn't that be more useful?"

Paul was content to pray and to disappear for Christ in the Sahara desert. Carlo then went on to ask himself: "What is my place in the great evangelizing work of the Church?" He answered his own question as follows:

> I understood that my place, too, was there, amid the ragged poor, mixing in the mob.
>
> Others in the church would have the task of evangelizing, building, feeding, preaching. The Lord asked me to be a poor man among the poor, a worker among workers....
>
> It's so difficult to judge!...
>
> But to one truth we must always cling desperately — to love!
>
> It's love which justifies our actions; love must initiate all we do. Love is the fulfillment of the law.
>
> If, out of love, Brother Paul has chosen to die on a desert track, by this he is justified.
>
> If, out of love, [others] built schools and hospitals, by this they were justified. If, out of love, Thomas Aquinas spent his life among books, by this he was justified....

I can only say, "Live love, let love invade you. It will never fail to teach you what you must do."[89]

Question to Consider

What might it look like for God's love to invade and fill you, guiding you to what you "must do"?

Prayer

Lord, I can see that there are a lot of things in me that need to change. Let your love invade me. Give me the courage to faithfully follow your unique path for my life — regardless of where it might lead, and regardless of the changes you want to make in me. In Jesus' name, amen.

Conclude with Silence (2 minutes)

Appendix A: The Lord's Prayer

Meditate on each phrase. Take your time; pause after each line.

Our

Father in heaven,

Hallowed be your name.

Your kingdom come.

Your will be done

On earth as it is in heaven.

Give us this day our daily bread.

Forgive us our trespasses

As we forgive those who trespass against us;

And lead us not into temptation,

But deliver us from evil ("the evil one").

Appendix B: Breath Prayer

Breath prayer is an ancient Christian practice dating back to at least the early centuries of the church. The famous "Jesus Prayer" is an example of a breath prayer. Developed from the parable of the Pharisee and the Tax Collector in Luke 18:9–14, it is drawn from the tax collector's desperate plea for mercy: "Lord Jesus Christ, Son of God, have mercy on me, a sinner." Each phrase of the prayer is prayed under the breath on an inhale or exhale. I have found breath prayer to be an especially helpful practice when I feel distracted as I come to be silent and still before the Lord.

Breath prayer is similar to silent prayer in that it can be done at any time, for we are always breathing! In Scripture, breath is a metaphor for the Spirit of God. It is through breath that God gives life (Genesis 2:7), and it is through breath that Jesus gives the Holy Spirit (John 20:22).

The following are a few guidelines[90] to help you practice breath prayer:

- Sit upright in a silent place. Draw your attention to your breathing.

- Breathe from your diaphragm, allowing your abdomen rise and fall easily. Don't force your breath or breathe too quickly.
- Whenever your thoughts wander, bring your attention back to your breath. As you inhale, ask God to fill you with the Spirit of life. As you exhale, release anything that is not of him.
- When your time of silence is over, pause to thank God for your time with him.

Appendix C: Top Ten FAQs about Practicing Silence

1. Why is practicing silence so hard?

Imagine having never exercised your entire life and then trying to sprint a mile. It would be very difficult. However, if you continued to practice, it would get much easier over time. The same is true when it comes to exercising the spiritual muscle that enables you to pay attention to God through silence. It is God who commands us to be still in his presence (Psalm 37:7; 46:10). This means God has also given us the capacity to attend to him in this way. In fact, every human being has a contemplative dimension that actually longs for silence with God. A relationship with God requires that we stop talking all the time so we can develop the capacity to simply enjoy being with him.

2. How is spending time in silence different from Eastern meditation, New Age practices, or secular programs on mindfulness?

We should not be surprised that other religions utilize the practice of silence. Many other faiths also have communal worship, sacred texts or scriptures, and spiritual disciplines, etc. The significant difference between Christian meditation and other kinds of meditation is that we are not attempting to empty our minds into nothingness or to achieve an altered state of consciousness. Instead, we practice silence to focus our minds on God and to spend time in his presence. This type of prayer is not new or New Age. Its roots extend as far back in Scripture as Moses and Elijah, continue into the New Testament with John the Baptist and Jesus, and have persisted throughout more than two thousand years of Christian history. In silence we are simply being with the God of Abraham, Isaac, and Jacob. Moreover, this kind of prayer is part of our larger prayer life that includes worship, confession, petitions, etc.

3. How much time should I spend in silence each day?

I used to recommend beginning with two minutes a day, but lately I've been recommending that people start with five minutes a day and slowly increase the time until they are spending ten to twenty minutes each day in silence. My practice is to spend twenty minutes in silence as part of my morning Office (time of prayer). For me, early morning—before the activities of the day begin—is best, but that is not possible for everyone. I also integrate briefer times (one to ten minutes) of silence during my midday and evening Offices. A great deal of research over the last fifteen years has confirmed how silence and meditation rewires our brains, helping us become more aware, more empathic, and reducing stress.[91]

4. What can I do when my mind wanders?

This is the number one challenge for most people. You are not alone! Our minds can wander a hundred times in a five-minute period. Here are the three things I do when my mind wanders. First, before entering silence, I spend time reading Scripture, a devotional passage, or writing in a journal if I have a lot on my mind. This helps to focus and settle my thoughts before I begin my time of silence. Second, when my thoughts wander, I redirect my attention to my breathing, focusing on both inhalation and exhalation as gifts of God. Focusing on the rhythm of breathing in and out is a practice used quite a bit among Orthodox Christians and is commonly talked about in secular settings as a tool for developing "mindfulness." And finally, I focus on one word, such as Abba or Jesus, to refocus my conscious thoughts on Christ. This helps to keep me anchored in him.

5. What should I do if I don't have a quiet place at home or at work?

It is possible to experience interior silence even when we are unable to have exterior silence. Believe it or not, I have practiced silence in such noisy places as Times Square, subway trains, city buses, airplanes, stairwells, park benches, highway rest stops, my car, on the beach, and empty church buildings. I know schoolteachers who use closets, sanitation workers who used their trucks, and students who use libraries.

6. What would help me to grow in this practice?

I sometimes light a candle as a symbol of Christ's presence with me. I use the timer on my phone each morning, setting it for twenty minutes. At other times of the day, I may set it for three or five minutes depending on my time constraints. Scripture is a core component of my time with God—either before or after my time of silence. Meditating on, memorizing, studying, and reading Scripture have become so much richer for me as I have created ample space to be still. I also have a special chair I use in my office, giving me a sense of sacred space that is set apart.

7. Am I doing it wrong if I don't I hear God speak when I am silent?
The goal of spending time in silence is not necessarily to hear from God but to be with God. When I spend time in silence, I am not looking for guidance, though it often comes. However, I do find that God says a lot when I am quiet! Part of maturing in Christ is not judging the quality of our time with him based on how we feel. The goal is to be with Jesus, not to have a "feel-good" experience. And the benefits of spending time in silence go beyond the time itself (for example, greater awareness of God and ourselves throughout the day, feeling more centered and less triggered, having a deeper sense of peacefulness, etc.). Just showing up to consistently be with Jesus in silence is an expression of trust and dependence on him.

8. What do I do if I don't have enough time and feel rushed?
I adjust to the time I have allotted. For example, if I have only ten minutes for midday prayer, I structure the limited time I have based on what I need in order to commune with Jesus. This may include more or less silence, reading of Scripture, etc. The goal is not to "get through" a reading or the time set aside for silence. Our aim is to be with Jesus with whatever time we have.

9. What should I do if I've practiced silence for a while but feel bored and want to quit?
There is a great deal to learn about the interior movements of your heart and silence with God. Getting started is often the most difficult step, much like starting an exercise routine or any other new habit that requires some planning and effort. However, if you stick with it, chances are you will wonder—as have so many others before you—how you ever lived without it. If you're feeling bored, I encourage you to seek out additional inspiration and resources.

You might begin by looking at the Centering Prayer materials of Thomas Keating (available online at www.contemplativeoutreach.org). And I would encourage you to look up the many evangelical authors who are now writing on the integration of silence, stillness, and solitude in the midst of our very active lives.

10. Why should I practice silence every day? Isn't once or twice a year on retreat enough?

Retreats are wonderful opportunities for us to "get away" from our routines and a powerful means to progress in our relationship with Jesus. An important question to ask on every retreat is what adjustments God might have for our lives. For example, How might I need to adjust my rhythms with God? What is his invitation for me in this next season? The fruit of retreats is to be found in our everyday practices.

I also believe all of us need a daily practice of silence and stillness. Why? Our goal is to cultivate our personal relationship with him—to be with God—surrendering our will to his will, our presence to his presence, and our actions to his actions each day. For this reason, silence and stillness with God are a foundational practice by which we actually position ourselves for God to do his transformative work in us.

Appendix D: Compline: Praying Before You Go to Sleep

Compline (pronounced "comp-line" or "comp-lin"), a going-to-sleep prayer of trust, is a wonderful way to end the day with God. For people like you and me who live outside a monastic community, it is the last of four daily Offices typically observed during the following time frames:

Morning Prayer: 6:00 a.m. – 9:00 a.m.
Afternoon Prayer: 11:00 a.m. – 2:00 p.m.
Evening Prayer: 5:00 p.m. – 8:00 p.m.
Compline: just before going to sleep

While I occasionally miss one or more of these in a day (especially Evening Prayer), the structure and flexibility of these time frames have transformed my spiritual life since I began observing the Offices in 2003. My Morning Prayer, for example, tends to be much longer than Afternoon or Evening Prayer, but the reminder to pause, even for only a few minutes, helps me remember God as the source, center, and goal of my life.

Compline is observed right before you go to sleep and is meant to be brief. You may read a portion of a Psalm (such as Psalm 31, 91,

131, or 134), do the Examen (review of the day with God), or pray the Lord's Prayer. I often use this simple prayer from *The Book of Common Prayer*: "May the Lord grant me and those I love a peaceful night and a perfect end." When Geri and I pray this together, we insert the names of each of our daughters, son-in-law, and grandchild after the phrase "those we love."

The particular beauty I appreciate most about Compline is the way it brackets my day with God. I begin with Morning Prayer and end with Compline. When I close my eyes to sleep, I release to God all the unfinished work of the day and trust him with my life. I am reminded of the fragileness of life and my dependence on him. When my eyes close to sleep, I am profoundly aware I may awake to see him face-to-face because he has called me home. Otherwise, I will awake the following morning to serve him for another day on earth.

Notes

Introduction

1. For more information about the Daily Office, see chapter 6 in Peter Scazzero, *Emotionally Healthy Spirituality: It's Impossible to Be Spiritually Mature, While Remaining Emotionally Immature* (Grand Rapids: Zondervan, 2017), chapter 6.
2. Timothy Fry, ed., *RB 1980: The Rule of St. Benedict in English* (Collegeville, Minn.: Liturgical Press, 1981), 65.
3. For a full explanation of loving union, see chapter 4 in Peter Scazzero, *The Emotionally Healthy Leader: How Transforming Your Inner Life Will Deeply Transform Your Church, Team, and the World* (Grand Rapids: Zondervan, 2015).
4. For additional resources, such as videos, a downloadable wallet-card, and testimonies of those who have benefited from practicing the Daily Office, visit www.emotionallyhealthy.org.

Week One: **The Problem of Emotionally Unhealthy Spirituality**

5. Quoted in Esther De Waal, *Lost in Wonder: Rediscovering the Spiritual Art of Attentiveness* (Collegeville: Liturgical Press, 2003), 19.
6. Mother Teresa, *A Simple Path* (New York: Ballantine Books, 1995), 7 – 8.

7. Eugene H. Peterson, *Under the Unpredictable Plant: An Exploration in Vocational Holiness* (Grand Rapids: Eerdmans, 1992), 15–16.
8. Thomas Merton, *The Wisdom of the Desert: Sayings from the Desert Fathers of the Fourth Century* (Boston: Shambhala, 1960, 2004), 1–2, 25–26.
9. R. Paul Stephens, *Down-to-Earth Spirituality: Encountering God in the Ordinary, Boring Stuff of Life* (Downers Grove: InterVarsity, 2003), 12.
10. Leighton Ford, *The Attentive Life: Discovering God's Presence in All Things* (Downers Grove: InterVarsity, 2008), 138–39, 173.
11. Scazzero, *Emotionally Healthy Spirituality*, 48–49.
12. Dan Allender and Tremper Longman III, *The Cry of the Soul* (Dallas: Word, 1994), 24–25.
13. Eugene Peterson, *The Contemplative Pastor: Returning to the Art of Spiritual Direction* (Grand Rapids: Eerdmans, 1989), 18–19.
14. Scazzero, *Emotionally Healthy Spirituality*, 34.

Week Two: **Know Yourself That You May Know God**

15. Scazzero, *Emotionally Healthy Spirituality*, 80–81.
16. Thomas Merton, *New Seeds of Contemplation* (New York: New Directions, 1987), 35.
17. Parker J. Palmer, *Let Your Life Speak: Listening to the Voice of Vocation* (San Francisco: Jossey-Bass, 2000), 10–11.
18. Gillian R. Evans, trans., *Bernard of Clairvaux: Selected Works, Classics of Western Spirituality* (Mahwah: Paulist Press, 1987), 47–94.

19. Richard J. Foster, *Streams of Living Water: Essential Practices from the Six Great Traditions of Christian Faith* (New York: HarperCollins, 1998), 25 – 32.
20. Henri Nouwen, *The Way of the Heart* (New York: Ballantine Books, 1981), 20.
21. Ibid., 25 – 28.
22. Palmer, *Let Your Life Speak*, 48 – 49.
23. Frederica Mathewes-Green, *First Fruits of Prayer: A Forty-Day Journey through the Canon of St. Andrew* (Brewster: self-published, 2006), xii – xiii.
24. M. Scott Peck, *A World Waiting to Be Born: Civility Rediscovered* (New York: Bantam Books, 1993), 112 – 13.
25. Anthony de Mello, *The Song of the Bird* (New York: Doubleday, 1982), 96.

Week Three: **Going Back in Order to Go Forward**

26. Scazzero, *Emotionally Healthy Spirituality*, 109 – 10.
27. Lori Gordon with Jon Frandsen, *Passage to Intimacy* (Self-Published: Revised Version, 2000), 157 – 58.
28. Thomas Keating, *Intimacy with God: An Introduction to Centering Prayer* (New York: Crossroads, 1996), 82 – 84.
29. John Michael Talbot with Steve Rabey, *The Lessons of Saint Francis: How to Bring Simplicity and Spirituality into Your Daily Life* (New York: Penguin Books, 1998), 246 – 47.
30. Scazzero, *Emotionally Healthy Spirituality*, 111 – 15.
31. Ibid.
32. Quoted in Os Guinness, *The Call: Finding and Fulfilling the Central Purpose of Your Life* (Nashville: Word, 1998), 52.
33. Chaim Potok, *The Chosen* (New York: Ballantine, 1967), 284–85.

34. Parker J. Palmer, introduction to *Leading from Within: Poetry That Sustains the Courage to Lead*, by Sam M. Intrator and Megan Scribner (San Francisco: Jossey-Bass, 2007), xxix – xxx.
35. Quoted in Ronald W. Richardson, *Family Ties that Bind: A Self-Help Guide to Change through Family of Origin Therapy* (Bellingham: Self-Counsel Press, 1995), 35.

Week Four: **Journey through the Wall**

36. Michael Harter, S.J., ed., *Hearts on Fire: Praying with Jesuits* (Chicago: Loyola Press, 1993, 2005), 102 – 3.
37. Brian Kolodiejchuk, M.C., ed., *Mother Teresa: Come Be My Light: The Private Writings of the Saint of Calcutta* (New York: Doubleday, 2007), 187, 211, 225.
38. Ibid., 215.
39. Scazzero, *Emotionally Healthy Spirituality*, 122 – 23.
40. Thomas Merton, *The Ascent to Truth* (New York: Harcourt Brace and Co., 1951), 188 – 89.
41. Wayne Muller, *Sabbath: Finding Rest, Renewal, and Delight in Our Busy Lives* (New York: Bantam, 1999), 187 – 88.
42. Richard Rohr with Joseph Martos, *From Wild Man to Wise Man: Reflections on Male Spirituality* (Cincinnati: St. Anthony Messenger Press, 1990, 1996, 2005), 2.
43. Peter Scazzero, *The Emotionally Healthy Church* (Grand Rapids: Zondervan, 2003), 167.
44. Henri Nouwen, *In the Name of Jesus: Reflections on Christian Leadership* (New York: Crossroads Publishing, 1991), 62 – 64.
45. Oswald Chambers, *My Utmost for His Highest*, ed. James Reimann (Grand Rapids: RBC Ministries, 1935, 1992), devotion for July 29.

Week Five: **Enlarge Your Soul through Grief and Loss**

46. Nicholas Wolterstorff, *Lament for a Son* (Grand Rapids: Eerdmans, 1987), 81.
47. Scazzero, *Emotionally Healthy Spirituality*, 136.
48. Gerald L. Sittser, *A Grace Disguised: How the Soul Grows through Loss* (Grand Rapids: Zondervan, 1995), 39, 44, 61 (cf. p. 37).
49. Joni Eareckson Tada and Steven Estes, *When God Weeps: Why Our Sufferings Matter to the Almighty* (Grand Rapids: Zondervan, 1997), 135 – 36.
50. *http://www.atthewell.com/itiswell/index.php*.
51. Parker Palmer, *Let Your Life Speak: Listening for the Voice of Vocation* (San Francisco: Jossey-Bass, 2000), 98 – 99.
52. Scazzero, *Emotionally Healthy Spirituality*, 148 – 49.
53. Eugene Peterson, *Leap Over a Wall: Earthly Spirituality for Everyday Christians* (New York: HarperCollins, 1997), 120 – 21.
54. Ken Gire, *The Weathering Grace of God: The Beauty God Brings from Life's Upheavals* (Ann Arbor: Vine Books: Servant Publications, 2001), 96 – 98.
55. Scazzero, *Emotionally Healthy Church*, 161 – 62.
56. Scazzero, *Emotionally Healthy Spirituality*, 151 – 52.

Week Six: **Discover the Rhythms of the Daily Office and Sabbath**

57. Merton, *New Seeds of Contemplation*, 14 – 15.
58. Scazzero, *Emotionally Healthy Spirituality*, 156, 155.
59. Ibid., 161.

60. Thomas Merton, *Conjectures of a Guilty Bystander* (New York: Doubleday, 1966), 86.
61. Thomas Merton, *Contemplative Prayer* (New York: Doubleday, Image Books, 1996), 29 – 30.
62. Wayne Muller, *Sabbath: Finding Rest, Renewal, and Delight in Our Busy Lives* (New York: Bantam Books, 1999), 69.
63. Ibid., 82 – 85.
64. Norman Wirzba, *Living the Sabbath: Discovering the Rhythm of Rest and Delight* (Grand Rapids: Brazos, 2006), 22 – 24.
65. Lynne M. Baab, *Sabbath Keeping: Finding Freedom in the Rhythms of Rest* (Downers Grove: InterVarsity, 2005), 17 – 19.
66. Eugene H. Peterson, *Working the Angles: The Shape of Pastoral Integrity* (Grand Rapids: Eerdmans, 1987), 49.

Week Seven: **Grow into an Emotionally Mature Adult**

67. Scazzero, *Emotionally Healthy Spirituality*, 193.
68. Ibid., 179 – 80.
69. Henri Nouwen, *Return of the Prodigal Son: A Meditation on Fathers, Brothers, and Sons* (New York: Doubleday, 1992), 17.
70. David G. Benner, *Sacred Companions: The Gift of Spiritual Friendship and Direction* (Downers Grove: InterVarsity, 2002), 47.
71. Michael Collopy, *Works of Love Are Works of Peace: Mother Teresa of Calcutta and the Missionaries of Charity* (San Francisco: Ignatius, 1996), 35.
72. Scazzero, *Emotionally Healthy Spirituality*, 181 – 83. I also recommend Malcolm Muggeridge, *Something Beautiful for God* (New York: Harper & Row, Image Edition, 1971), 119.
73. Anthony De Mello, *The Way to Love: The Last Meditations*

of Anthony De Mello (New York: Doubleday, Image Books, 1995), 131 – 32.

74. Henri Nouwen, *In the Name of Jesus*, 59 – 60.
75. Quoted in Rowan Williams, *Where God Happens: Discovering Christ in One Another* (Boston: Shambhala, 2005), 14.
76. For a full discussion, see Scazzero, *Emotionally Healthy Spirituality*, 184 – 93.
77. Scazzero, *Emotionally Healthy Spirituality*, 197 – 98.

Week Eight: **The Next Step: Develop a "Rule of Life"**

78. Benedicta Ward, *The Sayings of the Desert Fathers* (Kalamazoo: Cistercian, 1975), 3.
79. Merton, *Wisdom of the Desert*, 122.
80. Ibid., 44.
81. Dallas Willard, *Spirit of the Disciplines: Understanding How God Changes Lives* (San Francisco: Harper & Row, 1988), ix, 8.
82. Quoted in Robert Louis Wilken, *The Spirit of Early Christian Thought: Seeking the Face of God* (New Haven: Yale University Press, 2003), 302.
83. Judy Brown, "Fire." Widely available on the internet; see, e.g., www.judysorumbrown.com/blog/breathing-space. Used by permission.
84. Cited in Esther De Waal, *Lost in Wonder: Rediscovering the Spiritual Art of Attentiveness* (Collegeville: Liturgical Press, 2003), 21.
85. Timothy Fry, *Rule of St. Benedict 1980*, 15, 18 – 19.
86. Dale T. Irvin and Scott W. Sunquist, *History of the World Christian Movement: Volume 1: Earliest Christianity to 1453* (Maryknoll: Orbis Books, 2001), 236 – 37.

87. Adapted from the version of Patrick's famous prayer found at: www.ewtn.com/Devotionals/prayers/patrick.htm
88. Mark E. Thibodeaux, *Armchair Mystic: Easing into Contemplative Prayer* (Cincinnati: St. Anthony's Press, 2001), chapter 2.
89. Carlo Caretto, *Letters from the Desert, anniversary edition* (Maryknoll: Orbis Books, 1972, 2002), 108, 100, 23.

Appendix B: **Breath Prayer**

90. These guidelines are adapted from Daniel Wolpert, *Leading a Life with God: The Practice of Spiritual Leadership,* 2006. For additional resources on breath prayer, see Richard Foster's *Prayer: Finding the Heart's True Home* (New York: Harper Collins, 1992) and Marykate Morse's *A Guidebook to Prayer: 24 Ways to Walk with God* (Downers Grove: InterVarsity, 2013). For an Orthodox perspective, see, "Jesus Prayer: Breathing Exercises," by Bishop Kallistos-Ware, orthodoxprayer.org.

Appendix C: **Top Ten FAQs about Practicing Silence**

91. See, for example: Andrew Newberg and Mark Robert Waldman. How God Changes Your Brain (New York: Ballantine, 2009), and Mayo Clinic. "Meditation: A simple, fast way to reduce stress." Accessed 18 September 2013 at http://www.mayoclinic.com/health/meditation/HQ01070.

In this groundbreaking book, Peter Scazzero integrates a deep spirituality with Jesus to the crucial tasks of planning, creating healthy culture, team building, the healthy exercise of organizational power, transitions, and more. For good reason, this book has become a "must read" for leaders and teams around the world.

Chapter 1: The Problem of Emotionally Unhealthy Leadership

The Inner Life

Chapter 2: Face Your Shadow

Chapter 3: Lead Out of Your Marriage or Singleness

Chapter 4: Slow Down for Sabbath Delight

Chapter 5: Practice Sabbath Delight

The Outer Life

Chapter 6: Planning and Decision Making

Chapter 7: Culture and Team Building

Chapter 8: Power and Wise Boundaries

Chapter 9: Endings and New Beginnings

To download a free discussion guide, go to **www.emotionallyhealthy.org**

THE EMOTIONALLY HEALTHY LEADER

How Transforming Your Inner Life Will Deeply Transform Your Church, Team, And The World

9780310494577

ZONDERVAN®
.com

CHECKLIST | EMOTIONALLY HEALTHY **SPIRITUALITY** COURSE

SESSION #	EHS BOOK	DAY-BY-DAY	WORKBOOK	DVD (or live)
1. The Problem of Emotionally Unhealthy Spirituality	☐ Read Chapter 1	☐ Prayerfully read Intro & Week 1	☐ Read Intro and fill out Session 1	☐ Watch Session 1
2. Know Yourself That You May Know God	☐ Read Chapter 2	☐ Prayerfully read Week 2	☐ Fill out Session 2	☐ Watch Session 2
3. Going Back in Order to Go Forward	☐ Read Chapter 3	☐ Prayerfully read Week 3	☐ Fill out Session 3	☐ Watch Session 3
4. Journey through the Wall	☐ Read Chapter 4	☐ Prayerfully read Week 4	☐ Fill out Session 4	☐ Watch Session 4
5. Enlarge Your Soul through Grief and Loss	☐ Read Chapter 5	☐ Prayerfully read Week 5	☐ Fill out Session 5	☐ Watch Session 5
6. Discover the Rhythms of the Daily Office and Sabbath	☐ Read Chapter 6	☐ Prayerfully read Week 6	☐ Fill out Session 6	☐ Watch Session 6
7. Grow into an Emotionally Healthy Adult	☐ Read Chapter 7	☐ Prayerfully read Week 7	☐ Fill out Session 7	☐ Watch Session 7
8. Go the Next Step to Develop a "Rule of Life"	☐ Read Chapter 8	☐ Prayerfully read Week 8	☐ Fill out Session 8	☐ Watch Session 8

Congratulations on completing **The Emotionally Healthy (EH) Spirituality Course**, the first half of The EH Discipleship Courses.

Go to ***emotionallyhealthy.org*** to receive your **Certificate of Completion.**

Emotionally Healthy Spirituality

IT'S IMPOSSIBLE *to be* SPIRITUALLY MATURE, WHILE REMAINING EMOTIONALLY IMMATURE

UPDATED EDITION

Peter Scazzero

ZONDERVAN®

ZONDERVAN

Emotionally Healthy Spirituality, Updated Edition

Requests for information should be addressed to:
Zondervan, *3900 Sparks Dr. SE, Grand Rapids, Michigan 49546*

Zondervan titles may be purchased in bulk for educational, business, fundraising, or sales promotional use. For information, please email SpecialMarkets@Zondervan.com.

ISBN 978-0-310-34845-0 (hardcover)
ISBN 978-0-310-34849-8 (softcover)
ISBN 978-0-310-34857-3 (ebook)

Cover photo: Shutterstock® / © leonello calvetti
Author photos: Orlando Suazo
Interior illustration: 123RF® / Ion Popa
Interior design: Beth Shagene

Printed in the United States of America

21 22 23 24 25 26 27 28 29 30 /LSC/ 28 27 26 25 24

Contents

Introduction

When *Emotionally Healthy Spirituality* (EHS) was first published more than a decade ago, I hoped it would help people but I never imagined that the message it contained would resonate so deeply with readers across all denominational and theological lines and with churches around the world—from Africa to Asia, to Europe, to South and Central America, to the Mideast, to Australia and New Zealand, to North America. Nor could I have imagined that it would develop into *The Emotionally Healthy (EH) Spirituality Course*—with a workbook, a DVD, and an eight-week devotional book—or that churches would use it to implement EHS principles into their own DNA and discipleship culture.

When I am asked why I think the content of the book has spread so rapidly and found such a receptive audience, I often begin my response by describing how EHS was *lived* long before it was *written*. As a church, we have been practicing, refining, and absorbing the principles in this book for more than two decades. Fifteen hundred adults from seventy-three nations stream through our doors each week. This provides a very unique context for practicing this material in a community that represents the global church.

The other thing I point out is how EHS differs from more traditional approaches to discipleship. Many churches follow an approach to discipleship and ministry impact that looks something like this.

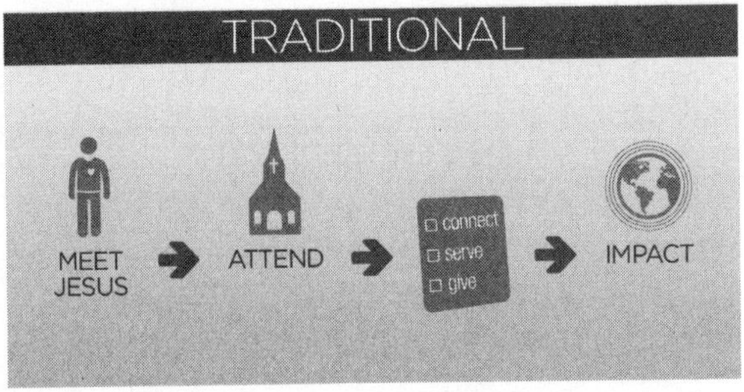

While the traditional approach typically focuses on providing helpful classes, engaging small groups, and ample opportunities to serve, the level of change in people's lives tends to be minimal. So is the impact.

In contrast, Emotionally Healthy Spirituality books and resources are designed to help people experience beneath-the-surface transformation—spiritually and emotionally. Why? Because deeply changed people have a more powerful and more sustainable impact in the world. Changed people change the world.

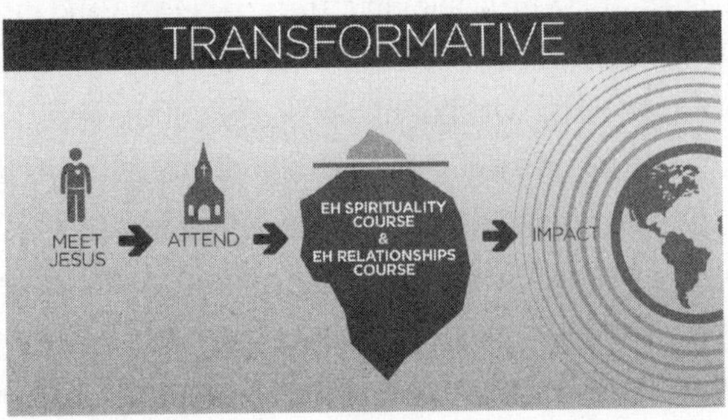

As a result of EHS, the transformation we experienced as a church—members and leaders—has led us to frontiers of life in the Holy Spirit that we could not have imagined. One recent example is my own leadership transition. After serving as senior pastor at New Life Fellowship for twenty-six years, and after a four-and-a-half-year succession process,[1] I shifted my role from senior pastor to teaching pastor/pastor-at-large. This has been a wonderful expansion and deepening for New Life. Other examples include the global impact our church has around the world, the creative outreach EHS has unleashed in people's witness to Christ in the marketplace, and the change it has produced in the culture and community in churches as a whole.

Now it's your turn. I believe with all my heart that the principles and practices that have changed my life and lives in churches all around the world can change your life as well.

This book (along with the EH Spirituality Course) is your invitation to a deeper and wider relationship with Jesus Christ, requiring you to journey into the unknown, much like Abraham did when he left his comfortable home in Ur. The combination of emotional health and contemplative spirituality—the heart of the message found on these pages—will unleash a revolution into the deep places of your life. This revolution will, in turn, transform all your relationships.

So I invite you to read these pages prayerfully . . . thoughtfully . . . slowly. Pause when you need to in order to absorb the glimpses of God and yourself that the Holy Spirit provides along the way. Write down how God speaks to you. When I read an edifying book God uses to speak to me, I write inside the back cover a few sentences about each insight along with the page number. This way I can go back later and easily review what God said for additional insight and direction. You have my permission to write all over the margins of this book, or you may want to keep a journal as you read.

Pray the prayers at the end of each chapter—slowly. Don't hurry. Each chapter could easily have been expanded into its own book. There is a lot of material here to chew on.

Let me also encourage you to use the Checklist for the Emotionally Healthy (EH) Spirituality Course found on the last page of the book. This will guide you, step by step, to implement the truths contained herein. Fill it out as you move through the Course and, when completed, go to emotionallyhealthy.org to receive your certificate of completion.

Most importantly, I encourage you to savor and cherish the Lord Jesus Christ as you meet him in these pages. The goal is to grow in your experience of Jesus, not merely add to your head knowledge about him.

John of the Cross, in the introduction of his book *The Living Flame of Love*, noted that everything he wrote about his life with God was "as far from the reality as is a painting from the living object represented."[2] Nonetheless, he ventured to write what he did know. In a similar way, I invite you to receive what you read here as a painting that directs you to a richer, more authentic encounter with the living God in Christ. The real fruit of this book will be measured by the positive changes you begin to experience in your relationships—with Jesus, with others, and with yourself.

A lack of emotional health in the early years of my ministry almost cost me everything—my marriage, my family, my work, and my own well-being. I am thankful to God for his mercy. This mercy enabled me not only to survive but to enjoy a richness and joy in the Christian life that I had given up believing was possible. If you are hungry for God to transform you as well as those around you, I invite you to continue reading.

CHAPTER 1

The Problem of Emotionally Unhealthy Spirituality

Something Is Desperately Wrong

Christian spirituality, without an integration of emotional health, can be deadly—to yourself, your relationship with God, and the people around you. I know. Having lived half my adult life this way, I have more personal illustrations than I care to recount.

The following is one I wish I could forget.

Faith and the Pool

I met John and Susan while speaking at another church. They were excited and enthusiastic about visiting New Life Fellowship Church in Queens where I was pastor. On a hot, humid July Sunday, they made the long, arduous drive from Connecticut, with all the predictable traffic, to sit through our three services. Between the second and third service John pulled me aside to let me know they hoped to get some time to talk with Geri and me.

I was exhausted. But my greater concern was what their pastor, a friend of mine, would think. What would they say to him if I simply sent them home? What might they say about me?

So I lied.

"Sure, I would love to have you for a late-afternoon lunch. I'm sure Geri would too!"

Geri, in her desire to be a "good pastor's wife," agreed to the lunch when I called, even though she too would have preferred to say no. John, Susan, and I arrived home about three o'clock in the afternoon. Within a few minutes, the four of us sat down to eat.

Then John began to talk . . . and talk . . . and talk. Susan said nothing.

Geri and I would occasionally glance at each other. We felt we had to give him time. But how much?

John continued to talk . . . and talk . . . and talk.

I couldn't interrupt him. He was sharing with such intensity about God, his life, his new opportunities at work. *Oh God, I want to be loving and kind, but how much is enough?* I wondered to myself as I pretended to listen. I was angry. Then I felt guilty about my anger. I wanted John and Susan to think of Geri and me as hospitable and gracious. Why didn't he give his wife a chance to say something? Or us?

Finally, Susan took a bathroom break. John excused himself to make a quick phone call. Geri spoke up once we were alone.

"Pete, I can't believe you did this!" she mumbled in an annoyed voice. "I haven't seen you. The kids haven't seen you."

I put my head down and slumped my shoulders, hoping my humility before her would evoke mercy.

It didn't.

Susan returned from the bathroom and John continued talking. I hated sitting at that kitchen table.

"I hope I'm not talking too much," John said unsuspectingly.

"No, of course not." I continued to lie on our behalf. I assured him, "It's great having you here."

Geri was silent next to me. I did not want to look over.

After another hour, Geri blurted out during a rare pause, "I haven't heard from Faith in a while." Faith was our three-year-old daughter.

John continued talking as if Geri hadn't said a word. Geri and I exchanged glances again and continued pretending to listen, occasionally stretching our necks to look outside the room.

Oh, I'm sure everything is all right, I convinced myself.

Geri, however, began to look very upset. Her face revealed tension, worry, and impatience. I could tell her mind was racing through options of where Faith might be.

The house was way too quiet. John continued talking.

Finally, Geri excused herself with what I could tell was an annoyed tone: "I have to go and check on our daughter."

She darted down to the basement. No Faith. The bedrooms. No Faith. The living and dining rooms. No Faith.

Frantically, she ran back into the kitchen. "Pete! Oh my God, I can't find her. She's not here!"

Horror gripped us both as our eyes locked for a nanosecond. We were both pondering the unthinkable: the pool!

Despite the fact that we lived in a two-family, semi-attached house with little space, we did have a small three-foot-high pool in our backyard for relief from the hot New York City summers. We ran to the backyard . . . and saw our worst fears realized.

There stood Faith in the middle of the pool with her back to us—our three-year-old daughter, naked, barely standing on tiptoes with water up to her chin, almost in her mouth.

At that moment I felt ourselves age five years.

"Faith. Don't move!" Geri yelled as we ran to pull her out of the pool. Somehow Faith had let herself up and down the ladder into the water without slipping. And she had kept herself standing on her tiptoes in the pool for who knows how long!

If she had faltered, Geri and I would have been burying our daughter. Geri and I were badly shaken—for days. I shudder even today as I write these words.

The sad truth about this incident is that nothing changed inside us. That would take five more years, a lot more pain, and a few more close calls.

How could I, along with Geri, have been so negligent? I look back in embarrassment at how untruthful and immature I acted with John and Susan, with God, with myself! John wasn't the problem; I was. Externally, I had appeared kind, gracious, and patient, when inwardly I was nothing like that. I so wanted to present a polished image as a good Christian that I cut myself off from what was going on within myself. Unconsciously I had been thinking: *I hope I am a good-enough Christian. Will this couple like us? Will they think we are okay? Will John give a good report of his visit to my pastor friend?*

Pretending was safer than honesty and vulnerability.

The reality was that my discipleship and spirituality had not touched a number of deep internal wounds and sin patterns—especially those ugly ones that emerged behind the closed doors of our home during trials, disagreements, conflicts, and setbacks.

I was stuck at an immature level of spiritual and emotional development. And my then-present way of living the Christian life was not transforming the deep places in my life.

And because of that, Faith almost died. Something was dreadfully wrong with my spirituality—but what?

Growing Up Emotionally Undeveloped

Very, very few people emerge out of their families of origin emotionally whole or mature. In my early years of ministry, I believed the power of Christ could break any curse, so I barely gave any thought to how the home I'd left long ago might still be shaping me. After all, didn't Paul teach in 2 Corinthians 5:17 that when you become a Christian, old things pass away and all things become new? But crisis taught me I had to go back and understand what those old things were in order for them to begin passing away.

My Italian-American family, like all families, was cracked and broken. My parents were children of immigrants and sacrificed themselves for their four children to enjoy the American dream. My dad, a baker by trade, worked endless hours, first in a New York City Italian pastry shop owned by my grandfather and later for a large baking distributor. His one overriding goal was for his children to study, graduate from college, and "make something of their lives."

My mom struggled with clinical depression and an emotionally unavailable husband. Raised under an abusive father, she suffocated under the weight of raising her four children alone. Her married life, like her childhood, was marked by sadness and loneliness.

My siblings and I emerged out of that environment scarred. We were emotionally underdeveloped and starved for affection and attention. We each left home for college, trying unsuccessfully not to look back.

From the outside our home, like so many others, appeared okay. It seemed better, at least, than most of my friends' situations. The house of cards, however, came tumbling down when I was sixteen. My older brother broke an invisible rule of our family by disobeying my father and quitting college. Even worse, he announced that Reverend and Mrs. Moon, founders of the Unification Church, were the true parents of humankind. For the next ten years he was declared dead and forbidden to return home. My parents were ashamed and crushed. They drew back from extended family and friends. The pressure and stress of his dramatic leaving exposed the large craters and holes in our family functioning. We splintered further apart.

It would take us almost two decades to begin recovering.

What is perhaps most tragic is that my dad's spirituality and loyal involvement in his church (he was the one member of our family with any spark of genuine faith) had little impact on his marriage and parenting. The way he functioned as a father, husband, and employee reflected his culture and family of origin rather than the new family of Jesus.

My family is undoubtedly different from yours. But one thing I've learned after thirty years of working closely with families is this: your family, like mine, is also marked by the consequences of the disobedience of our first parents as described in Genesis 3. Shame, secrets, lies, betrayals, relationship breakdowns, disappointments, and unresolved longings for unconditional love lie beneath the veneer of even the most respectable families.

Coming to Faith in Christ

Disillusioned and unsure of God's existence, by the age of thirteen I had left the church, convinced it was irrelevant to "real life." It was through a Christian concert in a small church and a Bible study on our university campus that, by God's grace, I became a Christian. I was nineteen. The enormity of God's love in Christ overwhelmed me. I immediately began a passionate quest to know this living Jesus who had revealed himself to me.

For the next seventeen years, I plunged headfirst into my new-found evangelical/charismatic tradition, absorbing every drop of discipleship and spirituality I could. I prayed and read Scripture. I consumed Christian books. I participated in small groups and attended church regularly. I learned about spiritual disciplines. I served eagerly with my gifts. I gave away money freely. I shared my faith with anyone who would listen.

Following college graduation, I taught high school English for one year and then worked for three years on staff with InterVarsity Christian Fellowship, a Christian ministry serving college students. Eventually, this led me to Princeton and Gordon-Conwell Theological seminaries, one year in Costa Rica to learn Spanish, and the planting of a multiethnic church in Queens, New York.

For those first seventeen years as a devoted follower of Christ, however, the emotional aspects of my humanity remained largely untouched. They were rarely talked about in Sunday school classes, small groups, or any church leadership settings. In fact, the phrase "emotional aspects of my humanity" seemed to belong in a professional counselor's vocabulary, not the vocabulary of the church.

Trying Different Approaches to Discipleship

Just as my ministry leadership seemed to be reaching full swing, Geri, my wife, slowly began to protest that something was desperately wrong—wrong with me and wrong with the church. I knew she might be right so I kept trying to implement different discipleship emphases that, to a certain degree, helped me. My conversation with myself went something like this:

"More Bible study, Pete. That will change people. Their minds will be renewed. Changed lives will follow."

"No. It is body life. Get everyone in deeper levels of community, in small groups. That will do it!"

"Pete, remember, deep change requires the power of the Spirit. That can only come through prayer. Spend more time in prayer yourself and schedule more prayer meetings at New Life. God doesn't move unless we pray."

"No, these are spiritual warfare issues. The reason people aren't really changing is you are not confronting the demonic powers in and around them. Apply Scripture and pray in Jesus' authority for people to be set free from the evil one."

"Worship. That's it. If people will only soak in the presence of God in worship, that will work."

"Remember Christ's words from Matthew 25:40. We meet Christ when we give freely to 'the least of these brothers and sisters of mine,' those sick, unknown, in prison. Get them involved in serving among the poor; they will change."

"No, Pete, you need people who hear God in an exceptional way and have prophetic insight. They will finally break the unseen chains around people."

"Enough, Pete. People don't really understand the grace of God in the gospel. Our standing before God is based on Jesus' record and performance, not our own. It is his righteousness, not ours! Pound it into their heads every day, as Luther said, and they'll change!"

There is biblical truth in each of these perspectives. I believe all of them have a place in our spiritual journey and development. You, no doubt, have experienced God and his presence through one or more of these in your walk with Christ.

The problem, however, is that you inevitably find, as I did, something is still missing. In fact, the spirituality of most current discipleship models often only adds an additional protective layer against people growing up emotionally. When people have authentic spiritual experiences—such as worship, prayer, Bible studies, and fellowship—they mistakenly believe they are doing fine, even if their relational life is fractured and their interior world is disordered. Their apparent "progress" then provides a spiritual reason for not doing the hard work of maturing.

They are deceived.

I know. I lived that way for almost seventeen years. Because of the spiritual growth in certain areas of my life and in those around me, I ignored the glaring signs of emotional immaturity that were everywhere in and around me.

In our more honest moments, most of us will admit that, much like an iceberg, we are made up of deep layers that exist well beneath our day-to-day awareness. As the following illustration shows, only about 10 percent of an iceberg is visible. This 10 percent represents the ways we conduct ourselves and the changes we make that others can see. We are nicer people, more respectful. We attend church and participate regularly. We "clean up our lives" somewhat by addressing any issues with alcohol and drugs to foul language to illicit behavior and beyond. We begin to pray and share Christ with others.

Iceberg Model

What Lies Beneath the Surface

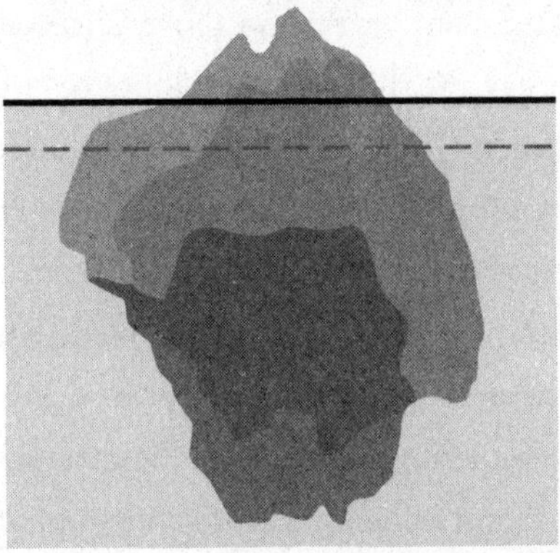

But the roots of who we are continue unchanged and unmoved.

Contemporary spiritual formation and discipleship models address some of that 90 percent below the surface. The problem is that a large portion (see below the dotted line) remains untouched by Jesus Christ until there is a serious engagement with what I call "emotionally healthy spirituality."

Getting My Attention through Pain

Three things finally dragged me, kicking and screaming, to open up to the notion of emotionally healthy spirituality.

First, I was not experiencing the joy or contentment Scripture promises us in Christ. I was unhappy, frustrated, overworked, and harried. God had brought me into the Christian life with the offer, "My yoke is easy and my burden is light" (Matthew 11:30), an invitation to a free and abundant life. But I wasn't feeling it.

A yoke in Jesus' time was made of wood, handmade to fit perfectly to the neck and shoulders of oxen and prevent chafing or cutting. In the same way, Jesus' assurance of a "light, easy yoke" can be translated as follows: "I have crafted a life for you, a yoke for you to wear that perfectly fits who you are. It is light and easy, I promise." The reality, however, is that after many years as an active Christian, I felt exhausted and in need of a break. My life was lived more out of reaction to what other people did or might do or what they thought or might think about me. I knew in my head we were to live to please God. Living like that was another matter. Jesus' yoke felt burdensome.

Second, I was angry, bitter, and depressed. For five years I had attempted to do the work of two or three people. We had two services in English in the morning and one in the afternoon in Spanish. I preached at all of them. When my associate in our afternoon Spanish congregation left the church with two hundred of the two hundred and fifty members to start his own church, I found myself hating him. I tried, without success, to forgive him.

I experienced the growing tension of a double life—preaching love and forgiveness on Sundays and cursing alone in my car on Mondays. The gap between my beliefs and my experience now revealed itself with terrifying clarity.

Third, Geri was lonely, tired of functioning as a single mom with our four daughters. She wanted more from our marriage and grew frustrated enough to confront me. She had finally come to a place where she would not accept my excuses, delays, or avoidant behavior. She had nothing else to lose.

Late one evening, as I was sitting on our bed reading, she entered the room and calmly informed me: "Pete, I'd be happier single than married to you. I am getting off this roller coaster. I love you but refuse to live this way anymore. I have waited. . . . I have tried talking to you. You aren't listening. I can't change you. That is up to you. But I am getting on with my life."

She was resolute: "Oh, yes, by the way, the church you pastor? I quit. Your leadership isn't worth following."

For a brief moment, I understood why people murder those they love. She had exposed my nakedness. A part of me wanted to strangle her. Mostly I felt deeply ashamed. It was almost too much for my weak ego to bear.

Nonetheless, this was probably the most loving thing Geri has done for me in our entire marriage. While she could not articulate it yet at that point, she realized something vital: emotional health and spiritual maturity are inseparable. It is not possible to be spiritually mature while remaining emotionally immature.

While I sincerely loved Jesus Christ and believed many truths about him, I was an emotional infant unwilling to look at my immaturity.

Geri's leaving the church pushed me over the brink to look beneath the surface of my iceberg to depths that were, until this time, too frightening to consider. Pain has an amazing ability to open us to new truth and to get us moving. I finally acknowledged the painful truth that huge areas of my life (or iceberg, if you prefer) remained untouched by Jesus Christ. My biblical knowledge, leadership position, seminary training, experience, and skills had not changed that embarrassing reality.

I was engaged in what I now characterize as "emotionally unhealthy spirituality." I was the senior pastor of a church, but I longed to escape and join the ranks of church leavers.

Respecting Your Full Humanity

God made us as whole people, in his image (Genesis 1:27). That image includes physical, spiritual, emotional, intellectual, and social dimensions. Take a look at the following illustration:

Different Parts/Components of Who We Are

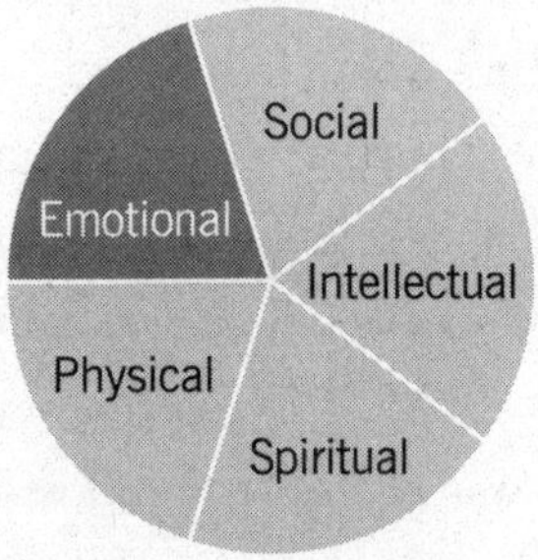

Ignoring any aspect of who we are as men and women made in God's image always results in destructive consequences—in our relationship with God, with others, and with ourselves. If you meet someone, for example, who is mentally or physically challenged, his or her lack of mental or physical development is readily apparent. An autistic child in a crowded playground standing alone for hours without interacting with other children stands out.

Emotional underdevelopment, however, is not so obvious when we first meet people. Over time, as we become involved with them, that reality becomes readily apparent.

I had ignored the "emotional component" in my seeking of God for seventeen years. The spiritual-discipleship approaches of the churches and ministries that had shaped me did not have the language, theology, or training to help me in this area. It didn't matter how many books I read or seminars I attended in the other areas—physical, social, intellectual, spiritual. It didn't matter how many years passed, whether seventeen or another thirty. I would remain an emotional infant until this was exposed and transformed through Jesus Christ. The spiritual foundation upon which I had built my life (and had taught others) was cracked. There was no hiding it from those closest to me.

When I finally discovered the link between emotional maturity and spiritual maturity, a Copernican revolution began for me and there was no going back. And I don't use the word *revolution* lightly. The spiritual pathway described in this book is radical. It cuts to the root of everything about our lives, including our entire approach to following Jesus.

Making the link between emotional and spiritual maturity transformed my personal journey with Christ, my marriage, parenting, and, ultimately, New Life Fellowship Church. If you accept the invitation to embark on this path, it will do the same for you. And only a revolution in the way we follow Jesus will bring about the profound and lasting change we long for in our lives. Without that kind of change, we're likely to find ourselves trapped in a spiritual rut similar to the one Jay, one of our church members, once described to me: "I was a Christian for twenty-two years. But instead of being a twenty-two-year-old Christian, I was a one-year-old Christian twenty-two times! I just kept doing the same things over and over and over again."

Diagnosing the Problem: The Top Ten Symptoms of Emotionally Unhealthy Spirituality

What exactly are the indicators, or symptoms, of an emotionally unhealthy spirituality? Before we explore the pathway that leads us out of our ruts and into a healthy spirituality, it is essential to clearly identify the primary symptoms of emotionally *unhealthy* spirituality—the patterns of thought and behavior that dig the ruts in the first place and then wreak havoc in our personal lives and our churches.

In short order, here are the top ten symptoms of emotionally *unhealthy* spirituality:

1. Using God to run from God
2. Ignoring anger, sadness, and fear
3. Dying to the wrong things
4. Denying the impact of the past on the present
5. Dividing life into "secular" and "sacred" compartments
6. Doing *for* God instead of being *with* God
7. Spiritualizing away conflict
8. Covering over brokenness, weakness, and failure
9. Living without limits
10. Judging other people's spiritual journey

1. Using God to Run from God

Few killer viruses are more difficult to discern than this one. On the surface, all appears to be healthy and working well, but it's not. This virus hides behind hours and hours spent reading one Christian book after another . . . engaging in endless Christian responsibilities outside the home . . . all that extra time devoted to prayer and Bible study. You might wonder how such things could be anything but good for the soul. Such Christian activities become detrimental when we use them in an unconscious attempt to escape pain.

In my case, using God to run from God happens when I create a great deal of "God-activity" in order to avoid difficult areas in my life God wants to change. I know I'm in trouble when I . . .

- Do God's work to satisfy me, not him
- Do things in God's name he never asked me to do
- Pray about God doing my will, not about me surrendering to his will
- Demonstrate "Christian behaviors" so significant people think well of me
- Focus on certain theological points out of concern for my fears and unresolved emotional issues rather than out of concern for God's truth
- Use biblical truth to judge and devalue others
- Exaggerate my accomplishments for God to subtly compete with others
- Make pronouncements like, "The Lord told me I should do this," when the truth is, "I *think* the Lord told me to do this"
- Use Scripture to justify the sinful parts of my family relationships, cultural values, and national policies, instead of evaluating them under God's lordship
- Hide behind God talk, deflecting the spotlight from my inner cracks, and become defensive about my failures
- Apply biblical truths selectively to avoid anything that would require making significant life changes

How about an example? John uses God to validate his strong opinions on issues ranging from the appropriate length of women's skirts in church to political candidates to gender roles to his inability to negotiate issues with fellow non-Christian managers at work. He does not listen to or check out the innumerable assumptions he makes about others. He quickly jumps to conclusions. His friends, family, and coworkers find him unsafe and condescending.

John then goes on to convince himself he is doing God's work by misapplying selected verses of Scripture. "Of course that person hates me," he says to himself. "All those who desire to be godly will suffer persecution." Ultimately, however, he is using God to run from God.

2. Ignoring Anger, Sadness, and Fear

Many Christians believe wholeheartedly that anger, sadness, and fear are sins to be avoided. When we feel these emotions, we're sure it's an indication that something is wrong with our spiritual life. Anger is dangerous and unloving toward others. Sadness indicates a lack of faith in the promises of God; depression surely reveals a life outside the will of God! And fear? The Bible is filled with commands to "not be anxious about anything" and "do not fear" (Philippians 4:6 and Isaiah 41:10).

So what do we do? We inflate ourselves with a false confidence to make those feelings go away. We quote Scripture, pray Scripture, and memorize Scripture—anything to keep ourselves from being overwhelmed by those feelings!

Like most Christians, I was taught that almost all feelings are unreliable and not to be trusted. They go up and down and are the last thing we should be attending to in our spiritual lives. It is true that some Christians live in the extreme of following their feelings in an unhealthy, unbiblical way. It is more common, however, to encounter Christians who do not believe they have permission to admit their feelings or express them openly. This applies especially to such "difficult" feelings as fear, sadness, shame, anger, hurt, and pain. And yet, how can we listen to what God is saying and evaluate what is going on inside when we cut ourselves off from our emotions?

To feel is to be human. To minimize or deny what we feel is a distortion of what it means to be image bearers of God. To the degree that we are unable to express our emotions, we remain impaired in our ability to love God, others, and ourselves well. Why? Because our feelings are a component of what it means to be made in the image of God. To cut them out of our spirituality is to slice off an essential part of our humanity.

To support what I mistakenly believed about God and my feelings I misapplied the following illustration:[1]

Used by permission.

I thought my spiritual life should head down the tracks beginning with the engine called "fact," which is what God said in Scripture. If I felt angry, for example, I needed to start with fact: "What are you angry about, Pete? So this person lied to you and cheated you. God is on the throne. Jesus was lied to and cheated too. So stop the anger."

After considering the fact of God's truth, I then considered my faith—the issue of my will. Did I choose to place my faith in the fact of God's Word? Or did I follow my feelings and "fleshly" inclinations, which were not to be trusted?

At the end of the train was the caboose and what was to be trusted least—my feelings. "Under no circumstances, Pete, rely on your feelings. The heart is sinful and desperately wicked. Who can understand it [see Jeremiah 17:9]? This will only lead you astray into sin."

When taken in its entirety, the practical implications of such an imbalanced and narrow belief system are, as we shall see later, enormous—a devaluing and repression of what it means to be both human and made in the image of God. Sadly, some of our misguided Christian beliefs and expectations have, as Thomas Merton wrote, "merely deadened our humanity, instead of setting it free to develop richly, in all its capacities, under the influence of grace."[2]

3. Dying to the Wrong Things

As Iraneus said many centuries ago, "The glory of God is a human being fully alive."

True, Jesus did say, "Whoever wants to be my disciple must deny themselves and take up their cross daily and follow me" (Luke 9:23). But when we apply this verse rigidly, without qualification from the rest of Scripture, it leads to the very opposite of what God intends. It results in a narrow, faulty theology that says, "The more miserable you are, the more you suffer, the more God loves you. Disregard your unique personhood; it has no place in God's kingdom."

We are to die to the sinful parts of who we are—such as defensiveness, detachment from others, arrogance, stubbornness, hypocrisy, judgmentalism, a lack of vulnerability—as well as the more obvious sins: Do not murder. Do not steal. Do not bear false witness. Speak the truth (Exodus 20:13–16 and Ephesians 4:25).

We are not called by God to die to the "good" parts of who we are. God never asked us to die to the healthy desires and pleasures of life—to friendships, joy, art, music, beauty, recreation, laughter, and nature. God plants desires in our hearts so we will nurture and enjoy them. Often these desires and passions are invitations from God, gifts from him. Yet somehow we feel guilty unwrapping these presents.

When I ask people, "Tell me about your wishes, hopes, and dreams," they are often speechless.

"Why do you ask?" they respond. "Isn't my only wish, hope, and dream supposed to be to serve Jesus?"

Not exactly. God never asks us to annihilate the self. We are not to become "non-persons" when we become Christians. The very opposite is true. God intends our deeper, truer self, which he created, to blossom as we follow him. God has endowed each of us with certain essential qualities that reflect and express him in a unique way. In fact, an essential part of the sanctification process—becoming more like

Jesus—is allowing the Holy Spirit to strip away the false constructs we have accumulated so our true selves in Christ can emerge.

4. Denying the Impact of the Past on the Present

When we come to faith in Jesus Christ, whether as a child, teenager, or adult, we are, in the dramatic language of the Bible, born again (John 3:3). The apostle Paul describes it this way: "The old has gone, the new is here!" (2 Corinthians 5:17).

These two verses and their meanings, however, are sometimes misunderstood. Yes, it is true that when we come to Christ, our sins are wiped away and we are given a new name, a new identity, a new future, a new life. It is truly a miracle. We are declared righteous before God through the life, death, and resurrection of Jesus (Philippians 3:9–10). The eternal, holy God of the universe is no longer our judge but our Father. That is the great news of the gospel. But we need to understand this does not mean that our past won't continue to influence us in different ways. For years, I was under the delusion that because I accepted Jesus, my old life was no longer in me. My past before Christ was painful. I wanted to forget it. I never wanted to look back. Life was so much better now that Jesus was with me.

I thought I was free.

Geri, after nine years of marriage, knew better. I will never forget the first time we made a genogram—a diagram outlining some of the patterns of our families. Our counselor at the time took about an hour to ask probing questions about the interactions between members of both of our families, to write two or three adjectives to describe our parents and their relationships.

When the counselor finished, he simply asked us, "Do you see any similarities between your marriage and your parents'?"

We both sat there dumbfounded.

We were evangelical Christians. We were committed and stable.

Our priorities and life choices were very different from that of our parents'. Yet, underneath the surface, our marriage bore a striking resemblance to that of our parents'. Gender roles; the handling of anger and conflict and shame; how we defined success; our view of family, children, recreation, pleasure, sexuality, grieving; and our relationships with friends had all been shaped by our families of origin and our cultures.

Sitting in that counselor's office that day, embarrassed by the state of our marriage, we learned a lesson we would never forget: even though we had been committed Christians for almost twenty years, our ways of relating mirrored much more our family of origin than the way God intended for his new family in Christ.

The work of growing in Christ (what theologians call *sanctification*) does not mean we don't go back to the past as we press ahead to what God has for us. It actually demands we go back in order to break free from unhealthy and destructive patterns that prevent us from loving ourselves and others as God designed.

5. Dividing Life into "Secular" and "Sacred" Compartments

Human beings have an uncanny ability to live compartmentalized, double lives.

Frank attends church and sings about God's love. On the way home he pronounces the death penalty over another driver. For Frank, Sunday church is for God. Monday to Saturday is for work.

Jane yells at her husband, berating him for his lack of spiritual leadership with the children. He walks away deflated and crushed. She walks away convinced she has fought valiantly in God's name.

Ken has a disciplined devotional time with God each day before going to work, but then does not think of God's presence with him all through the day at work or when he returns home to be with his wife and children.

Judith cries during songs about the love and grace of God at her church. But she regularly complains and blames others for the difficulties and trials in her life.

It is so easy to compartmentalize God, relegating him to "Christian activities" around church and our spiritual disciplines without thinking of him in the way we navigate our marriages, discipline our children, spend our money, enjoy our recreation, or even study for exams. According to Gallup polls and sociologists, one of the greatest scandals of our day is that "evangelical Christians are as likely to embrace lifestyles every bit as hedonistic, materialistic, self-centered and sexually immoral as the world in general."[3] The statistics are devastating:

- Church members divorce their spouses as often as their secular neighbors.
- Church members beat their wives as often as their neighbors.
- Church members' giving patterns indicate they are almost as materialistic as non-Christians.
- White evangelicals are the most likely people to object to neighbors of another race.
- Of the "higher-commitment" evangelicals, a rapidly growing number of young people think cohabitation is acceptable prior to marriage.[4]

Ron Sider, in his book *The Scandal of the Evangelical Conscience*, summarizes the level of our compartmentalization: "Whether the issue is marriage and sexuality or money and care for the poor, evangelicals today are living scandalously unbiblical lives. . . . The data suggest that in many crucial areas evangelicals are not living any differently from their unbelieving neighbors."[5] But you don't need a lot of statistics to know how true this is. Just ask Angela, a new member of our congregation whose question to me also explained why she had dropped out of church for five years: "Why is it that so many Christians make such lousy human beings?"

The consequences of this on our witness to Jesus Christ are incalculable, both for ourselves and the world around us. We miss out on the genuine joy of life with Jesus Christ that he promises (John 15:11). And the watching world shakes its head, incredulous that we can be so blind we can't see the large gap between our words and our everyday lives.

6. Doing for God Instead of Being with God

Being productive and getting things done are high priorities in Western culture. Praying and enjoying God's presence for no other reason than to delight in him was a luxury, I was told, that we could take pleasure in once we got to heaven. For now, there was too much to be done. People were lost. The world was in deep trouble. And God had entrusted us with the good news of the gospel.

For most of my Christian life, I wondered if monks were truly Christian. Their lifestyle seemed escapist. Surely they were not in the will of God. What were they doing to spread the gospel in a world dying without Christ? What about all the sheep who were lost and without direction? Didn't they know the laborers are few (Matthew 9:37)?

The messages were clear:

- Doing lots of work for God is a sure sign of a growing spirituality.
- It is all up to you. And you'll never finish while you're alive on earth.
- God can't move unless you pray.
- You are responsible to share Christ around you at all times or people will go to hell.
- Things will fall apart if you don't persevere and hold things together.

Are all these things wrong? No. But work *for* God that is not nourished by a deep interior life *with* God will eventually be contaminated by other things such as ego, power, needing approval of and from others, and buying into the wrong ideas of success and the mistaken belief that we can't fail. When we work for God because of these things, our experience of the gospel often falls off center. We become "human doings" not "human beings." Our experiential sense of worth and validation gradually shifts from God's unconditional love for us in Christ to our works and performance. The joy of Christ gradually disappears. Our activity for God can only properly flow from a life *with* God.

We cannot give what we do not possess. Doing for God in a way that is proportionate to our being with God is the only pathway to a pure heart and seeing God (Matthew 5:8).

7. Spiritualizing Away Conflict

Nobody likes conflict. Yet conflict is everywhere—from law courts to workplaces to classrooms to neighborhoods to marriages to parenting our children to close friendships to when someone has spoken or acted toward you inappropriately. But perhaps one of the most destructive myths alive in the Christian community today is the belief that smoothing over disagreements or "sweeping them under the rug" is part of what it means to follow Jesus. For this reason, churches, small groups, ministry teams, denominations, and communities continue to experience the pain of unresolved conflicts.

Very, very few of us come from families in which conflicts are resolved in a mature, healthy way. Most of us simply bury our tensions and move on. When I became a Christian I also became the great "peacemaker." I did anything to keep unity and love flowing in the church as well as in my marriage and family. I saw conflict as something that had to be fixed as quickly as possible. Like radioactive waste from a nuclear power plant, if not contained, I feared it might unleash terrible damage.

So I did what most Christians do: I lied a lot, both to myself and others.

What do you do when faced with the tension and mess of disagreements? Some of us may be guilty of one or more of the following:

- Say one thing to people's faces and then another behind their backs
- Make promises we have no intention of keeping
- Blame
- Attack
- Give people the silent treatment
- Become sarcastic
- Give in because we are afraid of not being liked
- "Leak" our anger by sending an email containing a not-so-subtle criticism
- Tell only half the truth because we can't bear to hurt a friend's feelings
- Say yes when we mean no
- Avoid and withdraw and cut off
- Find an outside person with whom we can share in order to ease our anxiety

Jesus shows us that healthy Christians do not avoid conflict. His life was filled with it! He was in regular conflict with the religious leaders, the crowds, the disciples—even his own family. Out of a desire to bring true peace, Jesus disrupted the false peace all around him. He refused to spiritualize conflict avoidance.

8. Covering Over Brokenness, Weakness, and Failure

The pressure to present an image of ourselves as strong and spiritually "together" hovers over most of us. We feel guilty for not measuring up, for not making the grade. We forget that not one of us is perfect and that we are all sinners. We forget that David, one of God's most beloved friends, committed adultery with Bathsheba and murdered her husband. Talk about a scandal! How many of us would not have erased that from the history books forever lest the name of God be disgraced?

David did not. Instead, he used his absolute power as king to ensure the details of his colossal failure were published in the history books for all future generations! In fact, David wrote a song about his failure to be sung in Israel's worship services and to be published in their worship manual, the psalms. (Hopefully, he asked Bathsheba's permission first!) David knew, "My sacrifice, O God, is a broken spirit; a broken and contrite heart you, God, will not despise" (Psalm 51:17).

Another of God's great men, the apostle Paul, wrote about God not answering his prayers and about his "thorn in [the] flesh." He thanked God for his brokenness, reminding his readers that Christ's power "is made perfect in weakness" (2 Corinthians 12:7–10). How many Christians do you know who would do such a thing today?

The Bible does not spin the flaws and weaknesses of its heroes. Moses was a murderer. Hosea's wife was a prostitute. Peter rebuked God! Noah got drunk. Jonah was a racist. Jacob was a liar. John Mark deserted Paul. Elijah burned out. Jeremiah was depressed and suicidal. Thomas doubted. Moses had a temper. Timothy had ulcers. And all these people send the same message: that every human being on earth, regardless of their gifts and strengths, is weak, vulnerable, and dependent on God and others.

For years I would observe unusually gifted people perform in extraordinary ways—whether in the arts, sports, leadership, politics, business, academics, parenting, or church—and wonder if somehow they had escaped the brokenness that plagues the rest of us. Now I know they hadn't. We are all deeply flawed and broken. There are no exceptions.

9. Living Without Limits

I was taught that good Christians constantly give and tend to the needs of others. I wasn't supposed to say no to opportunities to help or to requests for help because that would be selfish.

Some Christians are selfish. They believe in God and Jesus Christ, but live their lives as if God doesn't exist. They don't think or care about loving and serving others outside of their families and friends. That is a tragedy.

I meet many more Christians, however, who carry around guilt for never doing enough. "Pete, I spent two hours on the phone listening to him and it still wasn't enough," a friend recently complained to me. "It makes me want to run away."

This guilt often leads to discouragement. And this discouragement often leads Christians to disengagement and isolation from "needy people" because they don't know what else to do.

The core spiritual issue here relates to our limits and our humanity. We are not God. We cannot serve everyone in need. We are human. When Paul said, "I can do all this through him who gives me strength" (Philippians 4:13), the context was that of learning to be content in all circumstances. The strength he received from Christ was not the strength to change, deny, or defy his circumstances; it was the strength to be content in the midst of them, to surrender to God's loving will for him (Philippians 4:11–13).

Jesus modeled this for us as a human being—fully God yet fully human. He did not heal every sick person in the places he visited. He did not raise every dead person. He did not feed all the hungry beggars or set up job development centers for the poor of Jerusalem.

He didn't do it, and we shouldn't feel we have to. But somehow we do. Why don't we take appropriate care of ourselves? Why are so many Christians, along with the rest of our culture, frantic, exhausted, overloaded, and hurried?

Few Christians make the connection between love of self and love of others. Sadly, many believe that taking care of themselves is a sin, a "psychologizing" of the gospel taken from our self-centered culture. I believed that myself for years.

It is true we are called to consider others more important than ourselves (Philippians 2:3). We are called to lay down our lives for others (1 John 3:16). But remember, you first need a "self" to lay down.

As Parker Palmer said, "Self-care is never a selfish act—it is simply good stewardship of the only gift I have, the gift I was put on earth to offer others. Anytime we can listen to true self and give it the care it requires, we do it not only for ourselves, but for the many others whose lives we touch."[6]

10. Judging Other People's Spiritual Journey

"The monk," said one of the Desert Fathers, "must die to his neighbor and never judge him at all in any way whatever." He continued: "If you are occupied with your own faults, you have no time to see those of your neighbor."[7]

I was taught it was my responsibility to correct people in error or in sin and to always counsel people who were mixed up spiritually. I therefore felt guilty if I saw something questionable and did nothing to point it out. But I felt even guiltier when I was supposed to fix someone's problem and had to admit "I don't know how" or "I don't know what to say." Wasn't I commanded to be ready to give an answer for the hope that is in me (1 Peter 3:15)?

Of course, many of us have no trouble at all dispensing advice or pointing out wrongdoing. We spend so much time at it that we end up self-deceived, thinking we have much to give and therefore little to receive from others. After all, we're the ones who are right, aren't we? This often leads to an inability to receive from ordinary, less mature people than ourselves. We only receive from experts or professionals.

This has always been one of the greatest dangers in Christianity. It becomes "us versus them." In Jesus' day there was the superior "in group" of Pharisees who obeyed God's commands. And there was the inferior "out group" of sinners, tax collectors, and prostitutes.

Sadly, we often turn our differences into moral superiority or virtues. I see it all the time. We judge people for their music (too soft or too loud). We judge them for dressing up or dressing down, for the movies they watch and the cars they buy. We create never-ending groups to subtly categorize people:

- "Those artists and musicians. They are so flaky."
- "Those engineers. They are so cerebral. They're cold as fish."
- "Men are idiots. They're socially infantile."
- "Women are overly sensitive and emotional."
- "The rich are self-indulgent and selfish."
- "The poor are lazy."

We judge the Presbyterians for being too structured. We judge the Pentecostals for lacking structure. We judge Episcopalians for their candles and their written prayers. We judge Roman Catholics for their view of the Lord's Supper and Orthodox Christians from the Eastern part of the world for their strange culture and love for icons.

By failing to let others be themselves before God and move at their own pace, we inevitably project onto them our own discomfort with their choice to live life differently than we do. We end up eliminating them in our minds, trying to make others like us, abandoning them altogether or falling into a "Who cares?" indifference toward them. In some ways the silence of unconcern can be more deadly than hate. Like Jesus said, unless I first take the log out of my own eye, knowing that I have huge blind spots, I am dangerous. I must see the extensive damage sin has done to every part of who I am—emotion, intellect, body, will, and spirit—before I can attempt to remove the speck from the eye of another (Matthew 7:1–5).

The Revolutionary Antidote

The pathway to unleashing the transformative power of Jesus to heal our spiritual lives is found in the joining of emotional health and contemplative spirituality. (See Appendix B for a definition of emotional health and contemplative spirituality and why both are needed).

Now let me invite you to come with me for an exciting journey on the seven pathways of emotionally healthy spirituality. We will begin by looking at the essential first step of knowing yourself so that you may know God.

God, when I consider this chapter, the only thing I can say is, "Lord Jesus Christ, have mercy on me, a sinner." Thank you that I stand before you in the righteousness of Jesus, in his perfect record and performance, not my own. I ask that you would not simply heal the symptoms of what is not right in my life, but that you would surgically remove all that is in me that does not belong to you. As I think about what I have read, Lord, pour light over the things that are hidden. May I see clearly as you hold me tenderly. In Jesus' name, amen.

CHAPTER 2

Know Yourself That You May Know God

Becoming Your Authentic Self

Awareness of yourself and your relationship with God are intricately related. In fact, the challenge to shed our "old false" self in order to live authentically in our "new true" self strikes at the very core of authentic spirituality.

St. Paul, the apostle, expressed this as, "to put off your old self . . . and to put on the new self, created to be like God in true righteousness and holiness" (Ephesians 4:22, 24).

Augustine wrote in *Confessions*, in AD 400, "How can you draw close to God when you are far from your own self?" He prayed: "Grant, Lord, that I may know myself that I may know thee."

Meister Eckhart, a Dominican writer from the thirteenth century, wrote, "None can know God who does not first know himself."[1]

St. Teresa of Avila wrote in *The Way of Perfection*: "Almost all problems in the spiritual life stem from a lack of self-knowledge."

John Calvin in 1530 wrote in his opening of his *Institutes of the Christian Religion*: "Our wisdom . . . consists almost entirely of two parts: the knowledge of God and of ourselves. But as these are connected together by many ties, it is not easy to determine which of the two precedes and gives birth to the other."[2]

The vast majority of us go to our graves without knowing who we are. We unconsciously live someone else's life, or at least someone else's expectations for us. This does violence to ourselves, our relationship with God, and ultimately to others. The following personal story illustrates how dividing knowledge of God from knowledge of self can so easily keep us at a fixed level of spiritual/emotional development.

Geri Leaving—Again

Geri walked into the living room one day as I was reading the newspaper. "Pete, I want you to know that this summer I *am* going to the New Jersey shore."

She paused, waiting for me to react.

No, you aren't, I thought to myself.

I looked up from my newspaper and gave her an intimidating glare. She didn't flinch.

"I'm going to live at my mother's house for the month of July. . . . I leave in two weeks."

"You can't," I said firmly. I then raised my voice, hoping to intimidate her.

"You can't leave me alone all month by myself here in New York. It will wreck our marriage."

That was not true and I knew it. I was more concerned about being lonely, about looking foolish before others in the church. We had lived in densely populated Queens, New York City, for the previous ten years.

Geri was well prepared.

"For ten years I've wanted to go down to the beach during this horrific summer heat. My mom's house is three blocks from the ocean.

I've given in to your objections for ten years. I'm done. This is your issue . . . your problem. This is about you.

"I'm going," she quietly uttered, turning from me toward the kitchen.

My body screamed. I could feel my stomach knotting. My fingers formed into a fist. My neck and shoulders tightened.

This was not a discussion. It felt like a divorce.

I followed her into the kitchen. All the biblical arguments I had used the past ten years to keep Geri in New York raced through my mind:

God wants us together. One flesh . . . doing everything together. That's a great marriage.

It would be a bad witness to others. I'm senior pastor of the church. You're the pastor's wife. We are in this together . . . a team. God called us both here.

Women don't make these kinds of decisions without their husbands—or at least their agreement. This is unbiblical.

I shut my mouth without uttering an argument. I knew these simply camouflaged the true reasons why her spending four weeks in July at her mom's felt like four years and a divorce.

Geri had transformed the power dynamic of our marriage a year and a half earlier when she quit the church I pastored. This launched us into a crisis and the life-transforming journey of emotionally healthy spirituality.

She was back at New Life. Our marriage was doing well. We were babies on this new journey—together, I thought.

Why another bombshell?

She was right. It was my issue. I knew it—intellectually at least.

My emotions, however, were screaming.

We had four girls: Maria, age twelve; Christy, age ten; Faith, age seven; and Eva, age three. We lived on the first floor of a two-family, semi-attached house commonly referred to as a railroad apartment (meaning the rooms followed each other like railroad cars).

I used to wake up on summer mornings and jokingly say to Geri: "Listen to the sounds outside. [We could hear the cars from a busy six-lane highway only one block away.] Just close your eyes and imagine that is the surf pounding the beach."

She rarely found the comparison funny.

What was the hard truth from which I was running, buried deep beneath the surface of my life? There was more than one.

I wanted her to be the mom I'd never had—to not "abandon" me emotionally, to be there for the "wounded boy" inside her husband who was carrying out this great responsibility for God and our family. I also was concerned about what others thought of me. I could already imagine my Italian-American mother's reaction. Already Geri had broken many gender role expectations that had been passed on to me from generation to generation.

In my mind, I was already role-playing a conversation with my mother, in which she uttered in disbelief: "I have never heard of such a thing. I would never have done such a thing to my husband. Would never have dreamed of it!"

This was going to be way outside the box of generations of Scazzeros.

Our conversation was short that first day. I pouted. I sulked. I grew depressed.

But I knew she was right. This was great for her, for our four girls—and ultimately even for me. But I was a big, emotional baby, depending on her in inappropriate ways, reluctant to grow up.

What is really sad is that I was leading and pastoring a large church! I eventually stopped pouting. Over the next two weeks, we talked. Geri recognized the importance and value of our marriage, that it wasn't good to be apart unnecessarily. Between her coming back to church on Sundays and my going down to the shore for my days off, it really was only four days a week apart. That helped on one level.

Nonetheless, I struggled. And Geri went anyway. I hated it. She loved it.

Over time, however, I grew to enjoy the time alone also. God used it to "rewire my insides," repair some of the damage from my family of origin, and help me grow into my own person apart from Geri.

It turned out to be liberating.

The reality, however, was that my discipleship and spirituality had addressed neither my insecurities nor my understanding of myself. Breaking free would require learning to feel, learning to distinguish feeling and thinking, and finally, summoning the courage to follow my God-given "true self" rather than the voices and demands around me.

Feelings and the Beginning of a Revolution

Like many Christians today, I was taught that feelings are unreliable and not to be trusted. They go up and down and are the last thing we should be attending to in our spiritual lives. But that's an incorrect view.

Daniel Goleman, the author of *Emotional Intelligence*, defined *emotion* as "referring to a feeling and its distinctive thoughts, psychological and biological states, and range of propensities to act." What he meant is that God created human beings to feel a wide range of emotions. There are hundreds of emotions, each with their variations, blends, and hundreds of particular nuances. Researchers have classified them into eight main families:

- anger (fury, hostility, irritability, annoyance)
- sadness (grief, self-pity, despair, dejection, loneliness)
- fear (anxiety, edginess, nervousness, fright, terror, apprehension)
- enjoyment (joy, relief, contentment, delight, thrill, euphoria, ecstasy)

- love (acceptance, trust, devotion, adoration)
- surprise (shock, amazement, wonder)
- disgust (contempt, scorn, aversion, distaste, revulsion)
- shame (guilt, remorse, humiliation, embarrassment, chagrin)[3]

It never entered my mind that God might be speaking to me in the "feeling" realm in a way that did not compromise his truth. How could I listen to my desires, dreams, likes, and dislikes? Wouldn't they potentially take me the way of rebellion, away from God?

So I ignored them.

As I said in the previous chapter, most Christians do not think they have permission to consider their feelings, to name them, or express them openly. This applies especially to the more "difficult" feelings of fear, sadness, and anger. It was anger and depression, however, that finally got me to stop and admit something was desperately wrong. I could no longer stuff them. I began "leaking" all over my relationships at work and at home.

When we deny our pain, losses, and feelings year after year, we become less and less human. We transform slowly into empty shells with smiley faces painted on them. Sad to say, that is the fruit of much of our discipleship in our churches. But when I began to allow myself to feel a wider range of emotions, including sadness, depression, fear, and anger, a revolution in my spirituality was unleashed. I soon realized that a failure to appreciate the biblical place of feelings within our larger Christian lives has done extensive damage, keeping free people in Christ in slavery.

Our God Feels

The journey of genuine transformation to emotionally healthy spirituality begins with a commitment to allow yourself to feel. It is an essential part of our humanity and unique personhood as men and women made in God's image.

Scripture reveals God as an emotional being who feels—a Person. Having been created in his image, we too have the gift of experiencing emotions. Consider the following:

- "God *saw that it was good . . . very good*" (Genesis 1:25, 31). In other words, God delighted, relished, beamed with delight over us.
- "The LORD *regretted* that he had made human beings on the earth, and his heart was *deeply troubled*" (Genesis 6:6).
- "I, the LORD your God, am a *jealous* God" (Exodus 20:5).
- "For a long time I have kept silent, I have been quiet and held myself back. But now, like a woman in childbirth, *I cry out, I gasp and pant*" (Isaiah 42:14).
- "The *fierce anger* of the LORD will not turn back until he fully accomplishes the purposes of his heart" (Jeremiah 30:24).
- "I have *loved you with an everlasting love; I have drawn you with kindness*" (Jeremiah 31:3).
- "How can I hand you over, Israel? . . . My heart is changed within me; all my *compassion is aroused*" (Hosea 11:8).
- "He began to *be sorrowful and troubled*. Then he said to them, 'My soul is *overwhelmed with sorrow* to the point of death'" (Matthew 26:37–38).
- "He looked around them in *anger and, deeply distressed* at their stubborn hearts, said to the man, 'Stretch out your hand'" (Mark 3:5).
- "At that time Jesus, *full of joy* through the Holy Spirit . . ." (Luke 10:21). (Emphasis added throughout)

Take a few minutes and reflect on the implications of your God-given feelings. You are made in his image. God thinks. You think.

God wills. You will. God feels. You feel. You are a human being made in God's likeness. Part of that likeness is to feel.

At the very least, the call of discipleship includes experiencing our feelings, reflecting on our feelings, and then thoughtfully responding to our feelings under the lordship of Jesus.

You Feel—Even If You Are Unaware of It

The problem, however, is that we can't reflect and respond thoughtfully to our feelings if we don't know what they are. So much of our true selves is buried alive—sadness, rage, anger, tenderness, joy, happiness, fear, depression. Yet God designed our bodies to respond physiologically to those in the world around us.

God speaks to us through a knot in the stomach, muscle tension, trembling and shaking, the release of adrenaline into our bloodstream, headaches, and a suddenly elevated heart rate. God may be screaming at us through our physical body while we look for (and prefer) a more "spiritual" signal. The reality is that often our bodies know our feelings before our minds.

When I speak about the need to pay attention to our emotions, I often hear comments such as these:

- I am not very good at feelings. I really don't have time for this. Anyway, my family was more about doing.
- I don't know what I'm feeling. It's all a big blur.
- At times when I am about to interact with authority figures or somebody I don't know, I get physical sensations but I don't know why it is happening.
- Sometimes I am flooded by emotions that disorganize and confuse me.

- Sometimes after a difficult meeting with someone (e.g., conflict) I get depressed. I don't know why.
- Sometimes, during even a TV commercial, tears come to my eyes.
- When I am feeling bad, I can't tell if I am scared or angry.
- I carry an overwhelming feeling of being shameful, guilty, and/or defective.
- My family taught that nice girls don't get angry and big boys don't cry.

The problem for many of us comes when we have a "difficult" feeling such as anger or sadness. Unconsciously, we have a "rule" against those feelings. We feel defective because we ought not to be feeling the "wrong" things. We then lie to ourselves, sometimes convincing ourselves that we aren't feeling anything because we don't think we should be feeling it. We shut down our humanity.

So it was with me. I never really explored what I was feeling. I was not prepared to be honest about my emotions with God or myself. As a result I often said one thing with my words, but my tone of voice, facial expressions, and body posture said another. The problem is that when we neglect our most intense emotions, we are false to ourselves and close off an open door through which to know God.

I remember the awkwardness when I began to be honest about my feelings. Initially I wondered if I was betraying God or leaving Christianity. I feared that if I opened Pandora's box, I would get lost in a black hole of unresolved emotions. I was breaking an unspoken commandment of my family and my church tradition.

To my surprise, God was able to handle my wild emotions as they erupted after thirty-six years of stuffing them. I came alive like never before. And I rediscovered his love and grace—much like David, Job, and Jeremiah. I also began the journey to know myself that I might know God.

Discovering God's Will and Your Emotions

It wasn't until later that I began to learn of Ignatius of Loyola, the founder of the Jesuits, and his classic work on the importance of maintaining a balance between our reason (intellect) and feelings (heart). His development of a set of guidelines that respected the important place of emotions in discerning God's will has served believers for 450 years. He rightly emphasized the foundation of a complete commitment to do God's will, follow Scripture, and seek wise counsel. Yet, in addition, he provided excellent guidelines for sorting out how God speaks to us through the raw material of our emotions. The issue is not, by any means, to blindly follow our feelings, but to acknowledge them as a *part* of the way God communicates to us.

Ignatius explored the difference between *consolations* (those interior movements and feelings that bring life, joy, peace, and the fruit of the Spirit) and *desolations* (that which brings us "death," inner turmoil, disquiet, and "spiritual turbulence").[4] With this awareness of what we are feeling, Ignatius echoed the apostle John, who said "do not believe every spirit, but test the spirits to see whether they are from God" (1 John 4:1). Sometimes they are our fleshly desires or the enemy. Other times God is prodding us to a better choice. God intends that we mature in learning to recognize how he speaks and guides us through our feelings.

One of our greatest obstacles in knowing God is our own lack of self-knowledge. So we end up wearing a mask—before God, ourselves, and other people. And we can't become self-aware if we cut off our humanity out of fear of our feelings. This fear leads to unwillingness to know ourselves as we truly are and stunts our growth in Christ.

In *The Cry of the Soul*, Dan Allender and Tremper Longman summarize why awareness of our feelings is so important:

> Ignoring our emotions is turning our back on reality. Listening to our emotions ushers us into reality. And reality is where we meet God. . . . Emotions are the language of the soul. They are the cry that gives the heart a voice. . . . However, we often turn a deaf ear—through emotional denial, distortion, or disengagement. We strain out anything disturbing in order to gain tenuous control of our inner world. We are frightened and ashamed of what leaks into our consciousness. In neglecting our intense emotions, we are false to ourselves and lose a wonderful opportunity to know God. We forget that change comes through brutal honesty and vulnerability before God.[5]

Allow yourself to experience the full weight of your feelings. Allow them without censoring them. Then you can reflect and thoughtfully decide what to do with them. Trust God to come to you through them. This is the first step in the hard work of discipleship.

Once those "buried alive" emotions rose from the dead, I knew I could never go back to a spirituality that did not embrace emotional health. And when I finally allowed myself to begin asking, "How do I feel about the church, my life, different relationships around me?" before God and others, it released an outpouring that not only set me free but everyone around me.

The Great Temptation toward a False Self

I have spent years meditating on Jesus' temptations in the wilderness (Luke 4:1–13). They outline the three false identities or masks that Satan offers each one of us. And they show us the choices we, too, must make to remain faithful to our God-given unique life and identity.

Before the passage begins, we are given a snapshot of Jesus' understanding of who he is. Heaven opens. The Spirit descends like a dove. And Jesus' Father speaks audibly: "This is my Son, whom I love; with him I am well pleased" (Matthew 3:17). In other words: "You are lovable. You are good. It is so good that you exist."

Jesus has yet to perform miracles or to die on the cross for the sins of humanity. Nonetheless, he receives an experiential affirmation that he is deeply loved by his heavenly Father for who he is. This love is the foundation of his self-understanding and the root source of how he feels about himself.

Living and swimming in the river of God's deep love for us in Christ is at the very heart of true spirituality. Soaking in this love enables us to surrender to God's will, especially when it seems so contrary to what we can see, feel, or figure out ourselves. This experiential knowing of God's love and acceptance provides the only sure foundation for loving and accepting our true selves. Only the love of God in Christ is capable of bearing the weight of our true identity.

God has shaped and crafted us internally—with a unique personality, thoughts, dreams, temperament, feelings, talents, gifts, and desires. He has planted "true seeds of self" inside of us. They make up the authentic "us." We are also deeply loved. We are a treasure.

Three powerful temptations, however, threaten us. Each, in its own way, screams: "God's love for you will never be enough! You are not lovable. You are not good enough."

Temptation One: I Am What I Do (Performance)

The devil said to Jesus, "If you are the Son of God, tell these stones to become bread" (Matthew 4:3). Jesus had apparently done nothing for thirty years. He had not yet begun his ministry. He seemed like a loser. Nobody believed in him. He was hungry. What contribution had he made to the world?

Our culture asks the same question. What have you achieved? How have you demonstrated your usefulness? What do you do? Most of us consider ourselves worthwhile if we have scored sufficient successes—in work, family, school, church, relationships. When we don't, we may move harder and faster, go inward into depression out of shame, or perhaps blame others for our predicaments.

Thomas Merton, a Trappist monk and writer of the bestseller *Seven Storey Mountain*, tells of an occasion in his life:

> A few years ago a man who was compiling a book on success wrote and asked me to contribute a statement of how I got to be a success. I replied indignantly that I was not able to consider myself a success in any terms that had a meaning to me. I swore I had spent my life strenuously avoiding success. If it happened that I had once written a best-seller this was a pure accident, due to inattention and naiveté, and I would take very good care never to do the same thing again. If I had a message to my contemporaries, I said, it was surely this: be anything you like, be madmen, drunks . . . of every shape and form, but at all costs avoid one thing: success. I heard no more reply from him, and I am not aware that my reply was published.[6]

Merton understood how easily earthly success tempts us to find our worth and value outside of God's inexhaustible, free love for us in Christ.

Temptation Two: I Am What I Have (Possessions)

Jesus was taken to see all the magnificence and power of the earth. The devil basically said to him, "Look around you at what everyone else has. You don't have anything. How can you think you are somebody? How will you survive? You're a nobody." The devil played on profound issues of fear and the source of his security.

Our culture measures our success by what we own. Marketers now spend more than fifteen billion dollars each year seducing children and adolescents to believe they have to have certain toys, clothes, electronic devices, etc. Their very identities depend on it. As adults we measure ourselves through comparisons: Who has the most money? The most beautiful body? The most comfortable life? Often our sense of worth is tied to our positions at work—the money and perks. Who has the best education from what school, the most talents and awards, more degrees on their résumé? Who has the most attentive, handsome boyfriend or husband? The best-looking girl or wife?

A powerful example of this is found in the movie *Amadeus*. Antonio Salieri is the court musician whose soul is destroyed by envy, by not possessing enough. He longs to create music for God and to be famous. He is really good. The problem is that he is not as good as Mozart, who is a genius. Mozart possesses the ability to actually compose a symphony in his head, something few people in history have been able to do.

Rather than recognize Mozart's genius and bring it to the world, Salieri is angry at God for being so unfair. Tragically, he believes Mozart is loved by God, while he is not.

I understand Salieri. To define myself as a son immensely loved by God, to find my personal worth in my Abba Father, who says of me, "You are my son, Pete, whom I love; with you I am well pleased," apart from anything I do, is revolutionary. My culture, family of origin, and flesh tell me that only possessions and talents and applause from other people are sufficient for security. Jesus models surrender of my will to the love of the Father as the true anchor for who I am.

Temptation Three: I Am What Others Think (Popularity)

Some of us are addicted to what others think.

Satan invited Jesus to throw himself down from the highest spot of the temple that people might believe in him. At this point people did not think anything of Jesus. He was, in effect, invisible. How could he think he had worth and value?

Most of us place a higher premium on what other people think than we realize. What will I say or not say in a conversation? What school will my child attend? Who will I date? Do I tell that person he or she hurt me? What kind of career will I pursue? Our self-image soars with a compliment and is devastated by a criticism.

True freedom comes when we no longer need to be somebody special in other people's eyes because we know we are lovable and good enough.

M. Scott Peck illustrates the point through a story of meeting a classmate at his high school at the age of fifteen. The following are his reflections after a conversation with his friend:

> I suddenly realized that for the entire ten-minute period from when I had first seen my acquaintance until that very moment, I had been totally self-preoccupied. For the two or three minutes before we met all I was thinking about was the clever things I might say that would impress him. During our five minutes together I was listening to what he had to say only so that I might turn it into a clever rejoinder. I watched him only so that I might see what effect my remarks were having upon him. And for the two or three minutes after we separated my sole thought content was those things I could have said that might have impressed him even more. I had not cared a whit for my classmate.[7]

What is most startling in reading a detailed explanation of what goes on beneath the surface at the age of fifteen is that the same dynamics continue into the twenties, thirties, fifties, seventies, and nineties. We remain trapped in living a pretend life out of an unhealthy concern for what other people think.

The Deeply Entrenched False Self: Inside and Outside the Church

Consider the two following examples. While only the second one claims to be a follower of Christ, the core issues in their lives are not that different. The tragedy is, that for the Christian, years of following Christ did not change her false self. It remained deeply entrenched and untouched by the power of the gospel.

Joe DiMaggio

One of my heroes growing up was Joe DiMaggio, a baseball player for the New York Yankees. Although he played for my dad's generation, stories and legend circulated for decades throughout my childhood and teen years. They placed him firmly as "the greatest living baseball player" of the twentieth century, a larger-than-life hero in American sports history. Crowds erupted into applause at his very entrance into a restaurant or public event. News reporters, year after year, praised his extraordinary talent in baseball as if he were a god.

A final jewel was added to his earthly crown when one of the most beautiful women of his day—Marilyn Monroe—became his wife.

After Joe's death, however, a devastating biography of his life was published.

It related in vivid detail how Joe's "image management," right up to his dying days at the age of eighty-three, was all a mask. It hid an egocentric, competitive, greedy, selfish man driven by power and money. In *Joe DiMaggio: The Hero's Life*, Richard Ben Cramer details the "flatness" of Joe's life because of his commitment to "show nothing but a shiny surface of his own devising." Anyone who attempted to penetrate that surface was met with silence, exclusion, or rage. "The story of Joe DiMaggio the icon was well known. The story of DiMaggio the man had been buried."[8]

Who knows what negative core beliefs Joe might have carried within himself. I doubt Joe DiMaggio himself knew. However, one thing is sure: his life was both a lie and a tragedy.

What is perhaps more tragic is that so many of us who are followers of Jesus Christ also remain trapped within the layers of our false self.

Sheila Walsh

Sheila Walsh, Christian singer, writer, and former cohost of *The 700 Club* told her story of how, in 1992, her disconnected spirituality caused her to "hit the wall."

> One morning I was sitting on national television with my nice suit and inflatable hairdo and that night I was in the locked ward of a psychiatric hospital. It was the kindest thing God could have done to me.
>
> The very first day in the hospital, the psychiatrist asked me, "Who are you?"
>
> "I'm the co-host of the *700 Club*."
>
> "That's not what I meant," he said.
>
> "Well, I'm a writer. I'm a singer."
>
> "That's not what I meant. Who are you?"
>
> "I don't have a clue," I said.
>
> And he replied, "Now that's right and that's why you're here."

Sheila continued:

> I measured myself by what other people thought of me. That was slowly killing me.
>
> Before I entered the hospital, some of the *700 Club* staff said to me, "Don't do this. You will never regain any kind of platform. If

> people know you were in a mental institution and on medication, it's over."
>
> I said, "You know what? It's over anyway. So I can't think about that."
>
> I really thought I had lost everything. My house. My salary. My job. Everything. But I found my life. I discovered at the lowest moment of my life that everything that was true about me, God knew.[9]

At times our false self has become such a part of who we are that we don't even realize it. The consequences—fear, self-protection, possessiveness, manipulation, self-destructive tendencies, self-promotion, self-indulgence, and a need to distinguish ourselves from others—are harder to hide.[10]

Living your God-given life involves remaining faithful to your true self. It entails distinguishing your true self from the demands and voices around you and discerning the unique vision, calling, and mission the Father has given to you.[11] It requires listening to God from within yourself and understanding how he has uniquely made you. Knowing your personality, temperament, likes and dislikes, thoughts, and feelings all contribute to your discovery.

John Chrysostom, the golden-mouthed preacher and archbishop of Constantinople, described our work as follows: "Find the door of your heart, you will discover it is the door of the kingdom of God."

Jesus' True Self

It seemed that almost everyone had expectations, or a false self, to impose on Jesus' life. In living faithfully to his true self, he disappointed a lot of people. Jesus was secure in his Father's love, in himself, and thus was able to withstand enormous pressure. He left his family of origin and their expectations of a carpenter's son and became an inner-directed, separate adult. As a result, he disappointed his family. At one point, his mother and siblings wondered if he was out of his mind (Mark 3:21).

He disappointed the people he grew up with in Nazareth. When Jesus declared who he really was as the Messiah, they tried to push him off a cliff (Luke 4:28–29). He remained self-assured in his beliefs, regardless of the outrage of the crowds in his hometown.

He disappointed his closest friends, the twelve disciples. They projected onto Jesus their own picture of the kind of Messiah Jesus was to be. This did not include a shameful end to his life. They quit on him. Judas, one of his closest friends, "stabbed him in the back" for being true to himself. But even though they misunderstood him, Jesus never held it against them.

Jesus listened without reacting. He communicated without antagonizing. Yet he deeply disappointed the crowds. They wanted an earthly Messiah who would feed them, fix all their problems, overthrow the Roman oppressors, work miracles, and give inspiring sermons. Somehow Christ was able to serve and love them, again, without holding it against them.

He disappointed the religious leaders. They did not appreciate the disruption his presence brought to their day-to-day lives or to their theology. They finally attributed his power to demons. Nonetheless, Jesus was able to maintain a non-anxious presence in the midst of great stress.

Jesus was not *selfless*. He did not live as if *only* other people counted. He knew his value and worth. He had friends. He asked people to help him. At the same time Jesus was not *selfish*. He did not live as if nobody else counted. He gave his life out of love for others. From a place of loving union with his Father, Jesus had a mature, healthy "true self."

The pressure on us to live a life that is not our own is also great.

Powerful generational forces and spiritual warfare work against us. Yet living faithfully to our true self in Christ represents one of the great tasks of discipleship.

Differentiation—Living Faithful to Your True Self

One very helpful way to clarify this process of growing in our faithfulness to our true selves in a new way is through the use of a new term: *differentiation*. Developed by Murray Bowen, the founder of modern family systems theory, it refers to a person's capacity to "define his or her own life's goals and values apart from the pressures of those around them."[12] The key emphasis of differentiation is on the ability to think clearly and carefully as another means, besides our feelings, of knowing ourselves.

Differentiation involves the ability to hold on to who you are and who you are not. The degree to which you are able to affirm your distinct values and goals apart from the pressures around you (separateness) while remaining close to people important to you (togetherness) helps determine your level of differentiation. People with a high level of differentiation have their own beliefs, convictions, directions, goals, and values apart from the pressures around them. They can choose, before God, how they want to be without being controlled by the approval or disapproval of others. Intensity of feelings, high stress, or the anxiety of others around them does not overwhelm their capacity to think rationally.

I may not agree with you or you with me. Yet I can remain in relationship with you. I don't have to detach from you, reject you, avoid you, or criticize you to validate myself. I can be myself apart from you.

Read through my adaptation of Bowen's scale of differentiation beginning below. On the lower end of the scale are those with little sense of their unique God-given life. They need continual affirmation and validation from others because they don't have a clear sense of who they are. They depend on what other people think and feel in order to have a sense of their own worth and identity. Or out of fear of getting too close to someone and thus swallowed up, they may avoid closeness to others completely. Under stress they have little ability to distinguish between their feelings and their thought (intellectual) process.

Considering that Jesus was 100 percent true to himself, or "self-differentiated," where might you place yourself on this scale?

0 . . . . 25 . . . . 50 . . . . 75 100

0–25

- Can't distinguish between fact and feeling
- Emotionally needy and highly reactive to others
- Much of life energy spent in winning the approval of others
- Little energy for goal-directed activities
- Can't say, "I think . . . I believe . . ."
- Little emotional separation from their families
- Dependent marital relationships
- Do very poorly in transitions, crises, and life adjustments
- Unable to see where they end and others begin

25–50

- Some ability to distinguish between fact and feeling
- Most of self is a "false self" and reflected from others
- When anxiety is low, they function relatively well
- Quick to imitate others and change themselves to gain acceptance from others
- Often talk one set of principles/beliefs, yet do another

- Self-esteem soars with compliments or is crushed by criticism
- Become anxious (i.e., highly reactive and "freaking out") when a relationship system falls apart or becomes unbalanced
- Often make poor decisions due to their inability to think clearly under stress
- Seek power, honor, knowledge, and love from others to clothe their false selves

50–75

- Aware of the thinking and feeling functions that work as a team
- Reasonable level of "true self"
- Can follow life goals that are determined from within
- Can state beliefs calmly without putting others down
- Marriage is a functioning partnership where intimacy can be enjoyed without losing the self
- Can allow children to progress through developmental phases into adult autonomy
- Function well—alone or with others
- Able to cope with crises without falling apart
- Stay in relational connection with others without insisting they see the world the same

75–100

(Few people function at this level)

- Are principle oriented and goal directed—secure in who they are, unaffected by criticism or praise
- Are able to leave family of origin and become an inner-directed, separate adult

- Sure of their beliefs but not dogmatic or closed in their thinking
- Can hear and evaluate beliefs of others, discarding old beliefs in favor of new ones
- Can listen without reacting and communicate without antagonizing others
- Can respect others without having to change them
- Aware of dependence on others and responsibility *for* others
- Free to enjoy life and play
- Able to maintain a non-anxious presence in the midst of stress and pressure
- Able to take responsibility for their own destiny and life

Developing Your Authentic Self

We are so unaccustomed to being our true self that it can seem impossible to know where to begin. Thomas Merton describes well what we so often do:

> I . . . love to clothe this false self . . . and I wind experiences around myself with pleasures and glory like bandages in order to make myself visible to myself and to the world, as if I were an invisible body that could only become visible when something visible covered its surface. But there is no substance under the things with which I am clothed. I am hollow. . . . And when they are gone there will be nothing left of me but my own nakedness and emptiness and hollowness.[13]

Getting to your core requires following God into the unknown, into a relationship with him that turns your present spirituality upside down. God invites us to remove the false layers we wear to reveal our authentic self, to awaken the "seeds of true self" he has planted within us. The path we must walk is initially very hard. Powerful forces around and inside us work to smother the process of nurturing the seeds planted in each of us.[14] At the same time the God of the universe has made his home in us (John 14:23). The very glory God gave Jesus has been given to us (John 17:21–22). The Holy Spirit has been given to empower us that we might break free into our true selves in Christ.

By God's grace we are to be the freest people on earth!

The issue then is how to dismantle the false self and allow our true self in Christ to emerge. The following are four practical truths that can help us begin the radical transition of living faithful to our true self in Christ.

1. Pay Attention to Your Interior in Silence and Solitude

We want to be the men and women God has called us to be—our true selves in Christ.

Yet enormous distractions keep us from listening to our feelings, our desires, our dreams, our likes and dislikes. Many people around us would like to fix, save, advise, and set us straight into becoming the people they would like.[15]

We need to be alone so we can listen.

My journey into emotionally healthy spirituality began very simply. Each day, as part of my devotions with God, I would allow myself to feel emotion before God. Then I would journal. Over time I began to discern patterns and God's movements in a new way in my life.

Initially, I wondered if I was a heretic to make this part of my prayer life. Finally I determined that what was going on inside of me was true whether I was aware of it or not—so I may as well be aware of it.

I allowed myself to feel the full weight of my feelings, not censoring any of them. How did I feel about that critical comment a coworker had made to me while we were walking to our cars? Why was I angry? What was I afraid of? What was I excited about? What might be some of the depression I felt this afternoon?

I have been journaling ever since. I go back and read what I have written to review truths God told to me during that time.

This takes time. I slowed down the pace of my life considerably. From working six days a week (and about seventy hours), I slowed down to a five-day, forty-five-hour workweek. Over the years this led me quite naturally to the classic Christian disciplines of silence (escaping from noise and sounds) and solitude (being alone, without human contact). Silence and solitude are so foundational to emotionally healthy spirituality that they are a theme repeated throughout this book. We observe this from Moses to David to Jesus to all the great men and women of the faith who have gone before us.

Like you, I have countless demands pressing for my attention. With the hectic pace of our lives, the incessant noise of television, radio, computers, music, and our overloaded schedules, it is no wonder the ancient path of silence and solitude is lost to most believers in the West. But we must take the time. As the wise, old Abbot Moses said when a brother came to him for a good word, "Go, sit in your cell [a monk's room], and your cell will teach you everything."[16]

2. Find Trusted Companions

I don't know many people who shed layers of their false self in order that their true self might emerge unless they have a few trusted mature companions to help them along the way. Dietrich Bonhoeffer in his classic *Life Together* warned: "Let the person who cannot be alone beware of community. Let the person who is not in community beware of being alone."[17] We are to be "alone together," a "community of solitudes."[18]

John Cassian, in the fifth century, tells the story of a man named Hero who spent fifty years living as a hermit in the desert, free from all concerns of the world. When the other hermits would gather for worship on Sabbath or feast days, Hero refused to participate lest he give the impression he was relaxing his strict disciplines for God. One day Hero discerned God wanted him to jump into a deep well as a test of his faithfulness. He expected an angel to save him but fell to the bottom where he lay half dead. His fellow monks pulled him out, trying to convince him he had not actually heard God's voice—but it was useless. Even as he lay dying, they could not convince him that he had not heard the voice of God. "He went along so stubbornly with his own deception that he could not be persuaded, even when faced with death, that he had been deluded by the cleverness of demons." His pride was too great.[19]

In this journey of emotionally healthy spirituality, we are talking about radical change at the core of our being. At least two critical forces hinder such a profound shift. First, the pressure of others to keep us living lives that are not our own is enormous. And second, our own stubborn self-will is much deeper and more insidious than we think. The possibility of self-deception is so great that without mature companions we can easily fall into the trap of living in illusions.

My trusted companions have included mentors, spiritual directors, counselors, mature friends, and the members of our small group and leadership at New Life Fellowship Church. They have each helped me pay attention to God and see through my inconsistencies. Most significant, God has used Geri, my wife, to lovingly reflect back to me who I am. The following is one example.

Shortly before my forty-ninth birthday, Geri innocently suggested I use an illustration in a Sunday message that included mentioning my age.

"I would never do that," I gasped.

She looked stunned. "Why not?" she asked.

Then I blurted out something that surprised even me. "Well, you see, Geri, a year from now I will be fifty. Then ten years later I will be sixty. Eva [our then ten-year-old] keeps reminding me that my hair is turning gray even now."

Her eyes widened, realizing something deep was going on. "Well, I am embarrassed to be honest," I continued. I couldn't stop talking. I was getting more and more anxious. "Geri, the truth is I feel like I'm behind," I stammered. "I should have written this book when I was thirty-five, not at forty-nine. During my whole childhood I felt like I was behind . . . like I missed some major chunks of my life growing up . . . and I've been catching up ever since. I always feel different, kind of backwards. And I think that no matter what, I carry that with me."

Geri listened to my five-minute speech, realizing she was on holy ground. When I finished, she quietly replied, "This is pretty significant, Pete. You may want to get some time alone with God and reflect on that one."

"Sure," I answered, my head down. I left the room. I felt naked and silently hoped to be able to bury the topic.

God, of course, had other plans.

As I followed her question of why I could not admit my age freely, I was forced to acknowledge that sense of being backward and behind had long, intertwined roots reaching back from my family of origin that continued to impact me. God was peeling off another layer of my false self (what a lifelong process!). He was peeling off another layer of the onion that the true Pete in Christ might freely live.

Perhaps you may be thinking, "I don't have anyone to walk with me in this journey." If so, pray. Ask God for his person(s) during this season of your life. Let him surprise you. Often God seems to lead us to people who are very different from us and who are not pastors or leaders. Ask those you respect for suggestions. And pay attention to what he might be saying to you.

3. Move Out of Your Comfort Zone

Dying to your false self and allowing your true self to come out can be frightening. For some of us giving or receiving a compliment feels wrong. Others have an allergic reaction to being in the presence of angry people. For others to enter into conflict feels like death. To some asking for help feels like complete failure, and even thinking about disagreeing with a friend can send some into an evening of insomnia.

To begin to do things differently, especially in the beginning, will feel very awkward. For years I learned from leaders and consultants around the country how to lead a large, growing church. None of the training I received concerned itself with knowing myself. The problem was that running a large organization, overseeing budgets, and managing staff and deadlines and endless to-do lists crushed me. I was busy, very busy, and dying on the inside.

The true seeds God had placed within me—those which enjoyed preaching and teaching, creating, writing, contemplation with God, and loving people—struggled for space. I felt smothered. I was trapped. But this was God's will, wasn't it? Didn't all pastors of large churches manage large budgets and staff, constantly building and expanding the infrastructure of the organization?

Initially, it felt so wrong and strange to begin to think differently. I did not want to be a CEO or a manager. I longed to pastor and to live differently. Would the church then ask me to resign? Would people reject me?

The pain of living a life that was not God's will for me finally was greater than the pain of change. It took years of hurting to get me to listen to God from within myself, to allow myself to ask the question, "Am I living faithfully to the life God has asked me to live?"

So I slowly changed how it would look for me to serve Christ at New Life Fellowship.

And the church blossomed.

I realized that what Rumi said was true: "Inside you there's an artist you don't know about. . . . If you are here unfaithfully with us, you're causing terrible damage. If you've opened your loving to God's love, you're helping people you don't know and have never seen."[20]

I truly believe the greatest gift we can give the world is our true self living in loving union with God. In fact, how can we affirm other people's unique identities when we don't affirm our own? Can we really love our neighbors well without loving ourselves?

For this reason the famous Hasidic story of Rabbi Zusya remains so important for us today: Rabbi Zusya, when he was an old man, said, "In the coming world, they will not ask me: 'Why were you not Moses?' They will ask me, 'Why were you not Zusya?'"

Changing the way we have lived for twenty or forty or sixty years requires nothing short of a revolution.

4. Pray for Courage

When we differentiate into our true self in Christ, the change is always accompanied by a reaction from those close to us. We may meet with a countermove or "Change back!" consequence from other people when we give up our old ways of behaving and living.

Murray Bowen, the originator of the term *differentiation*, emphasizes that in families there is a powerful opposition when one member of that system matures and increases his or her level of differentiation. He argues that even a little growth can cause a reaction in those closest to him or her. In the same way, I have seen repeatedly that when anyone makes a change in themselves (becoming their true self in Christ), a few people around them often get upset.

Bowen describes the opposition in three stages:

- Stage One: "You are wrong for changing and here are the reasons why."
- Stage Two: "Change back and we will accept you again."
- Stage Three: "If you don't change back, these are the consequences" (which are then listed).[21]

At each season of our journey with Christ, whenever Geri and I have taken steps to more clearly define who we are and who we are not in Christ, there has always been a consequence. It will happen with you too. But keep making changes. Be willing to tolerate the discomfort necessary for growth. Pray for the Holy Spirit's power to continue. You are doing something that has never been done before in your history! In some cases you will be challenging deep multigenerational patterns. Expect that you may stir up some profound emotionality!

God and the Sound Barrier

When we choose to begin to make changes in our life, the pressure can feel like either our inner person or exterior life relationships will implode in the process. The shaking that happens in our life can be compared, I believe for each of us, to breaking the sound barrier for the first time. Both require great courage.

The year was 1947 and nobody had successfully broken the speed of sound—760 mph at sea level. There was a widely held belief of the existence of a "sound barrier," an invisible wall of air that would smash an airplane that tried to pierce the speed of Mach 1. In fact, a British plane, along with the pilot, had been blown to pieces in an attempt earlier that year to break the barrier. The plane could not sustain the pressure.

About that time, the United States Air Force was developing a project to put military pilots into space, but they first needed to punch through the sound barrier. Chuck Yeager was invited to be their test pilot. His boss, Colonel Boyd, informed him, "Nobody knows for sure what happens until somebody gets there. Chuck, you'll be flying into the unknown."[22]

The plane had the latest technology and design, but neither the air force nor the colonel could guarantee the outcome. Nobody had been there before.

In the same way, no other person has ever lived your life. You may be wondering what will happen if you engage in this journey of emotionally healthy spirituality, if you take seriously God's purpose for you to increasingly live faithfully out of the life he has given you.

After nine attempts, on October 14, 1947, Yeager finally broke the sound barrier. He wrote later about the experience: "I was thunderstruck. After all the anxiety, breaking the sound barrier turned out to be a perfectly paved speedway. . . . After all the anticipation it was really a let down. The 'unknown' was a poke through Jell-O."[23]

The point of this story is not that we live our life flying at high speeds. (My prayer is that you will slow down!) Hebrews 11 tells us that some people conquered kingdoms. Others were sawed in two for their faith. Only God knows your future. Yet you can be sure of one thing: your life, like Yeager's airplane, will shake in the process of you maturing into the person God intends. Why? The raw material of your life is unaccustomed to flying in order to break through the sound barrier. It will initially feel uncomfortable, as if the plane of your life is shaking from the pressure.

If you move forward, however, you will find that God is with you and behind you. His grace is sufficient. His power is accessible. And the unknown before you is really like poking through Jell-O.

Getting to know yourself so that you might know God is the adventure of a lifetime. You now have taken your first steps on the pathway toward an emotionally healthy spirituality. Let's go to the next chapter and explore a foundational issue of getting to know ourselves—going back in order to go forward.

And as Augustine prayed, "Grant, Lord, that I may know myself that I may know thee."

Lord, help me to be still before you. Lead me to a greater vision of who you are, and in so doing, may I see myself—the good, the bad, and the ugly. Grant me the courage to follow you, to be faithful to become the unique person you have created me to be. I ask you for the Holy Spirit's power to not copy another person's life or journey. "God, submerge me in the darkness of your love, that the consciousness of my false, everyday self falls away from [me] like a soiled garment. . . . May my 'deep self' fall into your presence . . . knowing you alone . . . carried away into eternity like a dead leaf in the November wind."[24] In Jesus' name, amen.

CHAPTER 3

Going Back in Order to Go Forward

Breaking the Power of the Past

Emotionally healthy spirituality is about reality, not denial or illusion. It is about embracing God's choice to birth us into a particular family, in a particular place, at a particular moment in history.

That choice granted to us certain opportunities and gifts. It also handed to us a certain amount of what I will call "emotional baggage" in our journey through life. For some of us this load was minimal; for others, it turned out to be a heavy one to carry. In fact, some of us are so accustomed to walking with such excess weight that we can't imagine living any other way.

True spirituality frees us to live joyfully in the present. It requires, however, going back in order to go forward. This takes us to the very heart of spirituality and discipleship in the family of God—breaking free from the destructive sinful patterns of our pasts to live the life of love God intends.

Frank

Frank works for a large corporation as a middle manager. Married with two teenage boys, Frank had been attending New Life Fellowship for more than a year when he asked if we could get together. Walking into the diner the following week, it was obvious he was visibly shaken and depressed.

"Hi, Frank, what's up?" I asked.

"Pete, you'll never believe it," he erupted immediately. "Maria told me last night that she wasn't sure she loved me anymore. I asked if there was another guy. She said no, but who knows."

His shoulders slumped. He looked down to the floor and continued. "You know I was never very good at this relationship thing, but I've done everything I could to be a good husband, a good father, a good provider. I don't know. . . . I pray. We pray. I have no idea what's happening."

They'd met in college and married soon after graduation. Frank then served as a pastor for ten years (in three different cities) before eventually going into business. He had recently been transferred to New York.

After a long silence, I wondered aloud, "Frank, what do you think precipitated this now—after being together so long?"

He pounced. "She's upset because I told her we might have to relocate again in two years. Well . . . she's always complaining, more than ever, of me being distant, emotionally unavailable, 'un-intimate'—whatever that is! She's also been really upset about my lack of involvement with the boys. It is just so hard for me! I try but then I slip back into my own world of work and church so quickly that . . . I don't know. . . . I've tried to make her happy." His voice trailed off to a whisper. "I don't know what to think. And I have no idea where to go from here."

Both Frank and Maria were raised in Christian homes. They know the Bible.

For years they have worshiped God and listened to thousands of sermons. They have attended small groups faithfully and served on their church worship team. They have gone away on Christian marriage retreats and attended leadership conferences.

Yet they are miserable. Why?

Why hasn't a lifetime of spirituality in the church, surrounded by the truth of Jesus Christ, transformed deeply their inner lives and marriage? Where is the rich, abundant fruit of a life well lived in God?

Why are so many of us living lives with deeply entrenched parts of us apparently untouched by the power and mercy of the Lord Jesus Christ? This entire book, I hope, begins to offer an answer to this challenge.

One critical ingredient, however, relates to our need to go back in order to go forward. This can be summed up in two essential biblical truths:

1. The blessings and sins of our families going back two to three generations profoundly impact who we are today.
2. Discipleship requires putting off the sinful patterns of our family of origin and relearning how to do life God's way in God's family.

The pathway to an emotionally healthy spirituality calls for these key biblical ingredients to be central in our understanding of what it means to be a follower of Jesus.

The Power of the Family

When the Bible uses the word *family*, it refers to our entire extended family over three to four generations. That means your family, in the biblical sense, includes all your brothers, sisters, uncles, aunts, grandparents, great-grandparents, great-uncles and aunts, and significant others going back to the mid-1800s!

While we are affected by powerful external events and circumstances through our earthly lives, our families are the most powerful group to which we will ever belong. Even those who left home as young adults, determined to "break" from their family histories, soon find that their family's way of "doing" life follows them wherever they go.

What happens in one generation often repeats itself in the next. The consequences of actions and decisions taken in one generation affect those who follow.

For this reason it is common to observe certain patterns from one generation to the next such as divorce, alcoholism, addictive behavior, sexual abuse, poor marriages, one child running off, mistrust of authority, pregnancy out of wedlock, an inability to sustain stable relationships, etc. Scientists and sociologists have been debating for decades whether this is a result of "nature" (i.e., our DNA) or "nurture" (i.e., our environment) or both. The Bible doesn't answer this question. It only states that this is a "mysterious law of God's universe."[1]

Consider the following:

God, in the giving of the Ten Commandments, connected this reality to the very nature of who he is: "You shall not make for yourself an image in the form of anything in heaven above or on the earth beneath or in the waters below . . . for I, the Lord your God, am a jealous God, *punishing the children for the sin of the parents to the third and fourth generation of those who hate me, but showing love to a thousand generations of those who love me and keep my commandments*" (Exodus 20:4–6, emphasis added).

God repeated the same truth again when Moses asked to see God's glory: "And he passed in front of Moses, proclaiming, 'The Lord, the Lord, the compassionate and gracious God, slow to anger, abounding in love and faithfulness. . . . *Yet he does not leave the guilty unpunished; he punishes the children and their children for the sin of the parents to the third and fourth generation*'" (Exodus 34:6–7, emphasis added).

When David murdered Uriah in order to marry his wife Bathsheba, God declared, *"Now, therefore, the sword will never depart from your house, because you despised me and took the wife of Uriah the Hittite to be your own"*

(2 Samuel 12:10, emphasis added). Family tensions, sibling rivalry, and internal strife marked his children, grandchildren, and great-grandchildren for generations.

Family patterns from the past are played out in our present relationships without us necessarily being aware of it. Someone may look like an individual acting alone—but they are really players in a larger family system that may go back, as the Bible says, three to four generations. Unfortunately, it is not possible to erase the negative effects of our history. This family history lives inside all of us, especially in those who attempt to bury it. The price we pay for this flight is high. Only the truth sets us free.

Frank and Maria—The Challenge Before Them

For Frank, to follow Christ and do the serious work of discipleship will require him to examine the impact of growing up in a U.S. Army family that moved every three to four years. His father was frequently deployed away from home six months at a time. The strain was more than his mother was willing to bear. Eventually, she ended the marriage.

Frank, as the oldest child, filled in the gap his father vacated—at least financially. He worked hard but had a lot of difficulty with friendships. The frequent moves scarred him. He had difficulty getting close to people or sustaining long-term friendships.

He rarely spoke with his dad.

You can see where I'm going with this, can't you? But Maria also has work to do. Why was she so drawn to Frank's stability and good work ethic? Her father was an alcoholic who became a Christian when she was ten. He then buried himself in men's softball and church activities. He remained emotionally absent. Maria, an only child and often lonely, became very close to her mom. They'd been best friends for years, although her marriage to Frank was now putting strain on their relationship.

Both Maria and Frank have a wonderful growth opportunity before them. But it will involve a break with the old way of living and relating they had learned from their families. The ways of relating and thinking they embody go back not only to their parents but their grandparents and great-grandparents!

For this reason Christ said, "Anyone who loves their father or mother [or culture or other significant influences or unhealthy church traditions] more than me is not worthy of me" (Matthew 10:37). He knew our families are flawed and our relationships and patterns of loving are broken due to sin. Regardless of our culture, country of origin, education, social class, or age, the early messages and scripts we took in from our histories powerfully influence our present relationships and behaviors as well as our self-esteem.

Abraham, Isaac, and Jacob

Genesis, the first book of the Bible, relates how the truth that sins and blessings are passed from generation to generation works out. On one level, the blessings given to Abraham because of his obedience passed from generation to generation—to his children (Isaac), grandchildren (Jacob), and great-grandchildren (Joseph and his brothers). At the same time we observe a pattern of sin and brokenness transmitted through the generations. Truly, more is caught than taught.

For example, we observe:

A PATTERN OF LYING IN EACH GENERATION

- Abraham lied twice about Sarah.
- Isaac and Rebecca's marriage was characterized by lies.
- Jacob lied to almost everyone; his name means "deceiver."
- Ten of Jacob's children lied about Joseph's death, faking a funeral and keeping a "family secret" for more than ten years.

FAVORITISM BY AT LEAST ONE PARENT IN EACH GENERATION

- Abraham favored Ishmael.
- Isaac favored Esau.
- Jacob favored Joseph and later Benjamin.

BROTHERS EXPERIENCING A CUTOFF FROM ONE ANOTHER IN EACH GENERATION

- Isaac and Ishmael (Abraham's sons) were cut off from one another.
- Jacob fled his brother Esau and was completely cut off for years.
- Joseph was cut off from his ten brothers for more than a decade.

POOR INTIMACY IN THE MARRIAGES OF EACH GENERATION

- Abraham had a child out of wedlock with Hagar.
- Isaac had a terrible relationship with Rebecca.
- Jacob had two wives and two concubines.

The Ten Commandments of Your Family

We often underestimate the deep, unconscious imprint our families of origin leave on us. In fact, my observation is that it is only as we grow older that we realize the depth of their influence. Each of our family members, or those who raised us through childhood, has "imprinted" certain ways of behaving and thinking into us. (Likewise our cultures, the media, our interpretation of events that happen to us also imprint us.) These behavioral patterns operate under a set of "commandments." Some of them are spoken and explicit. Most are unspoken. They were "hardwired" into our brains and DNA, so much so that apart from the intervention of God himself and biblical discipleship we simply bring these expectations into our closest relationships as adults.

Consider the following Ten Commandments tablet:

1. MONEY
- Money is the best source of security.
- The more money you have, the more important you are.
- Make lots of money to prove you "made" it.

2. CONFLICT
- Avoid conflict at all costs.
- Don't get people mad at you.
- Loud, angry, constant fighting is normal.

3. SEX
- Sex is not to be spoken about openly.
- Men can be promiscuous; women must be chaste.
- Sexuality in marriage will come easily.

4. GRIEF AND LOSS
- Sadness is a sign of weakness.
- You are not allowed to be depressed.
- Get over losses quickly and move on.

5. EXPRESSING ANGER
- Anger is dangerous and bad.
- Explode in anger to make a point.
- Sarcasm is an acceptable way to release anger.

6. FAMILY
- You owe your parents for all they've done for you.
- Don't speak of your family's "dirty laundry" in public.
- Duty to family and culture comes before everything.

7. RELATIONSHIPS
- Don't trust people. They will let you down.
- Nobody will ever hurt me again.
- Don't show vulnerability.

8. ATTITUDES TOWARD DIFFERENT CULTURES
- Only be close friends with people who are like you.
- Do not marry a person of another race or culture.
- Certain cultures/races are not as good as mine.

9. SUCCESS
- Is getting into the "best schools."
- Is making lots of money.
- Is getting married and having children.

10. FEELING AND EMOTIONS
- You are not allowed to have certain feelings.
- Your feelings are not important.
- Reacting with your feelings without thinking is okay.

You can easily add to this list. What messages did you receive about parenting? Gender roles? Marriage? Singleness? Physical affection and touch? How did your family view God, other churches, other faiths? It is essential that we reflect on the messages that were handed down to us, submitting them to Christ and his Word.

A common, deadly commandment that prevails inside and outside the church is, "You must achieve to be loved." In other words, we must be competent in the context of competition—in school, sports, recreation, work, neighborhood, church—to feel of worth and value. As a result, many people struggle with an "achievement addiction." It never seems like enough. We consistently feel inferior. Many of us know the experience of being approved for what we do. Few of us know the experience of being loved for being just who we are.

Take a few minutes and ponder your family's commandments on this issue. How have they impacted you and your relationships today? Our history has shaped our current lives profoundly. The cost of ignoring the impact of our past on our present life is costly.

God's desire for us to leave our families is similar to the desire he had for the Israelites to leave Egypt. Although the Israelites did physically leave the land of Egypt, a great deal of Egyptian culture and thinking remained in them. In the same way, we may choose to become Christ followers, but in reality we continue to follow, probably unconsciously, the commandments and rules we internalized in our families of origin.

The great problem, of course, is when our family's invisible scripts are contrary to Christ's. And when the family commandments passed on to us are so deeply imbedded in our DNA that we cannot even discern the difference, the result can be tragic.

Compartmentalization

In 1976 I became a Christian at the age of nineteen. God then transferred me into his family—the body of Christ. While I now was a new member of Christ's family, almost everything I had learned about life had come from my original family.

The issue of discipleship now was how to do life Christ's way.

Learning how to pray, read Scripture, participate in small groups, worship, and use my spiritual gifts were the easy part. Rooting out deeply ingrained messages, habits, and ways of behaving, especially under stress, would prove far more complex and difficult.

My family, like all families, had invisible, unspoken rules that were expected to be obeyed. These included, for example, gender roles, how and when to express anger, views of race and other cultures, the definition of success, how authority was to be treated, sexuality for men versus women, marriage expectations, and views of the church. They were things I didn't want to address, and therefore going back to go forward was something I resisted strongly. Geri would ask me questions about my family past, and I would argue: "What good would it do to look back? It would be too painful. I am just so grateful to be a new creation in Christ." Like most people, I did not want to betray my family. What kind of a Christian would dig up "dirt" and secrets on his own family—especially an Italian-American one?

Looking to the past illumines the present. But make no mistake about it; it is painful.

Because so few people do the hard work of going back in order to go forward, the symptoms of a disconnected spirituality are everywhere. The compartmentalization of our spirituality from the rest of our lives becomes necessary because there is so little integration. I know. I lived that way for years.

Let's go back to Frank and his slow awakening to how his past was impacting his present.

The Painful Fruit of a Disconnected Spirituality

In later coffee meetings at the local diner with Frank, I asked him to describe his family to me.

"Our marriage is really better than my parents', at least," he began. "My father's father was extremely abusive physically and an alcoholic.

But my father became a Christian. He seemed to come out of the mess of his family. Yet he struggled his whole life with some sort of sexual addiction. I don't know what. He rarely spoke about it.

"Actually we moved an average of every three years as my dad took on different assignments for the army. So I never really developed close friends anywhere. Our family revolved around my dad. It was almost like everyone kind of tiptoed around him, fearing his anger—especially Mom. Her whole life, really, was about him. She gave up all her wants and desires for him and us kids. She died recently. But I'm not sure she ever really lived. She just kind of existed.

"So getting close to Maria was really hard for me. I wanted something better for us. But it didn't seem to bother her. She never said anything before—at least until now!"

After a few meetings Frank felt safe enough to unload a secret he had been carrying for a number of years: "I was exposed to pornography at age twelve. You can imagine living on an army base at that age. I've struggled ever since. I feel crippled by it, actually. Accountability groups, confessions, prayer lines—it keeps coming back. I don't know. Who knows? It's overwhelming."

Again there was a long pause as he waited for my reaction.

"I did some work with a counselor a number of years ago for depression but we never really got to underlying issues. The pornography addiction just grew until I left the board I was serving on. I just felt shame all over. Then I started to get some victory—at least for a while—so I went back to serve on the board."

Frank's life resembled a jack-in-the-box. While he regularly stuffed down his feelings of being invisible as a child or the feelings of being dominated by his parents as a young child, they often "popped" out in the present. Frank felt like he was betraying his parents talking so openly about their "secrets," but the pain had finally grown so great he had little choice.

Because this is not part of the discipleship or spiritual formation programs in most of our churches, it often takes a crisis to move someone like Frank, or myself, to go in this direction. I have not met anyone who wants to carry the weight and pass on their unfinished sins and baggage to their children and their children's children.

It is against this backdrop that the glory and power of the Lord Jesus offers such incredible hope.

The Great News of Jesus Christ

The great news of Christianity is that your family of origin does not determine your future. God does! What has gone before you is not your destiny! The most significant language in the New Testament for becoming a Christian is "adoption into the family of God." It is a radical new beginning. When we place our faith in Christ, we are spiritually reborn by the Holy Spirit into the family of Jesus. We are transferred out of darkness into the kingdom of light.

The apostle Paul used the image of Roman adoption to communicate this profound truth, emphasizing we are now in a new and permanent relationship with a new Father. God becomes our Father. Our debts (sins) are canceled. We are given a new name (Christian), a new inheritance (freedom, hope, glory, the resources of heaven), and new brothers and sisters (other Christians) (Ephesians 1).

Jesus' mother and brothers arrived at a house where he was teaching, looking for him to come outside. Jesus replied to the crowd inside the house sitting at his feet: "'Who are my mother and my brothers?' . . . Then he looked at those seated in a circle around him and said, 'Here are my mother and my brothers! Whoever does God's will is my brother and sister and mother'" (Mark 3:33–35). The church for the believer was now the "first family."[2]

In the ancient world of Jesus, it was extremely important to honor one's mother and father. Jesus demonstrated that, even while hanging on the cross. He entrusted the care of his mother to the apostle John. Yet Jesus was direct and clear in calling people to a first loyalty to himself over their biological families, saying, "Anyone who loves his father or mother more than me is not worthy of me" (Matthew 10:37). Discipleship, then, is the putting off of the sinful patterns and habits of our families of origin and being transformed to live as members of Christ's family.

This is the Christian life. God's intention is that we grow up into mature men and women transformed by the indwelling presence of Christ. We honor our parents, culture, and histories but obey God.

Every disciple, then, has to look at the brokenness and sin of his or her family and culture. The problem is that few of us have reflected honestly on the impact of our family of origin and other major "earthquake" events in our histories.

Philosopher George Santanya said it well: "Those who cannot learn from the past are doomed to repeat it." For example, perhaps your family defined success by profession or education or money. Maybe there were underlying messages that in order to be loved, cared for, or accepted you needed to *do* certain behaviors. This impacted your view of yourself (i.e., your self-esteem).

In God's family, success is defined as being faithful to God's purpose and plan for your life. We are called to seek first his kingdom and righteousness (Matthew 6:33). Everything else, he promises, will be added to us. Moreover, God declares we are lovable. We are good enough in Christ (Luke 15:21–24).

Discipleship, then, is working these truths into our practical, everyday lives.

Sadly, when we look deep beneath the surface of our lives, most of us are not doing anything fundamentally differently from what our families did. God's intention, however, is that our local churches and parishes are to be places where, slowly but surely, we are re-parented in doing life Christ's way.

God intends that his new community of people be the place where we are set free. This requires recognizing the sad reality that all of us bring to our new community our old "Egyptian" ways of living and relating. The following is a glimpse into how this worked out for me.

The Scazzero-Ariola Family

On the next page is a simplified genogram of my family. Genograms are a way to draw our family trees in a way that looks at information about family members and their relationships over two to three generations.

All our families are broken and marred by the effects of the fall.

Mine is no different. On the bottom right you will notice the highlighted "Peter." I am the youngest of four children. Geri and I have four daughters. By looking to the right side of the genogram you will see my mom, Francis, with her parents, Crescenzo and Carmela, above her.

On the left side you will see my father, Joseph, and then his parents, Dominic and Pasqualina, above him.

To understand the dynamics of who I am, you have to look at my mother's family, especially the impact of her father. Her father, Crescenzo, had married my grandmother in an arranged marriage in order to come to the United States. He was a "womanizer" who lived as a "married bachelor." He sent his wife and children to work in an Italian pastry shop while he continued living his own separate life.

My mother cannot remember him ever saying her first name. Crescenzo would scream, for example: "Disgrace the family and I'll kill you." He would win a pony and give it to another man's child. When one of his friends expressed keen interest in my mom's pet dog (she was about ten years old), he gave him the dog as a gift, ignoring my mother's tears.

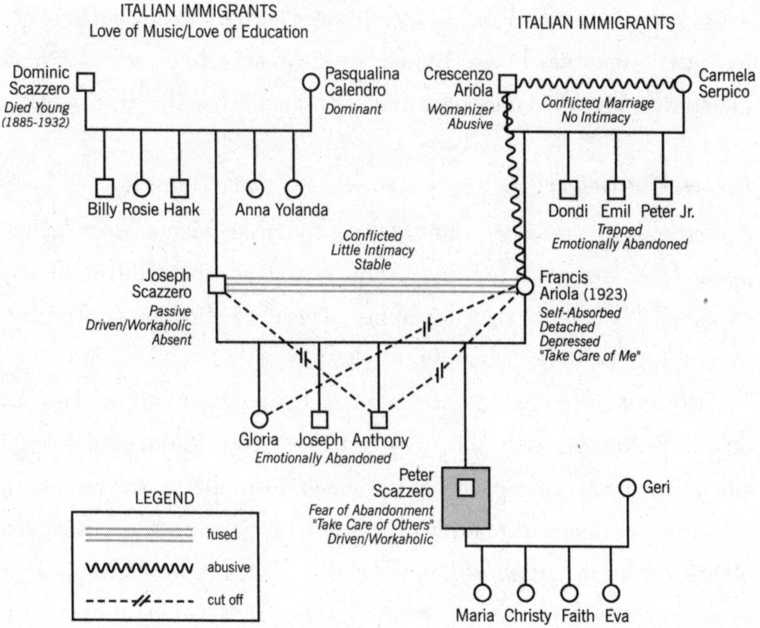

My dad worked for him in Ariola's pastry shop before marrying his daughter. He once remarked to me, "He treated his dogs better than his children."

Francis, my mom, was his only daughter. Her childhood and teen years were lonely, isolated, and tightly controlled. She never had a childhood and carried the emotional scars of her abuse into our family. Giving and receiving love, enjoying life, fun, laughter, playfulness, joy were unknown to her. She struggled with depression and feelings of profound loneliness her entire life.

My father was emotionally unavailable and absorbed in work and his hobbies. He delegated the raising of the family to my mom while he traveled. One of the tragedies of our family was that his marriage into my mom's family resulted in a cutoff from his own family that lasted more than twenty years.

What things then did I bring into my marriage with Geri and the walking out of my discipleship with Jesus? There are many, but here are five heavy "emotional bags" I unconsciously carried into my Christian life for years prior to understanding emotionally healthy spirituality.

I Over-Functioned

Along with my brothers, our role was to "make Mama happy" since my dad was absent for her. Even though we were the children, it was expected we would take care of her. There was little room to play, to have fun, or to be listened to.

When I became a Christian I naturally began to take care of others. Within one year of coming to Christ, I was leading our college Christian group, taking care of the sheep. I simply transferred being overly responsible in my family of origin to being overly responsible for others' salvation and growth in the church. Is it any wonder I became a pastor to care for others? Is it any wonder that I had great difficulty maintaining healthy, appropriate boundaries as an adult?

I Over-Performed

The experience of being Italian-American immigrants struggling to make it in the United States left an expectation on us: "You will make your parents proud; they have suffered so much for you to be able to succeed and go to college." The performance-based approval that ran strongly in the veins of our family now drove me to "work hard for Jesus." "Prove yourself" was the message.

We knew we were loved but always knew there was a line we could not cross. My brother Anthony, when he disobeyed my father, quit college and joined the Unification Church. He was disowned and forbidden to return home for years.

How many high-achieving, "successful" people are driven by a deeply seated shame and feeling of abandonment, silently crying out, "Notice me!"?

I Had Cultural, Not Biblical, Expectations for Marriage and Family

My beliefs regarding marriage and gender roles were shaped much more strongly by my family than Scripture. Of course Geri complained. But all the women in our extended family complained about their husbands. Wasn't that normal? Our marriage sure seemed better than most. I was "helping" with the kids, wasn't I?

I never observed a joyful, intimate couple investing in the quality of their own relationship before their relationships with their children. Women were to stay home with the children. Men led and made the major decisions for the family. I assumed that was God's way also.

I Resolved Conflict Poorly

Even though I taught workshops on conflict resolution and communication, the basic way I handled conflict and anger resembled my family of origin, not Christ's family. My mother raged and attacked. To avoid conflict, my dad the appeaser gave in to whatever my mom wanted. I took on my father's basic style, taking the blame whenever something was wrong in order to end any tension. I justified it as being like Christ, a sheep going to the slaughter. In doing so, however, I did not love well.

I Didn't Let Myself Feel

Finally, I did not know how to accept and process my own feelings, needs, and wants. I felt "invisible" in our family growing up, consistently taking care to keep the family together. So questions such as "What do you feel? What do you want? What do you need?" were never asked to me growing up. I was naturally drawn to certain biblical teachings (e.g., Luke 9:23 on denying yourself and John 15:13 on laying down your life for others) while ignoring others (e.g., remember to rest on the Sabbath day [see Exodus 20:8]).

A child doesn't say, "What's wrong with this environment where

I am growing up?" They think, *What's wrong with me?* So I grew up feeling inadequate, flawed . . . defective. *If people only knew*, I would think to myself.

I loved the message of Christ. No other religion in the world reveals a personal God who loves us for who we are, not what we do. His approval is without conditions. Yet for the first seventeen years of my discipleship the profound impact my family history had upon me blocked that truth from penetrating deeply into my experience. Like many people I meet, I lied to myself out of fear, twisting the truth to myself: *Oh, Pete, it wasn't that bad. How many people have it so much worse?*

The truth is that I did "lose a leg in my childhood." I cannot get that back. Yet because, by God's grace, I have gone back, I can walk. I may walk with a limp, but I am no longer crippled. I am free. But when I look back now and think about how I lived the first seventeen years of my Christian life, I am stunned . . . shocked . . . embarrassed. . . . There was so much needless pain!

The Present Is a Window into the Past

I have examined genograms that outline the major themes of people's pasts both at New Life Fellowship Church and around North America at seminars and conferences for more than a decade. Our church has people from China, Argentina, Lebanon, Poland, Greece, Indonesia, the Philippines, Haiti, India, and more than sixty other countries. We've done genograms for many of them. We have done genograms for poor people from the South Bronx and suburban megachurches in the United States, for Ivy League PhDs and high school dropouts.

Often people will say afterward, "Gee, Pastor Pete, I guess my family [or culture, or country] is just particularly messed up."

My answer is always the same: "No. All families are broken and fallen. There aren't any 'clean' genograms. None of us comes from perfect families with perfect parents. Most parents did the best they could with what they brought with them into adulthood. And it is likely that some of the things that did hurt us, such as criticism and rejection, were a result of what was handed to them by their families of origin rather than a reflection on us or their love for us."

Our fear of bringing secrets and sin into the light, however, drives many people to prefer the illusion that if they don't think about it, it somehow goes away. It doesn't. Unhealed wounds open us up to habitual sin against God and others.

Jane, for example, is a member of a Sunday school class. She often helps set up chairs and refreshments beforehand and cleans up when class is over. Her relationship with the primary authority figures in her life growing up—her father and mother—was strained. They were rarely home and highly critical. Also, she was abused sexually by an uncle as a teenager. Today, twenty-five years later, whenever an authority figure gives Jane suggestions or constructive criticism, she gets defensive and withdraws. She is unaware of how her unexamined past chains her to unloving, disrespectful ways of relating in the present.

The great news is that Jane can go back in order to go forward. In Christ she can emerge a freer, more whole, alive person.

You see, even the worst and most painful family experiences are part of our total identity. God had a plan in placing us in our particular families and cultures. And the more we know about our families, the more we know about ourselves—and the more freedom we have to make decisions about how we want to live. We can say: "This is what I want to keep. This is what I do not want to bring with me to the next generation."

If we ignore truth out of fear, we end up like Miss Havisham from Charles Dickens's novel *Great Expectations.* The daughter of a wealthy man, she received a letter on her wedding day at 8:40 a.m. that her husband-to-be was not coming. She stopped all clocks in the house at the precise time the letter arrived and spent the rest of her life in her bridal dress (it eventually turned yellow), wearing only one shoe (since she had not yet put on the other at the time of the disaster). Even as an old lady, she remained crippled by the weight of that crushing blow. It was as if "everything in the room and house had stopped." She decided to live in her past, not her present or future.

The Beaver System Model[3]

The Beaver System Model is one helpful, well-known way of looking at and understanding our families. Based primarily on how they understand their boundaries, families are able to classify themselves along five different levels of health.

Level Five: The Family in Pain

This is a severely disturbed family. Real leadership is totally lacking. Chaos, uncertainty, confusion, and turmoil are the adjectives that describe these homes. Conflicts are never dealt with or resolved. There is no ability to look at issues with clarity.

Level Four: The Borderline Family

This is a polarized family. Instead of anarchy, as in Level Five, a dictatorship rules here. Instead of no rules, this home has nothing but black-and-white rules. There are rigid ways of thinking, feeling, and behaving that are expected of all members. Individuals cannot say, "I disagree with what you said."

Level Three: The Rule-Bound Family

This family is not in chaos or under a dictatorship. It is healthier than Level Four. Feeling loved and good about oneself, however, depends on obeying the spoken and unspoken rules of the family. "If you loved me, you would do all the things you know will meet with my approval." There is an invisible referee, with the rules of the system being more important than the individual. A subtle level of manipulation, intimidation, and guilt permeates the home.

Levels Two and One: The Adequate Family and the Optimal Family
In these families there is an ability to be flexible and cherish each individual member while at the same time valuing a sense of closeness. Good feelings, trust, and teamwork by the parents enable members to work through difficulties and conflicts. What distinguishes Level Two families from Level One can be summed up in one word: delight. Level One families truly delight in being with one another.

Now ask yourself: Which of these five family categories best describes my experience growing up? How does my family of origin still impact me today? What are the areas I need to intentionally work on in order to move forward in Christ (e.g., boundaries, dealing with conflict, intimacy)?

Joseph—Modeling How to Go Back to Go Forward

One-fourth of the book of Genesis is about Joseph growing up into an emotionally and spiritually mature adult who lived out his unique destiny in God. As with many families, however, Joseph's family was characterized by great brokenness and sadness.

Joseph appears in Genesis 37 at the age of seventeen, the eleventh of twelve sons and the favorite of his father, Jacob. They were a complex, blended family with Jacob, his two wives and two concubines, and all their children living under one roof.

Joseph was immature, arrogant, and unaware of how his dreams and visions from God only further alienated him from his brothers. Their hatred of him grew to the point where they faked his death, saying he had been killed by a wild animal. Instead they sold him to Egypt as a slave, hopefully never to be heard from again.

In many ways the level and number of secrets in a family gives an indication of its level of health and maturity. Joseph's family, by that standard, was very sick. Joseph's father, grandfather, and great-grandfather all engaged in lying and half-truths, secrecy and jealousy. Now, they took this generational pattern to a new level.

Imagine the impact for Joseph. He lost his parents, siblings, culture, food, language, freedom, and hopes in one day! Then in Egypt, while serving as a slave in the home of Potiphar, he was falsely accused of rape and sent to prison for years. A door opened for his release while in the dungeon, but he was forgotten once again. He languished in prison for ten to thirteen years. What a waste! What betrayal! His life, to the age of thirty, appears to be a tragedy. If anyone should have been filled with bitterness and rage for so much family pain, it was Joseph!

Yet he remained faithful as a seeker and lover of God. Even when horrific events outside his control swirled around him, Scripture describes Joseph as "walking with God."

Then the incredible happened. Overnight, through the interpretation of a dream, Joseph was pulled from the pit of prison and made the second most powerful person in Egypt, the superpower of that day. He continued to walk with the Lord until his dying day, partnering with the God of Israel to be a blessing to his family of origin, Egypt, and the world. He honored and blessed the family that betrayed him.

Joseph went back to go forward. The question is how? What lessons can we learn from his life?

1. Joseph Had a Profound Sense of the Bigness of God

Repeatedly, Joseph affirmed the large, loving hand of God through all his pain and hardships. "It was not you who sent me here, but God," he repeatedly proclaimed (Genesis 45:8). In doing so he affirmed that God mysteriously leads us into his purposes through darkness and obscurity. God is the Lord God Almighty who has all history in his grip, working in ways that are mostly hidden to us on Earth. Joseph understood that in all things God is at work, in spite of, through, and against all human effort, to orchestrate his purposes.

God never loses any of our past for his future when we surrender ourselves to him. Every mistake, sin, and detour we take in the journey of life is taken by God and becomes his gift for a future of blessing.

Why did God allow Joseph to go through such pain and loss? We see traces of the good that came out of it in Genesis 37–50, but much remains a mystery. Most importantly, Joseph rested in God's goodness and love, even when circumstances went from bad to worse.

2. Joseph Admitted Honestly the Sadness and Losses of His Family

Most of us are resistant to going back and feeling the hurt and pain of our past. It can feel like a black hole or an abyss that might swallow us up. We wonder if we are only getting worse. Yet Joseph wept repeatedly when he reunited with his family. In fact, Scripture relates that he wept so loudly that the Egyptians heard him (Genesis 45:2). He did not minimize or rationalize the painful years. But out of his honest grieving of the pain, he truly forgave and was able to bless the brothers who betrayed him. And he took leadership of his family to the end of his days, providing for them financially, emotionally, and spiritually. He saw how God sent him ahead to Egypt to save their lives by a great deliverance (Genesis 45:7).

When Joseph did begin to prosper in Egypt after his long years of suffering, he gave his two children names that reflected the pain and sadness of his past. His first son was named Manasseh, from the Hebrew word for "forget," because God had enabled him to forget all his troubles. His second child was named Ephraim, from the Hebrew word for "fruitful," because God had made him fruitful in his new land of suffering (Genesis 41:50–52).

3. Joseph Rewrote His Life Script According to Scripture

Joseph had plenty of reason to say to himself, *I don't have a right to exist. My life is a mistake. I am worthless. I should never trust anyone. I shouldn't take risks. I shouldn't feel. It is too painful. I am a loser.* Yet he didn't.

Our families and traumatic events in our histories often hand us negative messages or scripts that unconsciously direct our lives. These decisions we make, often forgotten, are replayed over and over in adult situations—even when they are not necessary. For instance, who doesn't know someone who was hurt in a church and vowed to himself, "I will never trust any spiritual leader or church again!"?

Joseph was very aware of his past. Think of a play and a script being handed to an actor for a certain part. Most of us never examine the scripts handed to us by our past.

Joseph did. He thought about it. And then he opened the door to God's future by rewriting it with God.

It has been said that the real measure of our sense of self is when we are with our parents for more than three days. At that point we need to ask ourselves how old we feel. Have we gone back to our patterns of behaving more in line with our childhood, or have we broken free from our past to live in what God has for us now?

4. Joseph Partnered with God to Be a Blessing

Joseph could have destroyed his brothers with anger. Instead he joined with God to bless them. For those of us who have been deeply wounded like Joseph, that can feel like a difficult, almost impossible path.

Joseph made a choice. It is the same choice we make every day: Is God safe? Is God good? Can God be trusted?

Joseph had clearly developed a secret history over a long period of time in his relationship with God. His whole life was structured around following the Lord God of Israel. Then when the moment came for a critical decision, he was ready. In the same way, there are the *daily* choices centered around our own walks with God (which we shall talk about in later chapters) that are critical for us to serve as an instrument of blessing to many.

One Final Word: Our Need to Be "Alone Together"

The gravitational pull back to the sinful, destructive patterns of our family of origin and culture is enormous. A few of us live as if we were simply paying for the mistakes of our past. For this reason God has called us to make this journey with companions in the faith. Going back in order to go forward is something we must do in the context of community—with mature friends, a mentor, spiritual director, counselor, or therapist. We need trusted people in our lives of whom we can ask, "How do you experience me? Tell me the feelings and thoughts you have when you are with me. Please be honest with me." Prayerfully listening to their answers will go a long way toward healing and getting a perspective on areas of our lives that need to be addressed. Needless to say, this takes a lot of courage.

This work of going back in order to go forward for sure leads most of us to a Wall in our journey with Christ. We find ourselves disoriented, confused, and shaken by the unknown territory to which this leads. Thus, the next step into an emotionally healthy spirituality calls us to . . . journey through the Wall.

Lord, I believe you are a God with great purposes. You placed me into my particular family in a particular place in a particular time in history. I don't see what you see, but I ask you to show me, Lord, the revelation and purposes you have for me in your decision. I do not want to betray or be ungrateful for what was given to me. Yet at the same time, help me discern what I need to let go of from my past and what my essential discipleship issues are in the present that must be addressed.

Grant me courage; grant me wisdom to learn from the past but not be crippled by it. And may I, like Joseph, be a blessing to my earthly family, spiritual family, and the world at large. In Jesus' name, amen.

CHAPTER 4

Journey through the Wall

Letting Go of Power and Control

Every follower of Jesus at some point will confront the Wall—or, as the ancients called it, "the dark night of the soul." Emotionally healthy spirituality helps provide a (partial) roadmap of both how one goes through the Wall and what it means to begin living on the other side.

Failure to understand its nature results in great long-term pain and confusion. Receiving the gift of God in the Wall, however, transforms our lives forever.

The Christian Life as a Journey

The image of the Christian life as a journey captures our experience of following Christ like few others. Journeys involve movement, action, stops and starts, detours, delays, and trips into the unknown.

God called Abraham to leave his past life in Ur at the age of seventy-five and to embark on a journey. God called to Moses from a burning bush to begin a new phase of his journey at the age of eighty. God called the Israelites to leave Egypt and embark on a forty-year journey of personal transformation in the desert. God called David to leave the comforts of his job as a shepherd to conquer Goliath and to serve as king of Israel. God called Jeremiah to forty to fifty years of difficult work, standing firm for God's values in the midst of a rebellious people.

Jesus called the twelve disciples to a journey that would change their lives forever. Judas, however, grew disillusioned and got stuck along the way. He couldn't imagine what Jesus was up to, especially in surrendering himself to the authorities to be crucified! He could not see how anything good could emerge out of the disintegration of their powerful ministry that was helping so many people. Jesus' plan offended him.

Judas's "stuckness" eventually resulted in him quitting Christ altogether, resulting in perhaps history's saddest account of a wasted opportunity!

I meet many believers today who also are stuck. Some have dropped out altogether. Tragically, they fail to see the larger picture of the transforming work God seeks to do in them at their Wall. The disorientation and pain of their present circumstances blinds them. And they feel incapable of finding other companions for such a journey.

What most don't understand is that growth into maturity in Christ requires going through the Wall.

The Wall—Stages of Faith

Throughout church history great men and women such as Augustine, Teresa of Avila, Ignatius Loyola, Evelyn Underhill, and John Wesley have written about the phases of this journey to help us understand the larger picture, or map, of what God is doing in our lives. In *The Critical Journey: Stages in the Life of Faith*, Janet Hagberg and Robert Guelich developed a model that includes the essential place of the Wall in our journeys.[1] The following is my adaptation of their work.

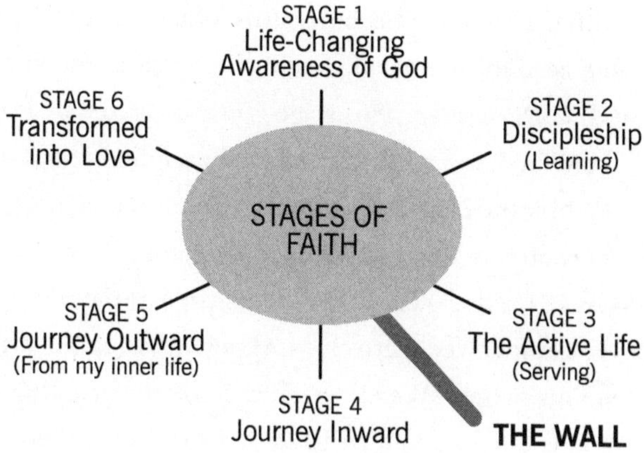

Used by permission.

Note that each stage builds naturally upon the other. In the physical world, babies must grow into young children and then into teenagers who become adult men and women. In a similar way, spiritually, each stage builds on the ones that go before it. We can't jump from the discipleship of Stage 2 to the journey outward of Stage 5.

An important difference, however, is that we can stagnate very easily at a certain stage and choose not to move forward in our journeys with Christ. We refuse to trust God into this unknown, mysterious place. We turn inward into ourselves. Our soil, ever so slowly, becomes hard (Mark 4:1–20).

It is important to remember that while we may identify with more than one stage (I always relate to Stages 2 and 3), or even if we find ourselves in transition between them, we will still tend to have a specific "home stage that best characterizes [our] life of faith now."[2]

Let's take a look at the stages:

STAGE 1: *Life-Changing Awareness of God.* This stage, whether in childhood or adulthood, is the beginning of our journey with Christ as we become aware of his reality. We realize our need for mercy and begin our relationship with him.

STAGE 2: *Discipleship.* This stage is characterized by learning about God and what it means to be a follower of Christ. We become part of a Christian community and begin to get rooted in the disciplines of the faith.

STAGE 3: *The Active Life.* This is described as the "doing" stage. We get involved, actively working for God, serving him and his people. We take responsibility by bringing our unique talents and gifts to serve Christ and others.

STAGE 4: *The Wall and Journey Inward.* Notice that the Wall and the Journey Inward are closely related. The Wall compels us into the Journey Inward. In some cases the Journey Inward eventually leads us to the Wall. Most importantly, remember it is God who brings us to the Wall.

STAGE 5: *Journey Outward.* Having passed through the crisis of faith and the intense inner journey necessary to go through the Wall, we begin once again to move outward to "do" for God. We may do some of the same active external things we did before (e.g., give leadership, serve, and initiate acts of mercy toward others). The difference is that now we give out of a new, grounded center of ourselves in God. We have rediscovered God's profound, deep, accepting love for us. A deep, inner stillness now begins to characterize our work for God.

STAGE 6: *Transformed into Love.* God continually sends events, circumstances, people, and even books into our lives to keep us moving forward on our journeys. He is determined to complete the work he began in us, whether we like it or not! His goal, in the language of John Wesley, is that we be made perfect in love, that Christ's love becomes our love

> both toward God and others. We realize love truly is the beginning and the end. By this stage, the perfect love of God has driven out all fear (1 John 4:18). And the whole of our spiritual lives is finally about surrender and obedience to God's perfect will.

I prefer the notions of seasons to stages when describing our life in Christ. We don't control the seasons; they happen to us. Winter, spring, summer, and fall come to us whether we like it or not.

So do Walls.

For most of us the Wall appears through a crisis that turns our world upside down. It comes, perhaps, through a divorce, a job loss, the death of a close friend or family member, a cancer diagnosis, a disillusioning church experience, a betrayal, a shattered dream, a wayward child, a car accident, an inability to get pregnant, a deep desire to marry that remains unfulfilled, a dryness or loss of joy in our relationship with God. We question ourselves, God, the church. We discover for the first time that our faith does not appear to "work." We have more questions than answers as the very foundation of our faith feels like it is on the line. We don't know where God is, what he is doing, where he is going, how he is getting us there, or when this will be over.

My Wall included a number of events piling up one after the other. It began with a feeling of betrayal during a church split in our Spanish congregation. This was followed by a long-lasting depression and loss of motivation to serve Christ, a marital crisis with Geri, and a careful look at how my family of origin had impacted who I was in the present. I had tried to go around, jump over, and then dig a hole under the Wall. None succeeded. I finally went forward *through* it because the pain of staying where I was felt unbearable.

On a certain level it is correct to say that Walls come to us in various ways throughout our lifetimes. It is not simply a one-time event that we pass through and get beyond. It appears to be something we return to as part of our ongoing relationship with God. We see this, for example, in Abraham waiting at the Wall for twenty-five years for the birth of his first child with his wife, Sarah. Ten to thirteen years later God led him again to another Wall—the sacrificing of that long-awaited son he loved, Isaac, on an altar. Consider Moses, Elijah, Nehemiah, Jeremiah, and Paul. Each appears to have gone through the Wall numerous times in their journey with God. "Unintentionally and unknowingly we fall back into imperfections. Bad habits are like living roots that return. These roots must be dug away and cleared from the garden of our soul. . . . This requires the direct intervention of God."[3] Note I said "gone through," not "gotten to." Because these men did make the journey to the other side of the Wall, so can we. When we make it through the Wall, we no longer have a need to be well known or successful, but to do God's will. We have now tasted what it means to live in union with the love of God through Christ in the Holy Spirit. We have learned, like the apostle Paul, "the secret of being content in any and every situation" (Philippians 4:12). We have become "whole and holy" (Ephesians 1:4 MSG). We have become, finally, our true selves in Christ.[4]

Stuck at the Wall—The Dark Night of the Soul

Without an understanding of the Wall in the journey, however, countless sincere followers of Christ stagnate there and no longer move forward with God's purpose for their lives. Some of us hide behind our faith to flee the pain of our lives rather than trust God to transform us through it. We utter platitudes like "in all things God works for the good" (Romans 8:28). We smile and sing contemporary praise songs about our victory in Jesus. We don't curse or get bitter toward

God. We keep it together to demonstrate to the weaker members of the body and the watching world that our faith is solid and strong.

The problem is that emotionally healthy faith admits the following:

- I am bewildered.
- I don't know what God is doing right now.
- I am hurt.
- I am angry.
- Yes, this is mystery.
- I am very sad right now.
- O God, why have you forsaken me?

The best way to understand the dynamics of the Wall is to examine the classic work of St. John of the Cross, *Dark Night of the Soul*, written over five hundred years ago.[5] He described the journey in three phases: beginners, progressives, and perfect. To move out of the beginning stage, he argued, required the receiving of God's gift of the dark night, or the Wall. This is the "ordinary way" we grow in Christ. A failure to understand this is one of the major reasons many start out well in their journeys but do not finish.

How do we know we are in "the dark night"? Our good feelings of God's presence evaporate. We feel the door of heaven has been shut as we pray. Darkness, helplessness, weariness, a sense of failure or defeat, barrenness, emptiness, dryness descend upon us. The Christian disciplines that have served us up to this time "no longer work." We can't see what God is doing and we see little visible fruit in our lives.

This is God's way of rewiring and "purging our affections and passions" that we might delight in his love and enter into a richer, fuller communion with him. God wants to communicate to us his true sweetness and love. He longs that we might know his true peace and rest. He works to free us from unhealthy attachments and idolatries of the world. He longs for an intimate, passionate love relationship with us. For this reason, John of the Cross wrote that God sends us "the dark night of loving fire" to free us. John listed the seven deadly spiritual imperfections of beginners that must be purified:

1. Pride: They have a tendency to condemn others and become impatient with their faults. They are very selective in who can teach them.
2. Avarice: They are discontent with the spirituality God gives them. They never have enough learning, are always reading many books rather than growing in poverty of spirit and their interior life.
3. Luxury: They take more pleasure in the spiritual blessings of God than God himself.
4. Wrath: They are easily irritated, lacking sweetness, and have little patience to wait on God.
5. Spiritual gluttony: They resist the cross and choose pleasures like children do.
6. Spiritual envy: They feel unhappy when others do well spiritually. They are always comparing.
7. Sloth: They run from that which is hard. Their aim is spiritual sweetness and good feelings.[6]

While in chapter 2 I talked about the critical importance of paying attention to our feelings in order to know God, the "dark night" protects us from worshiping them. This is one of the more common idolatries of the spiritual life.

St. John of the Cross knew the human tendency to become attached to feelings of and about God, mistaking them for God himself. These sensations, rich or empty, are not God but only messengers from God that speak to us of him. There is no other way, John of the Cross would say, for our souls to be strengthened and purified so that we don't worship our feelings than for God to remove them altogether.[7] This is God's way of rewiring our taste buds that we might taste of him ever more fully.

St. John wrote: "[God] is purging the soul, annihilating it, emptying it or consuming in it (even as fire consumes the mouldiness and the rust of metal) all the affections and imperfect habits which it has contracted its whole life. . . . These are deeply rooted in the substance of the soul. . . . At the same time, it is God who is passively working here in the soul."[8]

In addition to purging our will and understanding of the deadly sins mentioned above, God also adds something into our souls. He mysteriously infuses or imparts his love into us. God powerfully invades us when we persevere patiently through this suffering. Our great temptation is to quit or go backward, but if we remain still, listening for his voice, God will insert something of himself into our character that will mark the rest of our journey with him.[9]

Finding My Way through the Wall

For many years I failed to distinguish the "dark night of the soul" from trials and setbacks. This confusion hindered me from actually going through the Wall. I surmised I had suffered more than the average Christian. That surely qualified me for undeserved blessings, didn't it?

In 1994 I was pastoring two congregations in two languages—one in English in the morning and one in Spanish in the afternoon. Life was very difficult. There were constant crises and difficulties, but they were mostly due to a discipleship that did not include emotional health.

When the afternoon Spanish congregation split and two hundred people left to start another congregation, my dark night began. I was depressed and angry. For the first time in my Christian life I did not "feel" God's presence. The Bible turned to dust. My prayers seemed to bounce back from heaven. God was not delivering me!

I thought I had hit the bottom and could only go up.

I remember telling a former member of our church about this rock bottom I had hit.

"Rock bottom," she laughed. "You have no idea how much further you have to go!"

I was in so much pain that I was incredulous at such a statement, but she seemed to discern there was some deep cleansing that was needed in me. She was right. There would be more than two additional years of life in the "valley of the shadow of death" (Psalm 23:4 ESV). I thought it would never end. It would take our marriage hitting the Wall and Geri leaving the church I was pastoring to finally drive me to my knees. I remember asking God, "Is there anything else you want to rip out of me, you sadist?"

For that two-year period I continued my spiritual disciplines. I followed Jesus out of obedience. I served him as a leader, but everything in me wanted to quit. Quit God and quit his messed-up church forever. Little did I know he was both purging and implanting something into my person during that horror.

I still remember coming out of it. I began to crawl and to feel for the first time, saying to myself, "Something is different. Totally different. I cannot explain it, but I feel freer than ever from people's opinions, more clear about who I am, more certain of God and his love than ever!"

I hope this means God has no other "dark nights" for me. Biblical history seems to suggest this may not be the case.

How Long Will This Last?

It may be months. More probably, it may be a year or two . . . or more. Sorry. I know this is not what you want to read. Ultimately God chooses the length and level of intensity. He has a unique purpose for each of us, knowing how much there is to cleanse out of our inner being, and how much he wants to infuse of himself into us for his greater, long-term purposes. Our Father knows how much we can handle.

Actually, John of the Cross divides the dark night into two levels. The first level (which he terms "the night of the sense") is the one all of us encounter as we journey with Christ. The second ("the night of the spirit") is for a very few. He describes it as "violent and severe" as we "are dragged down and immersed again into a worse degree of affliction more severe and darker and more grievous . . . the brighter and purer is the supernatural and divine light, the more it darkens the soul."[10]

What is important here is to note that the trials we encounter each day are not the Wall or "the dark night of the soul." Trials are the traffic jams, annoying bosses, delayed airplane departures, car breakdowns, fevers, and barking dogs in the middle of the night.

James refers to this: "Consider it pure joy, my brothers and sisters, whenever you face trials of many kinds, because you know that the testing of your faith develops perseverance. Let perseverance finish its work so that you may be mature and complete, not lacking anything" (James 1:2–4).

Walls are David fleeing a jealous king for thirteen years in the desert. Walls are Abraham waiting twenty-five years for the birth of his first child, Isaac. Walls are Job losing his ten children, health, and possessions in a day!

Characteristics of Life on the Other Side

It can be difficult to discern precisely when we began the journey through the Wall and when we might be on the other side. I know many people who have been through great sufferings and hit formidable Walls. Yet the Walls did not change them. They only bounced off them. They returned to a similar, but different Wall later. Again they bounced off it, often more bitter and angry than before.

Ultimately, God is the One who moves us through the Wall. And with that comes mystery. How and when God takes us through is up to him. We make choices to trust God, to wait on God, to obey God, to stick with God, to remain faithful when everything in us wants to quit and run. But it is *his* slow, deep work of transformation in us, not ours.

So how do we know we are making progress or if we are, perhaps, even on the other side? The following are at least four dynamics to consider:

1. A Greater Level of Brokenness

Christians can be notoriously judgmental in the name of standing up for the truth. But people who have been through the Wall are broken. They have seen, as Karl Barth notes, that "the root and origin of sin is the arrogance in which man wants to be his own and his neighbor's judge."[11] Before we go through the Wall, we prefer to exercise the right to determine good and evil rather than leave this knowledge to God. Afterward, we know better.

I know. I am embarrassed when I think of how I regularly judged other people's journeys with Christ that were different from mine. I had an opinion and attitude about almost everyone who was different from me.

The first words uttered by Jesus in the New Testament were revolutionary: "Blessed are the poor in spirit, for theirs is the kingdom of heaven" (Matthew 5:3). The word he used described a beggar who had hit rock bottom, having been stripped of everything. Jesus was not describing a person in total destitution materially but one destitute of elevating themselves above others.

Picture a beggar. Not someone you might find on the streets of a

North American city, strolling along looking for change to buy beer or cigarettes. Rather, picture a person in such abject poverty that he is incapable of doing anything more than lying on a corner with a palm upraised, hoping someone will take pity on him. Picture someone who knows he will die unless someone has mercy upon him. Can you imagine that beggar saying:

- I wasn't always like this; I graduated high school.
- I don't like the way you are looking at me. Keep your money.
- I earn more money than the rest of these beggars.
- Look at what that other beggar on the corner is wearing. Doesn't he have any shame?

People on the other side of the Wall are freed from judging others.

Pride and our tendency to judge others is found in every corner of the world, in all cultures, workplaces, playgrounds, families, neighborhoods, sports teams, classrooms, marriages, homeless shelters, corporate boardrooms, and ten-year-olds' birthday parties. When we become Christians it does not automatically disappear. It only takes on a new face:

- I can't believe she calls herself a Christian.
- Megachurch members are superficial.
- Their church is small and dead.
- Look at what he is doing. He is not a Christian.

Another helpful way to measure your level of brokenness is to consider how "offendable" you are. (Yes, I realize *offendable* is not in the dictionary.) Imagine an inflated, bloated person who, when criticized, judged, or insulted, immediately pulls back and reacts. He either goes on the attack or decides we no longer exist.

Contrast that image with a broken person who is so secure in the love of God that she is unable to be insulted. When criticized, judged, or insulted, she thinks to herself, *It is far worse than you think!*

"Blessed is he who expects nothing, for he shall enjoy everything," said St. Francis of Assisi.[12] Few people enjoyed earthly things as well as him. He understood that no one can earn a star or a sunset, that gratitude and dependence on God are the very bedrock of reality. St. Francis, like others who have gone through the Wall, appreciated that we all depend, in every instant, upon the mercy of God.

That is one of the reasons I have integrated into my spiritual disciplines the Jesus Prayer. The words of the prayer, adapted from a parable of Jesus found in Luke 18:9–14, are: "Lord Jesus Christ, Son of God, have mercy on me, a sinner." Dating back to the sixth century, the Jesus Prayer has long been a foundation of Eastern Christian spirituality to help believers remain grounded and dependent on God throughout the day. By repeating the prayer throughout the day, synchronizing the syllables of these words with our heartbeat throughout the day, the intention is that our very lives will embody the richness of the prayer.[13]

2. A Greater Appreciation for Holy Unknowing (Mystery)

I like control. I like to know where God is going, exactly what he is doing, the exact route of how we are getting there, and exactly when we will arrive. I also like to remind God of his need to behave in ways that fit in with my clear ideas of him. For example, God is just, merciful, good, wise, loving. The problem, then, is that God is beyond the grasp of every concept I have of him. He is utterly incomprehensible. Yes, God is everything revealed in Scripture, but also infinitely more. God is not an object that I can determine, master, possess, or command.[14] And still I try to somehow use my "clear ideas" about God to give me power over him, to somehow possess him. Unconsciously, I make a deal with God that goes something like this: "I obey and keep my part of the bargain. Now you bless me. Do not allow any serious suffering."

God doesn't appreciate being demoted to the rank of our personal secretary or assistant. Remember who we are dealing with here: God is immanent (so close) and yet transcendent (so utterly above and far from us). God is knowable, yet he is unknowable. God is inside us and beside us, yet he is wholly different from us. For this reason Augustine wrote, "If you understand, it is not God you understand."[15]

Most of the time we have no idea what God is doing.

There is an old story about a wise man living on one of China's vast frontiers. One day, for no apparent reason, his son's horse ran away and was taken by nomads across the border. Everyone tried to offer consolation for the man's bad fortune, but his father, a wise man, said, "What makes you so sure this is not a blessing?"

Months later, the horse returned, bringing with her a magnificent stallion. This time everyone was full of congratulations for the son's good fortune. But now his father said, "What makes you so sure this isn't a disaster?"

Their household was made richer by this fine horse the son loved to ride. But one day he fell off his horse and broke his hip. Once again, everyone offered their consolation for his bad luck, but his father said, "What makes you so sure this is not a blessing?" A year later nomads invaded across the border, and every able-bodied man was required to take up his bow and go into battle. The Chinese families living on the border lost nine of every ten men. Only because the son was lame did father and son survive to take care of each other.

What appeared like a blessing and success has often turned out to be a terrible thing. What appeared to be a terrible event has often turned out to be a rich blessing.[16]

I, too, can honestly say that the more I know about God, the less I know about him.

Moses first saw God in a burning bush. God appeared in light (Exodus 3:2). Then God led Moses into the desert where he revealed himself in a pillar of cloud by day and fire by night. This was a mix of light and darkness (Exodus 13:21). Finally, God led Moses into the "thick darkness" of Mount Sinai where God spoke to him face to face (Exodus 20:21). As Gregory of Nyssa first noted, it was in this pure darkness that the Infinite Light of God dwelled. And the more Moses grew to know God, the wilder, more dazzling, and "unknown" this true and living God became to him.[17]

St. Thomas Aquinas in the 1200s wrote a twenty-volume work on God. He began his work: "This is the ultimate knowledge about God, to know that we do not know." At the end of his life, however, he had a vision of Christ in church. After that experience he stated, "I can no longer write, for God has given me such glorious knowledge that all contained in my works are as straw—barely fit to absorb the holy wonders that fall in a stable."[18]

One of the great fruits of the Wall is a childlike, deepened love for mystery. We can rest more easily and live more freely on the other side of the Wall, knowing that God is in control and worthy of our trust. Joyfully we can then sing with David: "He made darkness his covering, his canopy around him" (Psalm 18:11).

3. A Deeper Ability to Wait for God

An outgrowth of greater brokenness and holy unknowing is a greater capacity to wait upon the Lord. Going through the Wall breaks something deep within us—that driving, grasping, fearful self-will that must produce, that must make something happen, that must get it done for God (just in case he doesn't).

If I were to identify my greatest sins and errors of judgment in the last thirty years of following Christ, they would each go back to a failure to wait on the Lord. What does it truly mean when we read,

"Wait for the LORD; be strong and take heart and wait for the LORD" (Psalm 27:14)? Or "I wait for the LORD, my whole being waits, and in his word I put my hope. I wait for the Lord" (Psalm 130:5–6)?

From finishing people's sentences to starting new daughter churches too quickly, I have struggled to wait upon the Lord. God, I believe, extended my Wall (and then added a few smaller ones) to purge out of me this deep, stubborn willfulness to run ahead of him. While I kick and scream, God slowly teaches me to wait. Now I understand why this is such a consistent theme in Scripture.

Abraham learned to wait at his Wall. At seventy-five years old, he was told he would be a father of nations. After eleven years of waiting, he took matters into his own hands and birthed Ishmael through his maidservant Hagar (Genesis 16:1–4). God forced him to wait another fourteen years before the promised child was born. The public and private humiliation he suffered transformed him into a father of faith for all history.

Moses learned to wait at his Wall. After murdering a man and failing to deliver the Israelites, he spent the next forty years learning to wait on God. In the desert God transformed him into the meekest man on the earth (Numbers 12:3).

David learned to wait at his Wall. After a stunning victory over Goliath, David, innocent, was forced to flee the mighty army of King Saul for ten to thirteen years, losing his dreams, family, reputation, and earthly security. In the wilderness God transformed him into a man after his own heart (1 Samuel 16 through 2 Samuel 1).

Hannah learned to wait at the Wall. After years of infertility, unanswered prayers, and mocking from the second wife of her husband, God finally heard her prayers. Her years of pain and grief transformed her into the godly mother of Samuel who would transform a nation (1 Samuel 1 and 2).

Jesus learned to wait in obscurity and silence, both as a lowly carpenter's son and in the wilderness, resisting the temptation of the devil to act before his Father's time. Out of this waiting Jesus emerged from the wilderness in the power of the Spirit (Luke 4:14).We can trust God to do the same in us—if we will learn to wait on him.

4. A Greater Detachment

The critical issue on the journey with God is not "Am I happy?" but "Am I free? Am I growing in the freedom God gave me?"[19] Paul addressed this central issue of detachment in 1 Corinthians 7:29–31, calling us to a radical, new understanding of our relationship to the world:

> What I mean, brothers and sisters, is that the time is short. From now on those who have wives should live as if they do not; those who mourn, as if they did not; those who are happy, as if they were not; those who buy something, as if it were not theirs to keep; those who use the things of the world, as if not engrossed in them. For this world in its present form is passing away.

We are to live our lives as the rest of the world—marrying, experiencing sorrow and joy, buying things and using them—but always with awareness that these things in themselves are not our lives. We are to be marked by eternity, free from the dominating power of things.

Detachment is the great secret of interior peace. Along the way, in this journey with Christ, we get attached to (literally "nailed to") behaviors, habits, things, and people in an unhealthy way. For example, I love my home, my car, my books, Geri, our four daughters, our church, our comforts, and my good health. Like you, I rarely realize how attached I am to something until God removes it. Then the power struggle begins. I say, "God I must have that second car for convenience." God answers, "No, you don't need that. You need me!"

When we put our claws into something and we don't want to take them out, we are beyond enjoying them. We now *must* have them.

The Wall, more than anything else, cuts off our attachments to who we think we ought to be, or who we falsely think we are. Layers of our counterfeit self are shed. Something truer, that is Christ in and through us, slowly emerges.

Richard Rohr has written extensively about the five essential truths to which men must awaken if they are to grow up into their God-given masculinity and spirituality.[20] His conclusions, I believe, describe the powerful biblical truths all of us can now truly know as a result of going through the Wall and experiencing a greater detachment:

- Life is hard.
- You are not that important.
- Your life is not about you.
- You are not in control.
- You are going to die.[21]

A Final Word

Remember, God's purpose for us is to have a loving union with him at the end of the journey. We joyfully detach *from* certain behaviors and activities *for* the purpose of a more intimate, loving attachment to God. We are to enjoy the world, for God's creation is good. We are to appreciate nature, people, and all God's gifts, along with his presence in creation—without being ensnared by them. It has rightly been said that those who are the most detached on the journey are best able to taste the purest joy in the beauty of created things.

Thomas Merton summed up our challenge well: "I wonder if there are 20 men alive in the world now who see things as they really are.

That would mean that there were 20 men who were free, who were not dominated or even influenced by an attachment to any created thing or to their own selves or to any gift of God."[22]

The journey with Jesus calls us to a life of undivided devotion to him. This requires that we simplify our lives, removing distractions. Part of that will mean learning to grieve our losses and embrace the gift of our limits. To this we now turn in the next chapter.

Heavenly Father, teach me to trust you even when I do not know where you are going. Help me to surrender and not turn inward into myself out of fear. The storms and winds of life blow strongly all around me. I cannot see in front of me. Sometimes I feel like I am going to drown. Lord, you are centered, utterly at rest and peace. Open my eyes that I might see you are with me on the boat. I am safe.

Awaken me, Jesus, to your presence within me, around me, above me, and below me. Grant me grace to follow you into the unknown, into the next place in my journey with you. In your name, amen.

CHAPTER 5

Enlarge Your Soul through Grief and Loss

Surrendering to Your Limits

There is no greater disaster in the spiritual life than to be immersed in unreality. In fact the true spiritual life is not an escape from reality but an absolute commitment to it. Loss marks the place where self-knowledge and powerful transformation happen—if we have the courage to participate fully in the process. Loss and grief, however, cannot be separated from the issue of our limits as human beings.

Limits are behind all loss. We cannot do or be anything we want. God has placed enormous limits around even the most gifted of us. Why? To keep us grounded, to keep us humble. In fact, the very meaning of the word *humility* has its root in the Latin *humus*, meaning "of the earth."

Our culture routinely interprets losses as alien invasions that interrupt our "normal" lives. We numb our pain through denial, blaming, rationalizations, addictions, and avoidance. We search for spiritual shortcuts around our wounds. We demand others take away our pain. Yet we all face many deaths within our lives. The choice is whether these deaths will be terminal (crushing our spirit and life) or open us up to new possibilities and depths of transformation in Christ.

The Story of Us All

Jonathan Edwards, in a famous sermon on the book of Job, noted that the story of Job is the story of us all. Job lost everything in one day—his family, his wealth, his health (Job 1:13–2:8). Most of us experience our losses more slowly, over the span of a lifetime, until we find ourselves on the door of death, leaving *everything* behind.

We lose our youthfulness. No amount of plastic surgery, cosmetics, good diet, or exercise routine can stop the process of growing older.

We lose our dreams. Who has not lost dreams, dreams of a career or marriage or children for which we hoped?

We lose our routines and stability in transitions. Each time we change jobs, immigrate to a new country, or move is a loss. Our children grow more independent and more powerful as they move through their life transitions. Our influence and power decrease. Our parents age, and we become their caretakers.

Most of us, in one or more moments of our lives, experience catastrophic loss. Unexpectedly, a family member dies. A friend or son commits suicide. Our spouse has an affair. We find ourselves single again after a painful divorce or breakup. We are diagnosed with cancer. Our company suddenly downsizes and we find ourselves unemployed after twenty-five years of stable employment. Our child is born severely handicapped. A loyal friend betrays us. Infertility, miscarriages, broken friendships, loss of memory or mental acuity, abuse.

We grieve the many things we can't do, our limits. We experience greater or lesser losses from our families growing up. Some people, like me, "lost a leg in that war" during our childhood years and now walk with a limp.

Finally, we lose our wrong ideas of God and the church. (Thank God!) What makes this so difficult is how much we invested of our lives into a certain way of following Jesus, into certain applications of biblical truths, only to realize much of it was foolishness or perhaps even wrong. We feel betrayed by a church tradition, a leader, or even God himself. We realize God truly is much larger and more incomprehensible than we thought.

We lose our illusions about this new family of Jesus, the church. It is not the perfect family with perfect people as we expected. In fact, people disappoint us. At times, we are bewildered and shocked by their lack of awareness and sin (evil). Every person who lives in community with other believers, sooner or later, experiences this disillusionment and the grief that accompanies it.

Job

Job was the Bill Gates of his day. His wealth was staggering. The Bible tells us he had seven thousand sheep, three thousand camels (prestigious animals in his day), five hundred yoke of oxen, and five hundred donkeys, along with a large staff of employees. In today's world, we would see Job's face on the front page of *Forbes* magazine each year for being the richest person in the world. His assets would include a fleet of Rolls-Royces and Lexuses, private airplanes, impressive yachts, thriving businesses, and expansive real-estate holdings. "He was the greatest man among all the people of the East" (Job 1:3).

Job was also very godly, faithfully walking with God, delighting and obeying him with all his heart. "He feared God and shunned evil" (Job 1:1b). Today we would say he was one of the most well-known, respected Christian leaders of our day.

Suddenly, all the forces of heaven and earth, from the east, west, north, and south, came against Job. Enemies invaded. Lightning struck. A tornado unleashed her fury. By the end of the afternoon, the unthinkable had happened—the world's richest man had been reduced to poverty and his ten children had been killed in a terrible natural disaster.

Amazingly, Job neither sinned nor blamed God. He responded beautifully; he worshiped.

Then, as he attempted to get on his feet, Job's body was seized with "sore boils" from the soles of his feet to the top of his head. His skin darkened and shriveled. His sores became infected with worms. His eyes grew red and swollen. High fevers with chills only added to excruciating pain. Sleeplessness, delirium, and choking filled his days. His horrid sickness emaciated his body.[1]

Job moved outside the city walls to the town's garbage dump, the home for the city's outcasts. He sat alone, isolated and mourning his terrible, lonely fate.

Finally, his marriage tore asunder. After ten funerals and a husband hopelessly ill, Mrs. Job had had enough. Her recommendation to her husband: "Are you still maintaining your integrity? Curse God and die!" (Job 2:9).

What makes this story so bewildering is the undeserved nature of his suffering.

Job was innocent. There was no connection between his sin and the amount of pain he experienced. This seems terribly unfair.

Where is the love and goodness of God who would do this to faithful Job?

Getting Out of the Pain

How might you have responded to such cataclysmic loss? How might you have grieved if you were Job?

Grieving differs from family to family, from culture to culture.

What our families of origin consider acceptable ways of expressing emotions related to loss shape us. Our culture also plays a role for us—be it Native American, Latino, Chinese, Arab, African American, Jewish, Eastern European, or Caucasian. At one extreme, Americans of British ancestry tend to value a "no muss, no fuss" rationale of experiencing loss. Funerals, for example, are practical and pragmatic. As one sister said, explaining why she had not attended the funeral of her twin sister, "What would have been the point of spending money on the airfare to get there? She was already dead."

On the other extreme is where time stops forever. In places like Italy and Greece, women traditionally have worn black the rest of their lives after their husband's death. In Italian-American funerals (my background) family members might bang on the coffin with their fists, crying out the dead person's name or even jumping into the grave as the coffin is lowered into the ground.

Queen Victoria of England lost her husband, Albert, when she was forty-two. Obsessed that nothing would change, she continued to make Albert the center of her life. For years she slept with his nightshirt in her arms. She made his room a "sacred room" to be kept exactly as it had been when he was alive. Every day for the rest of her long life, she had the linens changed, his clothes laid out fresh, and water prepared for his shaving. On every bed on which Queen Victoria slept, she attached a photograph of Albert as he lay dead.[2]

In our culture, addiction has become the most common way to deal with pain. We watch television incessantly. We keep busy, running from one activity to another. We work seventy hours a week, indulge in pornography, overeat, drink, take pills—anything to help us avoid the pain. Some of us demand that someone or something (a marriage, sexual partner, an ideal family, children, an achievement, a career, or a church) take our loneliness away.

Sadly, the result of denying and minimizing our wounds over

many years is that we become less and less human, empty Christian shells with painted smiley faces. For some, a dull, low-level depression descends upon us, making us nearly unresponsive to all reality.

Much of contemporary Christian culture has added to this inhuman and unbiblical avoidance of pain and loss. We feel guilty for not obeying Scripture's commands to "rejoice in the Lord always" (Philippians 4:4) and to "come before him with joyful songs" (Psalm 100:2).

Deep down, many of us feel ashamed like Joe, a visitor to New Life, who said to me recently: "Feeling sad or depressed or anxious about the future has got to be due to my unbelief. This is not God. It has to be related to my sins. I just figured it was better I stay away from church and Christians for a while until I get over it."

Dropping Our Defensive Shields

Hilda, a young Jewish student, worked part time at a New York university. When a fellow student, a Christian, died of cancer, she attended the funeral. As the service began, the family announced that this would not be a time for mourning but a celebration. They remembered and thanked God for the gift of their daughter who died. They sang songs of praise. They quoted Scripture about God working all things together for good to those who love him (Romans 8:28). In disbelief, Hilda sat through the service, wondering, *Are these people for real? Do they have any emotions at all?*

By the time she returned to work the next day, she was angry, livid that the tragic loss of her friend had been treated so glibly. Finally, she exploded at lunch to another Christian acquaintance at her job who also attended the funeral, "Don't you people cry or mourn? I don't get it. Are you people human beings at all?!"

Certainly we are not to cry or mourn like those who are without hope in Christ. But we do cry and grieve. The wise teacher of

Ecclesiastes teaches us: "There is a time for everything, and a season for every activity under the heavens . . . a time to weep and a time to laugh, a time to mourn and a time to dance" (Ecclesiastes 3:1, 4). Jesus himself wept, both at the grave of Lazarus and for his people in Jerusalem (John 11:35 and Luke 19:41).

Jane, a member of our small group sometime ago, was becoming increasingly aware of how much she had lost in her childhood, teen, and young adult years. Our group was in the third week of exploring how both our families and ethnic histories have impacted our present lives. Jane looked terrified. For the first time in her life, she was turning toward her losses, not avoiding them.

One week, after our group, I asked her how she was doing. She responded, with her head down, in a whisper, "Pete, I keep thinking that if I continue going down this road of truly grieving my losses, I might die."

Turning toward our pain is counterintuitive. But in fact, the heart of Christianity is that the way to life is through death, the pathway to resurrection is through crucifixion. Of course, it preaches easier than it lives.

Gerald Sittser, in his book *A Grace Disguised*, reflects on the loss of his mother, wife, and young daughter from a horrific car accident. He chose not to run from his loss but to walk directly into the darkness, letting the experience of that overwhelming tragedy transform his life.

He learned that the quickest way to reach the sun and the light of day is not to run west chasing after it, but to head east into the darkness until you finally reach the sunrise.[3]

When we are children, creating a defensive wall to shield us from pain can serve as one of God's great gifts to us. If someone suffers emotional or sexual abuse as a young child, for example, denial of the assault on his or her exposed humanity serves as a healthy survival mechanism. Blocking out the pain enables him or her to endure such painful circumstances. It is healthy to not fully experience painful realities when we are that young so that we survive emotionally.

The transition into adulthood, however, requires that we mature through our "defense mechanisms" of denial in favor of honestly looking at what is true—at reality. Jesus himself said, "You will know the truth, and the truth will set you free" (John 8:32).

Unconsciously, however, we carry many defensive maneuvers into adulthood to protect ourselves from pain. And in adulthood, they block us from growing up spiritually and emotionally.

The following are a few common defenses:[4]

- *Denial* (or selective forgetting). We refuse to acknowledge some painful aspect of reality externally or internally. For example: "I feel just fine. It didn't bother me a bit that my boss belittled me . . . and that I got fired. I'm not worried in the least."
- *Minimizing*. We admit something is wrong, but in such a way that it appears less serious than it actually is: "My son is doing okay with God. He's just drinking once in a while," when in reality he is drinking heavily and rarely sleeping at home.
- *Blaming others*. We deny responsibility for our behavior and project it "out there" upon another: "The reason my brother is sick in the hospital is because the doctors messed up his medications!"
- *Blaming yourself*. We inwardly take on the fault: "It's my fault Mom doesn't take care of me and drinks all the time. It's because I'm not worth it."
- *Rationalizing*. We offer excuses, justifications, alibis to provide an inaccurate explanation of what is going on: "Did you know that John has a genetic disposition toward

rage that runs in his family? That's why the meetings aren't helping him."

- *Intellectualizing*. We give analysis, theories, and generalities to avoid personal awareness and difficult feelings: "My situation is not that bad compared to how others are suffering in the world. What do I have to cry about?"
- *Distracting*. We change the subject or engage in humor to avoid threatening topics: "Why are you so focused on the negative? Look at the great time we had as a family last Christmas."
- *Becoming hostile*. We get angry or irritable when reference is made to certain subjects: "Don't talk about Joe. He's dead. It's not going to bring him back."

Biblical Grieving in Job: God's Path to New Beginnings

Job models brilliantly for us how we are to grieve in the family of Jesus, regardless of our family, temperament, culture, or gender. He models for us five different phases of biblical grieving so central to our following of Jesus. It is a new, radical way for most of us.

1. Pay Attention

In the church we have little theology for anger, sadness, waiting, and depression. "How are you?" we are asked after a loss or disappointment in our lives. "Couldn't be better!" we exclaim confidently without thinking. "God's working all things for good. I just can't see it all yet!"

Job, on the other hand, screamed out in his pain, holding nothing back. He cursed the day of his birth: "May the day of my birth perish, and the night that said, 'A boy is conceived!' That day—may it turn to darkness. . . . If only my anguish could be weighed and all my misery be placed on the scales! It would surely outweigh the sand of the seas. . . . The arrows of the Almighty are in me, my spirit drinks in their poison; God's terrors are marshaled against me" (Job 3:3–4; 6:2–4).

He shouted at God. He prayed wild prayers. He told God exactly what he was feeling. For thirty-five chapters we read how he struggled with God. He doubted. He wept. He wondered where God was and why all this had happened to him. He did not avoid the horror of his predicament but confronted it directly.

Two-thirds of the psalms are laments, complaints to God. God grieved in Genesis for having created humanity (Genesis 6:6). David wrote poetry after the death of Saul and his best friend, Jonathan, commanding his army to sing a lament to God (2 Samuel 1:17–27). Jeremiah wrote an entire Old Testament book entitled Lamentations. Ezekiel lamented. Daniel grieved. Jesus wept over Lazarus and cried out in grief over Jerusalem (John 11:35 and Luke 13:34).

As men and women made in God's image, what has happened to us? One biblical scholar wrote, in an article entitled "God Damn God: A Reflection on Expressing Anger in Prayer": "The Psalms have often been called a school of prayer. If this is true, then it must be said that Christians, in recent years at least, have been quite selective in their approach to the curriculum. A significant number of psalms have been deemed unacceptable for use in worship. These are the cursing or imprecatory psalms."[5]

We are uncomfortable with such rare, confusing bluntness. When I became a Christian, I was taught that anger was a sin. Wanting to be like Jesus, I stuffed all feelings of irritation, annoyance, resentment, and hatred. They were sins, right?

Yes and no.

When we do not process before God the very feelings that make us human, such as fear or sadness or anger, we leak.[6] Our churches are filled with "leaking" Christians who have not treated their emotions as a discipleship issue. Grieving is not possible without paying attention to our anger and sadness. Most people who fill churches are "nice" and "respectable." Few explode in anger—at least in public. The majority, like me, stuff these "difficult feelings," trusting that God will honor our noble efforts. The result is that we leak through in soft ways such as passive-aggressive behavior (e.g., showing up late), sarcastic remarks, a nasty tone of voice, and the giving of the "silent treatment."

The following story from the movie *Ordinary People* (based on the novel by Judith Guest) illustrates the destructive consequences of refusing to wrestle with God in our sadness and anger. In the movie, Calvin and Beth Hutton are living the American dream in an affluent, Chicago suburb. Their beautiful home, along with their marriage, appears perfect. Calvin is a lawyer. Beth is a homemaker. Everything is in place.

The beauty of their stability begins to crumble when their oldest teenage son, Buck, drowns tragically in a boating accident. His younger brother, Conrad, who was with him when he drowned, feels responsible for his brother's death. Soon afterward, he attempts suicide and spends four months in a psychiatric hospital.

The movie opens a few months later with Conrad beginning his senior year in high school. He is depressed and trying to "control" himself. Neither Conrad nor his parents are able to speak openly of their profound loss and grief.

Conrad begins to see a psychiatrist twice a week and explores his interior. He slowly allows himself to be honest with his pain, his shame, his guilt about his brother's death. He admits the coldness he feels from his mother (Buck was her favorite son) and his preoccupation with "looking good" to others.

Calvin, his father, feels the increasing tension as Conrad begins to break invisible family rules and express himself. He finally attempts to speak honestly with his wife, Beth. "Wouldn't it be easier if we talked about it—in the open?" he asks.

Beth defends herself. "What are we going to talk about, for God's sake? I've already had enough changes in my life. Let's hold on to what we've got. I don't want to change. . . . I don't want any surprises. I want to hold on to what I've got. We'll solve our problems in the privacy of our own home."

It is too late, however. Even a three-week vacation "away from it all" does not stop the crumbling of the false shell that has masked the true reality of their family underneath.

Calvin finally begins speaking the truth to Beth: "We were going to our son's funeral and you were worrying about what I was wearing on my feet!"

Beth cannot, and will not, respond.

The movie finally ends with Calvin sitting alone in the early morning darkness at the dining room table, crying.

Beth enters and asks what's wrong.

He quietly answers, "You are beautiful and you are unpredictable. But you're so cautious. . . ."

Calvin pauses and takes a deep breath. "It would be all right if there hadn't been any mess. But you can't handle mess. You need everything neat and easy. I don't know. . . . Maybe you can't love anybody. So much Buck. When Buck died—it was as if you buried all your love with him and I don't understand that. . . . Maybe it wasn't even Buck. . . . Maybe it was just you. But whatever it was I don't know who you are, what we've been playing at. . . . So I was crying . . . because I don't know if I love you anymore, and I don't know what I am going to do without that."

Beth slowly turns away, walks up the stairs, and goes to their bedroom.

She breaks down briefly. Then she regains her composure as she packs her bags and leaves quietly in a taxi. The marriage ends.

Beth's refusal to pay attention to her pain and loss deaden her ability to love as well. Something has died within her.

Job's misery lasted for several months, perhaps several years. We do not know. What we do know is that he paid attention to both God and himself, choosing to enter the confusion of his personal "dark night of the soul" rather than to medicate himself. We enjoy the fruits of his decision to this day.

2. Wait in the Confusing In-Between

I hate waiting for subways, buses, airplanes, and people. Like most New Yorkers, I struggle not to finish other people's sentences. I talk too fast.

My greatest challenge in following Jesus Christ for over forty years has been waiting on God when things are confusing. I prefer control. I understand why Abraham, after waiting eleven years for God's promise of a son to come true, took matters in his own hands and had a baby the "natural way." Birthing Ishmaels is common in both our churches and personal lives. "Be still before the LORD and wait patiently for him" (Psalm 37:7) remains one of the most radical commands of our day. It requires enormous humility.

Job waited for a long time when the people closest to him quit. They did not have a big enough God or theology to walk through phase two of grieving—waiting in the confusing in-between. Job spent much time battling with his three religious friends—Eliphaz, Zophar, and Bildad—who were convinced Job was suffering because of his sin.

"That is the way God works," they argued time and time again. "You reap what you sow, Job, and you must have done some bad things. You need to repent so God can bless you once again. You are suffering due to your sin. Trouble comes to sinners."

Job's three friends represent "classic religion" or "legalism." It goes something like this: "The reason you are not healed is you don't pray enough, fast enough, read the Bible enough. You are suffering more than most because you have sinned more."

The problem with Job is that it wasn't true. He was an innocent sufferer. His friends had no room for the "confusing in-between," no room for mystery. Like many Christians today, they overestimated their grasp of truth. They played God and stood in God's shoes. Job had two fights going on: one with God and the other with his friends who kept quoting Scripture to him. They tried to fix Job and defend God, and in their attempt to explain what God was doing (which they did not understand), they tortured Job, who was already in great pain.

Do you know what it is like to feel worse after talking with some people who were trying to make you feel better?

The confusing in-between resists all earthly categories and quick solutions. It runs contrary to our Western culture that pervades our spirituality. It is for this reason we have such an aversion to the limits God places around us.

3. Embrace the Gift of Limits

I have wondered if the greatest loss we must grieve is our limits. It drives us to humility before God and others like little else. Great as Job was, he was not God. He, too, had to embrace his limits.

Consider the following list of your limits:

- *Your physical body.* Your body is dying and will return to dust one day. You must sleep, eat, and drink in order to live. All the plastic surgeons in the world, ultimately, cannot stop your aging process. We will finish our lives with unfinished goals and dreams.

- *Your family of origin.* Your family, ethnicity, country of birth, culture all gave you a gift and limits. Whether you had two parents, one parent, or were adopted, all of us enter adulthood with limits given to us by our families.
- *Your marital status.* Both marriage and singleness are limits given by God. If you have children, the number and kind of children is a limit.
- *Your intellectual capacity.* None of us is brilliant in literature, mathematics, engineering, carpentry, physics, and music at the same time.
- *Your talents and gifts.* Jesus has all the gifts. You may have ten. I may have three. Only Jesus has them all.
- *Your material wealth.* Even if you are a millionaire, you are limited in your resources. Our level of prosperity limits us.
- *Your raw material.* God has given you a certain personality, temperament, "unique self." I am a high feeler and an extrovert. That is both a gift and limit. It is great for writing and speaking and creating. It limits me in leading a large staff and church.
- *Your time.* You have only one life to live. You can't do it all. I would like to try living in Asia, Europe, Africa, and a rural area in the United States. I would like to try a few different professions. I can't. My time is running out.
- *Your work and relationship realities.* Our work remains "thorns and thistles" (Genesis 3:18). It is hard. We never totally finish. There is always a grief in never having complete fulfillment. Relationships will not be perfect until heaven. Who wouldn't like a perfect, loving church where everyone has the time, energy, and maturity to love everyone else perfectly! We must grieve that limit also or we will demand from them something they cannot give.

- *Your spiritual understanding.* "The secret things belong to the LORD our God" (Deuteronomy 29:29). God has revealed himself to us in his Son, Scripture, creation, and other ways, but so much of who he is remains incomprehensible.

John the Baptist models wonderfully for us what it means to embrace our limits. Crowds that formerly followed John for baptism switched their allegiances once Jesus began his ministry. They began leaving John to follow Jesus. Some of John's followers were upset about this dramatic turn of events. They complained to him, "Everyone is going to him" (John 3:26).

John understood limits and replied, "A person can receive only what is given them from heaven" (John 3:27). He was able to say, "I accept my limits, my humanity, my declining popularity. He must increase. I must decrease" (see John 3:30).

In contrast, many of us are like a baby. A baby screams for his mother to feed and take care of him. He is the center of the universe, with others existing to care for his needs. He suffers from grandiosity, arrogance, childishness. Growing up will require learning he is not the center of the universe. The universe does not exist to meet his every need.

That is a painful lesson for all of us to learn. Our egos tend to be so inflated that we act as if we were God. Often we have larger fantasies and wishes for ourselves than our real lives can support. As a result, we work frantically trying to do more than God intended. We burn out thinking we can do more than we can. We get stressed and blame others.

We run around frantically, convinced that the world—whether it be our churches, friends, businesses, or children—will stop if we stop. Others of us get depressed because our desires are so high and unachievable that it seems useless to do anything at all.[7]

Getting off our thrones and joining the rest of humanity is a must for growing up. A part of us hates limits. We won't accept them. This is part of the reason why grieving loss biblically is such an indispensable part of spiritual maturity. It humbles us like little else.

In fact, one of the great tasks of parenting and leadership is to help others accept their limits. This applies to the home, workplace, community, or church.

4. Climb the Ladder of Humility

Job emerged from his suffering transformed. He was a broken and changed man.

After his great loss and long time of waiting, God spoke to Job out of the storm of his life. For the first time, God referred to him four times as "my servant," suggesting a new level of intimacy and closeness with Job (Job 42). Job had the opportunity to take revenge on his three religious friends who tortured him with their proud, insensitive counsel. Instead he prayed and blessed them (Job 42:7–9). Throughout the process of waiting, Job made a choice. It was a choice to "climb the ladder of humility," something Jesus described as an indispensable quality for maturing in him (Matthew 5:3–10; Luke 14:7–11; 18:9–14).

St. Benedict, in the sixth century, developed a twelve-step ladder for growing in the grace of humility. His goal was perfect love and transformation of our entire personalities. I don't know too many Christians today seeking to climb this ladder. (Like anything else, this, too, can be misused. But I believe it is a powerful, time-tested tool when used with the other elements of emotional health.)

On the following page is my adaptation of St. Benedict's Ladder of Humility.[8]

St. Benedict's Ladder of Humility

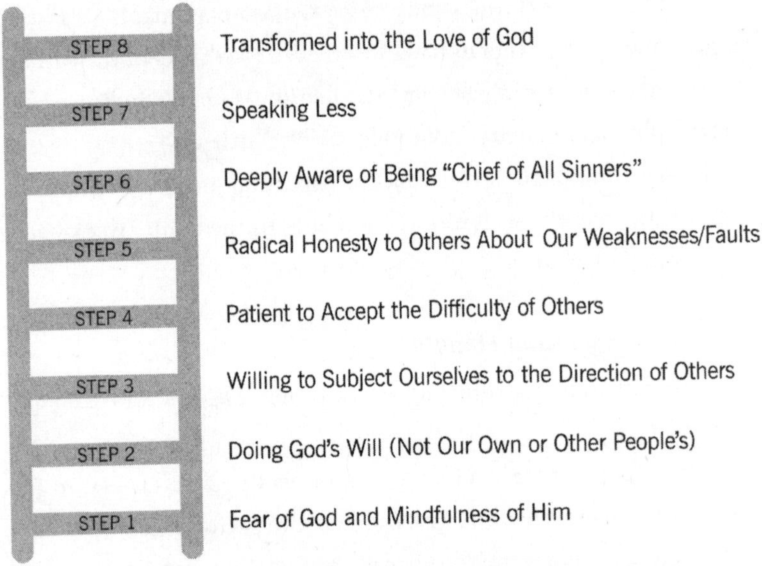

STEP 1: *Fear of God and Mindfulness of Him.* We often forget the presence of God, acting as if he were not present.

STEP 2: *Doing God's Will (Not Our Own or Other People's).* We recognize that surrendering our self-will to God's will for our lives touches the very heart of spiritual transformation.

STEP 3: *Willing to Subject Ourselves to the Direction of Others.* We are free to give up our arrogance and all-powerfulness and are open to accepting God's will as it comes through others. This may be a manager at work, or directions from a friend. And we do it without grumbling or an attitude.

STEP 4: *Patient to Accept the Difficulties of Others.* Life with others, especially when living in community, is full of aggravations. This requires we give others a chance to figure out their weakness in their own way in their own time.

STEP 5: *Radical Honesty to Others about Our Weaknesses/Faults.* We quit pretending to be something we are not. We admit our weaknesses and limitations to a friend, spouse, parent, or someone else who cares about our development.

STEP 6: *Deeply Aware of Being "Chief of All Sinners."* We see ourselves as potentially weaker and more sinful than anyone around us. We are the chief of all sinners. This is not self-hate or an invitation to abuse, but is meant to make us kind and gentle.

STEP 7: *Purposeful to Speak Less (with More Restraint).* This is near the top of the ladder, because it is seen as the outcome of a life that seeks God and is filled with wisdom. As the Rule of St. Benedict states: "The wise are known for their few words."

STEP 8: *Transformed into the Love of God.* Here, there is no haughtiness, no sarcasm, no putdowns, no airs of importance. We are able to embrace our limits and those of others. We are fully aware of how fragile we are and are under no illusions. We are at home with ourselves and content to rely on the mercy of God. Everything is a gift.

Let the Old Birth the New

Good grieving is not just letting go, but also letting it bless us. Job did just that. The old life for Job was truly over. That door remained closed. That is the great grief about our losses. There is finality. We can't get it back. Yet when we follow Job's path and . . .

1. Pay Attention
2. Wait in the Confusing In-Between
3. Embrace the Gift of Limits

4. Climb the Ladder of Humility
5. Let the Old Birth the New . . . *in his time*

. . . we will be blessed. That is the lesson of Job. As he followed the difficult path of allowing his losses to enlarge his soul for God, God blessed him superabundantly. Not only was he spiritually transformed but "the LORD restored his fortunes and gave him twice as much as he had before. . . . The LORD blessed the latter part of Job's life more than the former part." His wealth was doubled. God gave him ten children once again and he lived till a ripe old age (Job 42:10–17).

This account is meant to encourage us to trust the living God with the many mini-deaths that we experience in our lives. The central message of Christ is that suffering and death bring resurrection and transformation. Jesus himself said, "Very truly I tell you, unless a kernel of wheat falls to the ground and dies, it remains only a single seed. But if it dies, it produces many seeds" (John 12:24).

But remember, resurrection only comes out of death—real death.

Our losses are real.

And so is our God, the living God.

A New Relationship with God

There are many rich fruits that blossom in our lives as a result of embracing our losses. The greatest, however, concerns our relationship to God. We move from a "Give me, give me, and give me" prayer life to an intimate, loving prayer life characterized by loving union with God.[9] When we grieve God's way, we are changed forever.

In the next chapter, we will examine more closely two disciplines in the history of God's people—the Daily Office and the Sabbath—and why they are so essential to a mature prayer life as well an emotionally healthy spirituality.

Lord Jesus, when I think about my losses, it can feel that I have no skin to protect me. I feel raw, scraped to the bone. I don't know why you have allowed such pain. Looking at Job helps, but I must admit that I struggle to see something "new being birthed out of the old." Lord, grant me the courage to feel, to pay attention, and then to wait on you. You know that everything in me resists limits, humility, and the cross.

So I invite you, Father, Son, and Holy Spirit, to make your home in me as you describe in John 14:23, to freely roam and fill every crevice of my life. And may the prayer of Job, finally, be mine: "My ears had heard of you but now my eyes have seen you." In Jesus' name, amen.

CHAPTER 6

Discover the Rhythms of the Daily Office and Sabbath

Stopping to Breathe the Air of Eternity

We live in a blizzard. And few of us have a rope.

In his book *A Hidden Wholeness*, Parker Palmer relates a story about farmers in the Midwest who would prepare for blizzards by tying a rope from the back door of their house out to the barn as a guide to ensure they could return safely home. These blizzards came quickly and fiercely and were highly dangerous. When their full force was blowing, a farmer could not see the end of his or her hand. Many froze to death in those blizzards, disoriented by their inability to see. They wandered in circles, lost sometimes in their own backyards. If they lost their grip on the rope, it became impossible for them to find their way home. Some froze within feet of their own front door, never realizing how close they were to safety.

To this day, in parts of Canada and the Great Plains, meteorologists counsel people that, to avoid getting lost in the blinding snow when they venture outside, they tie one end of a long rope to their house and grasp the other end firmly.[1]

Many of us have lost our way, spiritually, in the whiteout of the blizzard swirling around us. Blizzards begin when we say yes to too many things. Between demands from work and family, our lives fall somewhere between *full* and *overflowing*. We multitask, so much so that we are unaware we are doing three things at once. We admire people who are able to accomplish so much in so little time. They are our role models.

At the same time many of us are overscheduled, tense, addicted to hurry, frantic, preoccupied, fatigued, and starved for time. Cramming as much as possible into our to-do lists, we battle life to make the best use of every spare minute we have.

Yet not much changes. Our overproductivity becomes counter-productive. We end our days exhausted from work and raising children. And then our "free time" on weekends becomes filled with more demands in an already-overburdened life.

We listen to sermons and read books about slowing down and creating margin in our lives.[2] We read about the need to rest and recharge our batteries. Our workplaces offer seminars on increased productivity through replenishing ourselves.

But we can't stop. And if we aren't busy, we feel guilty that we waste time and are not productive.

We go through the motions of doing so many things as if there is no alternative way of spending our days. It is like being addicted—only it is not to drugs or alcohol but to tasks, to work, to doing. Any sense of rhythm in our daily, weekly, and yearly lives has been swallowed up in the blizzard of our lives.

Add to this the storms and trials of life that blow into our lives unexpectedly and catch us off guard, and we wonder why so many of us are disoriented and confused.

We need a rope to lead us home.

God *is* offering us a rope to keep us from getting lost. This rope consistently leads us back home to him, to a place that is centered and rooted. This rope can be found in two ancient disciplines going back thousands of years—the Daily Office and Sabbath. When placed inside present-day Christianity, the Daily Office and Sabbath are groundbreaking, countercultural acts against Western culture. They are powerful declarations about God, ourselves, our relationships, our beliefs, and our values.

Stopping for the Daily Office and Sabbath is not meant to add another to-do to our already busy schedules. It is the resetting of our entire lives toward a new destination—God. It is an entirely new way of being in the world.

The Daily Office and Sabbath are ropes that lead us back to God in the blizzards of life. They are anchors for living in the hurricane of demands. When done as a "want to" rather than a "have to," they offer us a rhythm for our lives that binds us to the living God.

They are nothing short of revolutionary disciplines for Christians today.

The Inadequacy of Our Present Ropes

Today we teach young Christians eager to develop their relationship with God to have devotions or a quiet time. Normally this consists of ten to thirty minutes a day spent reading the Bible, praying, and perhaps reading something from a devotional book. Along with church on Sundays and perhaps involvement in a small group, we hope this will enable them to withstand the blizzard swirling around them.

It won't.

Within a couple of hours after being with God in the morning, I easily forgot God was active in my everyday affairs. By lunch I was grumpy and short with people. By late afternoon God's presence had disappeared from my consciousness. By the time dinner was over, he felt a long way off. After observing my behavior for a couple of hours, my wife and children were always wondering, "What happened to Dad's Christianity?" And by nine o'clock at night, I was asking myself the same question!

I wanted to pay attention to God all through the day. I longed to be carried in his presence like Brother Lawrence wrote about in *Practicing the Presence of God*. The emotional health integration Geri and I had worked on for years had dramatically changed people's lives.

But something continued to elude us. We knew the answer related to a further slowing down the pace of people's lives and their balancing of activity and contemplation. Yes, embracing our limits was helpful, but something was still missing.

There are many great spiritual disciplines—the prayer of examen, retreats, spiritual direction, service, fellowship in small groups, worship, giving, Bible study, devotional reading, centering prayer, fasting, Scripture memorization, *lectio divina*, confession, journaling, intercession, to name a few.[3] They are each wonderful tools and gifts to help us follow Jesus. Many are essential threads in a strong rope to keep us centered and lead us home in the midst of blizzards.

The Daily Office and the Sabbath, however, offer us a rhythm powerful enough to anchor us. Whatever catastrophic blizzard may be blowing in our lives, the Daily Office and Sabbath enable us to hang onto the rope (that is, God himself) so we can safely make our way home.

Stopping to Surrender

At the heart of the Daily Office and the Sabbath is stopping to surrender to God in trust. Failure to do so is the very essence of the sin in the Garden of Eden. Adam and Eve legitimately worked and enjoyed their achievements in the garden. They were to embrace their limits, however, and not eat from the tree of the knowledge of good and evil. They were not to try to see and know that which belongs to the Almighty God. God was teaching them that, "after the full flowering of their achievements and activities, they [were] invited, not to be active, not to accomplish, but to surrender in trust. . . . Action, then passivity; striving, then letting go, doing all one can do and then being carried . . . only in this rhythm is the spirit realized."[4]

As theologian Robert Barron argued, at the heart of original sin is the refusal to accept God's rhythm for us.[5] The essence of being in God's image is our ability, like God, to stop. We imitate God by stopping our work and resting. If we can stop for one day a week, or for mini-Sabbaths each day (the Daily Office), we touch something deep within us as image bearers of God. Our human brain, our bodies, our spirits, and our emotions become wired by God for the rhythm of work and rest in him.[6]

The Daily Office and Sabbath serve as ropes so we might live in a rhythmic and joyful way even in the midst of blizzards.

The Discovery of an Ancient Treasure: The Daily Office

The term *Daily Office* (also called *fixed-hour prayer*, *Divine Office*, or *liturgy of the hours*) differs from what we label today as *quiet time* or *devotions*. When I listen carefully to most people describe their devotional life, the emphasis tends to be on "getting filled up for the day" or "interceding for the needs around me." The root of the Daily Office is not so much a turning to God to get something but to be *with* Someone. The word *Office* comes from the Latin word *opus*, or "work." For the early church, the Daily Office was always the "work of God." Nothing was to interfere with that priority. It was "an act of offering . . . by the creature to the Creator . . . prayers of praise offered as a sacrifice of thanksgiving and faith to God and as sweet-smelling incense . . . before the throne of God."[7]

I first observed and experienced the Daily Office during a one-week visit with Trappist monks in Massachusetts. The basic structure of Trappist life includes four elements—prayer, work, study, and rest. Yet it was their intentional arranging of their lives around the prayers of the Daily Office that moved me. This was their means to remain aware of God's presence while they worked and to maintain healthy balance in their lives.

During my time with the monks, we met seven times a day, remembering God through reading and singing the Scriptures, especially the psalms and prayer. Our daily schedule looked like this:

Vigils: 3:45 a.m. (middle of the night)
Lauds: 6:00 a.m. (predawn)
Prime: 6:25 a.m. ("First" hour—in their case it was Mass)
Sext: 12:15 p.m. ("Sixth" hour)
None: 2:00 p.m. ("Ninth" hour)
Vespers 5:40 p.m. ("Evening" hour)
Compline: 7:40 p.m. (before bed)

We chanted so many psalms (they sing all one hundred and fifty each week), read so much Scripture, and spent so much time in silence that by day three of my first week I felt like I had been transported into another world. I cannot imagine what that would do to a person's spiritual life if they engaged in that kind of spiritual discipline 365 days a year, year after year, decade after decade.

I did not join the monks in their six hours of manual work, but spent that time taking naps! I was too physically exhausted. (My body was not accustomed to getting up at 3:15 a.m.) Yet I was sure of one thing: this rhythm of pausing for the Daily Office offered a key to unlocking the secret of paying attention to God and being carried in his presence throughout the day unlike anything I had experienced in almost thirty years of following Christ.

What surprised me most in conversations with them was how much we had in common in our love for Christ and our desire to be transformed by that love and into that love. They, too, struggled with the balance of "Mary" and "Martha," contemplation and activity.

This experience with the Trappists launched me on a journey over the next two years to visit a variety of Roman Catholic, Protestant, and Orthodox monastic communities to learn more. From Taizé, France, to the Northumbrian community in England to the monks of New Skete in upstate New York, Geri and I participated in all kinds of variations of the Daily Office. And I read church history—a lot of it—trying to understand how this might apply to schoolteachers, police officers, lawyers, social workers, contractors, students, financial advisors, and stay-at-home moms seeking to follow Jesus in a place like New York City.

More importantly, I was trying to figure out how it might apply to me—a husband and father of four daughters with a full-time job as a pastor of a very active church with enormous demands on my time. How might I integrate this in the midst of soccer games, teachers meetings, tuition decisions, parenting issues, neighboring relationships, and faucet leaks?

David practiced set times of prayer seven times a day (Psalm 119:164). Daniel prayed three times a day (Daniel 6:10). Devout Jews in Jesus' time prayed two to three times a day. Jesus himself probably followed the Jewish custom of praying at set times during the day. After Jesus' resurrection, his disciples continued to pray at certain hours of the day (Acts 3:1 and 10:9ff).

About AD 525, a good man named Benedict structured these prayer times around eight Daily Offices, including one in the middle of the night for monks. The Rule of St. Benedict became one of the most powerful documents in shaping Western civilization. At one point in his Rule, Benedict wrote: "On hearing the signal for an hour of the divine office, the monk will immediately set aside what he has in hand and go with utmost speed. . . . Indeed, nothing is to be preferred to the Work of God [that is, the Daily Office]."[8]

All these people realized that stopping for the Daily Office to be with God is the key to creating a continual and easy familiarity with God's presence the rest of the day. It is the rhythm of stopping that makes the "practice of the presence of God," to use Brother Lawrence's phrase, a real possibility.

I know it does for me. The great power in setting apart small units of time for morning, midday, and evening prayer infuses into the rest of my day's activities a deep sense of the sacred, of God. All the time is his. The Daily Office, practiced consistently, actually eliminates any division of the sacred and the secular in our lives.

The Central Elements of the Daily Office

God has built us each differently. What works for one person will not for another. Geri and I approach our Daily Offices very differently. I prefer more structure, enjoy written prayers, pray the psalms often, and love the rhythm of four Offices per day.

Geri utilizes a variety of tools, books, and methods to approach her Daily Office each day. She will skip an Office without any guilt whatsoever. She aims at three Offices a day and enjoys great flexibility to what she does in her time with God. For example, it is not uncommon for Geri to go outside and breathe in the presence of God in creation.

You choose the length of time for your Offices. The key, remember, is regular remembrance of God, not length. Your pausing to be with God can last anywhere from two minutes to twenty minutes to forty-five minutes. It is up to you.

You also choose the content of your Offices. A number of possible resources are available that you may want to utilize—*The Divine Hours* by Phyllis Tickle, *Celtic Daily Prayer* by the Northumbria Community, and *A Guide to Prayer for All Who Seek God* by Norman Shawchuck and Rueben P. Job are three excellent examples.[9] Many of us also utilize the daily examen of St. Ignatius for compline (see appendix C). *Compline* refers to the final office/prayer time at the completion of the day before going to sleep.

Yet four elements, I believe, need to be found in any Office, regardless of what approach you ultimately choose. The Office can be done together or alone.

1. Stopping

This is the essence of a Daily Office. What is more important than the number of offices each day is that our time with God be unhurried so that what we read or pray has time to sink deeply into our spirits. We stop our activity and pause to be with the living God. Central to the challenge of stopping at midday, for example, is to trust that God is on the throne. He rules. I don't. At each Office I give up control and trust God to run his world without me.

2. Centering

Scripture commands us: "Be still before the Lord and wait patiently for him" (Psalm 37:7) and "Be still, and know that I am God" (Psalm 46:10). We move into God's presence and rest there. That alone is no small feat. For this reason I often spend five minutes centering down so I can let go of my tensions, distractions, and sensations and begin resting in the love of God. I follow James Finley's guidelines for these times:[10]

- Be attentive and open
- Sit still
- Sit straight
- Breathe slowly, deeply, and naturally
- Close your eyes or lower them to the ground

When you find your mind wandering, let your breathing bring you back. As you breathe in, ask God to fill you with the Holy Spirit. As you breathe out, exhale all that is sinful, false, and not of him.

A second tool I use when my mind wanders is to pray the Jesus Prayer: "Lord Jesus Christ, Son of God, have mercy on me, a sinner." If nothing else happens during a Daily Office, it is a call to mindfulness, an invitation to pay attention to what our short, earthly lives are all about.

3. Silence

Dallas Willard called *silence* and *solitude* the two most radical disciplines of the Christian life. Solitude is the practice of being absent from people and things to attend to God. Silence is the practice of quieting every inner and outer voice to attend to God. Henri Nouwen said that "without solitude it is almost impossible to live a spiritual life."[11]

These are probably the most challenging and least practiced disciplines among Christians today. We live in a world of noise and distractions. Most of us fear silence. Studies say that the average group can only bear fifteen seconds of silence. Most of our church services confirm this.

When God appeared to Elijah after his suicidal depression and flight from Jezebel, he told him to stand and wait for the presence of the Lord to pass by. God did not appear in ways he had in the past. God was not in the wind (as with Job), an earthquake (as at Mount Sinai with the giving of the Ten Commandments), or fire (as in the burning bush with Moses).

God finally revealed himself to Elijah in "a sound of sheer silence," which is the literal translation of 1 Kings 19:12. The translation often used for this text—"a still small voice" or "gentle whisper"—does not capture the original Hebrew. But what could translators do? How do you *hear* silence?

The silence after the chaos, for Elijah and for us, is full of the presence of God. God did speak to Elijah out of the silence, and he speaks also to us. While it is not the objective of the Office, it is a natural result.

4. Scripture

The psalms are the foundation of almost any Daily Office book you will find available today. They have served as the prayer book of the church through the centuries. Jesus quoted psalms more than any other book except Isaiah. The prayers of the Psalter cover the entire gamut of our life experience—from anger to rage to trust to praise. A good Daily Office guide will also lead you to Old and New Testament readings that both reflect the church calendar year and a balanced diet of spiritual food. I often conclude each Daily Office by slowly and thoughtfully praying the Lord's Prayer.

There are many other rich spiritual practices you can integrate into your Daily Office—*lectio divina* (meditation on Scripture), centering prayer, singing along with a worship CD, reading through the Bible in a year, readings from devotional classics, to name a few.[12]

A good rule to follow when dealing with tools and techniques is this: If it helps, do it. If it does not help you, do not do it—including the Daily Office! If reading the psalms helps you, then great. Do it. If reading the psalms has become routine and dead for you, then don't. Maybe it is time for you to meditate on one phrase, such as "You hem me in behind and before, and you lay your hand upon me" (Psalm 139:5) and sit in silence. Be attentive in your heart to what God is doing inside of you. Learn from others. Remember: we go through seasons. And most important, let God be your guide.

The purpose of the Daily Office is to remember God and commune with him all through our days. Keep that clearly in mind as you develop structures and habits that fit you. We are constantly tempted to think God will love us more if we pray more, do the Daily Office often, and keep the Sabbath. Remember grace, which reminds us there is nothing we can do or not do that would cause God to love us any more than he does right now.

We have been experimenting with how to integrate the Daily Office into our lives within our active local church in New York City. In appendix A is a simple tool we have used to help individuals and small groups get started in pausing for the Daily Office throughout the day.[13]

A Second Ancient Treasure: Sabbath-Keeping

The word *Sabbath* comes from the Hebrew word that means "to cease, to stop working." It refers to doing nothing related to work for a twenty-four hour period each week. It refers to this unit of time around which we are to orient our entire lives as "holy," meaning "separate, a cut above" the other six days (Genesis 2:2–3).[14] Sabbath provides for us now an additional rhythm for an entire reorientation of our lives around the living God. On Sabbaths we imitate God by stopping our work and resting.

Make no mistake about it: keeping the command to Sabbath is both radical and extremely difficult in our everyday lives. It cuts to the core of our spirituality, the core of our convictions, the core of our faith, the core of our lifestyles.

Our culture knows nothing of setting aside a whole day (twenty-four hours) to rest and delight in God. Like most, I always considered it an optional extra, not something absolutely essential to discipleship. But as we've discussed, living in a fallen world is much like being in a blizzard. Without the Sabbath, we easily find ourselves lost and unsure of the larger picture of God and our lives. I am convinced that nothing less than an understanding of Sabbath as a *command* from God, as well as an incredible invitation, will enable us to grab hold of this rope God offers us.

God's Command for Rhythm in our Lives

Keeping the Sabbath in Scripture is a commandment—right next to refraining from lying, murdering, and committing adultery. Sabbath is a gift from God we are invited to receive.

Israel lived as slaves in Egypt for over four hundred years. They never had a day off. They were treated as tools of production to make pyramids. They were "doing" machines. They worked seven days a week all year long. Imagine how deeply ingrained activism and overwork must have been for them! They had never observed or experienced a rhythm of work and rest. They had neither permission nor the choice to do so. Living meant performing tasks, with one day blurring into the next.

When God called Israel out of Egypt, he affirmed they were sacred human beings made in his image. He then showed them how to live according to their God-given nature. In effect, God said, "It may feel awkward at first, but as a fish is created to live in water, I created you to live according to this design."

The longest and most specific of the Ten Commandments is the fourth. Let's take a look at all of them in comparison:

- You shall have no other gods before me.
- You shall not make for yourself an image in the form of

anything in heaven above or on the earth beneath or in the waters below.

- You shall not misuse the name of the LORD your God.
- Remember the Sabbath day by keeping it holy. Six days you shall labor and do all your work, but the seventh day is a Sabbath to the LORD our God. On it you shall not do any work, neither you, nor your son or daughter, nor your male or female servant, nor your animals, nor any foreigner residing in your towns. For in six days the LORD made the heavens and the earth, the sea, and all that is in them, but he rested on the seventh day. Therefore the LORD blessed the Sabbath day and made it holy.
- Honor your father and your mother.
- You shall not murder.
- You shall not commit adultery.
- You shall not steal.
- You shall not give false testimony against your neighbor.
- You shall not covet. (Exodus 20:1–17)

God worked. We are to work. God rested. We are to rest. After completing his work of creating the heavens and earth, God rested on the seventh day. It was the climax of God's week in Genesis 1:1–2:4, and it is to be the climax of ours.

Before the Israelites entered the Promised Land, Moses proclaimed further that the very act of ceasing from work in the midst of all the surrounding nations was a sign of their liberation by God (Deuteronomy 5:13ff). By the very act of refusing to succumb to the enormous pressure of Western culture around us, we, too, serve as a sign of a free people. We have been called out of a world trying to prove its worth and value by what it does or possesses. We are deeply loved by God for who we are, not for what we do.

The Sabbath calls us to build the doing of nothing into our schedules each week. Nothing measurable is accomplished. By the world's standards it is inefficient, unproductive, and useless. As one theologian stated, "To fail to see the value of simply being with God and 'doing nothing' is to miss the heart of Christianity."[15]

The Sabbath was always a hallmark of the Jews throughout their history. This one act, perhaps more than any other, kept them from the pressure of the powerful cultures that have sought to assimilate them. For this reason it is often said that, for thirty-five hundred years, the Sabbath has kept the Jews more than Jews have kept the Sabbath.

This is certainly not the case with Christians living in the twenty-first century.

Sabbath, when lived, is our means as the people of God to bear witness to the way we understand life, its rhythms, its gifts, its meaning, and its ultimate purpose in God. Observing the Sabbath, we affirm: "God is the center and source of our lives. He is the beginning, the middle, and the end of our existence." We trust God to provide and care for us.

Eugene Peterson points out even though Sabbath has been one of the most abused and distorted practices of the Christian life, we cannot do without it. "Sabbath is not primarily about us or how it benefits us; it is about God and how God forms us. . . . I don't see any way out of it; if we are going to live appropriately in the creation we must keep the Sabbath."[16]

The Four Principles of Biblical Sabbath

One of the great dangers of faithfully observing Sabbath is legalism. What about pastors, nurses, doctors, police officers, and others who must work on Sundays? Jesus observed Sabbath but he also healed the sick and preached sermons on that day. What might be work for you may be different for someone else. Some people will have to choose another day besides Saturday or Sunday (depending on your church tradition) if it is to be a day without work.

The key is to set a regular rhythm of keeping the Sabbath every seven days for a twenty-four-hour block of time. Traditional Jewish Sabbath begins at sundown on Friday and ends on sundown Saturday. I know many Christians who begin their Sabbath precisely at 6:00 p.m. or 7:00 p.m. on Saturday until the same time the following day. Others, like myself, choose a day of the week. The apostle Paul seemed to think one day would do as well as another (Romans 14:1–17). What is important is to select a time period and protect it!

The following are four foundational qualities of biblical Sabbaths that have served me well in distinguishing a "day off" from a biblical Sabbath. A secular Sabbath is to replenish our energies and make us more effective the other six days. A "day off" produces positive results but is, in Eugene Peterson's words, "a bastard Sabbath."[17] I commend them to you as you develop a biblical framework for Sabbath that fits your particular life situation, temperament, calling, and personality.

1. Stop

Sabbath is first and foremost a day of "stopping." "To stop" is built into the literal meaning of the Hebrew word *Sabbath*. Yet most of us can't stop until we are finished with whatever it is we think we need to do. We need to complete our projects and term papers, answer our emails, return all phone messages, complete the balancing of our checkbooks to pay our bills, finish cleaning the house. There's always one more goal to be reached before stopping.

On Sabbath I embrace my limits. God is God. He is indispensable. I am his creature. The world continues working fine when I stop.

I've hated stopping my entire life. When I was a college and seminary student, I had too much homework to stop for one twenty-four-hour period. When I taught high school English, I had too many papers to grade to stop. When I was learning Spanish in Costa Rica, I couldn't stop if I was going to learn the language. If I was going to be responsive to the needs of the people in our church and still have time to pray and study, I needed to work at least half of my Sabbath, didn't I?

We think, *Maybe I will stop when our children grow into adults and are on their own, when I have enough saved to buy our first home, when I retire and* . . . The list goes on.

We stop on Sabbaths because God is on the throne, assuring us the world will not fall apart if we cease our activities. Life on this side of heaven is an unfinished symphony. We accomplish one goal and then immediately are confronted with new opportunities and challenges. But ultimately we will die with countless unfinished projects and goals. That's okay. God is at work taking care of the universe. He manages quite well without us having to run things. When we are sleeping, he is working. So he commands us to relax, to enjoy the fact that we are not in charge of his world, that even when we die, the world will continue on nicely without us. Every Sabbath reminds us to "be still, and know that [he is] God" (Psalm 46:10) and to stop worrying about tomorrow (Matthew 6:25–33).

The core spiritual issue in stopping revolves around trust. Will God take care of us and our concerns if we obey him by stopping to keep the Sabbath?

The story is told of a wagon train of Christians traveling on their way from St. Louis to Oregon. They observed the habit of stopping for the Sabbath during the autumn, but as winter approached the group began to panic in fear they would not reach their destination before the snows began. A number of members of the group proposed they quit the practice of stopping for the Sabbath and travel seven days a week. This caused an argument in the community until it was finally decided to divide the wagon train into two groups. One group would observe the Sabbath day as before and not travel. The other would press on.

Which group arrived in Oregon first? Of course—the ones who kept the Sabbath. Both the people and their horses were so rested by their Sabbath observance they could travel much more efficiently the other six days.[18]

When I trust God and obey his commands, he provides. Jesus takes our loaves and fishes that we offer him, even though they are insufficient to feed the multitudes, and somehow miraculously and invisibly multiplies them. We can trust him enough to stop.

2. Rest

Once we stop, the Sabbath calls us to rest. God rested after his work. We are to do the same—every seventh day (Genesis 2:1–4). What do we do to replace all we are now stopping during our Sabbath time? The answer is simple: whatever delights and replenishes you.

For example, in my case, work relates to my vocation as pastor of New Life Fellowship Church, along with writing and speaking. For this reason, Saturday rather than Sunday is my Sabbath. I purposely engage in ideas and people that get my mind off even the thought of work! That includes napping, working out, going for long walks, reading a novel, watching a good movie, going out for dinner. I avoid the computer and cell phone.

For me to enjoy Sabbath rest on Saturday, however, requires I have another day of the week to do the tasks of life that consume my energy or fill me with worry. For example, planning my week, paying bills, balancing our checkbook, cleaning the house, fighting traffic and crowds to shop, doing loads of laundry are all work I need to do a different day of the week.

The following list gives you nine possibilities to consider replacing with rest. The primary one, of course, is rest from work. But you may want to also pick one or two others over the next couple of months as you develop your practice of Sabbath keeping. Consider resting from:

- work
- physical exhaustion
- hurriedness
- multitasking
- competitiveness
- worry
- decision making
- catching up on errands
- talking
- technology (e.g., cell phones, TV, computers, social media)

When we stop and rest, we respect our humanity and the image of God in us. We are not nonstop human beings. Sadly, it often takes a physical illness such as cancer, a heart attack, the flu, or a severe depression to get us to rest. We don't serve the Sabbath. The Sabbath serves us.

3. Delight

A third component to biblical Sabbath revolves around delighting in what we have been given. God, after finishing his work of creation, proclaimed that "it was very good" (Genesis 1:31). God delighted over his creation. The Hebrew phrase communicates a sense of joy, completion, wonder, and play. This is particularly radical in a culture like ours, both secular and Christian, that is "delight deficient." Because of the way pleasure and delight have been so distorted by our culture, many of us as Christians struggle with receiving joy and pleasure.

On Sabbaths we are called to enjoy and delight in creation and its gifts. We are to slow down and pay attention to our food, smelling and tasting its riches. We are to take the time to see the beauty of a tree, a leaf, a flower, the sky that has been created with great care by our God. He has given us the ability to see, hear, taste, smell, and touch, that we might feast with our senses on the miraculousness of life. We are, as William Blake wrote, "to see a world in a grain of sand and a heaven in a wild flower."[19]

I will never forget the first time I took pleasure in warm water running over my hands in a McDonald's restroom on a Sabbath. I slowly dried my hands, rubbing them together under the drier as the water dissipated. I did not run out of the restroom, drying my hands on my pants as I walked to the car. I did not skip putting soap all over my hands. I relished the present moment and tasted the Sabbath gift of simply washing my hands!

On Sabbaths God also invites us to slow down to pay attention and delight in people. In the Gospels, Jesus modeled a prayerful presence with people—whether it was a Samarian woman, the widow at Nain, the rich young ruler, or Nicodemus. He seemed "into" the beauty of men and women crafted in God's image. This has become a spiritual discipline for me. I try, for example, to walk slowly, leaving lots of free space and time on Sabbaths so I can stop for unexpected conversations with neighbors, family, and shopkeepers. I ask God for the grace to leave the frenzied busyness around me and be a contemplative presence for others.

Finally, Sabbath delight invites us to healthy play. The word chosen by the Greek Fathers for the perfect, mutual indwelling of the Trinity was *perichoerisis*. It literally means "dancing around."[20] Creation and life are, in a sense, God's gift of a playground to us. Whether it be through sports, dance, games, looking at old family photographs, or visiting museums, nurturing our sense of pure fun in God also is part of Sabbath.

4. Contemplate

The final quality of a biblical Sabbath is, of course, the contemplation of God. The Sabbath is always "holy to the LORD" (Exodus 31:15). Pondering the love of God remains the central focus of our Sabbaths. Throughout Jewish and Christian history, Sabbath has included worship with God's people where we feast on his presence, the reading and study of Scripture, and silence. For this reason, Saturdays (if your tradition gathers on that day) or Sundays remain the ideal time for Sabbath keeping whenever possible.

Every Sabbath also serves as a taste of the glorious eternal party of music, food, and beauty that awaits us in heaven when we see him face to face (Revelation 22:4). On every Sabbath, we experience a sampling of something greater that awaits us. Our short earthly lives are put in perspective as we look forward to the day when God's kingdom will come in all its fullness and we will enter an eternal Sabbath feast in God's perfect presence. We will taste his splendor, greatness, beauty, excellence, and glory far beyond anything we ever experienced or dreamed.

As with stopping, resting, and delighting, we will need to prepare in advance how to do this. Is it any wonder that the Jewish people traditionally had a Day of Preparation for the Sabbath? There was food to buy, clothes to wash for the children, and final preparations to be made. What will it mean to prepare yourself for worship, to receive the Word of God? What time do you need to go to bed the night before? When might you have times of silence and solitude or prayer during the day? What final items do you need to resolve so you can have an uncluttered Sabbath?

Devout Jews today have numerous customs related to their Friday Shabbat meal as a family. They maintain various traditions, from the lighting of candles to the reading of psalms to the blessing of children to the eating of the meal to the giving of thanks to God. Each is designed to keep God at the center of their Sabbath.[21]

There are an amazing variety of Sabbath possibilities before you. It is vitally important you keep in mind your unique life situation as you work out these four principles of Sabbath keeping into your life. Experiment. Make a plan. Follow it for one to two months. Then reflect back on what changes you would like to make. There is no one right way that works for every person.

Sabbath is like receiving the gift of a heavy snow day every week. Stores are closed. Roads are impassable. Suddenly you have the gift of a day to do whatever you want. You don't have any obligations, pressures, or responsibilities. You have permission to play, be with friends, take a nap, read a good book. Few of us would give ourselves a "no obligation day" very often.

God gives you one—every seventh day.

Think about it. He gives you over seven weeks (fifty-two days in all) of snow days every year! And if you begin to practice stopping, resting, delighting, and contemplating for one twenty-four-hour period each week, you will soon find your other six days becoming infused with those same qualities. I suspect that has always been God's plan.[22]

Sabbath Vacations and Other Applications

God knew that if the people of Israel were to be true to their calling and purpose, they would need more than weekly Sabbaths. They would need longer stretches of time to stop, to rest, to delight in and contemplate him. For this reason God built into their national economic and political life entire Sabbatical *years*. God commanded all Israel to give the land a "Sabbath of rest" one year in every seven

(Leviticus 25:1–7). Since he knew this would require great faith, God promised that what they harvested in year six would be enough to feed them for two whole years. They were to trust God for his provision.[23] In much the same way, the Sabbath principle has a number of rich applications to help us survive the blizzards of life today.

First, each of us takes a vacation every year, for one, two, three, or more weeks. Consider viewing that time as a longer Sabbath gift from God. Geri and I take the four principles of Sabbath—stop, rest, delight, and contemplate—to structure our vacations. We take into account our different needs, our children, our resources, and plan accordingly. This has utterly transformed our vacations over the past several years. If you go this route, one thing is for sure: you will not return from your vacations in need of another vacation.

Second, consider spending a few days at a spiritual retreat with a group or attending a training conference. Treat it as a sabbatical. You may want to simply go away overnight for a personal retreat with God every four to six months for a longer sabbatical. Or take some time away from work to go on a mission trip to serve with a group from your church, looking to the four principles of Sabbath as a way to structure your time.

Third, if you are actively serving in a ministry at your church—whether it be as a small-group leader, a children's worker, a musician on the worship team, an usher—consider taking a rest after six or seven years. Even if you love it, do it. Take the time for a sabbatical *to* the Lord, not a vacation *from* church. Follow the same biblical principles applied to weekly Sabbaths. Prepare. Sketch out a plan. Talk it over with your pastor or a friend. Model a rhythm of life.

Finally, if you are a pastor or Christian leader, I want to encourage you to take time for sabbatical rest every seven or eight years. To be providing leadership in God's church is a demanding task. The soil needs to be replenished and to lie dormant for a season. I have taken three separate three-to four-month sabbaticals (seven to eight years apart) beginning in 1996. They transformed my life, my marriage, and the church I pastor. I continue to feed others out of the rich fruit of those sabbaticals.

Geri jokes at times, "I have been married to four different men the last thirty-two years, all of them named Pete Scazzero, and New Life Fellowship Church has had at least four pastors, all of whom were Pete Scazzero."

Gripping the Rope during Our Blizzards

God invites us to grab on to his rope in the blizzard of life. He seeks to lead us back home to him. Sabbath keeping and the Daily Office summon us to slow down to God's rhythm. For when we are busier than what God requires, as Thomas Merton has written, we do violence to ourselves:

> There is a pervasive form of contemporary violence . . . activism and overwork. The rush and pressure of modern life are a form, perhaps the most common form, of its innate violence. To allow oneself to be carried away by a multitude of conflicting concerns, to surrender to too many demands, to commit oneself to too many projects, to want to help everyone in everything, is to succumb to violence. . . . It kills the root of inner wisdom which makes work fruitful.[24]

And in doing violence to ourselves, we are unable to love others in and through the love of Christ. This leads us to the topic of our next chapter: growing into an emotional adult who loves others well.

Lord, help me to grab hold of you as my rope in the blizzard today. I need you. The idea of stopping to be with you one, two, or three times a day seems overwhelming, but I know I need you. Show me the way. Teach me to be prayerfully attentive to you. This idea of Sabbath will require a lot of change in the way I am living life. Lead me, Lord, in how to take the next step with this. Help me trust you with all that will remain unfinished, to not try to run your world for you. Set me free to begin reorienting my life around you and you alone. In Jesus' name, amen.

CHAPTER 7

Grow into an Emotionally Mature Adult

Learning New Skills to Love Well

In Dostoevsky's novel *The Brothers Karamazov*, a wealthy woman asks an elderly monk how she can know if God exists. He tells her no explanation or argument can achieve this, only the practice of "active love." She then confesses that sometimes she dreams about a life of loving service to others. At such times she thinks perhaps she will become a Sister of Mercy, live in holy poverty, and serve the poor in the humblest way. But then it crosses her mind how ungrateful some of the people she would serve are likely to be. They would probably complain that the soup she served wasn't hot enough or that the bread wasn't fresh enough or the bed was too hard. She confesses that she couldn't bear such ingratitude—and so her dreams about serving others vanish, and once again she finds herself wondering if there is a God.

To this the wise monk responds, "Love in practice is a harsh and dreadful thing compared to love in dreams."[1]

Loving well is the goal of the Christian life. This is easier in our dreams than in practice. It requires that we grow into emotional adulthood in Christ, the rewards of which are rich beyond measure.

The Problem of Emotional Immaturity

Many people know the truths of the Bible relatively well. They can recite many of the Ten Commandments and articulate key principles for Christian living. They believe wholeheartedly they should be living them. The problem is they don't know how!

The following is one simple, common scenario:

> Jessica is a gifted manager in her company. She has been a Christian for fifteen years and loves spending time with God. When the vice president of her company was making schedules for managers to meet with clients out of town, he asked Jessica to pick the weeks she would prefer to travel over the next three months. Within the week Jessica emailed him the dates and eagerly awaited his confirmation. None arrived. Jessica called his office the following week.
>
> His administrative assistant answered. "Well, according to the schedule I have in front of me, the next three months are all full," she said. "I guess this means he doesn't need you right now. But thanks for calling."
>
> Jessica sat stunned in her chair. "Thank you," she replied robotically and hung up.
>
> For the next two weeks Jessica wrestled with God and herself. She asked God for forgiveness for the anger she was feeling. She tried to figure out why the vice president had changed his mind. She humbled herself to God. She cried out in prayer for love toward her coworkers. She lost sleep.
>
> Finally, she concluded God was dealing with her stubborn self-will.
>
> Over time Jessica distanced herself from the vice president and other managers, avoiding them whenever possible. During

the next two years she worked hard, but she felt like she had hit a ceiling in how far she could go with this company. Eventually, she took a position with another company.

Jessica is committed to her personal relationship with Jesus Christ. She practices spiritual disciplines. The problem, however, is that her commitment to Jesus Christ does not include relating to people in an emotionally mature way. Instead, she misapplies biblical truth and follows, most probably, the relational skills learned unconsciously in her family growing up.

What assumptions is she making about her vice president? His administrative assistant? About God's will for her life? What might she have done to prevent her pain? To preserve her relationships at work?

Unless Jessica receives equipping in this area, she will likely repeat the same pattern over and over again.

We learn many skills to be competent in our careers and at school. We don't learn, however, the skills necessary to grow into an emotionally mature adult who loves well. The Bible is clear what we are to do. Part of growing into an emotionally mature Christian is learning how to apply practically and effectively the truths we believe. For example:

- How can I be quick to hear and slow to speak?
- How can I be angry and not sin?
- How can I watch my heart above all else (since that is the place from which life flows)?
- How can I speak the truth in love?
- How can I be a true peacemaker?
- How can I mourn?
- How can I not bear false witness against my neighbor?
- How can I get rid of all bitterness, rage, and envy?

The end result of an inability to walk out our beliefs is that our churches and relationships within the church are not qualitatively any different from the world around us.

Emotional Infants, Children, Adolescents, and Adults

Jesus preached great messages to the multitudes. Yet he knew that would not be enough for people to truly "get it." So he chose twelve disciples with whom he lived day and night for three years. He modeled how his teaching worked out practically. He had them practice. He supervised. He imparted power.

Jesus knew inspiration was not enough.[2]

I have spent all my adult life giving inspiring sermons about God's heart for us to love people. I have preached messages about how Jesus saw each human being as infinitely precious and a treasure in God's sight. I have quoted Mother Teresa of Calcutta's inspiring quote about "loving one person at a time," and Thomas Merton's revelation that people "were walking around shining like the sun."[3] But I have found that telling people to love better and more is not enough. They need practical skills incorporated into their spiritual formation to grow out of emotional infancy into emotional adulthood. It is easy to grow physically into a chronological adult. It is quite another to grow into an emotional adult. Many people may be, chronologically, forty-five years old but remain an emotional infant, child, or adolescent.

The question then is: How do I distinguish between them? The following is a brief summary of each:[4]

EMOTIONAL INFANTS

- Look for others to take care of them
- Have great difficulty entering into the world of others

- Are driven by need for instant gratification
- Use others as objects to meet their needs

EMOTIONAL CHILDREN

- Are content and happy as long as they receive what they want
- Unravel quickly from stress, disappointments, trials
- Interpret disagreements as personal offenses
- Are easily hurt
- Complain, withdraw, manipulate, take revenge, become sarcastic when they don't get their way
- Have great difficulty calmly discussing their needs and wants in a mature, loving way

EMOTIONAL ADOLESCENTS

- Tend to often be defensive
- Are threatened and alarmed by criticism
- Keep score of what they give so they can ask for something later in return
- Deal with conflict poorly, often blaming, appeasing, going to a third party, pouting, or ignoring the issue entirely
- Become preoccupied with themselves
- Have great difficulty truly listening to another person's pain, disappointments, or needs
- Are critical and judgmental

EMOTIONAL ADULTS

- Are able to ask for what they need, want, or prefer—clearly, directly, honestly
- Recognize, manage, and take responsibility for their own thoughts and feelings

- Can, when under stress, state their own beliefs and values without becoming adversarial
- Respect others without having to change them
- Give people room to make mistakes and not be perfect
- Appreciate people for who they are—the good, bad, and ugly—not for what they give back
- Accurately assess their own limits, strengths, and weaknesses and are able to freely discuss them with others
- Are deeply in tune with their own emotional world and able to enter into the feelings, needs, and concerns of others without losing themselves
- Have the capacity to resolve conflict maturely and negotiate solutions that consider the perspectives of others

The Spiritual Discipline of Practicing the Presence of People

As emotionally mature Christian adults, we recognize that loving well is the essence of true spirituality. This requires that we experience connection with God, with ourselves, and with other people. God invites us to practice his presence in our daily lives. At the same time, he invites us "to practice the presence of people," within an awareness of his presence, in our daily relationships.[5] The two are rarely brought together.

Jesus' profound, contemplative prayer life with his Father resulted in a contemplative presence with people. He saw every person he met as someone new who never existed before, something original and unique. In fact, this ability to pay attention and really listen to people was at the very heart of his mission. It could not help but move him to compassion. In the same way, out of our contemplative time with God, we, too, are invited to be prayerfully present to people, revealing their beauty to themselves.

The religious leaders of Jesus' day, the "church leaders" of that time, never made that connection. They were diligent, zealous, and absolutely committed to having God as Lord of their lives. They memorized the entire books of Genesis, Exodus, Leviticus, Numbers, and Deuteronomy. They prayed five times a day. They tithed all their income and gave money to the poor. They evangelized. But they never delighted in people. They did not link loving God with the need to be diligent, zealous, and absolutely committed to growing in their ability to love people. For this reason they criticized Jesus repeatedly for being a "glutton and a drunkard, a friend of tax collectors and sinners" (Matthew 11:19). He delighted in people and life too much.

Jesus refused to separate the practice of the presence of God from the practice of the presence of people. When pushed to the wall to separate this unbreakable union, Jesus refused. He summarized the entire Bible for us: "'Love the Lord your God with all your heart and with all your soul and with all your mind.' This is the first and greatest commandment. And the second is like it: 'Love your neighbor as yourself.' All the Law and the Prophets hang on these two commandments" (Matthew 22:37–40).

Our Great Problem

I can't help but experience life with me at the center of my universe. With my eyes I look out on the world. With my ears I hear what is going on. I can only feel, want, and experience what I am feeling, wanting, and experiencing. I naturally want the people around me to give up themselves and become what I want them to be. I prefer those close to me to think, feel, and act toward the world in the same way I do. I prefer the illusion of sameness when really we are very different from each other. I want other people's worlds to be like mine. I even act the same way in my relationship with God, walking out my spirituality as if I am the center of the universe.

For this reason, M. Scott Peck argues that we are all born narcissists and that learning to grow out of our narcissism is at the heart of the spiritual journey.[6]

When Geri and I were married we lit what is recognized today as the unity candle. There were two separate candles representing our separate lives. After taking our vows, we lit a third candle and extinguished the two separate ones. This symbolized we were now "one."

"We are one," we proclaimed to our family and friends.

The question we didn't answer was: "Which one?" For the first nine years of our marriage, I unconsciously answered that question with: "Yes, Geri and I are one, and I *am* the one!"

To grow spiritually, a Copernican revolution must take place in the way we perceive ourselves in relation to others. When Copernicus removed human beings from the center of the universe and said we revolve around the sun, not vice versa, it sent a shock wave through Western civilization. To discover the "otherness" of a spouse, friend, boss, child, and coworker and to see them as separate, unique human beings—without losing yourself—is also a Copernican revolution of emotional maturity.

I-It Relationships

In 1923, the great Jewish theologian Martin Buber wrote a brilliant but difficult to read book, called *I and Thou.*[7] Buber described the most healthy or mature relationship possible between two human beings as an "I-Thou" relationship. In such a relationship I recognize that I am made in the image of God and so is every other person on the face of the earth. This makes them a "Thou" to me. Because of that reality, every person deserves respect—that is, I treat them with dignity and worth. I do not dehumanize or objectify them. I affirm them as having a unique and separate existence apart from me.

See the following circles illustrations:

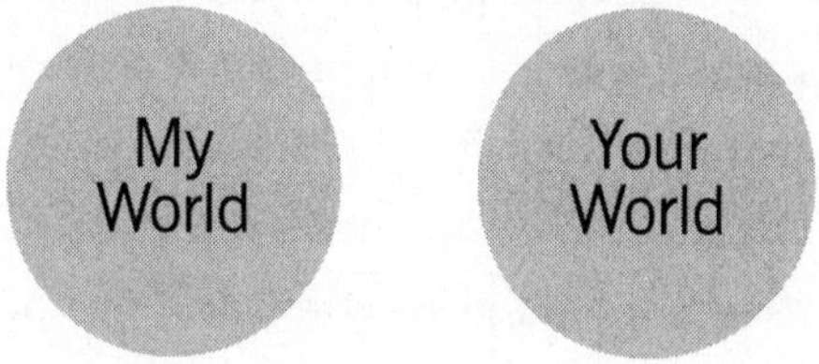

Though you are different from me—a "You" or "Thou"—I still respect, love, and value you.

Buber argued that in most of our human relationships we lose sight of others as separate from us. We treat people as objects, as an "It" (to use Buber's word). In the I-It relationship I treat you as a means to an end—as we might use a toothbrush or car.

What might that look like?

- I walk in and dump my work on my secretary without saying hello.
- I move people around on an organizational chart at a staff meeting as if they were objects or subhuman.
- I talk about people in authority as if they were subhuman.
- I treat Geri or our children as if they are not in charge of their own freedom, dreams, autonomy; I expect them to be the picture I have of them in my head.
- I am threatened when someone disagrees with my political views.
- I listen to my neighbors' problems and help them with chores around their house hoping they will attend the Christmas outreach at our church. They don't . . . and I move on to someone else.

The result of I-It relationships is that I get frustrated when people don't fit into my plans. The way I see things is "right." And if you don't see it as I do, you are not seeing things the "right" way. You are wrong.

Recognizing the uniqueness and separateness of every other person on earth is so pivotal to emotional maturity. We so easily demand that people view the world the way we do. We believe our way is *the* right way. Augustine defined sin as the state of being "caved in on oneself."

Instead of using our God-given power to orient ourselves to God and other human beings, we focus inward. For this reason when Dante, in his famous *Inferno*, arrived at the very pit of hell, ice dominated, not fire. The coldness spoke of the death, the inwardness, the coldness of sin. Satan was stuck, frozen in ice, and weeping from all six of his eyes.[8] C. S. Lewis described hell in *The Great Divorce* as a place where each person lives in isolation, millions of miles apart from one another, because they can't get along.[9]

I-Thou Relationships

True relationships, said Buber, can only exist between two people willing to connect across their differences. God fills that in-between space of an I-Thou relationship. God not only can be glimpsed in genuine dialogue but penetrates their in-between space. See the following diagram:

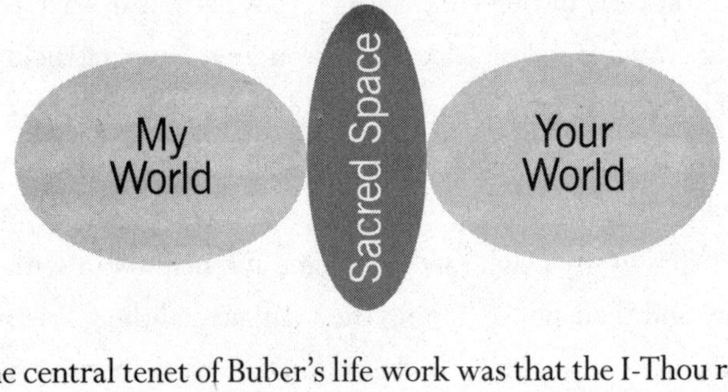

The central tenet of Buber's life work was that the I-Thou relationship between persons intimately reflects the I-Thou relationship humans have with God. Genuine relationship with any Thou shows traces of the "eternal Thou."[10] For this reason, when we love someone well as emotional adults, treating them as a Thou, not an It, it is such a powerful experience. When genuine love is released in a relationship, God's presence is manifest. The separate space between us becomes sacred space.

Jessica's relationship with her vice president was not what Buber would characterize as I-Thou. Jessica did not have the skills and emotional maturity to resolve this conflict maturely. She also did not have the ability to state her own feelings and beliefs without thinking adversarially. The end result was an isolation and coldness in her relationships at work that resembled hell more than heaven.

Emotional Maturity and Conflict

Practicing the "I-Thou" in our relationships leads to another aspect of emotional maturity. It informs our capacity to resolve conflicts maturely and negotiate solutions as we consider other people's perspectives.

At the heart of true peacemaking is acknowledgment, once again, that we are human beings made in God's image. Likeness to our Creator, along with Christ's example, puts us on paths that desire to live in the truth and not in pretense, even when that means a conflict may result. Yet most Christians I meet are poor at resolving conflict. There are at least two reasons for this: the first relates to wrong beliefs about peacemaking and the second relates to a lack of training and equipping in this area.

Ignoring Conflict—False Peacemaking

A tragically misinterpreted verse in the New Testament is Jesus' proclamation: "Blessed are the peacemakers, for they will be called children of God" (Matthew 5:9). Most people think that Jesus calls us in this verse to be pacifiers and appeasers who ensure that nobody gets upset. We are to keep the peace, ignoring difficult issues and problems, making sure things remain stable and serene.

When, out of fear, we avoid conflict and appease people, we are false peacemakers. For example:

Karl is upset about the behavior of his spouse who constantly comes home late after work. He says nothing. Why? He thinks he is being like Christ by not saying anything, although he does give her a cold shoulder. He is a false peacemaker.

Pam disagrees with her coworkers at lunch when they slander her boss. She is afraid to speak up. She goes along. *I don't want to kill the atmosphere by speaking up and disagreeing*, she thinks. She is a false peacemaker.

Bob goes to dinner with ten other people. He is tight financially, so he orders only a salad and appetizer. Meanwhile, the other nine order appetizers, steak, wine, and desserts. When the bill comes, someone says, "Let's divide up the bill equally. It will take forever to figure it out." Everyone agrees. Bob is dying on the inside but won't say anything. He is a false peacemaker.

Yolanda is engaged. She would like more time to rethink her decision but is afraid that her fiancé and his family will get angry. She goes through with the wedding. She is a false peacemaker.

Ellen loves her parents. They are both quite critical about how she raises her children. Each holiday is filled with tension. Ellen doesn't say anything because she doesn't want to hurt their feelings. She is a false peacemaker.

Sharon thinks her boyfriend is irresponsible but feels bad for him. *He has had so much pain already in his life*, she thinks. *How can I add to that?* So she backs down from telling him the truth about the way his behavior is slowly killing their relationship. The relationship dies a slow death. She is a false peacemaker.

The problem with all these scenarios is that the way of true peace will never come through pretending what is wrong is right! True peacemakers love God, others, and themselves enough to disrupt false peace. Jesus models this for us.

Embracing Conflict—The Path to True Peace

Conflict and trouble were central to the mission of Jesus. He disrupted the false peace all around him—in the lives of his disciples, the crowds, the religious leaders, the Romans, those buying and selling in the temple. He taught that true peacemaking disrupts false peace even in families: "Do not suppose that I have come to bring peace to the earth. I did not come to bring peace, but a sword. For I have come to turn 'a man against his father, a daughter against her mother, a daughter-in-law against her mother-in-law—a man's enemies will be the members of his own household'" (Matthew 10:34–36).

Why? You can't have the true peace of Christ's kingdom with lies and pretense. They must be exposed to the light and replaced with the truth. This is the mature, loving thing to do.

In the Beatitudes, Jesus explains to us the characteristics we need to display if we are to engage in true peacemaking—poverty of spirit, meekness, purity of heart, mercy, etc. (Matthew 5:3–11). He also follows the call to true peacemaking by stating that persecution will follow for those of us who follow him in this.

Nonetheless, unresolved conflicts are one of the greatest tensions in Christians' lives today. Most of us hate them. We don't know what to do with them. Instead of risking any more broken relationships, we prefer to ignore the difficult issues and settle for a "false peace," hoping against hope they will somehow go away. They don't. And we all learn, sooner or later, that you can't build Christ's kingdom on lies and pretense. Only the truth will do.

Learning Skills to Be True Peacemakers

Many of us believe loving well is learned automatically, that it is just a "feeling." We underestimate the depth of our bad habits and what is needed to sustain long-term, Christlike change in our relationships.

This belief led Geri and me, some years ago, to begin learning from a variety of sources, gathering exercises and tools, so people could learn how to practice the I-Thou with others. Our desire was to help followers of Jesus obey the command to love well. We wanted to move people from defensiveness, reactivity, and fear to openness, empathy, and vulnerability. We realized they needed to experience a new kingdom-way of relating that was outside their comfort zone. Practicing new skills like the ones that follow will cause a level of discomfort initially. They are easy to understand but difficult to implement. But by repeatedly practicing mature, godly behaviors, we have seen people freed from lifelong cycles of emotional immaturity.[11] They have served as a helpful link in moving people into becoming mothers and fathers of the faith.

We have collected a number of tools and exercises. The following, however, are a few we use in all kinds of relationships—our marriage, parenting, staff team, and wider church. They each provide, in their own way, a means to help people move out of an I-It way of relating to others into an I-Thou relationship. They each, in their own way, contribute to helping us follow Christ in becoming true peacemakers and lead us to love well.

Speaking and Listening

Speaking and listening is the essence of having an I-Thou relationship with another person. Everyone knows that communication is essential to all relationships. People take courses in high school, college, and beyond to learn more about it. Yet few people do it well. This is especially true under stress and in conflict.

For many of us, our childhood was an experience of invisibility. For this reason, simply being the speaker and expressing your wishes and hopes can be a very healing, powerful experience. Moreover, this process of speaking and listening creates a fresh connection between two people, slowing them both down.

I encourage you to see the following structure as a spiritual practice of meeting God through your time with this person. Ask God to help you be prayerfully present. Ask him to help you receive this person as if they were Jesus. How might Jesus Christ want to come to you through this person? Ask God to clear the noise from your mind so you can be still enough to enter the speaker's world.

AS THE SPEAKER

- Talk about *your* own thoughts, *your* own feelings (speak in the "I").
- Be brief. Use short sentences or phrases.
- Correct the other person if you believe he or she has missed something.
- Continue speaking until you feel you've been understood.
- When you don't have anything else to say, say, "That's all for now."

AS THE LISTENER

- Put your own agenda on hold. Be quiet and still as you would before God.
- Allow the other person to speak until he or she completes a thought.
- Reflect accurately the other person's words back to him or her. You have two options: paraphrase in a way the other person agrees is accurate or use his or her own words.
- When it appears the speaker is done, ask, "Is there more?"

- When they are done ask them: "Of everything you have shared, what is the most important thing you want me to remember?"

The purpose of repeating back what the other person says is to be sure you are hearing them accurately. This requires you as the listener to put your ideas and responses on hold. Validate the other person, letting them know that you really see and understand his or her world and point of view. You recognize they are different. Typical validation phrases might include: "That makes sense . . ." or "I can see that because . . ." or "I can understand that because . . ."

The Bill of Rights[12]

Respect is not a feeling. It is how we treat another person. Regardless of how we might feel about another human being, they are made in God's image and of infinite value and worth. The following Bill of Rights has remained posted on our refrigerator and in our lives for years. Next to each "right" are examples from our family's life.

BILL OF RIGHTS

Respect means I give myself and others the right to:

- *Space and privacy* (e.g., knocking on doors before entering, not opening one another's mail, respecting each other's needs for quiet and space);
- *Be different* (e.g., allowing preferences for food, movies, volume of music, and how we spend our time);
- *Disagree* (e.g., making room for each person to think and see life differently);
- *Be heard* (e.g., listening to each other's desires, opinions, thoughts, feelings, etc.);
- *Be taken seriously* (e.g., listening and being present to one another);

- *Be given the benefit of the doubt* (e.g., checking out assumptions rather than judging one another when misunderstandings arise);
- *Be told the truth* (e.g., counting on the truth when asking each other for information—from "Did you study for the test that you failed?" to "Why were you late coming home?");
- *Be consulted* (e.g., checking and asking when decisions will affect others);
- *Be imperfect and make mistakes* (e.g., leaving "room" for breaking things, forgetting things, letting each other down unintentionally, failing tests when we have studied, etc.);
- *Courteous and honorable treatment* (e.g., using words that don't hurt, asking before using, consulting when appropriate, treating each other as I-Thou's); and
- *Be respected* (e.g., taking one another's feelings into account)

Stop Mind Reading[13]

The ninth commandment reads: "You shall not give false testimony against your neighbor" (Exodus 20:16). To check out assumptions, or *stop mind reading,* as we like to call it, is a very simple but powerful tool that eliminates untold conflicts in relationships. It enables me to check out whether what I'm thinking or feeling about you is true. It enables me to clarify potential misunderstandings.

Every time I make an assumption about someone who has hurt or disappointed me without confirming it, I believe a lie about this person in my head. This assumption is a misrepresentation of reality. Because I have not checked it out with the other person, it is very possible I am believing something untrue. It is also likely I will pass that false assumption around to others.

When we leave reality for a mental creation of our own doing (hidden assumptions), we create a counterfeit world. When we do this, it can properly be said that we exclude God from our lives because

God does not exist outside of reality and truth. In doing so we wreck relationships by creating endless confusion and conflict. Jessica, in our opening illustration of this chapter, made all sorts of assumptions about why the boss failed to schedule her to meet with clients. The Bible has much to say about not taking on the role of judge to others (Matthew 7:1–5).

Following are some important steps in using this tool with another person:

- Reflect on something you suspect the other person thinks or feels but hasn't told you.
- Ask: "Do I have your permission to check out an assumption I am making?" or "May I have permission to read your mind?" (If he or she grants it, then you can proceed.)
- Say: "I think you think . . ." or "I assume you are thinking . . ." (fill in the blank). When you finish, ask them: "Is this correct?"
- Give the other person an opportunity to respond.

You can use this with employees, employers, spouses, friends, roommates, coworkers, parents, and children. The list is endless.

***Clarify Expectations*[14]**

Unmet and unclear expectations create havoc in our places of employment, classrooms, friendships, dating relationships, marriages, sports teams, families, and churches. For example:

- Of course you're coming to the family event. We're important to you, aren't we?
- I never knew the job involved all that. You never told me.

- My adult son should know I need him to come over and fix things. I shouldn't have to ask.
- I'm so disillusioned. I expected that a good marriage just happened naturally.
- I'm the only one caring for my aging parents. My siblings expect me to do everything.
- If she really cared about me, she would call me.
- In a good church everyone should be friendly and supportive when someone is hurting.

We expect other people to know what we want before we say it (especially if they are invested in the relationship). The problem with most expectations is that they are:

- unconscious—we have expectations we're not even aware of until someone disappoints us;
- unrealistic—we may have illusions about others. For example, we think a spouse, a friend, or a pastor will be available at all times to meet our needs;
- unspoken—we may have never told our spouse, friend, or employee what we expect, yet we are angry when our expectations are not met; and
- un-agreed upon—we may have had our own thoughts about what was expected, but it was never agreed upon by the other person.

Expectations are only valid when they have been mutually agreed upon. We all know the unpleasant experience of other people having expectations we never agreed to.

In order for expectations to be established, they must first be:

- conscious (I have to become aware of the expectations I have for the other person);
- realistic (I have to ask myself if my expectations regarding the other person are realistic);
- spoken (I have to speak my expectations clearly, directly, and respectfully to the other person); and
- agreed upon (in order for my expectations to be valid, the other person must be aware of and agree to them; otherwise it is simply a hope).

Think of an expectation you have of a spouse, friend, roommate, boss, family member, or coworker. Ask yourself: Am I conscious of what it is? Is it realistic? Has it been spoken? Have they also agreed to this? Initiate conversation with them and seek to come to a mutually agreed upon expectation. Now think of a person who may have an unconscious, unrealistic, unspoken, and un-agreed upon expectation of you. Sit down with them and discuss it. Seek to come to a mutually agreed upon expectation.

Allergies and Triggers

We are familiar with physical allergies to certain foods or pollen, but less familiar with our emotional allergies. An emotional allergy is an intense reaction to something in the present that reminds us, consciously or unconsciously, of an event from our history.

Examples of emotional allergies might be the response I used to have when Geri wanted to go away for weekends with her girlfriends in the early years of our marriage. I would have an allergic reaction. It reminded me of early feelings of my parents' emotional unavailability. The circumstances were very different, but the feeling was the same.

Another example is when Theresa sees her husband watching television instead of parenting the children with her and she gets very angry. She attacks and belittles him because he unconsciously reminds her of her father who left her home when she was seven years old, leaving her and her mom to fend for themselves.

As you can see, what happens most often in an allergic reaction is that we end up treating the person with whom we are in a relationship now as if they were someone from our past. We treat them like an It.

The PAIRS organization has developed a helpful exercise ("Healing the Ledger") we encourage people to take part in, either with another person or by themselves:[15]

- An emotional allergy you trigger in me is . . .
- When this allergy happens, what I think or tell myself is . . .
- When this allergy happens, I feel . . .
- When this allergy happens, what I think and feel about myself for even having these feelings is . . .
- When this happens inside me, the behavior you then see from me is . . .
- What this allergy relates to in my history is . . .
- When this allergy happens, you remind me of . . .
- The price we are paying for this in our relationship is . . .
- The words from the past that I needed, the words that I wish had been said to me, are . . .

Many people realize through this exercise how much they still live in the past and project it into present relationships. Once we begin to see this connection, we can begin making different choices that are more loving, emotionally adult responses rather than allergic reactions.

The Church as a New Culture

One of the greatest gifts we can give our world is to be a community of emotionally healthy adults who love well. This will take the power of God and a commitment to learn, grow, and break with unhealthy, destructive patterns that go back generations in our families and cultures—and in some cases, our Christian culture also.

Remember, Jesus formed a community with a small group from Galilee, a backward province in the ancient world. They were neither spiritually nor emotionally mature. Peter, the point leader, had a big problem with his mouth and was a bundle of contradictions. Andrew, his brother, was quiet and behind the scenes. James and John were given the name "sons of thunder" because they were aggressive, hot-headed, ambitious, and intolerant. Philip was skeptical and negative. He had limited vision. "We can't do that," summed up his faith when confronted by the problem of feeding the five thousand. Nathanael Bartholemew was prejudiced and opinionated. Matthew was the most hated person in Capernaum, working in a profession that abused innocent people. Thomas was melancholy, mildly depressive, and pessimistic. James, son of Alphaeus, and Judas, son of James, were nobodies. The Bible says nothing about them. Simon the Zealot was a freedom fighter and terrorist in his day. Judas, the treasurer, was a thief and a loner. He pretended to be loyal to Jesus before finally betraying him.

Most of them, however, did have one great quality: they were willing. That is all God asks of us.

In the next chapter, we will bring together all the principles we've considered throughout this book as we look at creating a "rule of life" to enable us to walk out all we have talked about so far. So stay with me.

Lord Jesus Christ, Son of God, have mercy on me. I am aware of how often I treat people as Its, as objects, instead of looking at them with the eyes and heart of Christ. I have unhealthy ways of relating that are deeply imbedded in me. Please change me. Make me a vessel to spread mature, steady, reliable love so that people with whom I come in contact sense your tenderness and kindness.

Deliver me from false peacemaking that is driven by fear. Lord Jesus, help me love well like you. Grow me, I pray, into an emotionally mature adult through the Holy Spirit's power. In Jesus' name, amen.

CHAPTER 8

Go the Next Step to Develop a "Rule of Life"

Loving Christ Above All Else

In *The Book of the Dun Cow,* Walter Wangerin creates a fantasy world of animals living in community around a chicken coop. Chauntecleer, the rooster of the coop, is the leader in charge of guiding the other animals who depend on him. The peace of the kingdom is broken when Ultimate Evil, in the form of Wyrm, threatens to destroy the coop community through the release of "licorice-length black and poisonous snakes." The community is held together by Chauntecleer as he crows the Daily Office, a gift he has received and disciplined out of the memory of his own history. He will eventually use force and violence to destroy Wyrm. But in this battle against evil, the community around the chicken coop is only able to fight because of their faith and the spiritual exercises they practice, all of which appear on the surface to be a waste of time against such enormous evil.

We, too, are called to order our lives around spiritual practices and disciplines—that is, a "Rule of Life," something utterly foreign to the world around us. It is a call to order our entire life in such a way that the love of Christ comes before all else. And in doing so, like Chauntecleer, the very quality of our lives holds the possibility of being transformed into a gift to our families, friends, coworkers, and communities.

The Ancient Treasure of a Rule of Life

Please don't be intimidated by the word *rule*. The word comes from the Greek for "trellis." A trellis is a tool that enables a grapevine to get off the ground and grow upward, becoming more fruitful and productive. In the same way, a Rule of Life is a trellis that helps us abide in Christ and become more fruitful spiritually.[1] A Rule of Life, very simply, is an intentional, conscious plan to keep God at the center of everything we do. It provides guidelines to help us continually remember God as the Source of our lives. It includes our unique combination of spiritual practices that provide structure and direction for us to intentionally pay attention and remember God in everything we do. The starting point and foundation of any Rule is a desire to be with God and to love him.

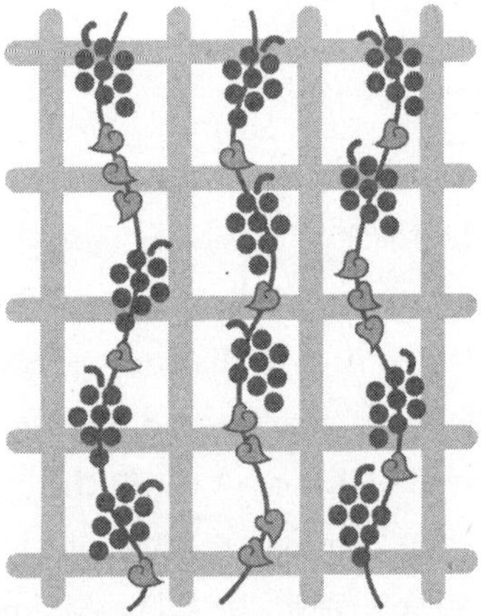

Very few people have a conscious plan for developing their spiritual lives. Most Christians are not intentional, but rather functional, like cars on autopilot. Our crammed schedules, endless to-do lists, demanding jobs and families, constant noise, information bombardment, and anxieties keep us speeding up, not slowing down. We have routines to manage other parts of our lives. For example, each morning we may get up, feed the cat, then make coffee, exercise, get dressed for work, and eat breakfast.

The reality, however, is that every person has an unconscious Rule for developing his or her spiritual life. We each have our values and ways of doing things. This may include, for example, attending a church on Sundays, participating in a small group, serving in a ministry, and/or ten minutes for prayer and Bible reading before going to bed.

However, our present spiritual practices are not enough to keep us afloat in the ocean of the beast, the Babylon of our twenty-first-century world. Fighting against such a strong current, without the anchor of a Rule of Life, is almost impossible. Eventually we find ourselves unfocused, distracted, and adrift spiritually.

Is it any wonder that most people live off other people's spirituality rather than taking the time to develop their own direct experience of God? Most Christians talk about prayer but don't pray. Most believe the Bible as the Word of God but have little idea what it says. Our goals for our children differ little from those of "pagans" who do not know God. Like the world, we, too, grade people based on their education, wealth, beauty, and popularity.

Nurturing a growing spirituality with depth in our present-day culture will require a thoughtful, conscious, intentional plan for our spiritual lives. To plan well, however, requires we go back to Daniel and early church history to consider the roots of this hidden treasure.

Daniel's "Rule of Life"

Nebuchadnezzar and his Babylonian armies, with their gods, conquered Jerusalem and carried off most of the city's inhabitants as slaves. One of those was a young teenager named Daniel. Cut off from his family, teachers, friends, food, culture, and language, Daniel was brought into the Babylonian court of the king and sent to the best university in the land. He studied a completely foreign and pagan way of viewing the world—history, mathematics, medicine, religion, literature. He learned about myths, astrology, sorcery, and magic—all things banned in Israel. Pagan priests and counselors educated him in their wisdom and religion. In Babylon's effort to assimilate Daniel, they even changed his name.

Babylon had one simple goal: to eliminate Daniel's distinctiveness as a God follower and absorb him into the values of their culture.

How did Daniel resist the enormous power of Babylon? He was not a cloistered monk living behind walls. He had heavy job responsibilities with people giving him orders. He had a minimal support system, and, I imagine, a very long to-do list each day.

What Daniel did have was a plan, a Rule of Life. He did not leave the development of his interior life to chance. He knew "going to church on Sundays, along with a fifteen-minute daily quiet time" would never be enough. He knew what he was up against. While we know little of the specifics, it is clear that he oriented his entire life around loving God. He renounced certain activities, such as eating the king's contaminated food (Daniel 1), and engaged in others, such as the Daily Office (Daniel 6). Daniel somehow fed himself spiritually and blossomed into an extraordinary man of God in this hostile environment. He knew resisting the beast of Babylon and thriving required a plan that would enable him to pay attention to God.

A Short History of the "Rule"

From the end of the third century to the fifth century, men and women withdrew from society into the deserts of Egypt, Syria, and Arabia to seek God. They wanted to free themselves from any distractions between them and God. A number of these monks later formed communities and organized their daily life around an agreed-upon plan consisting of work, prayer, and study of Scripture. They called this plan a Rule of Life.

Pachomius (AD 290–345) wrote the first known "Rule of Life" for his monastic communities in Egypt. Others followed with shorter and longer rules. Spiritual seekers from the Western church, most notably John Cassian, learned from these Desert Fathers and returned home to develop their own Rule of Life. Finally, this climaxed with Benedict (AD 480–547), who wrote the most widely known of monastic rules: the Rule of St. Benedict. The Rule of St. Benedict has not only shaped Western monasticism for the last fifteen hundred years but continues to guide tens of thousands of people around the world today from all church traditions.

The great, buried gift in a Rule of Life is its goal of regulating our entire lives in such a way that we truly prefer the love of Christ above all things.

Getting Started—The Big Picture

God has made each of us unique and different. Our goal is the same: union with God in Christ, transformation into his image, and the freeing of our hearts from anything that stands in the way of Christ living in and through us. How we get there will vary, depending on our personality, gift mix, temperament, geographic location, and particular calling from God. In addition, God will have different practices and emphases at different seasons and phases of our lives.

St. Francis of Assisi, for example, would spend weeks alone in his hermitage and then travel for weeks preaching the message of Jesus to anyone who would listen.

Catherine Doherty helped develop Madonna Houses where members spent three days each week alone with God in *poustinias* (the Russian word for "desert"), and four days out serving the people.[2]

While an infinite number of variations exist for a Rule of Life, I like to see a panoramic view of the big picture first. The following is a suggested list of twelve elements (which I explain in greater detail in the next section) to consider as you begin to develop your personal Rule of Life.

PRAYER

1. Scripture
2. Silence and Solitude
3. Daily Office (Prayer)
4. Study

REST

1. Sabbath
2. Simplicity
3. Play and Recreation

WORK/ACTIVITY

1. Service and Mission
2. Care for the Physical Body

RELATIONSHIPS

1. Emotional Health
2. Family
3. Community (Companions for the Journey)

You may want to add new elements (e.g., hospitality) and/or delete others. I have placed the elements under four broad categories—Prayer, Rest, Work, and Relationships. You may prefer to place Study, for example, under Rest or Work. Or you may favor placing Care for the Physical Body under the category of Rest. The choice is yours.

Developing an intentional Rule of Life takes trial and error. You will need to learn a great deal about yourself as well as about each foundational area mentioned above. For example, what kinds of spiritual practices bring you closer to God? Which drive you away from him? How can you discern the right combination for your particular Rule of Life?

My personal Rule of Life is a prayer document that constantly changes. It is a "live" work in progress—always. For example, due to my highly intuitive, conscientious temperament, I rarely write down my goals and commitments. For me, it can easily become a "have to" rather than a "want to" out of love for Christ.

Give yourself lots of time for the slow development of what works best for you. As you examine your life, you may notice many areas that need work. The best approach is to start with only one or two elements for the first few months. Then, after you experience some success with those, you will want to add another building block to your Rule. Or you may want to stay with the same element to work on over a long period of time. An example under Prayer might look something like this:

- Pray the Jesus prayer ("Lord Jesus Christ, Son of God, have mercy on me, a sinner") each day at work, several times a day.
- Take five minutes for silence at lunch three times a week.
- Practice the Ignatian prayer of examen three nights a week before going to bed.
- Fast for one meal every Wednesday during Lent.

If possible, find a companion for this journey. It may be a spiritual director, a mentor, a trusted friend, a mature Christian, or a small group. This will serve to keep you on track.

Don't be hard on yourself. St. Benedict writes at the beginning of his Rule of Life:

> Therefore we intend to establish a school for the Lord's service. . . . Do not be daunted immediately by fear and run away from the road that leads to salvation. It is bound to be narrow at the outset. But as we progress in this way of life and in faith, we shall run on the path of God's commandments, our hearts overflowing with the inexpressible delight of love.[3]

The Elements of a Rule of Life

Scripture

God speaks to us in and through the Word. Your plan during one season of your life may be reading through the Bible in a year or following the lectionary of Scripture readings from the Book of Common Prayer. In recent years I have moved to a reflective meditation on smaller portions of Scripture. *Lectio divina*, the ancient practice of contemplative reading, has become a weekly practice for me. This begins with reading a short passage of Scripture and then reflecting on it, allowing it to quietly work on you, as leaven in bread or water on a stone. The key is to read slowly, chewing over the words and allowing them to feed and transform you. This has led me also to prayerfully memorize small portions of Scripture each week.

Silence and Solitude

It is said of Abbot Agathon, one of the Desert Fathers: "For three years he carried a stone in his mouth until he learned to be silent." I think I could use a few good rocks myself! This is one of the most challenging and least practiced disciplines among Christians today. When we are silent, we come face to face with our addiction to being in control and always trying to fix things. As Dallas Willard says, "Silence is frightening because it strips us as nothing else does, throwing us upon the stark realities of our life. It reminds us of death, which will cut us off from this world and leave only us and God."[4]

I often integrate my times of silence into the Daily Office each day. I seek to take between five and twenty minutes, a few times a week, to "be still before the LORD and wait patiently for him" (Psalm 37:7). This continues to be the core of my cutting edge for growing in Christ.

Daily Office

As you read in the previous chapter, this spiritual practice has a rich history in both Scripture and church history. I need structure, spontaneity, and variety in the way I approach the Daily Office each day. For example, I've used Phyllis Tickle's *Divine Hours* to provide a skeletal structure for morning, midday, evening prayer, and compline, as well as the lectionary in the Book of Common Prayer. I love praying the psalms as the central part of my Daily Office. I also like having a devotional classic available as part of my morning Office each day. Many people pray with nature, setting aside time in silence to examine a leaf, a flower, a tree, the grass, the sky, giving God praise for his creation.[5]

Study

Few people recognize that spending intentional time reading and studying is a spiritual discipline. Yet these, too, are an important way of encountering God in new ways. One of the most striking features of the Rule of St. Benedict is that three hours a day were set aside for reading and reflection. He didn't say someone should be sent around the monastery to see if people were doing their work. But he did want someone to go around seeing if the monks were doing their reading and study! And this was in AD 550 when many of the monks had to learn to read first! Benedict understood an important principle:

growing, maturing Christians are always exploring, reading, and learning. Study may include digging into Scripture through inductive Bible study or other helpful tools, reading books, or attending workshops, classes, and seminars. Listening to teachings from people ahead of you spiritually may also be included here. Consider studying not simply for information but for the purpose of formation in Christ. Pray back to God what you are learning. I love to read so I could easily have moved Study under the category of Rest. Yet I can think of a few friends who would move Study immediately to Work.

Sabbath

Develop a rhythm of setting apart one twenty-four-hour period each week. Most of us work a five-day week but need another day for doing the activities of life that are "work" for us. That might include paying bills, fixing your car, working on your house or apartment, or finishing your homework if you are a student. Take some time to reflect on the four characteristics of biblical Sabbaths—stop, rest, delight, contemplate. What will it mean for you to stop and rest rather than use this as one more day to "get things done"? One key to my Sabbath is to purposely not think about New Life Fellowship Church, my place of work, nor look at emails or my answering machine. Waste time and don't look at the clock.

For those of us who work on Sundays, we need to carefully choose and stick with another day of the week. When our children were younger, I chose Saturdays (in most weeks) because my children were off from school on that day. Yes, my commitment had a significant impact on them and what I was willing to do! Getting out of New York City to the beauty of nature is an important part of our Sabbaths.

Trust God to run the universe without you. Begin to look at your weeks as preparing for Sabbath! Ask yourself, "What kinds of activities bring me joy and delight? What truly replenishes me?" Take a nap. Enjoy God. Do something totally different from your work. Finally, when you plan your vacation this coming year, apply the principle of Sabbath. See it as an extended Sabbath to the Lord. Plan, in advance, how you will balance the four elements of biblical Sabbaths—stopping, resting, delighting, and contemplating—during that time.

Simplicity

The primary issue here is to remove distractions and remain free from attachments. "Live as free of complications as possible [so] you're free to concentrate on simply pleasing the Master" (1 Corinthians 7:32 MSG). For this reason our children were not in three sports at one time while learning violin. We are careful to not buy every new electronic or technological item to help us save time. Instead of having five credit cards, we have one. Instead of cooking elaborate meals and having a house that is always perfectly clean, we have made choices to let that go. We are no longer involved in fifteen projects at the same time in our service for Christ. We do less, but do it better than before. We also got rid of our cable a number of years ago and opted for a DVD player instead.

The principle of tithing—that is, the giving away of 10 percent of our income—is also an important component to simplicity. It teaches us to let go of what is not necessary and to remain dependent on God as our security and source. Jesus himself taught that "where your treasure is, there your heart will be also" (Matthew 6:21). It is not a law as it was in the Old Testament, but it is a powerful principle that serves to keep us detached from the power of money. It also forces us to handle our money more carefully. We have been increasing our financial giving percentage each year as part of our Rule of Life and have seen God work miracle after miracle in providing for us. Get out of all unhealthy debt by attending a money-management seminar.

Play and Recreation

The key here is to engage in activities that are pure and healthy and that breathe life into you. Many Christians, in particular, are "fun deficient." We perhaps didn't grow up in families or environments that included play and recreation as a valid part of life. This requires planning and preparation. For example, many people, due to lack of planning, will watch a movie to relax, only to realize they feel worse spiritually, not better, when it is over.

Make no mistake: It is revolutionary to enjoy healthy pleasure. I believe this is a profound theological issue touching on how we view God, life, and creation. For this reason, each New Year's Eve our church hosts some sort of a non-alcoholic, intergenerational event that is fun! And I am convinced fun is one of Geri's spiritual gifts to the body of Christ. She summarizes part of her life mission as: "Life can be difficult, so have fun whenever you can to the glory of God." Remember Ecclesiastes 3:4: there is "a time to weep and a time to laugh, a time to mourn and a time to dance."

Service and Mission

The question here is, in what way(s) is God inviting me to serve him at this stage of my journey? In what way can I use my time, talents, resources, and gifts for others? What passions and desires has God placed within me? Every church and community has numerous opportunities to serve. This may also include volunteering to feed the homeless and hungry, looking for a person in a lonely social situation and finding ways to include her in your life, or mentoring a young person or new believer in Christ. Under this category I would include commitment to the poor and marginalized; to bridging racial, cultural, and economic barriers; to working for justice and the environment; to world missions. For some of us, our challenge is to do something for others outside of our comfort zone. For others, like me, the issue is limits. How can I embrace my God-given limits and not go beyond what he is asking me to do?

Care for the Physical Body

Many of us take poor care of the bodies God has given us. Yet caring for our bodies can be as spiritual as prayer or worship. What might you want to include in your Rule of Life about exercise? How many times a week will you exercise? What will you do? What about your work habits? Are you eating a balanced, healthy, nutritious diet? What is the effect of certain foods on your energy level? Do you get adequate rest and sleep? Scripture says sleep is a gift of God (Psalm 127:2). When is the last time you went to the doctor for an annual checkup?

What might be one area you want to include in your Rule of Life now? It may be that you want to begin to listen to your body and how God might be speaking to you through it. For example, a headache, knot in your stomach, inability to sleep, and the resulting exhaustion may be God calling you to slow down or to change directions. Listening to our bodies can be an important way to listen to God.

When we care for our bodies, we acknowledge the holiness of all of life and honor the fact that God is within us.

Emotional Health

This has been part of my Rule of Life for the last twenty-plus years. For a couple of years, it was as simple as paying attention to my feelings and journaling them to God a few times a week. Then I would ask God how he might be speaking to me through them.

It may be that you recognize you have a lot of unprocessed grief due to losses from your past. You may want to make that part of your plan over the next year. This may include reading, journaling, meeting with a trusted friend or counselor, or going on a personal "grief retreat." Part of your plan may include joining a small group that works through this book slowly. You may want to join a group that focuses on practical relational skills such as resolving conflict well or healthy communication practices.

Growth in understanding your sexuality, both as a single or married person, would come under this element. Geri and I continue to mature in this part of our Rule of Life. We read broadly and attend training events or courses that challenge us to grow in new ways. But like anything else, this, too, takes intentionality.

Family

This element applies both to people married and single. Marriage, parenting, and our relationship with our family of origin are all crucial discipleship issues. For example, when our four daughters were younger, what did *I* need to learn to grow in my parenting skills? And what did I want *them* to learn before they transitioned into young adulthood? It is very easy for me to fall into passive patterns. What can I do to invest in our marriage this coming year? One of Geri's passions is the outdoors—hiking, camping, and enjoying the beauty of God's creation. I am content in a library or bookstore. While I enjoy our time outdoors together, it requires a plan to get me started.

Geri and I are best friends. We love our marriage. Yet we continue to search out opportunities, separately and together, to build into our relationship. If you are single, what is your plan to relate to your parents (or stepparents), your siblings? What kind of relationship would you like to have with them? What are one or two steps you can take to get there?

Community (Companions for the Journey)

Under this heading in your personal Rule of Life, you will want to ask yourself about the kind of companions you need for this next stage of your journey. If you are not part of a church, for example, you will want to ask God for direction and investigate places where you can both give and receive. What other support networks might you need inside or outside your local church? We recommend that everyone in our church connect relationally through a small group. Geri and I lead a small group in our home. We enjoy these relationships, but I am their pastor! So in my case, for example, I meet regularly with two of the elders of our church about my spiritual life. I also have a long-term mentor who is older and wiser in God. While he lives in another state, we exchange phone calls and occasional visits. I also see a spiritual director every month or two. This provides a time for peaceful listening with another, more experienced person about how God is moving in my life. Again, be open and be creative on how God might want you to walk this out during this season of your journey.

Reread or rethink your Rule of Life regularly. St. Augustine wanted his read once a week! Minimally, you will want to review and revisit your Rule of Life every year.

Again, begin slowly working on only one or two elements at a time. Be willing to make mistakes, try again, and learn new things. You may want to try sketching out a Rule of Life for a four-week period such as Advent or during Lent.

Remember, as Benedict wrote fifteen hundred years ago, "Your way of acting should be different from the world's way. The love of Christ must come before all else." Keep that before you and you won't go too far off.

Broader Applications of a "Rule of Life"

The focus of this chapter has been on the development and application of a Rule of Life for your personal, interior growth in God. That, for me, is one very clear application of a rich treasure in church history that is available to us today. The following are three other significant applications to consider.

The Local Church

Every church has values, practices, and habits they take for granted. Each is unique and has her way of doing things. People join a church and become part of her family. In some ways it is correct to say that every church has a Rule of Life. The problem is that it is often unconscious. The challenge is to identify and authenticate what that is and be clear about it. That definition provides boundaries for the church community in a way that provides safety and clarity. Then we can invite people to follow Christ under this particular broad Rule of Life. Broad categories for a church then might include:

- history and particular gifts of the local church (mission statement);
- worship;
- equipping;
- small groups and community;
- authority;
- Lord's Supper and baptism;
- hospitality;
- new members;
- the poor and marginalized;
- serving the larger community;
- emotional health; and
- world missions.

Then, within the broad Rule of our community, we invite each member to continually work on the specifics of their personal Rule of Life.

Task Group or Small Group

Task groups, such as worship teams or mission groups, will often agree on a certain Rule of Life as a group for following Christ—either orally or in writing. A small group, for an agreed-upon period of time, may commit together to certain practices and habits to follow Christ.

The Family

A few people have been led to apply the development of a Rule of Life for their family. Geri and I have not done that, but I can see how clarifying what we do as a family could release great energy and focus. It sure sounds like a great idea!

Live Faithfully the Life God Has Given You

God has a different path for each of us.

My prayer is that you would be faithful to yours. It is a tragedy to live someone else's life.

I know. I did it for years.

I would like to close with a story from Carlo Carretto (1910–1988), a member of the Little Brothers of Jesus community, who lived among Muslims in North Africa for ten years. He wrote that one day he was traveling by camel in the Sahara desert and came across about fifty men laboring in the hot sun to repair a road. When Carlo offered them water, to his surprise, he saw among them his friend Paul, another member of his Christian community.

Paul had been an engineer in Paris working on the atomic bomb for France. God had called him to leave everything and become a Little Brother in North Africa. At one point Paul's mother came asking Carlo for help understanding her son's life.

"I have made him an engineer," she said. "Why can't he work as an intellectual in the church? Wouldn't that be more useful?"

Paul was content to pray and to disappear for Christ in the Sahara Desert.

Carlo then went on to ask himself: "What is my place in the great evangelizing work of the Church?" He answers his own question:

> My place was there—among the poor. Others would have the task of building, feeding, preaching. . . . The Lord asked me to be a poor man among the poor, a worker among workers. It is difficult to judge others . . . but the one truth we must cling desperately to is love.
>
> It is love that justifies our actions. Love must initiate all we do.
>
> If out of love Brother Paul has chosen to die on a desert road, then he is justified. If out of love . . . others build schools and hospitals, they are justified. If out of love . . . scholars spend their lives among books, they are justified. . . . The Lord asked me to be a poor man among the poor, a worker among workers. . . .
>
> I can only say, "Live love, let love invade you. It will never fail to teach you what you must do."[6]

In the same way, it is my prayer that God give you the courage to faithfully live your unique life in Christ. And may love invade you. It will never fail to teach you what you must do.

Lord, after reading this chapter, I just need to be with you—for a long time. I know that at other times I have rushed and cut you short, but I can see there are a lot of things in me that need to change. Let this time be different, Lord. Show me what one small step I can take to begin to build a life around you. Help me pay attention to your voice. By faith, I obey, trusting that even small changes will grow into powerful winds of the Holy Spirit blowing through and overtaking all of the areas of my life. Thank you. In Jesus' name, amen.

APPENDIX A

Excerpt from *Emotionally Healthy Spirituality Day by Day*

Introduction

I wrote *Emotionally Healthy Spirituality Day by Day* for churches doing The EHS Course (*The Emotionally Healthy Spirituality Course*). We call the book the core of The EHS Course because it slows us down to develop our own relationship with Jesus, introducing us to silence, solitude, and rhythms in a world that rarely stops.

Each of the eight weeks of Daily Offices is based on a corresponding chapter from this book. The two sample Offices included here are based on Chapter 1, "The Problem of Emotionally Unhealthy Spirituality."

DAY 1: MORNING/MIDDAY OFFICE

Silence, Stillness, and Centering before God (2 minutes)

Scripture Reading: Mark 11:15 – 17

On reaching Jerusalem, Jesus entered the temple courts and began driving out those who were buying and selling there. He overturned the tables of the money changers and the benches of those selling doves, and would not allow anyone to carry merchandise through the temple courts. And as he taught them, he said, "Is it not written: 'My house will be called a house of prayer for all nations'? But you have made it 'a den of robbers.'"

Devotional

Jesus' intense anger and overturning of the tables in the temple courts ought to make us gasp. He knows that if we don't get to God, invaluable treasures will be lost or obscured. We lose the space where we experience God's unfailing love and amazing forgiveness. We lose an eternal perspective on what is important and what is not. We lose compassion. We gain the world but lose our souls (Mark 8:36 – 37).

Be Free for God

I have a need
of such clearance
as the Savior effected in the temple of Jerusalem
a riddance of clutter
of what is secondary
that blocks the way

to the all-important central emptiness
which is filled
with the presence of God alone.
—Jean Danielou[5]

Question to Consider

How would you describe "what is secondary" in your life, the thing that might be "blocking the way" to experiencing God?

Prayer

Lord, help me to see how much I lose when I lose you. My perspective on my life and all of life gets distorted when I don't make space for you, obscuring your love for me. Your love is better than life, and truly I long for more tastes of that love. In Jesus' name, amen.

Conclude with Silence (2 minutes)

DAY 1: MIDDAY/EVENING OFFICE

Silence, Stillness, and Centering before God (2 minutes)

Scripture Reading: 1 Samuel 15:22 – 23

But Samuel replied:

"Does the LORD delight in burnt offerings and sacrifices
as much as in obeying the LORD?
To obey is better than sacrifice,
and to heed is better than the fat of rams.
For rebellion is like the sin of divination,
and arrogance like the evil of idolatry.
Because you have rejected the word of the LORD,
he has rejected you as king."

Devotional

Saul, the first king of Israel, did not know much about silence or listening to God. Like David, he was a gifted, anointed, successful military/political leader. Yet unlike David, we never see him seeking to be with God. In this passage, Samuel the prophet reprimands Saul for doing many religious acts (i.e., offering burnt offerings and sacrifices) but not quieting himself enough to listen, or "to heed" God (v. 22).

> We all must take the time to be silent and to contemplate, especially those who live in big cities like London and New York, where everything moves so fast. . . . I always begin my prayer in silence, for it is in the silence of the heart that God speaks. God is the friend of silence—we need to listen to God because it's not what we say but what He says to us and through us that matters. Prayer feeds the soul—as blood is to the body, prayer is to the soul—and it brings you closer to God. It also gives you a clean and pure heart. A clean heart can see God, can speak to God, and can see the love of God in others.
>
> —Mother Teresa[6]

Question to Consider

How could you make more room in your life for silence in order to listen to God?

Prayer

Unclutter my heart, O God, until I am quiet enough to hear you speak out of the silence. Help me in these few moments to stop, to listen, to wait, to be still, and to allow your presence to envelop me. In Jesus' name, amen.

Conclude with Silence (2 minutes)

APPENDIX B

Defining Emotional Health and Contemplative Spirituality

A person can grow emotionally healthy without Christ. In fact, I can think of a number of non-Christian people who are more loving, balanced, and civil than many church members I know (including myself!). At the same time, a person can be deeply committed to contemplative spirituality, even to the point of taking a monastic vow, and remain emotionally unaware and socially maladjusted.

How can this be?

Few Christians committed to contemplative spirituality integrate the inner workings of emotional health. At the same time few people committed to emotional health integrate contemplative spirituality. Both are powerful, life-changing emphases when engaged in separately. But *together* they offer nothing short of a spiritual revolution, transforming the hidden places deep beneath the surface. When emotional health and contemplative spirituality are interwoven together in an individual's life, a small group, a church, a university fellowship, or a community, people's lives are dramatically transformed. They work as an antidote to heal the symptoms of emotionally unhealthy spirituality described in chapter 1.

Defining Emotional Health and Contemplative Spirituality

Emotional health is concerned with such things as:[1]

- naming, recognizing, and managing our own feelings;
- identifying with and having active compassion for others;
- initiating and maintaining close and meaningful relationships;
- breaking free from self-destructive patterns;
- being aware of how our past impacts our present;
- developing the capacity to express our thoughts and feelings clearly;
- respecting and loving others without having to change them;
- asking for what we need, want, or prefer clearly, directly, and respectfully;
- accurately self-assessing our strengths, limits, and weaknesses and freely sharing them with others;
- learning the capacity to resolve conflict maturely and negotiate solutions that consider the perspectives of others;
- integrating our spirituality with our sexuality in a healthy way;
- grieving well.

Contemplative spirituality, on the other hand, is concerned with slowing down to be with God, focusing on such practices as:[2]

- awakening and surrendering to God's love in any and every situation;
- positioning ourselves to hear God and remember his presence in all we do;

- communing with God, allowing him to fully indwell the depth of our being;
- practicing silence, solitude, and a life of unceasing prayer;
- resting attentively in the presence of God;
- understanding our earthly life as a journey of transformation toward ever-increasing union with God;
- finding the true essence of who we are in God;
- loving others out of a life of love for God;
- developing a balanced, harmonious rhythm of life that enables us to be aware of the sacred in all of life;
- adapting historic practices of spirituality that are applicable today;
- allowing our Christian lives to be shaped by the rhythms of the Christian calendar rather than the culture; and
- living in committed community that passionately loves Jesus above all else.

The combination of emotional health and contemplative spirituality addresses what I believe to be the missing piece in much of contemporary Christianity. When practiced together, they unleash the Holy Spirit inside us in order that we might know experientially the power of an authentic life in Christ.

Both Are Needed

The following[3] illustrates well how contemplation and emotional health are different and yet overlap. In a very real sense, both are necessary for loving God, loving ourselves, and loving others. For this reason, these form the outer circle around the diagram.

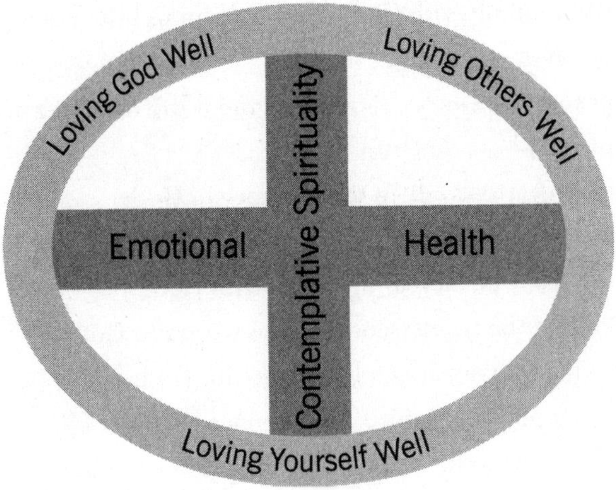

The greatest commandments, Jesus said, are that we love God with all our heart, mind, strength, and soul and that we love our neighbor as ourselves (Matthew 22:37–40). Contemplation has been defined in many ways throughout history. Brother Lawrence called it "the pure loving gaze that finds God everywhere." Francis de Sales described it as "the mind's loving, unmixed, permanent attention to the things of God." For this reason, contemplation is the vertical line going upward toward God that cuts through emotional health. We are not simply about experiencing a better quality of life through emotional health. Awareness of and responding to the love of God is at the heart of our lives. We are first and foremost about God revealed in Christ.

At the same time, contemplation is not simply about our relationship with God. It is ultimately the way we see and treat people and the way we look at ourselves. Our relationship with God and relationship with others are two sides of the same coin. If our contemplation or "loving union with God" does not result in a loving union with people, then it is, as 1 John 4:7–21 says so eloquently, not true. Moreover, it is about seeing God in *all* of life, not just in what we might consider the spiritual aspects of life.

Emotional health, on the other hand, concerns itself primarily with loving others well. It connects us to our interior life, making possible the seeing and treating of each individual as worthy of respect, created in the image of God and not just as an object to use. For this reason, self-awareness—knowing what is going on inside of us—is indispensable to emotional health and loving well. In fact, the extent to which we love and respect ourselves is the extent to which we will be able to love and respect others.

At the same time, emotional health is not only about ourselves and our relationships. It also impacts our image of God, including our ability to hear God's voice and discern his will.

Allow me to share a personal story that illustrates how the tools of *both* emotional health and contemplative spirituality are essential to truly break free from our dysfunctions and illusions. I worked for several years on understanding the impact my family history had on my present relationships. While in an advanced program in marriage and family, my class was given the assignment of interviewing every living member of our families. The goal was to put together the jigsaw puzzle of our family history, to uncover any secrets, and to understand ourselves more accurately within the context of our families. God used that experience to make me aware of numerous generational patterns that negatively impacted my relationship with Geri, our daughters, my coworkers at New Life Fellowship, and myself. By the power of the Holy Spirit, I was able to make specific positive changes for Christ.

Two years later, during a lengthy time of silence and solitude (one of the gifts of contemplative spirituality), I found myself feeling angry at God. I not only yelled at God, I cursed him! I called him a liar. "Your yoke is not easy and light!" I screamed aloud. (Don't worry. I was by myself.) And even though I felt angry, I wondered where the anger was coming from.

This led me to weeks of meditating and pondering Jesus' invitation:

"Come to me, all you who are weary and burdened, and I will give you rest. . . . For my yoke is easy and my burden is light" (Matthew 11:28, 30). Over time, I realized that underneath my preaching countless sermons on God's grace and love, I perceived God as a perfectionist—a demanding taskmaster. But was it really him? Or was it part of my past I was unwilling to look at?

I came to realize during this time of solitude that the god I was serving reflected my earthly parents more than the God of Scripture. "I am never enough," was how I often felt in my family growing up. Almost unconsciously, I had transferred that perspective to my heavenly Father. No matter what I did, all I could hear God saying to me was, "It is never enough, Pete." I had never made that connection before.

I was stunned!

My point is this: There are powerful breakthroughs that can take place deep below the surface of our lives when the riches of both contemplative spirituality *and* emotional health are joined together. I have seen this again and again in my own life and in the lives of countless others. Together, they form a refining fire in which God's love burns away what is false and unreal and his fierce and purifying love sets us free to live in the truth of Jesus.

APPENDIX C

The Prayer of Examen

An Adaptation of St. Ignatius Loyola's Examen

A classic spiritual practice developed by Ignatius Loyola (1491–1556) is called the "Prayer of Examen." It is a prayerful reflection of your experience with Jesus over a specific time period. The goal is simple: increased awareness and attentiveness to the presence of God in your daily life.

While it is normally done at the end of each day, it can be prayed at any time. Get in a comfortable position and still yourself. Recall you are in the presence of God, inviting the Holy Spirit to guide you as you review the events of your day. Walk through the events in your day (or yesterday's events if it is morning). Imagine yourself watching your day on a fast-forwarded DVD with Jesus. Let Jesus stop the DVD at any part of the day so you might reflect on it.

Notice those times when you were aware of God's presence, when you felt you were moving toward God. How did you feel when you were open and responsive to God's guidance? Give God thanks for those times.

End with prayer for grace to be more aware of God's presence.

Close the time with a prayer of thanks for this time with God.

Notes

Introduction

1. This process of succession is explained fully in the book *The Emotionally Healthy Leader*, chapter 9, "Endings and New Beginnings."
2. Saint John of the Cross, quoted in Kieran Kavanaugh, ed., *John of the Cross: Selected Writings, Classics of Western Spirituality* (Mahwah, NJ: Paulist Press, 1987), 292.

CHAPTER 1: The Problem of Emotionally Unhealthy Spirituality

1. Bill Bright, "The Four Spiritual Laws" (New Life Publications, 1995), 12.
2. Thomas Merton, *Thoughts in Solitude* (Boston: Shambhala Publications, 1956), 13.
3. Quoted in Ron Sider, *The Scandal of the Evangelical Conscience: Why Are Christians Living Just Like the Rest of the World?* (Grand Rapids: Baker Books, 2005), 13.
4. Ibid., 17–27.
5. Ibid., 28–29.
6. Parker Palmer, *Let Your Life Speak: Listening for the Voice of Vocation* (San Francisco: Jossey-Bass, 2000), 30–31.
7. Quoted in Rowan Williams, *Where God Happens: Discovering Christ in One Another* (Boston: Shambhala Publications, 2005), 14.

CHAPTER 2: Know Yourself That You May Know God

1. Meister Eckhart, *The Complete Mystical Works of Meister Eckhart*, ed. and trans. Maurice O'C. Walshe (New York: Crossroad Publishing, 2009), 251.
2. John Calvin, *Institutes of the Christian Religion, Volume 1* (Grand Rapids: Eerdmans Publishing Company, 1957), 37.
3. Daniel Goleman, *Emotional Intelligence: Why It Can Matter More than IQ* (New York: Bantam Books, 1995), 199–200.

4. For a great introduction to Ignatius's teachings on discernment and our emotions, see Thomas H. Green, *Weeds Among the Wheat: Discernment: Where Prayer and Action Meet* (Notre Dame, IN: Ave Maria Press, 1984). See also the sermon series "Discovering the Will of God" available at www.emotionallyhealthychurch.com.
5. Dan Allender and Tremper Longman III, *The Cry of the Soul* (Dallas: Word, 1994), 24–25.
6. Quoted in James Finley, *Merton's Palace of Nowhere: A Search for God Through Awareness of the True Self* (Notre Dame, IN: Ave Maria Press, 1978), 54.
7. M. Scott Peck, *A World Waiting to Be Born: Civility Rediscovered* (New York: Bantam Books, 1993), 112–113.
8. Richard Ben Cramer, *Joe DiMaggio: The Hero's Life* (New York: Simon and Schuster, 2000), 519.
9. *Leadership* (Summer 2002), 52–53.
10. M. Robert Mulholland Jr., *The Deeper Journey: The Spirituality of Discovering Your True Self* (Downers Grove, IL: InterVarsity Press, 2006). See chapters 2 and 3 for a detailed analysis of these consequences.
11. I am using the words *true self* in a way similar to M. Robert Mulholland Jr. (see previous endnote). In footnote 1 of chapter 2 in *The Deeper Journey*, Mulholland states: "Self is used here not in the contemporary sense of the psychological 'self,' an implicitly reductionistic term, but in the larger biblical sense of personhood framed within the context of a life lived in relationship with God, in community with others and as part of creation."
12. Michael Kerr and Murray Bowen, *Family Evaluation: The Role of the Family as an Emotional Unit That Governs Individual Behavior and Development* (New York: Norton Press, 1988), 97–109.
13. Merton, *New Seeds of Contemplation*, 35.
14. Parker Palmer, *A Hidden Wholeness: The Journey Toward an Undivided Life* (San Francisco: Jossey-Bass, 2004), 80–84.
15. Ibid., 114–115.
16. Benedicta Ward, trans., *The Sayings of the Desert Fathers* (Kalamazoo, MI: Cistercian Study Series, 1975), 139.
17. Dietrich Bonhoeffer, *Life Together* (New York: HarperCollins, 1954), 78.
18. Palmer, *A Hidden Wholeness*, 57.
19. John Cassian, *The Conferences*, trans. Boniface Ramsey (Mahwah, NJ: Paulist Press, 1997), 87–89.
20. Coleman Barks, trans., *The Illuminated Rumi* (New York: Doubleday, 1997), 80.

21. Bowen's material is summed up in Harriet Lerner, *The Dance of Anger: A Woman's Guide to Changing the Pattern of Intimate Relationships* (New York: Harper and Row, 1985), 34.
22. Chuck Yeager and Leo Janos, *Yeager: An Autobiography* (New York: Bantam Books, 1985), 154.
23. Ibid., 165.
24. Thomas Merton, *The Ascent to Truth* (New York: Harcourt Brace and Co., 1951), 238.

CHAPTER 3: Going Back in Order to Go Forward

1. See Judith Rich Harris, *The Nurture Assumption: Why Children Turn Out the Way They Do* (New York: Touchstone, 1998). The "nurture" proponents argue that what children learn in early years about relationships and rules for living life sets the pattern for the rest of their lives. The "nature" proponents look at genetic factors and biology. Judith Harris has argued that it is neither. Rather, she states that our peer groups of childhood and adolescence shape our behavior and attitudes for life.
2. See Rodney Clapp, *Families at the Crossroads: Beyond Traditional and Modern Options* (Downers Grove, IL: InterVarsity Press, 1993) and Ray Anderson and Dennis Guernsey, *On Being Family: A Social Theology of the Family* (Grand Rapids: Eerdmans, 1985), 158.
3. For an excellent explanation and description of the five levels of the Beaver system of classifying families, see Maggie Scarf, *Intimate Worlds: Life Inside the Family* (New York: Random House, 1995).

CHAPTER 4: Journey through the Wall

1. Janet O. Hagberg and Robert A. Guelich, *The Critical Journey: Stages in the Life of Faith* (Salem, WI: Sheffield Publishing Company, 2005).
2. Ibid., 9.
3. Merton, *The Ascent to Truth*, 188–189.
4. For a concise, readable summary of God's goal for the destination of our journeys, see David G. Benner, *Sacred Companions: The Gift of Spiritual Friendship and Direction* (Downers Grove, IL: InterVarsity Press, 2002). For a sermon series I preached on Journeying through the Wall, go to www.emotionallyhealthychurch.com.
5. St. John of the Cross, *Dark Night of the Soul*, trans. E. Allison Peers (New York: Image, Doubleday Publishing), 1959.
6. Ibid., 36–90.

7. Gerald G. May, *The Dark Night of the Soul: A Psychiatrist Explores the Connection Between Darkness and Spiritual Growth* (New York: HarperCollins, 2004), 90.
8. St. John of the Cross, *The Dark Night of the Soul*, 106, 115.
9. This is the key teaching from James 1:3–4 when he writes about rejoicing in trials: "The testing of your faith develops perseverance. Let perseverance finish its work so that you may be mature and complete, not lacking anything." The Greek word translated "not lacking anything" carries with it the notion of God imparting or infusing something of his character into us through the process of difficulties and severe trials.
10. St. John of the Cross, *The Dark Night of the Soul*, 113, 117.
11. Karl Barth, *Church Dogmatics*, vol. 3, *The Doctrine of Reconciliation: Part One* (Edinburgh: T. & T. Clark, 1956), 231–234.
12. G. K. Chesterton, *St. Francis of Assisi* (New York: Image Books, Doubleday, 1957), 67.
13. Helen Bacovcin, trans., *The Way of a Pilgrim and The Pilgrim Continues His Way* (New York: Doubleday, 1978).
14. Merton, *The Ascent of Truth.*
15. Adapted from Robert Barron, *And Now I See: A Theology of Transformation* (New York: Crossroad Publishing, 1998), 148.
16. Wayne Muller, *Sabbath: Finding Rest, Renewal, and Delight in Our Busy Lives* (New York: Bantam, 1999), 187–188.
17. Everett Ferguson and Abraham J. Malherbe, trans., introduction and notes, *Gregory of Nyssa: The Life of Moses* (New York: Paulist Press, 1978), 94–97.
18. See G. K. Chesterton, *Saint Thomas Aquinas: "The Dumb Ox"* (New York: Image Books, Doubleday, 1956), 116, along with http://en.wikipedia.org/wiki/Thomas_Aquinas.
19. Basil Pennington, *Thomas Merton, Brother Monk: The Quest for True Freedom* (New York: Continuum Publishing, 1997), 15–16.
20. Richard Rohr, *Adam's Return: The Five Promises of Male Initiation* (New York: Crossroad Publishing, 2004).
21. Ibid., 152–166.
22. Merton, *New Seeds*, 203.

CHAPTER 5: Enlarge Your Soul through Grief and Loss

1. John E. Hartley, *The Book of Job: The New International Commentary on the Old Testament* (Grand Rapids: Eerdmans, 1988), 82–83.
2. Froma Walsh and Monica McGoldrick, eds., *Living Beyond Loss: Death in the Family* (New York: W. W. Norton & Company, 1991), 105–106.

3. Gerald L. Sittser, *A Grace Disguised: How the Soul Grows Through Loss* (Grand Rapids: Zondervan, 1995), 33–34.
4. For a partial list, see James E. Loder, *The Logic of the Spirit: Human Development in Theological Perspective* (San Francisco: Jossey-Bass Publishers, 1998), 183–184.
5. Sheila Carney, "God Damn God: A Reflection on Expressing Anger in Prayer," *Biblical Theology Bulletin*, 13, no. 4 (October 1983), 116.
6. See Lori Gordon with Jon Frandsen, *Passage to Intimacy* (self-published, revised version, 2000), 40. I am grateful to PAIRS for this insight.
7. Robert Moore and Douglas Gillette, *King, Warrior, Magician, Lover: Rediscovering the Archetypes of the Mature Masculine* (San Francisco: HarperCollins, 1990), 23–47.
8. See Timothy Fry, ed., *RB 1980: The Rule of St. Benedict in English* (Collegeville, MN: 1981), 32–38.
9. For a fuller explanation of the distinction between a prayer life characterized by "Gimme, gimme, gimme" and a prayer life that is relational, see Larry Crabb, *The Papa Prayer: The Prayer You've Never Prayed* (Nashville: Integrity, 2006), 34–35.

CHAPTER 6: Discover the Rhythms of the Daily Office and Sabbath

1. For an example, see http://www.lambtononline.com/winter_storms.
2. See the excellent book by Richard Swenson, *Margin: How to Create the Emotional, Physical, Financial, and Time Reserves You Need* (Colorado Springs: NavPress, 1992).
3. Countless good resources are available on spiritual disciplines. See Adele Ahlberg Calhoun, *Spiritual Disciplines Handbook: Practices That Transform Us* (Downers Grove, IL: InterVarsity Press, 2005); Tony Jones, *The Sacred Way: Spiritual Practices for Everyday Life* (Grand Rapids: Zondervan, 2005); and of course the classic by Richard Foster, *Celebration of Discipline* (New York: Harper and Row, 1986).
4. Robert Barron, *And Now I See*, 37. I am thankful to Barron for the insight that the core sin of the garden is the sin that leads us to take things into our own hands.
5. Ibid., 38.
6. James Loder, *The Logic of the Spirit: Human Development in Theological Perspective* (San Francisco: Jossey-Bass Publishers, 1998).
7. Phyllis Tickle, *The Divine Hours: Prayers for Autumn and Wintertime* (New York: Doubleday, 2000), xii.
8. Timothy Fry, *RB 1980*, 65.

9. A very readable and accessible three-volume series for the Daily Office is Phyllis Tickle, *The Divine Hours: Prayers for Autumn and Wintertime: A Manual for Prayer* (New York: Doubleday, 2001), *The Divine Hours: Prayers for Springtime: A Manual for Prayer* (New York: Doubleday, 2001), and *The Divine Hours: Prayers for Summertime: A Manual for Prayer* (New York: Doubleday, 2000). I know many people who also use Norman Shawchuck and Rueben P. Job, *A Guide to Prayer for All Who Seek God* (Nashville: Upper Room Publishing, 2003) and The Northumbria Community, *Celtic Daily Prayer* (San Francisco: HarperCollins, 2002). I also like to follow along the readings of the psalms as laid out in the lectionary from the Book of Common Prayer.
10. James Finley, *Christian Meditation: Experiencing the Presence of God* (London: Society for Promoting Christian Knowledge, 2004), chapters 8–12.
11. Henri Nouwen, *Making All Things New* (San Francisco: Harper and Row, 1981), 69.
12. For a great introduction to other approaches you can integrate into your Daily Office, see Tony Jones, *The Sacred Way: Spiritual Practices for Everyday Life* (Grand Rapids: Zondervan, 2005).
13. This Daily Office is based on sermon series on both the Ten Commandments and the Beatitudes that I preached at New Life Fellowship Church. They are available at www.emotionallyhealthychurch.org.
14. For an excellent study on the word *holy*, see R. C. Sproul, *The Holiness of God* (Wheaton, IL: Tyndale House Publishers, 1985), 53–65.
15. This comes from Catholic theologian Leonard Doohan. It is quoted in an excellent book on Sabbath: Lynne M. Baab, *Sabbath Keeping: Finding Freedom in the Rhythms of Rest* (Downers Grove, IL: InterVarsity Press, 2005), 20.
16. Eugene Peterson, *Christ Plays in Ten Thousand Places: A Conversation in Spiritual Theology* (Grand Rapids: Eerdmans, 2005), 116–118.
17. Eugene Peterson, *Working the Angles: The Shape of Pastoral Integrity* (Grand Rapids: Eerdmans, 1987), 46.
18. Marva Dawn, *Keeping the Sabbath Wholly: Ceasing, Resting, Embracing, Feasting* (Grand Rapids: Eerdmans, 1989), 65–66.
19. Quoted in Wendell Berry, *Life Is a Miracle: An Essay Against Modern Superstition* (Washington, DC: Counterpoint, 2000), 115.
20. Tilden Edwards, *Sabbath Time* (Nashville: Upper Room Books, 1992), 66.
21. Dr. Siang-Yang Tan, *Rest: Experiencing God's Peace in a Restless World* (Ann Arbor, MI: Servant Publications, 2000), 101–104.
22. I preached a four-part series on each of these components of biblical Sabbaths. They are available at www.emotionallyhealthychurch.com.

23. Every fifty years they were to take two years of Sabbath, adding to the one year a second called the Year of Jubilee (Leviticus 25:8–55). Again, God knew the people would be afraid to take such a step of faith. So he promised he would provide enough harvest in the forty-ninth year so they could eat for three full years! Can you imagine?
24. Thomas Merton, *Conjectures of a Guilty Bystander* (New York: Doubleday, 1968), 86.

CHAPTER 7: Grow into an Emotionally Mature Adult

1. *Sojourners* (July 2004), http:www.sojo.net/index.cfmaction-magazine .article&issue=sojo4070&article=040723.
2. See Robert Coleman, *The Master Plan of Evangelism* (Grand Rapids: Revell, 1963).
3. Merton, *Conjectures of a Guilty Bystander*, 156–158.
4. Visit our website (www.emotionallyhealthy.org) to take a free personal assessment that will help you to determine if you are an emotional infant, child, adolescent, or adult. Or see chapter 4 in Scazzero, *The Emotionally Healthy Church*.
5. I first came across the phrase "practicing the presence of people" in Mike Mason, *Practicing the Presence of People: How We Learn to Love* (Colorado Springs: WaterBrook Press, 1999).
6. M. Scott Peck, *A World Waiting to Be Born: Civility Rediscovered* (New York: Bantam Books, 1993), 108, 112.
7. Martin Buber, *I and Thou*, trans. Walter Kaufmann (New York: Charles Scribner's Sons, 1970).
8. Dante Alighieri, *The Divine Comedy*, vol. 1, trans. Mark Musa (New York: Penguin Books, 1984), 381.
9. C. S. Lewis, *The Great Divorce* (New York: Macmillan Company, 1946), 16–25.
10. Kenneth Paul Kramer with Mechthild Gawlick, *Martin Buber's I and Thou: Practicing Living Dialogue* (Mahwah, NJ: Paulist Press, 2003), 24.
11. Research has been done on how, when focusing attention away from negative behaviors and toward positive ones, people have been able to make permanent changes in their neural pathways. For an interesting study, see Jeffrey M. Schwartz and Sharon Begley, *The Mind and the Brain: Neuroplasticity and the Power of Mental Force* (New York: Regan Books, HarperCollins, 2002).
12. Pat Ennis, *The Third Option: Ministry to Hurting Marriages*, Topic #1, "Respect," 1–17.

13. I learned this tool from Lori Gordon, *PAIRS: Semester Course Handbook* (Weston, FL: PAIRS Foundation, 2003).
14. Pat Ennis, *The Third Option: Ministry to Hurting Marriages*, Teachers Manual, Topic #3, "Expectations," 1–9.
15. Lori Gordon with Jon Frandsen, *Passage to Intimacy*, 245, 246.

CHAPTER 8: Go the Next Step to Develop a "Rule of Life"

1. Jane Tomaine, *St. Benedict's Toolbox: The Nuts and Bolts of Everyday Benedictine Living* (Harrisburg, PA: Morehouse Publishing, 2005), 5.
2. Catherine Doherty, *Poustinia: Encountering God in Silence, Solitude and Prayer* (Combermere, Ontario, Canada: Madonna House Publications, 1993), 70.
3. Fry, *Rule of St. Benedict*, prologue, 45, 48–49.
4. Dallas Willard, *The Spirit of the Disciplines: Understanding How God Changes Lives* (San Francisco: HarperCollins, 1988), 63.
5. See Daniel Wolpert, *Creating a Life with God: The Call of Ancient Prayer Practices* (Nashville: Upper Room Books, 2003), 138–147.
6. Carlo Caretto, *Letters from the Desert*, anniversary edition (Maryknoll, NY: Orbis Books, 1972, 2002), 108, 100, 23.

APPENDIX A: Excerpt from Emotionally Healthy Spirituality Day by Day

1. Quoted in Esther De Waal, *Lost in Wonder: Rediscovering the Spiritual Art of Attentiveness* (Collegeville, MN: Liturgical Press, 2003), 19.
2. Mother Teresa, *A Simple Path* (New York: Ballantine Books, 1995), 7–8.

APPENDIX B: Defining Emotional Health and Contemplative Spirituality

1. Defining and measuring emotional health or intelligence is a massive field with a wide range of opinions on what constitutes emotional maturity. Alongside my own reflections I have gleaned from such sources as Lori Gordon, *PAIRS Semester Course*, PAIRS International, curriculum guide for trainers, 437; Joseph Ciarrochi, Joseph P. Forgas, and John Mayer, eds., *Emotional Intelligence in Everyday Life: A Scientific Inquiry* (New York: Psychology Press, 2001): and Cary Cherniss and Daniel Goleman, eds., *The Emotionally Intelligent Workplace: How to Select for, Measure, and Improve Emotional Intelligence in Individuals, Groups and Organizations* (San Francisco: Jossey-Bass, 2001). A very accessible resource is Cary Cherniss and Mitchel Adler, *Promoting Emotional Intelligence in Organizations: Make Training in*

Emotional Intelligence Effective (Alexandria, VA: The American Society for Training and Development, 2000).

2. For a brief but helpful description of the contemplative stream through church history, see Richard Foster, *Streams of Living Water: Celebrating the Great Traditions of Christian Faith* (San Francisco: HarperSanFrancisco, 1998), 23–58. See also Tony Jones, *The Sacred Way: Spiritual Practices for Everyday Life* (Grand Rapids: Zondervan, 2005); Joan Chittister, *Wisdom Distilled from the Daily: Living the Rule of St. Benedict Today* (San Francisco: HarperSanFrancisco, 1990); Daniel Wolpert, *Creating a Life with God: The Call of Ancient Prayer Practices* (Nashville: Upper Room Books, 2003); and Robert E. Webber, *Ancient-Future Time: Forming Spirituality Through the Christian Year* (Grand Rapids: Baker Books, 2004).
3. I am thankful to Jay Feld for the initial diagram, which was then expanded into its present form.

Acknowledgments

Although this book was written by me, the material was birthed with Geri, my best friend and wife for the last thirty-three years. We have lived the insights of this book separately, as a married couple, and as parents of our four daughters—Maria, Christy, Faith, and Eva—and Jesse, our son-in-law.

I would like to thank the family of New Life Fellowship Church in Queens, New York City, where I was the senior pastor for twenty-six years. This book was written out of the reality of our life together as a multiracial, multiethnic community committed to serving the poor and marginalized. The content of this book emerged out of this soil; their openness to the Holy Spirit and passion for the Lord Jesus is a gift. I want to express specific appreciation to the elders, staff, leaders, members, and close friends of New Life, and to all those who read drafts and portions of this book along the way (there are too many to mention by name). Thank you all.

I want to thank the entire staff of Zondervan/HarperCollins with whom we have been partners for the last thirteen years. Without your partnership, EHS would not be the gift that it is around the world. I am especially grateful to Sandy Vander Zicht who has been a wonderful friend, champion, and editor. Thank you to Tom Dean, John Raymond, and David Morris from the Zondervan team who have helped to make EHS what it is today. Thank you also to my agent, Chris Ferebee, who has been a gift and a guide through the entire process.

Finally, I want to thank Ruth Zsolani, who currently serves as executive director of EHS, and to Rich Villodas, lead pastor of New Life Fellowship Church, who is leading the charge to contextualize EHS for the next generation.

About the Author

Peter Scazzero is the founder of New Life Fellowship Church in Queens, New York City, a large, multiracial church with more than seventy-three countries represented. After serving as senior pastor for twenty-six years, he now serves as a teaching pastor/pastor-at-large. He is the author of *The Emotionally Healthy Leader* and the bestselling *The Emotionally Healthy Church*. He is also the coauthor of *The Emotionally Healthy Spirituality Course* and *The Emotionally Healthy Relationships Course*.

Pete is cofounder, along with his wife Geri, of Emotionally Healthy Spirituality, a global ministry active in over twenty-five countries. He holds a Master of Divinity from Gordon-Conwell Theological Seminary and a Doctor of Ministry in Marriage and Family.

For more information, visit emotionallyhealthy.org, or connect with Pete on Twitter @petescazzero or Facebook.

Leader's Resource Vault

Access a treasure chest of exclusive content designed to equip you to lead *The Emotionally Healthy Discipleship Course* effectively in your church or ministry.

In the Leader's Resource Vault you and your team will receive:

- Planning timelines
- Session schedules
- Training videos and resources
- Presentation decks
- Certificates of completion for participants
- Top 25 FAQ's people ask
- Marketing & promotional graphics

Access to a Certified EH Discipleship Course Coach:

- Customize a plan for your specific ministry context
- Build on areas of strength in your ministry
- Receive specific tools to ensure the Course develops disciple-makers and leaders

Exclusive Resources:

- Have your ministry posted publicly on a national map
- Access to On-line Q&A session with author Pete Scazzero
- Networking with other Point Leaders in an EHD Private Facebook Group

CHECKLIST | EMOTIONALLY HEALTHY **SPIRITUALITY** COURSE

SESSION #	EHS BOOK	DAY-BY-DAY	WORKBOOK	DVD (or live)
1. The Problem of Emotionally Unhealthy Spirituality	☐ Read Chapter 1	☐ Prayerfully read Intro & Week 1	☐ Read Intro and fill out Session 1	☐ Watch Session 1
2. Know Yourself That You May Know God	☐ Read Chapter 2	☐ Prayerfully read Week 2	☐ Fill out Session 2	☐ Watch Session 2
3. Going Back in Order to Go Forward	☐ Read Chapter 3	☐ Prayerfully read Week 3	☐ Fill out Session 3	☐ Watch Session 3
4. Journey through the Wall	☐ Read Chapter 4	☐ Prayerfully read Week 4	☐ Fill out Session 4	☐ Watch Session 4
5. Enlarge Your Soul through Grief and Loss	☐ Read Chapter 5	☐ Prayerfully read Week 5	☐ Fill out Session 5	☐ Watch Session 5
6. Discover the Rhythms of the Daily Office and Sabbath	☐ Read Chapter 6	☐ Prayerfully read Week 6	☐ Fill out Session 6	☐ Watch Session 6
7. Grow into an Emotionally Healthy Adult	☐ Read Chapter 7	☐ Prayerfully read Week 7	☐ Fill out Session 7	☐ Watch Session 7
8. Go the Next Step to Develop a "Rule of Life"	☐ Read Chapter 8	☐ Prayerfully read Week 8	☐ Fill out Session 8	☐ Watch Session 8

Congratulations on completing **The Emotionally Healthy (EH) Spirituality Course**, the first half of The EH Discipleship Courses.

Go to ***emotionallyhealthy.org*** to receive your **Certificate of Completion.**

Emotionally Healthy Spirituality

WORKBOOK

The Emotionally Healthy (EH) Discipleship Courses

The Emotionally Healthy (EH) Spirituality Course

Emotionally Healthy Spirituality

Emotionally Healthy Spirituality Workbook

Emotionally Healthy Spirituality Day by Day

Emotionally Healthy Spirituality DVD

The Emotionally Healthy (EH) Relationships Courses

Emotionally Healthy Relationships Workbook

Emotionally Healthy Relationships Day by Day

Emotionally Healthy Relationships DVD

Other Resources by Pete and/or Geri Scazzero

The Emotionally Healthy Woman (book, workbook, and DVD)

The Emotionally Healthy Leader

The Emotionally Healthy Church (book and workbook)

Emotionally Healthy Spirituality

DISCIPLESHIP THAT DEEPLY CHANGES
YOUR RELATIONSHIP WITH GOD

UPDATED EDITION

WORKBOOK
EIGHT SESSIONS

Peter and Geri Scazzero

ZONDERVAN®

ZONDERVAN

Emotionally Healthy Spirituality Workbook, Updated Edition

This title is also available as a Zondervan ebook.

Requests for information should be addressed to:
Zondervan, *3900 Sparks Dr. SE, Grand Rapids, Michigan 49546*

ISBN 978-0-310-08519-5

Cover photography: Shutterstock
Author photos: Orlando Suazo
Interior design: Beth Shagene
Interior iceberg illustration: 123RF® / Ion Popa

First Printing March 2017 / Printed in the United States of America

HB 08.20.2021

Contents

Introduction

The Emotionally Healthy Spirituality Course (or *The EH Spirituality Course*) is a plan for discipleship that deeply changes our relationship with God.

The EH Spirituality Course does this in two ways:

1. Addressing directly the reality that emotional maturity and spiritual maturity are inseparable, that it is not possible to be spiritually mature while remaining emotionally immature.
2. Equipping people in a personal, firsthand relationship with Jesus by incorporating stillness, silence, and Scripture as daily life rhythms.

The goal of this workbook, along with its companion resources—*The EH Spirituality Course* video, the *Emotionally Healthy Spirituality* book, and the *Emotionally Healthy Spirituality Day by Day* devotional—is to help you implement the eight core biblical truths and principles that make up *The EH Spirituality Course.* On the last page of the workbook you will find a checklist to keep you on track as you move through the Course. Fill it out along the way and, when completed, go to emotionallyhealthy.org to receive your certificate of completion.

Each of the eight truths explored in these sessions could easily have been expanded into their own course. We have kept them together, however, to serve as an introduction into a life with God that goes beyond "tip of the iceberg spirituality" into transformation through Christ that touches the depth of your being.

How to Use This Workbook

Before Session 1

- Purchase the *Emotionally Healthy Spirituality* book, *Emotionally Healthy Spirituality Day by Day*, and this workbook.
- Read chapter 1 of the *Emotionally Healthy Spirituality* book.
- A 5-minute video that introduces how to use *Emotionally Healthy Spirituality Day by Day* can be found at www.emotionallyhealthy.org/ehscourse or on YouTube.

Throughout the Study

Before each group meeting, read the chapters from the *Emotionally Healthy Spirituality* book that correspond with each session in this workbook. Another core element of *The EH Spirituality Course* is to prayerfully read the devotionals found in *Emotionally Health Spirituality Day by Day* during the week that follows the study.

Each session is divided into six sections:

- Introduction
- Growing Connected
- Video: Opening Presentation
- Group Discussion
- Application
- Video: Closing Summary

This is followed by a Between-Sessions Personal Study that is based on questions from the Daily Offices found in the *Emotionally Healthy Spirituality Day by Day* devotional.

Space is provided throughout for you to record your responses, questions, or other insights that God may be bringing to you during your meeting time as well as during your personal study time between meetings.

The Leader's Guide found in the back of this workbook provides extremely helpful information to supplement the studies. We especially encourage you to avail yourselves of this valuable material. Additional resources for *The EH Spirituality Course* can be found at www.emotionallyhealthy.org/courses.

Note

Pete's video presentations for each session are available wherever books/DVDs are sold or by digital video through sites such as: CBD.com, amazon.com, vimeo.com, Gotothehub.com, and studygateway.com.

Suggested Guidelines for the Group

Be Prepared

To get the most out of your time together, we ask that you read the chapters in *Emotionally Healthy Spirituality* that correspond with each session. Please also bring your workbook and the *EH Spirituality Day by Day* book with you to each meeting.

Speak for Yourself

We encourage you to share and use "I" statements. We are only experts on ourselves. For example: Instead of saying, "Everyone is busy," say, "I am busy." Instead of saying, "We all struggle with forgiving," say, "I struggle with forgiving."

Respect Others

Be brief in your sharing, remaining mindful that there are time limitations and others may want to share.

No Fixing, Saving, No Setting Other People Straight

Respect people's journeys and trust the Holy Spirit inside of them to lead them into all truth—in his timing. Resist the temptation to offer quick advice as people share in the group.

Turn to Wonder

If you feel judgmental or defensive when someone else is sharing, ask yourself: *I wonder what brought him/her to this belief? I wonder what he/she is feeling right now? I wonder what my reaction teaches me about myself?*

Trust and Learn from Silence

It is okay to have silence between responses as the group shares, giving members the opportunity to reflect. Remember, there is no pressure to share.

Observe Confidentiality

In order to create an environment that is safe for open and honest participation, anything someone shares within the group should not be repeated outside of the group. However, feel free to share your own story and personal growth.

Punctuality

Resolve to arrive on time.

SESSION 1

The Problem of Emotionally Unhealthy Spirituality

Before your first group meeting, read chapter 1 of the *Emotionally Healthy Spirituality* book.

Daily Office (10 minutes)

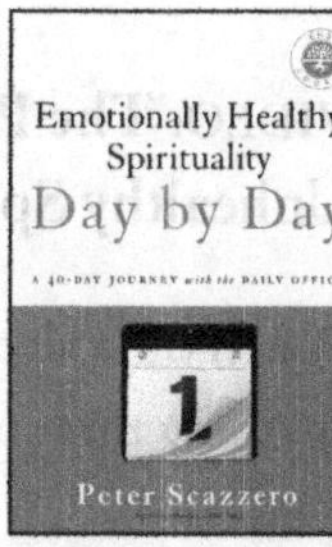

Do one of the Daily Offices from Week 1 of *Emotionally Healthy Spirituality Day by Day* to begin your session. **(Leaders, please see point number two in the "General Guidelines" on page 124.)**

Introduction (3 minutes)

Emotional health and spiritual maturity cannot be separated. It is not possible to be spiritually mature while remaining emotionally immature.

When we ignore the emotional component of our lives, we move through the motions of Christian disciplines, activities, and behaviors, but deeply rooted behavioral patterns from our pasts continue to hinder us from an authentic life of maturity in Christ.

We often neglect to reflect on what is going on inside us and around us (emotional health) and are too busy to slow down to be with God (contemplative spirituality).[1] As a result, we run the high risk of remaining stuck as spiritual infants, failing to develop into spiritually/emotionally mature adults in Christ.

Jay, one of our church members, described it best: "I was a Christian for twenty-two years. But instead of being a twenty-two-year-old Christian, I was a one-year-old Christian twenty-two times! I just kept doing the same things over and over and over again."

In order to facilitate a sense of safety at each small group table, please turn to pages 11–12 as the "Suggested Guidelines for the Group" are read aloud.

Growing Connected (10 minutes)

1. Share your name and a few words about what makes you feel fully alive (e.g., nature, music, sports, reading).

VIDEO: The Problem of Emotionally Unhealthy Spirituality (19 minutes)

Watch the video segment for Session 1 and use the space provided to note anything that stands out to you.

NOTES

Group Discussion (45 minutes)

Starters (10 minutes)

2. The following are the top ten symptoms of emotionally *unhealthy* spirituality. As the list that begins below is read aloud, put a check mark next to the one or two symptoms that are most relevant in your life today. Afterward, turn to another person and each share the one symptom that most applies to your spiritual life today.

☐ **1. Using God to run from God**
(Example: I fill my life with Christian activities to avoid addressing difficult issues in my life.)

☐ **2. Ignoring the emotions of anger, sadness, and fear**
(Example: I am rarely honest with myself and/or others about the feelings, hurts, and pains beneath the surface of my life.)

☐ **3. Dying to the wrong things**
(Example: I tend to deny healthy, God-given desires and pleasures of life such as friendships, joy, music, beauty, laughter, and nature. At the same time, I find it difficult to die to my self-protectiveness, defensiveness, lack of vulnerability, and judgmentalism.)

☐ **4. Denying the past's impact on the present**
(Example: I rarely consider how my family of origin and significant people/events from my past have shaped my present.)

☐ **5. Dividing life into "secular" and "sacred" compartments**
(Example: I easily compartmentalize God to "Christian activities" while usually forgetting about him when I am working, shopping, studying, or recreating.)

☐ **6. Doing for God instead of being with God**
(Example: I tend to evaluate my spirituality based on how much I am doing for God.)

☐ **7. Spiritualizing away conflict**
(Example: I usually miss out on true peace by smoothing over disagreements, burying tensions, and avoiding conflict, rather than disrupting false peace as Jesus did.)

☐ **8. Covering over brokenness, weakness, and failure**
(Example: I have a hard time speaking freely about my weaknesses, failures, and mistakes.)

☐ **9. Living without limits**
(Example: Those close to me would say that I often "try to do it all" or "bite off more than I can chew.")

☐ **10. Judging the spiritual journeys of others**
(Example: I often find myself occupied and bothered by the faults of those around me.)

Bible Study: 1 Samuel 15:7–24 (35 minutes)

In this story we meet King Saul, the first king of Israel, and Samuel, God's prophet who brings God's word to Saul. King Saul had been instructed by God earlier in verse 3 to "attack the Amalekites and totally destroy all that belongs to them." (Note: The Amalekites were a wicked, sinful culture known for their destructiveness). Saul, however, gives in to the wishes of his fighting men and does *only part* of God's will. Read aloud 1 Samuel 15:7–24.

> 7 Then Saul attacked the Amalekites all the way from Havilah to Shur,
> near the eastern border of Egypt. 8 He took Agag king of the Amalekites
> alive, and all his people he totally destroyed with the sword. 9 But Saul
> and the army spared Agag and the best of the sheep and cattle, the fat calves and lambs—everything that was good. These they were unwilling to destroy completely, but everything that was despised and weak they totally destroyed.

[10] Then the word of the LORD came to Samuel: [11] "I regret that I have made Saul king, because he has turned away from me and has not carried out my instructions." Samuel was angry, and he cried out to the LORD all that night.

[12] Early in the morning Samuel got up and went to meet Saul, but he was told, "Saul has gone to Carmel. There he has set up a monument in his own honor and has turned and gone on down to Gilgal."

[13] When Samuel reached him, Saul said, "The LORD bless you! I have carried out the LORD's instructions."

[14] But Samuel said, "What then is this bleating of sheep in my ears? What is this lowing of cattle that I hear?"

[15] Saul answered, "The soldiers brought them from the Amalekites; they spared the best of the sheep and cattle to sacrifice to the LORD your God, but we totally destroyed the rest."

[16] "Enough!" Samuel said to Saul. "Let me tell you what the LORD said to me last night."

"Tell me," Saul replied.

[17] Samuel said, "Although you were once small in your own eyes, did you not become the head of the tribes of Israel? The LORD anointed you king over Israel. [18] And he sent you on a mission, saying, 'Go and completely destroy those wicked people, the Amalekites; wage war against them until you have wiped them out.' [19] Why did you not obey the LORD? Why did you pounce on the plunder and do evil in the eyes of the LORD?"

[20] "But I did obey the LORD," Saul said. "I went on the mission the LORD assigned me. I completely destroyed the Amalekites and brought back Agag their king. [21] The soldiers took sheep and cattle from the plunder, the best of what was devoted to God, in order to sacrifice them to the LORD your God at Gilgal."

[22] But Samuel replied:

"Does the LORD delight in burnt offerings and sacrifices
as much as in obeying the LORD?

To obey is better than sacrifice,
and to [listen] is better than the fat of rams.
23 For rebellion is like the sin of divination,
and arrogance like the evil of idolatry.
Because you have rejected the word of the LORD,
he has rejected you as king."

24 Then Saul said to Samuel, "I have sinned. I violated the LORD's command and your instructions. I was afraid of the men and so I gave in to them."

3. In verse 11, what do you notice about God and Samuel's responses to Saul's failure to fully obey?

How does this differ from Saul's response in verses 12–13?

4. Reread verses 12 and 24. What might have been going on beneath the surface of Saul's life (iceberg) that he was unaware of?

5. Reread verses 22–23. Describe in your own words how Samuel explains Saul's disobedience.

6. List one or two examples of how you go through the motions of making "burnt offerings" and "sacrifices" rather than obeying the word of the Lord (e.g., acting or speaking from fear of what others think, or being one person at church and another person at work or home, or not having a place in your life to be still and listen to the Lord)?

7. Note the seriousness of verse 23a. What positive step(s) could Saul have taken to become aware of his own iceberg and hear God in his situation? What might be one positive step for you?

In what ways can you relate, or not relate, to Saul?

Application (15 minutes)

After the following paragraphs and questions 8 and 9 are read aloud, take 5 minutes to journal your response to those questions in the space provided. Then share your response to question 10 in groups of two or three.

Not only was Saul unaware of what was going on inside of him, he also did not cultivate a contemplative life with God. His "doing" for God did not flow from his "being" with God.

In the same way, our "doing" for Jesus must flow from our "being" with him. Far too often, we live vicariously off other people's spirituality and relate to God while busily "on the run."

8. What challenges keep you from slowing down your life to be with God?

9. The diagram below provides an illustration of a spiritual life where our activity (i.e., our doing) is out of balance with our contemplative life (i.e., our inner life with Jesus).

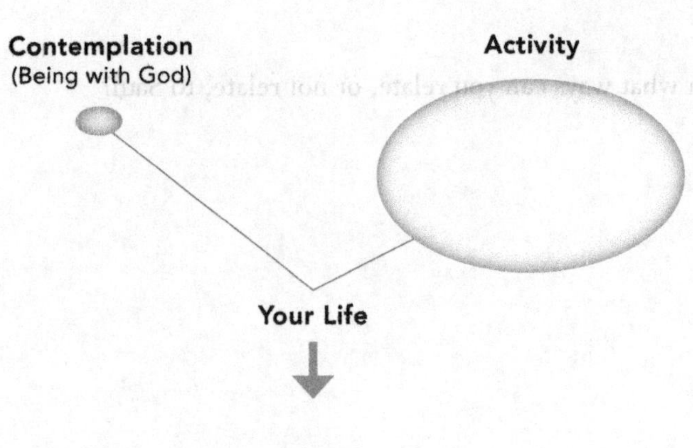

Now, using two circles like the ones in the diagram, draw your own diagram to illustrate how your activities (your doing) balance with your contemplative life (your being with God).[2]

10. The remaining sessions of *The EH Spirituality Course* will address ways we can make changes in our lives. At this point, what might be one or two simple steps you can take toward beginning to slow down your life and balance your two circles?

VIDEO: Closing Summary (6 minutes)

Watch the closing video summary for Session 1 and use the space provided to note anything that stands out to you.

NOTES

Between-Sessions Personal Study

SESSION 1

Read chapter 2 of the book *Emotionally Healthy Spirituality*, "Know Yourself That You May Know God." Use the space provided to note any insights or questions you might want to bring to the next group session.

Prayerfully read Week 1 of the devotional *Emotionally Healthy Spirituality Day by Day*, "The Problem of Emotionally Unhealthy Spirituality." Use the space provided to answer the Questions to Consider and/or to journal your thoughts each day.

Day 1 Questions to Consider:

How would you describe "what is secondary" in your life, the thing that might be "blocking the way" to experiencing God?

How could you make more room in your life for silence in order to listen to God?

Day 2 Questions to Consider:

What internal or external storm might God be sending into your life as a sign that something is not right spiritually?

How do you hear the words of the apostle John today: "Do not love the world or anything in the world" (1 John 2:15)?

Day 3 Questions to Consider:

In what way(s) has God put your life or plans "out of joint" so that you might depend on him?

What might be one way your "busyness" blocks you from listening and communing with the living God?

Day 4 Questions to Consider:

What things are "worrying" and "upsetting" you as you begin this day?

What are you angry about today? Sad about? Afraid of? Pour out your responses before God, trusting in him as David did.

Day 5 Questions to Consider:

What is one step you can take today to slow down and live more attentively to the voice of Jesus?

How might brokenness or weakness in your life today present an opportunity for God's power to be demonstrated?

SESSION 2

Know Yourself That You May Know God

Daily Office (8 minutes)

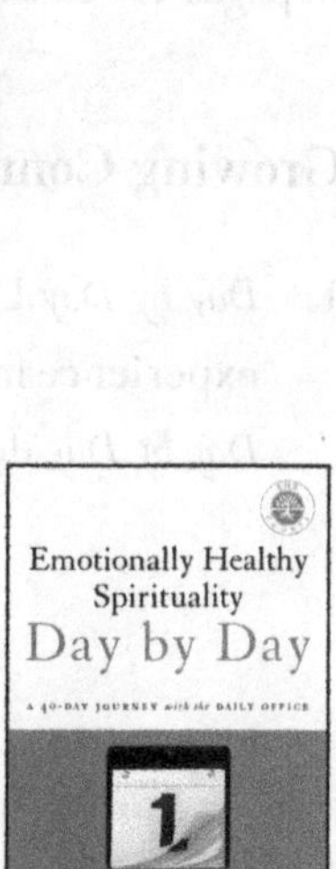

Do one of the Daily Offices from Week 2 of *Emotionally Healthy Spirituality Day by Day* to begin your session. **(Leaders, please see point number two in the "General Guidelines" on page 124.)**

Introduction (3 minutes)

Self-awareness is intricately related to our relationship with God. In fact, the challenge of Scripture to shed our old "false" self in order to live authentically in our new "true" self strikes at the very core of true spirituality.

In AD 500, Augustine wrote in *Confessions*, "How can you draw close to God when you are far from your own self?" He prayed: "Grant, Lord, that I may know myself that I may know thee."

In 1530, John Calvin wrote in his opening of the *Institutes of the Christian Religion*: "Our wisdom . . . consists almost entirely of two parts: the knowledge of God and of ourselves. But as these are connected together by many ties, it is not easy to determine which of the two precedes and gives birth to the other."

The vast majority of us go to our graves without knowing who we are. Without being fully aware of it, we live someone else's life, or at least someone else's expectations for us. This does violence to ourselves, to our relationship with God, and ultimately to others.

In order to facilitate a sense of safety at each small group table, please turn to pages 11–12 as the "Suggested Guidelines for the Group" are read aloud.

Growing Connected (17 minutes)

1. *Day by Day* Debrief: What obstacles, difficulties, or successes did you experience in meeting with God this past week using the *EH Spirituality Day by Day* devotional? Have two or three people share. (7 minutes)

2. Describe your dream job. (10 minutes. Depending on group size, you may have to divide the group in two.)

VIDEO: Know Yourself That You May Know God (13 minutes)

Watch the video segment for Session 2. Use the space provided to note anything that stands out to you.

NOTES

Group Discussion (45 minutes)

Starters (10 minutes)

After the following paragraph is read aloud, complete question 3 on your own.

The journey of genuine transformation to emotionally healthy spirituality begins with a commitment to allow yourself to feel. Feelings are an essential part of our humanity and unique personhood as men and women created in God's image. Scripture reveals God as an emotional being who feels as a person. Having been created in his image, we also are created with the gift to feel and experience emotions. Some of us may have learned that feelings are not to be trusted; that they are dangerous and can lead us away from God's will for us. While it is true that we are not to be led by our emotions, they do serve a critical function in our discipleship and discernment of God's will.

3. Journal your response to the questions on the next page in the space provided. Your concern can be something from the past, present, or future. Consider areas such as finances, health, relationships, work, etc. (5 min.)

- What are you angry about?

- What are you sad about?

- What are you anxious about?

- What are you glad about?

4. Share in groups of two or three what it was like to journal your feelings? (5 min.)

Bible Study: 1 Samuel 17:26–45 (35 minutes)

In this famous story, the army of Israel faced the great army of the Philistines. For forty days, the Philistine hero Goliath, described as nine feet tall and dressed in powerful weaponry, challenged any Israelite soldier to come out and fight him. When the Israelites saw him, however, "they all fled from him in great fear" (1 Samuel 17:24). We pick up the story after David hears, for the first time, Goliath's humiliating challenge to Israel's army. Listen carefully as the story from 1 Samuel 17:26–45 is read aloud.

[26] David asked the men standing near him, "What will be done for the man who kills this Philistine and removes this disgrace from Israel? Who is this uncircumcised Philistine that he should defy the armies of the living God?"

[27] They repeated to him what they had been saying and told him, "This is what will be done for the man who kills him."

[28] When Eliab, David's oldest brother, heard him speaking with the men, he burned with anger at him and asked, "Why have you come down here? And with whom did you leave those few sheep in the wilderness? I know how conceited you are and how wicked your heart is; you came down only to watch the battle."

[29] "Now what have I done?" said David. "Can't I even speak?" [30] He then turned away to someone else and brought up the same matter, and the men answered him as before. [31] What David said was overheard and reported to Saul, and Saul sent for him.

[32] David said to Saul, "Let no one lose heart on account of this Philistine; your servant will go and fight him."

[33] Saul replied, "You are not able to go out against this Philistine and fight him; you are only a young man, and he has been a warrior from his youth."

[34] But David said to Saul, "Your servant has been keeping his father's sheep. When a lion or a bear came and carried off a sheep from the flock, [35] I went after it, struck it and rescued the sheep from its mouth. When it turned on me, I seized it by its hair, struck it and killed it. [36] Your servant has killed both the lion and the bear; this uncircumcised Philistine will be like one of them, because he has defied the armies of the living God. [37] The Lord who rescued me from the paw of the lion and the paw of the bear will rescue me from the hand of this Philistine."

Saul said to David, "Go, and the Lord be with you."

[38] Then Saul dressed David in his own tunic. He put a coat of armor on him and a bronze helmet on his head. [39] David fastened on his sword over the tunic and tried walking around, because he was not used to them.

"I cannot go in these," he said to Saul, "because I am not used to them." So he took them off. [40] Then he took his staff in his hand, chose five smooth stones from the stream, put them in the pouch of his shepherd's bag and, with his sling in his hand, approached the Philistine.

[41] Meanwhile, the Philistine, with his shield bearer in front of him, kept coming closer to David. [42] He looked David over and saw that he was little more than a boy, glowing with health and handsome, and he despised him. [43] He said to David, "Am I a dog, that you come at me with sticks?" And the Philistine cursed David by his gods. [44] "Come here," he said, "and I'll give your flesh to the birds and the wild animals!"

[45] David said to the Philistine, "You come against me with sword and spear and javelin, but I come against you in the name of the LORD Almighty, the God of the armies of Israel, whom you have defied."

5. In your own words, what are some of David's thoughts and feelings when he hears Goliath's challenge to Israel (v. 26)?

6. What are some of the accusations and messages David receives from the people around him?

   - From his own family (v. 28)

   - From Saul (vv. 33, 38)

   - From Goliath (vv. 41–45)

7. What feelings might you be experiencing if you were David (*ex.*: in response to an older sibling, a person in authority over you, or a competent and intimidating person like Goliath)?

8. What enables David to live out of his true self against the powerful forces and pressures that seek to mold him into someone he is not?

9. Where in your life, or with whom, is it difficult to be your true self (*ex.*: to speak honestly, say "no," or not be afraid of what others think)?

Application (15 minutes)

Take five minutes alone to prayerfully journal your responses to the questions below. (5 min.)

10. What might it look like for you to take off armor that you are currently wearing that does not fit you?

11. Many of us are so unaccustomed to distinguishing our true self from our false self that it may seem difficult to know where to begin. Complete the following sentence, and then share it with your group as a first step: *What I am beginning to realize about myself is . . .*

12. Share your responses in groups of two or three. (10 min.)

VIDEO: Closing Summary (6 minutes)

Watch the closing video summary for Session 2 and use the space provided to note anything that stands out to you.

NOTES

Between-Sessions Personal Study

SESSION 2

Read chapter 3 of the book *Emotionally Healthy Spirituality*, "Going Back in Order to Go Forward." Use the space provided to note any insights or questions you might want to bring to the next group session.

Prayerfully read Week 2 of the devotional *Emotionally Healthy Spirituality Day by Day*, "Know Yourself So That You May Know God." Use the space provided to answer the Questions to Consider and/or to journal your thoughts each day.

Day 1 Questions to Consider:

What might be one specific way that you give in to expectations of others rather than being faithful to what Jesus has for you?

What might be one false layer or bandage God is inviting you to remove today?

Day 2 Questions to Consider:

What do you think might be one of your "birthright" gifts from God that has been ignored in your life?

Where do you see yourself on Bernard's list of the four degrees of love?

Day 3 Questions to Consider:

What impresses you most about the story of Anthony's life?

What temptation(s) or trials do you find yourself in today that God may be using as a furnace to help develop your interior life?

Day 4 Questions to Consider:

What would it look like to respect yourself in light of your God-given limits?

What is one area of your inner person that the fire of God's presence might want to burn away (*ex.*: selfishness, greed, bitterness, impatience)?

Day 5 Questions to Consider:

How might it change your day today if you were to cease looking for human approval and begin seeking only the approval of God?

In what area of your life might you be living as a chicken when God, in reality, has made you an eagle?

SESSION 3

Going Back in Order to Go Forward

Daily Office (8 minutes)

Do one of the Daily Offices from Week 3 of *Emotionally Healthy Spirituality Day by Day* to begin your session. **(Leaders, please see point number two in the "General Guidelines" on page 124.)**

Introduction (1 minute)

Emotionally healthy spirituality involves embracing God's choice to birth us into a particular family, in a particular place, at a particular moment in history.

That choice to embrace our past grants us certain opportunities and gifts. It also hands us a certain amount of "emotional baggage" for our journey through life. For some of us this load is minimal; for others, it is a heavy burden to carry.

True spirituality frees us to live joyfully in the present. Living joyfully, however, requires going back in order to go forward. This process takes us to the very heart of spirituality and discipleship in the family of God—breaking free from the destructive sinful patterns of our past in order to live the life of love that God intends.

Growing Connected (10 minutes)

1. *Day by Day* Debrief: What obstacles, difficulties, or successes did you experience in meeting with God this past week using the *EH Spirituality Day by Day* devotional? Have two or three people share.

2. How would you describe the family atmosphere you grew up in? Try to use just a word or two (*ex.*: affirming, complaining, critical, approachable, angry, tense, cooperative, competitive, close, distant, fun, serious).

VIDEO: Going Back in Order to Go Forward (13 minutes)

Watch the video segment for Session 3. Use the space provided to note anything that stands out to you.

NOTES

Group Discussion (40 minutes)

Starters (7 minutes)

3. Our need to go back in order to go forward can be summed up in two essential biblical truths:

   - The blessings and sins of our families going back two to three generations profoundly impact who we are today.
   - Discipleship requires putting off the sinful patterns of our family of origin and relearning how to do life God's way in God's family.

   What concerns or fears might you have in looking back at your family of origin to discern unhealthy patterns and themes? Explain.

Bible Study: Genesis 50:15–21 (33 minutes)

Read aloud the introductory paragraphs and then answer question 4.

The "family" is an emotional system of two to four generations who move through life together in different places at different times. When we are born into families, we inherit their ways of relating, their values, and their ways of living in the world. (Adopted children inherit not only birth family traits but draw on traits from their adoptive family.) Your family's story and your individual story cannot be separated.

Joseph is an excellent example of that reality. He was born into a complex, blended family where his father Jacob, Jacob's two wives, two concubines, and their children, all lived under one roof. Joseph was Jacob's favored son. As a result, his brothers grew jealous, leading them to sell Joseph to a merchant who took him to Egypt. The brothers never expected to hear from Joseph again. After he was sold, Joseph's life became very difficult. For the next ten to thirteen years, Joseph lived first as a slave, and later, as a prisoner falsely accused of rape.

4. Imagine yourself in Joseph's shoes sitting in a prison cell without any hope of freedom. What thoughts, feelings, or doubts might you have about your family? About yourself? About God?

Now read aloud the next paragraph and Scripture passage before discussing the remaining questions.

Through God's miraculous intervention, Joseph was pulled from the pit of prison and made the second most powerful person in Egypt. Later, when his brothers came to Egypt for food during a famine in Israel, Joseph invited them to return for their father and live in Egypt—which they gladly did. But after Jacob died, the brothers began to worry. Read Genesis 50:15–21.

> 15 When Joseph's brothers saw that their father was dead, they said, "What if Joseph holds a grudge against us and pays us back for all the wrongs we did to him?" 16 So they sent word to Joseph, saying, "Your father left these instructions before he died: 17 'This is what you are to say to Joseph: I ask you to forgive your brothers the sins and the wrongs they committed in treating you so badly.' Now please forgive the sins of the servants of the God of your father." When their message came to him, Joseph wept.
>
> 18 His brothers then came and threw themselves down before him. "We are your slaves," they said.
>
> 19 But Joseph said to them, "Don't be afraid. Am I in the place of God? 20 You intended to harm me, but God intended it for good to accomplish what is now being done, the saving of many lives. 21 So then, don't be afraid. I will provide for you and your children." And he reassured them and spoke kindly to them.

5. What assumptions are the brothers making about Joseph in verse 15?

6. Why do you think Joseph weeps (v. 17)?

7. Joseph chooses to break the "normal" way his family deals with hurt feelings and conflict by forgiving his brothers. How might you have responded if you were in Joseph's position? (Be sure to honestly put yourself in Joseph's shoes).

8. Slowly, reread verses 19–21. Here we see Joseph's response to the enormous losses he experienced in his life. Carefully consider the different aspects of this response noted below. As you think about your own life story, which one speaks the most to you and why?

   - "Don't be afraid."
   - "Am I in the place of God?"
   - "You intended to harm me, but God intended it for good."

Application (25 minutes)

Complete question 9 on your own. Then answer questions 10–12 as a group before closing together in prayer.

9. Joseph had a rich sense of being part of his family of origin and how it had shaped his life—both good and bad. We must honestly face the truths about our family of origin as well. Prayerfully complete the chart on the following page even if you have done a similar exercise before. We often receive new insights when we ponder and reflect on our family's impact on us at different times.

    - First, list the life messages you received from each of your parents or caretakers (*ex.*: Don't be weak. Education is everything. You must achieve to be loved. Don't be sad; things could be worse. Make a lot of money. Don't trust people; they will hurt you.).
    - Next, list any "earthquake" events that sent "aftershocks" into your extended family (*ex.*: abuse, premature or sudden deaths/losses, divorces, shameful secrets revealed, etc.).
    - Review the three separate boxes and summarize what messages about life/yourself/others you internalized. Then fill in the bottom box, "Cumulative messages I received."

Father (Caretaker)

Messages received about life:

Mother (Caretaker)

Messages received about life:

"Earthquake" events in family history:

-
-
-
-
-

Cumulative messages I received:

10. Share with the group the message(s) you received. How do those messages compare with the messages below that reflect who you are in the new family of Jesus?

- It is good that you exist.
- You are lovable.
- You are good enough.
- You are a joy.
- You have nothing left to prove.
- Your needs are a delight.
- You are allowed to make mistakes.

11. What might be one specific message from your family of origin that God has revealed to you today that you want to change as part of your "hard work of discipleship"?

VIDEO: Closing Summary (7 minutes)

Watch the closing video summary for Session 3 and use the space provided to note anything that stands out to you.

NOTES

Between-Sessions Personal Study

SESSION 3

Read chapter 4 of the book *Emotionally Healthy Spirituality*, "Journey through the Wall." Use the space provided to note any insights or questions you might want to bring to the next group session.

Prayerfully read Week 3 of the devotional *Emotionally Healthy Spirituality Day by Day*, "Going Back in Order to Go Forward." Use the space provided to answer the Questions to Consider and/or to journal your thoughts each day.

Day 1 Questions to Consider:

What invitation might God be offering to you out of the failures and pain of your past?

What heavy "raft" might you be carrying as you seek to climb the mountains God has placed before you?

Day 2 Questions to Consider:

What false self are you struggling with that Christ wants you to die to, so that you can truly live?

What most impacts you from the story about Francis? How is God speaking to you through that?

Day 3 Questions to Consider:

What would it look like for you to surrender the pains of your past (mistakes, sins, setbacks, and disappointments) to God today?

What pains in your life are waiting to be acknowledged and grieved?

Day 4 Questions to Consider:

What space in the world (for which the past has prepared you) is waiting to be filled by you?

Can you name ways in which you learned the pain of others by suffering your own pain?

Day 5 Questions to Consider:

How might the words from Exodus 14:14–15—"The Lord will fight for you, you need only to be still" and "move on"—apply to you today?

In Psalm 131:1, David prays: "I do not concern myself with great matters or things too wonderful for me." How do you hear these words?

SESSION 4

Journey through the Wall

Daily Office (8 minutes)

Do one of the Daily Offices from Week 4 of *Emotionally Healthy Spirituality Day by Day* to begin your session. **(Leaders, please see point number two in the "General Guidelines" on page 124.)**

Introduction (1 minute)

Emotionally healthy spirituality requires that you go through the pain of the Wall—or, as the ancients called it, "the dark night of the soul." Just as a physical wall stops us from moving ahead, God sometimes stops us in our spiritual journey through a spiritual Wall in order to radically transform our character. Often, we are brought to the Wall by circumstances and crises beyond our control.

Regardless of how we get there, every follower of Jesus at some point will confront the Wall. Failure to understand and surrender to God's working in us at the Wall often results in great long-term pain, ongoing immaturity, and confusion. Receiving the gift of God in the Wall, however, transforms our lives forever.

Growing Connected (10 minutes)

1. *Day by Day* Debrief: What obstacles, difficulties, or successes did you experience in meeting with God this past week using the *EH Spirituality Day by Day* devotional? Have two or three people share.

2. In this season of your life, what is the greatest obstacle that you face? Explain.

VIDEO: Journey through the Wall (13 minutes)

Watch the video segment for Session 4. Use the space provided to note anything that stands out to you.

NOTES

Group Discussion (50 minutes)

Starters (15 minutes)

Read aloud the following excerpt from the book *Emotionally Healthy Spirituality* before answering question 3.

> For most of us, the Wall appears through a crisis that turns our world upside down. It comes, perhaps, through a divorce, a job loss, the death of a close friend or family member, a cancer diagnosis, a disillusioning church experience, a betrayal, a shattered dream, a wayward child, a car accident, an inability to get pregnant, a deep desire to marry that remains unfulfilled, a spiritual dryness or a loss of joy in our relationship with God. We question ourselves, God, and the church. We discover for the first time that our faith does not appear to "work." We have more questions than answers as the very foundation of our faith feels like it is on the line. We don't know where God is, what he is doing, where he is going, how he is getting us there, or when this will be over. . . . It (the Wall) is not simply a one-time event that we pass through and get beyond. It appears to be something we return to as part of our ongoing relationship with God. (pp. 101–102, *Updated Edition*)

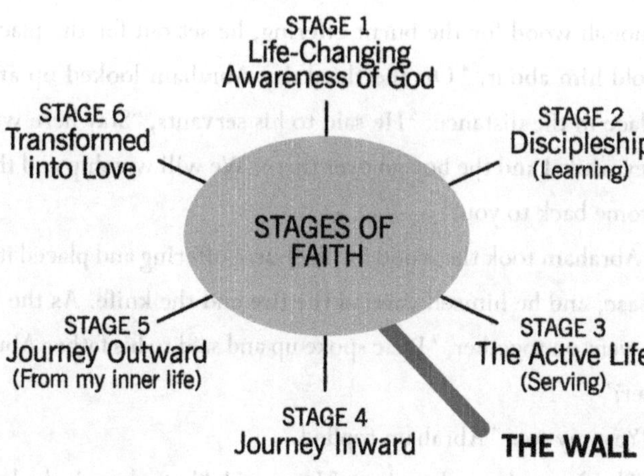

3. If you have been through a Wall, briefly share one way it impacted you and your view of God.

Bible Study: Genesis 22:1–14 (35 minutes)

Read aloud the introductory paragraph and Scripture passage, and then discuss the questions that follow.

Abraham, in his earthly pilgrimage with God, appeared to go through a number of Walls. His greatest one, however, came when God asked him to do the unthinkable—to kill his only son Isaac. Read Genesis 22:1–14:

1 Some time later God tested Abraham. He said to him, "Abraham!"

"Here I am," he replied.

2 Then God said, "Take your son, your only son, whom you love—Isaac—and go to the region of Moriah. Sacrifice him there as a burnt offering on a mountain I will show you."

3 Early the next morning Abraham got up and loaded his donkey. He took with him two of his servants and his son Isaac. When he had cut enough wood for the burnt offering, he set out for the place God
had told him about. 4 On the third day Abraham looked up and saw
the place in the distance. 5 He said to his servants, "Stay here with the donkey while I and the boy go over there. We will worship and then we will come back to you."

6 Abraham took the wood for the burnt offering and placed it on his son Isaac, and he himself carried the fire and the knife. As the two of
them went on together, 7 Isaac spoke up and said to his father Abraham, "Father?"

"Yes, my son?" Abraham replied.

"The fire and wood are here," Isaac said, "but where is the lamb for the burnt offering?"

[8] Abraham answered, "God himself will provide the lamb for the burnt offering, my son." And the two of them went on together.

[9] When they reached the place God had told him about, Abraham built an altar there and arranged the wood on it. He bound his son Isaac and laid him on the altar, on top of the wood. [10] Then he reached out his hand and took the knife to slay his son. [11] But the angel of the LORD called out to him from heaven, "Abraham! Abraham!"

"Here I am," he replied.

[12] "Do not lay a hand on the boy," he said. "Do not do anything to him. Now I know that you fear God, because you have not withheld from me your son, your only son."

[13] Abraham looked up and there in a thicket he saw a ram caught by its horns. He went over and took the ram and sacrificed it as a burnt offering instead of his son. [14] So Abraham called that place The LORD Will Provide. And to this day it is said, "On the mountain of the LORD it will be provided."

4. How would you hear the words in verse 2: "Take your son, your only son, whom you love . . . sacrifice him"?

5. What aspects of "the dark night" might have been tormenting Abraham's soul as he bound his son Isaac and laid him on the altar? (*ex.*: weariness, sense of failure, defeat, emptiness, dryness, unbelief, guilt, disillusionment, abandonment by God)

6. In light of this story, how is your image (or idea) of God challenged?

7. What are some possible reasons you have a hard time accepting and moving through Walls? (Note: Speak in the "I.")

8. In order to grow in Christ, every believer must go through Walls, or "dark nights of the soul." This is God's way of rewiring and "purging our affections and passions" that we might delight in his love and enter into a richer, fuller communion with him. In this way he frees us from unhealthy attachments and idolatries of the world. How might this larger perspective serve as an encouragement to you today?

9. This Wall gave Abraham a revelation of God that would change him and his relationship with God forever. He came to know God as Provider in even the most desperate of situations (v. 14). How might this encourage you in any current Walls you are facing?

Application (15 minutes)

Take about 5 minutes to complete question 10 on your own.

10. When God takes us through a Wall, we are changed. The following are four primary characteristics of life found on the other side of the Wall.

    - A greater level of brokenness
    - A greater appreciation for holy unknowing (mystery)
    - A deeper ability to wait on God
    - A greater detachment (from the world)

    Journaling can be a powerful tool to help clarify areas of life where God desires to bring transformation. It illuminates what is going on inside of us. Few tools get us to the "issue beneath the issue" like journaling.

    Choose one characteristic from the above list where you sense God is seeking to work in you now. Use the space provided to journal your thoughts and feelings regarding how God is birthing something new in you and/or helping you shed incomplete or immature ideas about him.

11. Form groups of two and share how you sense God might be working in you now.

VIDEO: Closing Summary (10 minutes)

Watch the closing video summary for Session 4 and use the space provided to note anything that stands out to you.

NOTES

Between-Sessions Personal Study

SESSION 4

Read chapter 5 of the book *Emotionally Healthy Spirituality*, "Enlarge Your Soul through Grief and Loss." Use the space provided to note any insights or questions you might want to bring to the next group session.

Prayerfully read Week 4 of the devotional *Emotionally Healthy Spirituality Day by Day*, "Journey through the Wall." Use the space provided to answer the Questions to Consider and/or to journal your thoughts each day.

Day 1 Questions to Consider:

What does it mean for you to trust in the slow work of God today?

What treasures might there be in such "darkness" or difficulties in your own life today?

Day 2 Questions to Consider:

What might be some unhealthy attachments or "idols" God wants to remove from your life in order to lead you to deeper, richer communion with him?

What things or people are you rooting your identity in that God may want to dig up so that your identity might be replanted in him?

Day 3 Questions to Consider:

Have you experienced any "terrible" circumstances that (in time) actually turned out to be a rich blessing?

What words or phrases from the Richard Rohr quote most speak to you? Why?

Day 4 Questions to Consider:

How is God inviting you to wait on him today?

In your own words, speak to God about your willingness to go where he leads you. What joys and/or fears accompany your willingness?

Day 5 Questions to Consider:

What is one thing God might want you to unlearn today?

What words speak to you most from the prayer found in the midday/evening Office of Week 4? Why?

SESSION 5

Enlarge Your Soul through Grief and Loss

Daily Office (8 minutes)

Do one of the Daily Offices from Week 5 of *Emotionally Healthy Spirituality Day by Day* to begin your session. **(Leaders, please see point number two in the "General Guidelines" on page 124.)**

Introduction (1 minute)

Loss is a place where self-knowledge and powerful transformation can happen—if we have the courage to participate fully in the process.

We all face many "deaths" within our lives. Our culture routinely interprets these losses and griefs as alien invasions and interruptions to our "normal" lives. The choice is whether these deaths will be terminal (crushing our spirit and life) or will open us up to new possibilities and depths of transformation in Christ.

Growing Connected (13 minutes)

1. *Day by Day* Debrief: What obstacles, difficulties, or successes did you experience in meeting with God this past week using the *EH Spirituality Day by Day* devotional? Have two or three people share.

2. As you were growing up, how did you deal with your disappointments? Give one example.

VIDEO: Enlarge Your Soul through Grief and Loss (13 minutes)

Watch the video segment for Session 5. Use the space provided to note anything that stands out to you.

NOTES

Group Discussion (50 minutes)

Starters (15 minutes)

3. Briefly share one loss you have experienced this past year. How has this loss impacted you?

Bible Study: Matthew 26:36–44 (35 minutes)

Read aloud the introductory paragraph and Scripture passage, and then discuss the questions that follow.

The end of Jesus' vibrant, popular, earthly life and ministry was an enormous loss to his disciples and followers. It was also, as we shall see, an enormous loss for Jesus. Read Matthew 26:36–44:

> 36 Then Jesus went with his disciples to a place called Gethsemane, and
> he said to them, "Sit here while I go over there and pray." 37 He took
> Peter and the two sons of Zebedee along with him, and he began to be
> sorrowful and troubled. 38 Then he said to them, "My soul is overwhelmed
> with sorrow to the point of death. Stay here and keep watch with me."
>
> 39 Going a little farther, he fell with his face to the ground and prayed, "My Father, if it is possible, may this cup be taken from me. Yet not as I will, but as you will."
>
> 40 Then he returned to his disciples and found them sleeping.
> "Couldn't you men keep watch with me for one hour?" he asked Peter.
> 41 "Watch and pray so that you will not fall into temptation. The spirit
> is willing, but the flesh is weak."
>
> 42 He went away a second time and prayed, "My Father, if it is not possible for this cup to be taken away unless I drink it, may your will be done."
>
> 43 When he came back, he again found them sleeping, because their
> eyes were heavy. 44 So he left them and went away once more and prayed
> the third time, saying the same thing.

4. Following is a list of common defenses we often use to protect ourselves from grief and loss. Checkmark the common defenses that you sometimes use:

   - ☐ Denial
   - ☐ Minimizing (admitting something is wrong but in such a way that it appears less serious than it actually is)
   - ☐ Blaming others (or God)
   - ☐ "Over-spiritualizing"
   - ☐ Blaming oneself
   - ☐ Rationalizing (offering excuses and justifications)
   - ☐ Intellectualizing (giving analysis and theories to avoid personal awareness or difficult feelings)
   - ☐ Distracting
   - ☐ Becoming hostile
   - ☐ Medicating (with unhealthy addictions or attachments to numb our pain)

5. It is important for us to remember that Jesus was both fully human and fully God. Spend a few moments focusing on Jesus in verses 36–41. In contrast to the checklist in question 4, what were some of the ways he dealt with and moved through his losses?

6. What about Jesus' example of grieving most speaks to you about embracing your own grief and loss?

Application (20 minutes)

Take 5–7 minutes on your own to journal your answers to questions 7–9 below.

7. Using the chart that follows, choose two or three age ranges of your life, and write down your significant losses during those years.

GRIEF CHART

Age (in years)	Losses/Disappointments Experienced	Your Response at the Time
3–12		
13–18		
19–25		
26–40		
41+		

8. What was the experience of filling out the chart like for you? Did it reveal anything new to you? Explain.

9. One of the central messages of Christianity is that suffering and death bring resurrection and new life. Are there any losses you have not yet embraced where new life is still waiting to be birthed?

10. Break into groups of two or three people and share your answers to questions 8 and 9.

VIDEO: Closing Summary (8 minutes)

Watch the closing video summary for Session 5 and use the space provided to note anything that stands out to you.

NOTES

Between-Sessions Personal Study

SESSION 5

Read chapter 6 of the book *Emotionally Healthy Spirituality*, "Discover the Rhythms of the Daily Office and Sabbath." Use the space provided to note any insights or questions you might want to bring to the next group session.

Prayerfully read Week 5 of the devotional *Emotionally Healthy Spirituality Day by Day*, "Enlarge Your Soul through Grief and Loss." Use the space provided to answer the Questions to Consider and/or to journal your thoughts each day.

Day 1 Questions to Consider:

What does it mean for you to pray, "Yet not as I will, but as you will"?

How can you see God enlarging your soul through your losses?

Day 2 Questions to Consider:

In what ways is God bringing you to your knees before him through difficulties and setbacks in your life today?

What about Horatio Spafford and his relationship with Christ moves you the most?

Day 3 Questions to Consider:

What "road closed" sign is before you today that may be God's way of redirecting you to something new?

Name one or two limits God has placed in your life today as a gift.

Day 4 Questions to Consider:

What might it mean for you to mature by entering the painful reality of your losses rather than avoiding them?

How would it change your prayer life to bring to God what is *actually* in you and not what you think *ought* to be in you?

Day 5 Questions to Consider:

In what way(s) are you tempted to spin or cover over your losses and miss God's deeper work in your interior?

How is God coming to you through the "mini-deaths" in your life now?

SESSION 6

Discover the Rhythms of the Daily Office and Sabbath

Daily Office (8 minutes)

Do one of the Daily Offices from Week 6 of *Emotionally Healthy Spirituality Day by Day* to begin your session. **(Leaders, please see point number two in the "General Guidelines" on page 124.)**

Introduction (1 minute)

Many of us are eager to develop our relationship with God. The problem, however, is that we can't seem to stop long enough to be with him. And if we aren't busy, we feel guilty that we are wasting time and not being productive. It is like being addicted—not to drugs or alcohol—but to tasks, work, and doing.

But God is offering us a way to deeply root our lives in him. This can be found in two ancient disciplines going back thousands of years—the Daily Office and Sabbath. When placed inside present-day Christianity, the Daily Office and Sabbath are groundbreaking, countercultural acts that go against the grain of our fast-paced Western culture.

Stopping for the Daily Office and Sabbath is not meant to add another "to-do" to our already busy schedules. It is the resetting of our entire lives toward a new destination—God himself. These practices enable us to stay attuned to God's presence throughout our days and weeks.

Growing Connected (10 minutes)

1. *Day by Day* Debrief: What obstacles, difficulties, or successes did you experience in meeting with God this past week using the *EH Spirituality Day by Day* devotional? Have two or three people share.

2. On a scale of 1 to 10 (1 = least busy to 10 = very busy), how busy are you? And where on the scale would you like to be?

VIDEO: Discover the Rhythms of the Daily Office and Sabbath (13 minutes)

Watch the video segment for Session 6. Use the space provided to note anything that stands out to you.

NOTES

Group Discussion (45 minutes)

Starters (10 minutes)

3. What is one practice you do on a daily/weekly basis that helps you stay connected to God?

Bible Study: Daniel 6:6–10; Exodus 20:1–17 (35 minutes)

Read aloud the introductory paragraph and the Daniel passage, and then answer questions 4–6. Then read aloud the Ten Commandments from Exodus 20:1–17 before answering questions 7–9.

After being forcibly removed from his country and home, Daniel was given a prestigious education and high-level job in government. The pressure on him to conform to the worldly, pagan values of Babylon was great. The following example gives us insight into one of the secrets of his faithful devotion to God. Read Daniel 6:6–10.

6 So these administrators and satraps went as a group to the king and said: "May King Darius live forever! 7 The royal administrators, prefects, satraps, advisers and governors have all agreed that the king should issue an edict and enforce the decree that anyone who prays to any god or human being during the next thirty days, except to you, Your Majesty, shall be thrown into the lions' den. 8 Now, Your Majesty, issue the decree and put it in writing so that it cannot be altered—in accordance with the law of the Medes and Persians, which cannot be repealed." 9 So King Darius put the decree in writing.

10 Now when Daniel learned that the decree had been published, he went home to his upstairs room where the windows opened toward Jerusalem. Three times a day he got down on his knees and prayed, giving thanks to his God, just as he had done before.

4. Reread verse 10 aloud. How do the words in this verse speak to you?

5. How do you think this practice anchored Daniel in God and enabled him to resist the great pressure he was facing?

6. What are the greatest obstacles preventing you from stopping to be with God once or twice a day?

These are the Ten Commandments as recorded in Exodus 20:1–17:

> [1] And God spoke all these words:
>
> [2] "I am the LORD your God, who brought you out of Egypt, out of the land of slavery.
>
> [3] "You shall have no other gods before me.
>
> [4] "You shall not make for yourself an image in the form of anything in heaven above or on the earth beneath or in the waters below. . . .
>
> [7] "You shall not misuse the name of the LORD your God, for the LORD will not hold anyone guiltless who misuses his name.
>
> [8] "Remember the Sabbath day by keeping it holy. [9] Six days you shall labor and do all your work, [10] but the seventh day is a Sabbath to the LORD your God. On it you shall not do any work, neither you, nor your son or daughter, nor your male or female servant, nor your animals, nor any foreigner residing in your towns. [11] For in six days the LORD made the heavens and the earth, the sea, and all that is in them, but he rested on the seventh day. Therefore, the LORD blessed the Sabbath day and made it holy.
>
> [12] "Honor your father and your mother, so that you may live long in the land the LORD your God is giving you.
>
> [13] "You shall not murder.
>
> [14] "You shall not commit adultery.
>
> [15] "You shall not steal.
>
> [16] "You shall not give false testimony against your neighbor.
>
> [17] "You shall not covet your neighbor's house. You shall not covet your neighbor's wife, or his male or female servant, his ox or donkey, or anything that belongs to your neighbor."

7. Reread the fourth commandment in verses 8–11. Biblical Sabbaths are a 24-hour block of time each week with four characteristics (see next page) that distinguish this time from a "day off."

- **Stop:** "To stop" is built into the literal meaning of the Hebrew word. We have limits. God is on the throne running the world. We are called to let go and trust him.
- **Rest:** Once we stop, we are called to rest from our work and our "doings."
- **Delight:** We are to slow down so we can enjoy what we have been given.
- **Contemplate:** We seek to see the invisible in the visible—to recognize the hidden ways the miracle of life is all around us in his gifts to us.

What 24-hour period might work for you at this phase of your journey to practice Sabbath?

8. What do you need to stop that relates to your work—paid and unpaid?

9. What activities, places, and/or people create rest and delight for you?

Application (25 minutes)

10. Review the "Sabbath FAQs" on pages 88–91. Pick one question from among that list. In groups of two or three, discuss with one another the response to your question.

11. In the space provided, take a few minutes to journal one small step you can take to begin to incorporate Sabbath as a spiritual formation practice?

12. Share that step with one other person.

VIDEO: Closing Summary (9 minutes)

Watch the closing video summary for Session 6 and use the space provided to note anything that stands out to you.

NOTES

Sabbath FAQs

1. Why do I need to keep Sabbath for a whole 24-hour period each week?

God created us in his image for a rhythm of work and rest. When we violate that rhythm, we do violence to our own souls. Moreover, we are not defined by what we do or what we produce. We are defined by God's unconditional love for us in Christ Jesus. Therefore, we don't keep Sabbath to earn God's love. Rather, Sabbath is God's gift to keep us centered and rooted in that amazing reality. It is not an accident that this essential spiritual formation practice is found in the fourth commandment of the Ten Commandments.

2. How do I go about deciding what specific activities are acceptable and unacceptable on the Sabbath?

Reflect on the following questions as you sort out God's pathway for you:

- What do I need to stop that relates to my work—paid and unpaid?
- What activities create delight and rest for me?
- How can I structure my day to cultivate a greater awareness of God in my life and in the world?
- What might help me see God's goodness and miracles all around me today?

Lynne Baab says, "Whatever we choose to do for Sabbath needs to give us rest and life over time. The challenge is discernment, experimenting to find what works for us and the people we love, what helps us catch our breath and remember who we are as God's beloved."

3. Do I need a day-off and a Sabbath?

You will need at least a half–day, or several hours, to prepare for Sabbath. Part of the Sabbath experience is the preparation time. What needs to happen before Sabbath starts so you (or your family) can experience true rest on the day itself? A basic list of what needs to get done before Sabbath starts might include getting the errands and chores of life done (e.g., food shopping, laundry, errands, cleaning the house, bringing closure to your work, final phone calls, paying bills). These things make Sabbath more restful and communicate the order and peace many of us long for.

4. What do I do about my tendency to perfectionism?

We don't ever get Sabbath "right." Sabbath is a day to let go of perfectionism and let God run the universe. Inconsistencies, bad choices, and learning from our mistakes are part of the point. Do your best to stop working, letting God worry about what you're not doing right, taking your focus off yourself so you can rest in him.

5. Isn't Jesus our Sabbath-rest? Is this another works-righteousness?

Jesus reinforced the gift of Sabbath amid all the abuses of his day. He reminds us, "The Sabbath was made for people, not people for the Sabbath" (Mark 2:27). To keep Sabbath is to exercise one's freedom, to declare oneself to be neither a tool to be "employed" nor a beast to be burdened. Sabbath-keeping is an invitation to rest because God rested. This rest serves as a sign of contemplation and abundance. God's gifts to humanity are so generous that we are able to rest. Our rest indicates that we depend completely on the God who redeemed us from sin, death, and evil.

6. How do I cease from the work of parenting?

You cannot stop changing diapers, of course. But you can cease from tidying up, cooking, doing laundry, and running errands. You can do some things together as a family. You can hire a babysitter, so you and your spouse can get time alone. Or you can take time alone for yourself, leaving parenting to your spouse. Then, you take the children and give equal time to him/her.

7. What do I do about my children who aren't interested in Sabbath?

The important thing to remember is that this is not a day of deprivation. Sabbath is to be a delight. Rather than simply taking things away, think about things you can add (e.g., special desserts, a movie, a creative family activity—depending on the ages of your children). It doesn't have to be a forced family day. If your children are older, they are going to naturally want to connect with their friends. That is okay. You will go through many transitions in keeping Sabbath, depending on your children's ages and temperaments. But, whenever possible, remember this is a wonderful opportunity to build rhythm, intentionality, and sacred traditions into your family.

8. What about sports and extracurricular activities my children may be involved in?

There may be some activities you want to eliminate because of the stress involved. But there may be others (e.g., if your child loves soccer) that you will continue, but you will do so in a different spirit. You may go to the soccer game but you are doing it without multitasking, talking on the phone, reading emails, or reading work-related paperwork at halftime or during time outs. You can focus on enjoying the game, other parents, or the very gift of the human body able to participate in athletics.

9. How, like Jesus, can we exercise compassion on the Sabbath without turning it into work?

The Jews have long believed that showing compassion on the Sabbath reflects the glorious abundance of the day. We rest from work in order to turn our hearts toward God, and God is always concerned with human need. When we stop for Sabbath, it may happen that we become more attentive to the problems of the world around us. This ultimately leads us to show more, not less, compassion. Maybe the Good Samaritan was on his Sabbath! Just be careful that it is not a "should." Rejoice in small acts of caring, allowing them to connect us to our compassionate God.

10. Which day is the Sabbath? Sunday or Saturday? I have heard different views.

Paul addresses this very issue in the Jew/Gentile/multicultural church in Romans 14:1–8. He writes: "One man considers one day more sacred than another; another considers every day alike. Each one should be fully convinced in his own mind. He who regards one day as special, does so to the Lord . . ." I believe the key principle is keeping a rhythm for the same day of the week each week. Doing it around the Sunday gathering of worship is clearly best when possible, I believe, as this is part of our contemplation.

11. Can I serve at church as a volunteer? Should I stop?

Yes, you can serve in your community. Except for a very, very few, our work is not at our church. We work as secretaries, social workers, teachers, lawyers, accountants, moms/dads at home, students, etc. Serving in our church community is not our job. Hopefully, there is delight in serving Christ as a children's worker, usher, greeter, etc. It is also important to remember that showing mercy and compassion was the missing element Jesus brought back into God's original intention of Sabbath-keeping. Treating people like Christ—whether children, youth, or adults—is the heart of what we seek to do in our churches.

Between-Sessions Personal Study

SESSION 6

Read chapter 7 of the book *Emotionally Healthy Spirituality*, "Grow into an Emotionally Mature Adult." Use the space provided to note any insights or questions you might want to bring to the next group session.

Prayerfully read Week 6 of the devotional *Emotionally Healthy Spirituality Day by Day*, "Discover the Rhythms of the Daily Office and Sabbath." Use the space provided to answer the Questions to Consider and/or to journal your thoughts each day.

Day 1 Questions to Consider:

Pause and consider your day. What "seeds" from God might be coming to you that you don't want to miss?

How do you hear the invitation to "stop and surrender to God in trust" today?

Day 2 Questions to Consider:

When can you set aside some time for extended, uninterrupted silence to hear God?

How might you be busier than God requires?

Day 3 Questions to Consider:

What keeps you from silence?

How do the rhythms you see in nature (spring, summer, fall, winter, day, night) speak to you about the kind of rhythms you desire for your own life?

Day 4 Questions to Consider:

What is your greatest fear in stopping for a 24-hour period each week?

How might Sabbath-keeping (for an entire 24-hour period) or a Daily Office (a mini-Sabbath for a few minutes) provide for you a taste of eternity?

Day 5 Questions to Consider:

How will you allow God to lead you to the "quiet waters" of rest this week so that you experience his unconditional love and acceptance?

How might the truth that God doesn't want to use you, but to enjoy you, give you a vision for celebrating Sabbath?

SESSION 7

Grow into an Emotionally Mature Adult

Daily Office (8 minutes)

Do one of the Daily Offices from Week 7 of *Emotionally Healthy Spirituality Day by Day* to begin your session. **(Leaders, please see point number two in the "General Guidelines" on page 124.)**

Introduction (1 minute)

The goal of the Christian life is to love well. Jesus was aware that true spirituality included not only loving God, but also the skill of loving others maturely.

Growing into an emotionally mature Christian person includes experiencing each individual, ourselves included, as sacred, or as Martin Buber put it, as a "Thou" rather than an "It." Becoming emotionally mature requires learning, practicing, and integrating such skills as speaking respectfully, listening with empathy, negotiating conflict fairly, and uncovering the hidden expectations we have of others . . . just to name a few.

As we will see in today's Bible study on the parable of the Good Samaritan, both self-respect and compassion for others are part of a life rooted in "I-Thou" relating.

Growing Connected (10 minutes)

1. *Day by Day* Debrief: What obstacles, difficulties, or successes did you experience in meeting with God this past week using the *EH Spirituality Day by Day* devotional? Have two or three people share.

2. As a group, brainstorm two lists (on a whiteboard, if one is available): qualities that describe emotional immaturity and qualities that describe emotional maturity. As you think about these qualities, consider how we treat/view ourselves and how we treat/view other people.

Emotional Immaturity	Emotional Maturity

VIDEO: Grow into an Emotionally Mature Adult (13 minutes)

Watch the video segment for Session 7. Use the space provided to note anything that stands out to you.

NOTES

Group Discussion (45 minutes)

Starters (10 minutes)

3. Why do you think we can be committed and "growing" in Christ and yet not be growing in our ability to be "prayerfully present" or loving toward others?

Bible Study: Luke 10:25–37 (35 minutes)

Read the introductory paragraph and Scripture passage, and then discuss the questions that follow.

Who can hear a story on the news about someone getting mugged, robbed, stripped naked, and left for dead in an alleyway without being affected? These real-life stories also happened in the days of Jesus. And Jesus told a parable recorded in Luke 10:25–37 that imagines one such disturbing story—with an unusual twist.

25 On one occasion an expert in the law stood up to test Jesus. "Teacher,"
he asked, "what must I do to inherit eternal life?"
26 "What is written in the Law?" he replied. "How do you read it?"
27 He answered, "'Love the Lord your God with all your heart and
with all your soul and with all your strength and with all your mind';
and, 'Love your neighbor as yourself.'"
28 "You have answered correctly," Jesus replied. "Do this and you
will live."
29 But he wanted to justify himself, so he asked Jesus, "And who is
my neighbor?"
30 In reply Jesus said: "A man was going down from Jerusalem to
Jericho, when he was attacked by robbers. They stripped him of his
clothes, beat him and went away, leaving him half dead. 31 A priest
happened to be going down the same road, and when he saw the man,
he passed by on the other side. 32 So too, a Levite, when he came to the
place and saw him, passed by on the other side. 33 But a Samaritan, as he
traveled, came where the man was; and when he saw him, he took pity
on him. 34 He went to him and bandaged his wounds, pouring on oil and
wine. Then he put the man on his own donkey, brought him to an inn
and took care of him. 35 The next day he took out two denarii and gave
them to the innkeeper. 'Look after him,' he said, 'and when I return, I
will reimburse you for any extra expense you may have.'
36 "Which of these three do you think was a neighbor to the man
who fell into the hands of robbers?"
37 The expert in the law replied, "The one who had mercy on him."
Jesus told him, "Go and do likewise."

4. According to Martin Buber, the great Jewish theologian, we treat people as an "It" when we use them as means to an end or as objects. We treat people as a "Thou" when we recognize each person as a separate human being made in God's image and treat them with dignity and respect.[3] If you were the priest or Levite, what are some of the

reasons you may have passed by this man and treated him as an "It" instead of a "Thou"?

5. Look back at verses 31–33. What did the Samaritan see and feel that the priest and Levite did not?

6. On your own, journal your thoughts on the following questions for two minutes. Then have one or two volunteers share their responses.

 - Can you think of a time when you were seen in a negative light, treated as inferior, or passed over as invisible? How did it feel?

 - Who have you been taught not to see (i.e., to treat as an "It")?

7. Reread verses 33–36. The Samaritan's compassion led him to stop and help the hurting man. At the same time, how did he demonstrate self-respect and awareness of his limits?

8. What are some of your challenges when it comes to loving your neighbor and loving yourself?

9. In light of how God is coming to you through this study, how do you hear the words in verse 37 to "go and do likewise"?

Application[4] (25 minutes)

Read aloud the introductory paragraphs below. Answer questions 10 and 11 on your own. Then, in groups of two or three, answer question 12 and close in prayer.

One way of growing in the area of loving others well, and treating ourselves and others as a "Thou," is to understand how we manage our expectations in relationships.

EXPECTATIONS are ASSUMPTIONS about what someone SHOULD do. Every time we make an assumption about someone without checking it out, it is likely we are treating them as an "It" and not a "Thou." Why? We are jumping to conclusions without having checked out the assumption. Consider how you feel when someone is angry with you because you didn't fulfill their expectations, yet they never communicated this expectation to you. They simply assumed you should know.

Unmet and unclear expectations can create havoc in our places of employment, classrooms, friendships, dating relationships, marriages, sports teams, families, and churches. We expect other people to know what we want before we say it. The problem with most expectations is that they are:

- **Unconscious:** We may have expectations we're not even aware of until we are disappointed by someone.
- **Unrealistic:** We may develop unrealistic expectations by watching TV, movies, or other people/resources that give false impressions.
- **Unspoken:** We may have never told our spouse, friend, or employee what we expect, yet we are angry when our "expectations" are not met.
- **Un-agreed upon:** We may have had our own thoughts about what was expected, but those thoughts were never agreed upon by the other person.

10. Think of a recent, simple expectation that went unmet and made you angry or disappointed. (*Ex.*: I expected my husband to accompany me to my office party this past weekend; I expected to socialize with members of my small group outside the meeting times; I expected my teenagers to put their dirty dishes in the dishwasher; I expected my boss to give me at least a 5 percent cost of living raise last year.) Write yours down.

11. Now compare that unmet expectation with the inventory questions below:

 - **Conscious:** Were you conscious (aware) you had this expectation?

 - **Realistic:** Is the expectation realistic regarding the other person?

 - **Spoken:** Have you clearly spoken the expectation to them or do you just think "they should know"?

 - **Agreed upon:** Has the other person agreed to the expectation?

Remember this principle: Expectations are only valid when they have been mutually agreed upon. These are the expectations we have a right to expect.

12. Break into groups of two or three and respond to the following two questions:

 - What did you discover about your expectations?

- What step(s) can you take to make your expectations conscious, spoken, realistic, and agreed upon so that you are relating in an "I-Thou" way?

VIDEO: Closing Summary (7 minutes)

Watch the closing video summary for Session 7 and use the space provided to note anything that stands out to you.

NOTES

Between-Sessions Personal Study

SESSION 7

Read chapter 8 of the book *Emotionally Healthy Spirituality*, "Go the Next Step to Develop a 'Rule of Life.'" Use the space provided to note any insights or questions you might want to bring to the next group session.

Prayerfully read Week 7 of the devotional *Emotionally Healthy Spirituality Day by Day*, "Grow into an Emotionally Mature Adult." Use the space provided to answer the Questions to Consider and/or to journal your thoughts each day.

Day 1 Questions to Consider:

What is one step you can take to place yourself (with all your flaws) in the hands of Jesus, inviting him to mold you into a spiritually and emotionally mature disciple?

How can you "practice the presence of people," within an awareness of his presence today?

Day 2 Questions to Consider:

Which words from Henri Nouwen's quotation about the prodigal son speak to you?

What is the biggest challenge you face in being still before the Lord?

Day 3 Questions to Consider:

How can you begin to see Jesus Christ in the people you meet this week?

Take a few moments and consider the people you will encounter today. What might it look like for you to slow down and treat each one as a "Thou" rather than an "It"?

Day 4 Questions to Consider:

What sometimes distracts you from seeing the people you are with as they really are?

What might be one way you can let go of power and control, and, in love, choose to serve someone today?

Day 5 Questions to Consider:

Is there someone God is calling you to stop judging? What might it look like to bless and extend mercy to them?

Where are you experiencing tensions in relationships that you are afraid to disrupt?

SESSION 8

Go the Next Step to Develop a "Rule of Life"

Daily Office (8 minutes)

Do one of the Daily Offices from Week 8 of *Emotionally Healthy Spirituality Day by Day* to begin your session. **(Leaders, please see point number two in the "General Guidelines" on page 124.)**

Introduction (1 minute)

If we are to nurture a heart that treats every person, ourselves included, as a "Thou" instead of "It," we need to be intentional about our lives. By ordering our lives to contemplate the love of Christ and to receive the love of Christ, we will be able to give the love of Christ away to others. In this way, he transforms our lives into a gift to our families, friends, coworkers, and communities.

The problem again, however, is our busyness and lack of intentionality. Often, we find ourselves unfocused, distracted, and spiritually adrift. Few of us have a conscious plan for intentionally developing our spiritual lives.

Nurturing a growing spirituality in our present-day culture calls for a thoughtful, conscious, purposeful plan. To do this well requires us to uncover another ancient buried treasure—a "Rule of Life."

Growing Connected (12 minutes)

1. *Day by Day Debrief*: What obstacles, difficulties, or successes did you experience in meeting with God this past week using the *EH Spirituality Day by Day* devotional? Have two or three people share.

2. Before we launch fully into our final session, it is important that we pause and consider the past seven sessions:

   - The Problem of Emotionally Unhealthy Spirituality
     (Saul—emotionally unaware and not cultivating his relationship with God)
   - Know Yourself That You May Know God
     (David—courageously living out of his true self)
   - Going Back in Order to Go Forward
     (Joseph—transformed by a very difficult past)
   - Journey through the Wall
     (Abraham—trusting God in a "dark night of the soul")
   - Enlarge Your Soul through Grief and Loss
     (Jesus in Gethsemane—embracing God's will)
   - Discover the Rhythms of the Daily Office and Sabbath
     (Daniel—anchoring himself in God)
   - Grow into an Emotionally Mature Adult
     (The Good Samaritan—modeling an "I-Thou" heart to others)

   In light of how God has been coming to you throughout these sessions, complete the following sentence (and then briefly share with the group as time permits):

   I am beginning to realize . . .

VIDEO: Go the Next Step to Develop a "Rule of Life" (13 minutes)

Watch the video segment for Session 8. Use the space provided to note anything that stands out to you.

NOTES

Group Discussion (25 minutes)

Starters (10 minutes)

3. Take about 5 minutes to think about your life in terms of prayer, rest, work/activity, and relationships. In each box, write one specific thing you are currently doing in each of these four areas to nurture your relationship with Jesus. Then briefly take turns sharing your "nurture" habits with the group.

Prayer	**Rest**
Work/Activity	**Relationships**

Bible Study: Acts 2:42–47 (15 minutes)

Have a volunteer(s) read the introductory paragraph and Scripture passage, and then discuss the questions that follow.

The Rule of Life will be introduced as we study the first Christian community in the book of Acts. The word *rule* comes from the Greek word for "trellis." A trellis is a tool that enables a grapevine to get off the ground and grow upward, becoming more fruitful and productive. In the same way, a Rule of Life is a trellis that helps us abide in Christ and become more fruitful spiritually.[5] Read Acts 2:42–47:

> 42 They devoted themselves to the apostles' teaching and to fellowship, to the breaking of bread and to prayer. 43 Everyone was filled with awe at the many wonders and signs performed by the apostles. 44 All the believers were together and had everything in common. 45 They sold property and possessions to give to anyone who had need. 46 Every day they continued to meet together in the temple courts. They broke bread in their homes and ate together with glad and sincere hearts, 47 praising God and enjoying the favor of all the people. And the Lord added to their number daily those who were being saved.

4. In the book of Acts, we are given a window into the life of the first community of believers soon after the coming of the Holy Spirit at Pentecost when three thousand people came to faith in Christ. What speaks to you from this passage?

5. Based on this one passage, how would you describe this community's Rule of Life? Describe the activities/disciplines they used to grow and mature in Christ.

Application (43 minutes)

Read the introductory paragraphs as well as question 6 (pages 116–117), and answer question 6 on your own (15 minutes). Then follow the instructions provided for questions 7 and 8.

Now it is time for you to begin developing your own personal Rule of Life. The following story and questions are meant to help you discern what may be getting in the way of developing a way of life that keeps you closely connected to God.

In his book *A Hidden Wholeness*,[6] Parker Palmer relates a story about farmers in the Midwest who would prepare for blizzards by tying a rope from the back door of their house out to the barn as a guide to ensure they could return safely home. These blizzards came quickly and fiercely and were highly dangerous. When their full force was blowing, a farmer could not see the end of his or her hand. Many froze to death in those blizzards, disoriented by their inability to see. They wandered in circles, lost sometimes in their own backyards. If they lost their grip on the rope, it became impossible for them to find their way home. Some froze within feet of their own back door, never realizing how close they were to safety.

Many of us are wandering amidst the blizzards of life and have lost our way spiritually.

6. Spend time alone with God around the following questions:
    - What is the nature of your blizzard at this time?

    - What contributes to your blizzard? What does it look like? Feel like?

    - What does that blizzard obscure? What gets "lost"?

- We each need a rope to keep us connected to God. Notice that every rope is actually made up of a series of smaller, intertwined threads. In light of your life at this time, what "threads" do you want to make up your rope (Rule of Life)?

7. After your time alone, get into groups of two. Share what you discovered in your time alone. (10 minutes)

8. Return to your small group and invite those who would like to share how God is coming to them regarding the blizzard and their own personal "Rule of Life"? (13 minutes)

VIDEO: Closing Summary (8 minutes)

Watch the closing video summary for Session 8 and use the space provided to note anything that stands out to you.

NOTES

Personal Study for the Coming Days

SESSION 8

Prayerfully read Week 8 of the devotional *Emotionally Healthy Spirituality Day by Day*, "Go the Next Step to Develop a 'Rule of Life.'" Use the space provided to answer the Questions to Consider and/or to journal your thoughts each day.

Day 1 Questions to Consider:

What is your plan, in the midst of your busy day, for not leaving the nurture of your interior life with God to chance?

How and why do you think finding time alone with God in silence might "teach you everything"?

Day 2 Questions to Consider:

What spoke to you when you read about the lifestyle of the early Christians in Acts and the way they sought to follow the life of Jesus?

Where can you find the time in your week to "gaze on the infinite beauty of God"?

Day 3 Questions to Consider:

What difference might it make if you were to practice "building open spaces" into your life?

In what ways might God be searching for you today—knocking on the door of your life?

Day 4 Questions to Consider:

What might it look like for you to "run on the path of God's commandments"?

What lines from Patrick's prayer speak to you? Carry them in your heart today.

Day 5 Questions to Consider:

What fears are you carrying that you can release to your Abba Father today?

What might it look like for God's love to invade and fill you, guiding you to what you must do?

Leader's Guide

The EH Spirituality Course, of which this workbook is a part, provides an indispensable foundation to integrate the larger, deeper, beneath-the-surface discipleship paradigm of Emotionally Healthy Spirituality into the life of your church.

Overview of the Course

The EH Spirituality Course has been designed and structured to offer a high-quality teaching experience in a large group setting while at the same time offering close community support within a small group.

Why?

At New Life Fellowship Church and churches around the world, we realized that this content was so critical that it needed to be offered in a centralized format that would ensure a high-quality experience for participants.

First, we wanted every newcomer and member to grasp our core elements of following Jesus in a way that deeply transforms us. And, secondly, we wanted to ensure the long-term integration of EHS into every aspect of the church. The radical, introductory call of discipleship found in the *EH Spirituality Course* serves as both an entry point and an essential bridge into the larger EHS vision. For this reason, the *EH Spirituality Course* is offered at least one or two times a year in churches (along with the *EH Relationships Course*).

The EH Spirituality Course equips us in a discipleship paradigm that deeply changes **our relationship with God**. *The EH Relationships Course* then deeply changes **our relationship with others**. The two Courses together form the foundation of a powerful discipleship strategy.

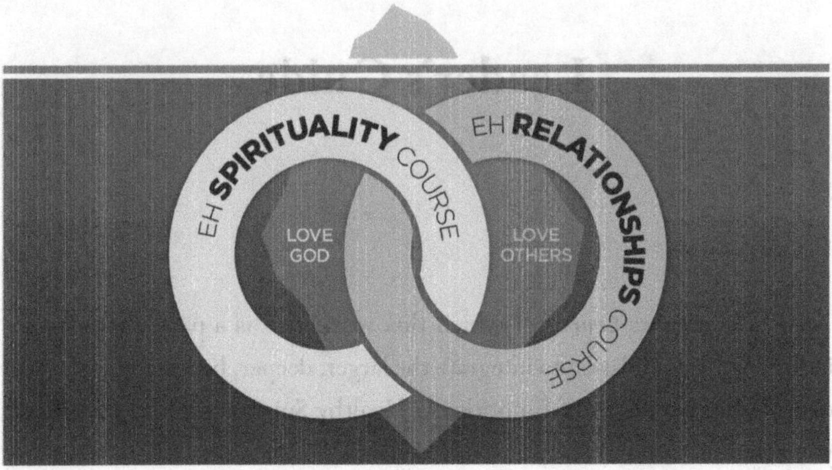

At New Life Fellowship Church our discipleship strategy builds on these two Courses. Go to www.emotionallyhealthy.org to download a variety of excellent, free resources to help you serve as the Point Leader of the course or a Small Group Table Leader.

General Guidelines

1. Be sure to work through the workbook content before each session. Becoming familiar with the material and instructions will allow you to comfortably lead your group. You will also want to read the corresponding chapter(s) of the *Emotionally Healthy Spirituality* book before each session. If possible, we recommend you watch the video segments as well.
2. The Point Leader, or another appointed person, will need to select a Daily Office to open each session. The initial large-group Daily Office (for Session 1) is particularly challenging because it will be the first exposure to silence and stillness for many people. Have them turn to the appropriate page in the *EH Spirituality Day by Day*

book and explain to them the elements of the Office before you begin. Refer to the Silence and Stillness guidelines below or display them on a PowerPoint slide as a brief orientation. While the Office may be difficult for some people, it will set a tone for the Course's centrality on being with Jesus. Specific suggestions on how to lead these Offices each week, and what you might say each week as an introduction, can be found at www.emotionallyhealthy.org/courses/the-ehs-course/.

SILENCE & STILLNESS GUIDELINES

The Lord will fight for you; you need only to be still. Ex 14:14

- **Sit down and take a few deep breaths to settle into the silence.**
- **Choose a very simple prayer to express your openness and desire for God.**
  (e.g. Abba, Father, Holy Spirit, Jesus, Here I am Lord)
- **Close your eyes and offer this prayer to Jesus, allowing His will and love full access in your life.**
- **When you become distracted, offer again your simple prayer back to God.**

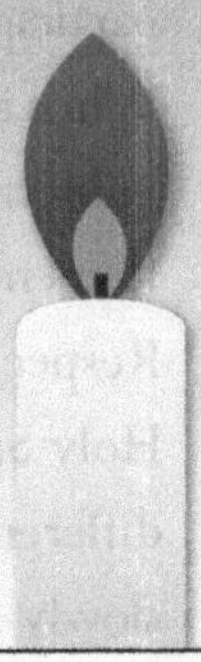

3. Have extra copies of this workbook, the *Emotionally Healthy Spirituality* book, and the *Emotionally Healthy Day by Day* devotional available for each participant to purchase at the first two sessions. Make scholarships available, if possible, for those who need financial assistance.
4. Each session—a combination of doing a Daily Office together, the video presentation and discussion, group and individual activities—will require 90–120 minutes to complete. Respect everyone by beginning and ending on time.
5. Set up the meeting room in a way that will comfortably seat all participants, preferably at a table so that everyone can see each other. Arrive at least 15 minutes ahead of time to greet group members individually as they come in.

6. The nature of this material easily lends itself to lengthy sharing. One of your greatest challenges as the Small Group Table Leader will be to keep the group focused and to share within the time frames allotted for each part of the session. Remember that each of these sessions could easily have been expanded into its own course. We have kept them together to serve a biblical framework that serves as an introduction into a life with God that goes beyond "tip of the iceberg spirituality." The implementation of these truths will involve the rest of people's lives.
7. If your table small group is large, you may want to break into smaller groups of three to four people so that everyone has a chance to participate.
8. When appropriate, it will be helpful if you lead by example—being vulnerable and open with life examples from your own journey. Remember, we are only experts on *our own* journey.
9. Respect where each person is in their journey with Christ. The Holy Spirit will prompt and lead each person differently and at different paces through this material. Remember that people change slowly—that includes you!
10. Being with Jesus is the core of *The EH Spirituality Course.* Learning the practice of silence to listen and *be with God* two or three times a day is the core discipline leading to a deep personal transformation. You will want to be sure to faithfully meet with God each day in the silence and stillness using *Emotionally Healthy Spirituality Day by Day: A 40 Day Journey with the Daily Office* and encourage participants to do the same.

    Beginning in Session 2, the following question is asked in the "Growing Connected" section: What obstacles, difficulties, or successes did you experience with God this week using the *EH Spirituality Day by Day* devotional?

Additional Suggestions[7]

1. Avoid answering your own questions. Feel free to rephrase a question.

2. Encourage more than one answer to each question. Ask, "What do the rest of you think?" or "Anyone else?"
3. Try to be affirming whenever possible. Let people know you appreciate their contributions.
4. Try not to reject an answer. If it is clearly wrong, ask, "What in the passage led you to that conclusion?"
5. Avoid going off on tangents. If people wander off course, gently bring them back to the subject at hand.

Specific Guidelines for Each Session

SESSION 1: The Problem of Emotionally Unhealthy Spirituality

In addition to the general guidelines, here are a few other key items for each session that you may find helpful.

Before the Session

- Read chapter 1 of the book *Emotionally Healthy Spirituality.*
- Select a Daily Office from Week 1 of *Emotionally Healthy Spirituality Day by Day* to begin the session. You will need 2–3 minutes to introduce the ideas of the Daily Office and stillness/silence. See point 2 under General Guidelines, pages 124–125.

Introduction

- Be sure to read aloud the "Suggested Guidelines for the Group" (pages 11–12) at the first two sessions.

Growing Connected

- This first "Growing Connected" section is longer than most to allow time for the Suggested Guidelines to be reviewed and for people to get to know one another with the second question: "Share your name and a few words about what makes you feel fully alive." You will want to think about this beforehand so you can give a concrete example from your own life.

Bible Study

- The command to "totally destroy everything," including women and children, presents a difficult moral and theological problem for the modern reader. Shortly after leaving Egypt, the Israelites "weary and worn out" were attacked by the Amalekites (Exodus 17:8–16). After God granted his people victory, he promised to completely destroy the Amalekites from the face of the earth (see also Deuteronomy 25:17–18). Now, through Saul, God determines to carry out his threat. You may want to mention three reasons for such a command. First, Israel was functioning as an instrument of God's judgment on a wicked, utterly sinful culture. Second, Israel needed to eliminate all forms of temptation that might corrupt and prevent them from being God's chosen instrument in the world. This drastic action was needed to maintain holiness (Deuteronomy 7:1–6; 20:16–18). Finally, in Hebrew the phrase "totally destroy" means "to devote to Yahweh." The spoils, then, were surrendered and dedicated to God and were in some way a sacrifice to God.
- (*Question* 7) For those who have not read the book, you will want to explain the iceberg illustration found on page 17 of chapter 1 of *Emotionally Healthy Spirituality*.

SESSION 2: Know Yourself That You May Know God

In addition to the general guidelines, here are some other helpful items to note by section:

Before the Session

- Read chapter 2 of the book *Emotionally Healthy Spirituality*.
- Select a Daily Office from Week 2 of *Emotionally Healthy Spirituality Day by Day* to begin the session. Again, take extra time as needed to explain the Daily Office and stillness/silence. See point 2 under General Guidelines.

Introduction

- Again, read aloud the "Suggested Guidelines for the Group" (pages 11–12).

Growing Connected

- Have copies of the *Emotionally Healthy Spirituality Course Workbook*, the *Emotionally Healthy Spirituality* book, and *Emotionally Healthy Spirituality Day by Day* devotional available for newcomers.
- (*Question 1*) This is the first time you'll debrief on the readings from *EH Spirituality Day by Day* that the group did the past week. Allow two or three people to share. We recommend about 7 minutes for debriefing and 10 minutes for question 2.
- (*Question 2*) Keep in mind that this question about people's dream job often offers to the speaker, as well as the group, a glimpse of their "true self" in surprising ways.

Starters

- You may want to reread the section "Discovering God's Will and Your Emotions" in *Emotionally Healthy Spirituality* (pages 48–49) for a brief summary of the role of feelings in discerning God's will.
- (*Questions 3 and 4*) This exercise may bring up significant pain in some of the members of the group (*ex.*: unresolved anger, sadness that has not been grieved, shame that has been masked). Remember that this is a limited exercise with one goal—to help people *begin* to be aware of how much is going on inside of them. This is not the time to fix or give advice. Giving people space to express their feelings is a gift enough. If "Pandora's box" opens for a member of the group, thank the person for their awareness and vulnerability and let them know that you would be glad to talk with them after the meeting, if they would like. It is important to recognize your role as facilitator/small group leader and not a professional counselor. In some cases, you may want to direct them to get the help they need beyond the limits of your group.

Bible Study

- One very helpful way to clarify this process of growing into our true selves in a new way is through use of a new term: *differentiation*. It refers to a person's capacity to "define his or her own life's goals and values apart from the pressures of those around them." The key emphasis of differentiation is the ability to think clearly and carefully as another means, besides our feelings, of knowing ourselves.

  It involves the ability to separate who you are from who you are not. The degree to which you are able to affirm your distinct values and goals apart from the pressures around you (separateness), while remaining close to people important to you (togetherness), helps determine your level of differentiation. People who are highly differentiated—such as David in this Bible account—can choose how they want to behave without being controlled by the approval or disapproval of others. Intensity of feelings, high stress, or the anxiety of others around them does not overwhelm their capacity to think intelligently.

  If you have additional time in your group, you can add the following question:

  David's ability to have a solid sense of who he was and who he wasn't in the midst of great trials and pressure is, in modern terminology, called *differentiation*. If David had been less differentiated, how might he have responded to his brothers, to Saul, and to Goliath?

SESSION 3: Going Back in Order to Go Forward

In addition to the general guidelines, here are some other helpful items to note by section:

Before the Session

- Read chapter 3 of the book *Emotionally Healthy Spirituality*.
- Select a Daily Office from Week 3 of *Emotionally Healthy Spirituality Day by Day* to begin the session.

Bible Study

- (*Question 6*) There is no way we can know for sure why Joseph weeps, but numerous possibilities exist. Perhaps he weeps because he knows that Jacob never left instructions that he should not harm the brothers. Maybe he realizes that they will never really change; they are still lying. Or it could be that they are finally admitting their terrible cruelty and sins against Joseph, and Joseph is weeping because his pain is finally validated or acknowledged. It could be that these are tears of joy as he realizes this is the fulfillment of his dream from Genesis 37, or that all the pain of his life has led to the truth of this moment when he must make a momentous decision of whether or not to forgive.

Application

- (*Question 9*) Encourage those who may have done work on their family of origin in some other setting, or even filled out the chart prior to the group meeting, to prayerfully ponder this exercise again. God often surprises us with fresh insights when we have space to contemplate these messages before him.

SESSION 4: Journey through the Wall

In addition to the general guidelines, here are some other helpful items to note by section:

Before the Session

- Read chapter 4 of the book *Emotionally Healthy Spirituality.*
- Select a Daily Office from Week 4 of *Emotionally Healthy Spirituality Day by Day* to begin the session.

Starters

- (*Question 3*) It usually takes a while (sometimes a long while!) to share about a Wall in a person's life. In light of only having a limited time for this question, you may want to use the time to share about a Wall that *you* have experienced, modeling how to do this in a limited time frame. We have found, at times, a well thought out testimony can sometimes be better than open sharing at this point. That may mean, however, that only two or three people will have time to share.

Bible Study

- (*Question* 7) We often carry within us inaccurate beliefs, or ideas, about God. For example, we take "Take delight in the LORD and he will give you the desires of your heart" (Psalm 37:4) to mean that if we are doing all we think God wants, then only good things will follow. The problem is that this contradicts other Scriptures such as our text here. Abraham was, as far as Scripture indicates, doing God's will. Yet it surely was not the desire of Abraham's heart to kill his son! Job is another classic example. He is an innocent sufferer—what makes his life so bewildering is the undeserved nature of his pain. The principle that we reap what we sow (Galatians 6:7–8) did not apply to Job, as his friends argued in Job chapters 3–37. For this reason, embracing our Walls frequently results in a crisis of faith for many believers rather than a doorway to transformation.

SESSION 5: Enlarge Your Soul through Grief and Loss

In addition to the general guidelines, here are some other helpful items to note by section:

Before the Session

- Read chapter 5 of the book *Emotionally Healthy Spirituality.*
- Select a Daily Office from Week 5 of *Emotionally Healthy Spirituality Day by Day* to begin the session.

Bible Study

- (*Question* 5) Jesus felt deeply his sorrow and pain. He did not "spin" or spiritualize it away. Jesus openly admitted his grief to those close to him and asked for their support. He repeatedly prayed to his Father for an alternative, but finally accepted the Father's "no." We see him move through a process from struggling to accept the Father's will to finally rising up to embrace it.

Application

- (*Question 9*) Two questions frequently come up in relation to grieving.
  1. How do I know I am grieving or if I should be grieving?

     One way to know if you are grieving is when you experience some of the following symptoms that normally accompany the stages of grieving—depression, anger, disbelief, yearning, bargaining. On the other hand, if you go through a significant loss but do not experience any of the above feelings, you may need a mature, objective outsider to help you move through the process.
  2. How do I know when I am done grieving?

     There are many factors that impact the amount of time needed to grieve. For example, the deeper the loss, the more time needed to grieve. The loss felt when a child leaves home and goes off to college is very different from the loss experienced should that child die tragically. Another factor is to respect how God has crafted each of us differently. The time you need and I need may be very different. One key principle is to not censor your emotions that come bubbling up as a result of the loss. Allow yourself, like Jesus and David, to feel them deeply before God. Censoring certain feelings because they are "bad" will only prolong or abort the discipleship process needed for long-term transformation in our lives.

SESSION 6: Discover the Rhythms of the Daily Office and Sabbath

In addition to the general guidelines, here are some other helpful items to note by section:

Before the Session

- Read chapter 6 of the book *Emotionally Healthy Spirituality*. The key word in this session is the word *rhythms*—in our days and weeks. Since we have been modeling Daily Offices each week, and talking about people's progress each week in developing a daily rhythm, the focus of this study will be on Sabbath. For more information on Sabbath, see www.emotionallyhealthy.org/courses/free-resources/.
- Select a Daily Office from Week 6 of *Emotionally Healthy Spirituality Day by Day* to begin the session.

Starters

- (*Question 3*) The Daily Office is a learned practice that takes time. For some it will be difficult; for others it will not be long enough. Others will struggle with all their interior noise. Be ready for a wide variety of responses. Hopefully, many will have adjusted comfortably to the rhythm of the Daily Office if they have been doing it since the Course began.

Bible Study

- (*Question 5*) The concept of the Daily Office has a rich history going back to David, Daniel, the Jews during Jesus' time, and the early church. It is the rhythm of stopping to be with God at set times so that we can "practice the presence of God" all through our day when we are active. Daniel seamlessly models this for us. Jesus, of course, does this for us as well as we observe him getting alone to pray often (Luke 4:42–44; 5:12; 6:12–13; 11:1).

Application

- The specific questions people have may go beyond the FAQs listed on pages 88–91. It is okay to say, "I don't know" and be comfortable in your own process of practicing Sabbath. For a larger treatment of the subject of Sabbath, read chapter 4, "Practice Sabbath Delight," in *The Emotionally Healthy Leader* (Zondervan, 2015). Another great resource is Wayne Mueller's *Sabbath: Finding Rest, Renewal, and Delight in Our Busy Lives* (New York: Bantam, 1999). Free sermons on Sabbath can also be found at www.emotionallyhealthy.org/media/sermons/. Finally, remember that the goal of this session is to provide people with an introduction to Sabbath, not to provide an exhaustive study.

SESSION 7: Grow into an Emotionally Mature Adult

In addition to the general guidelines, here are some other helpful items to note by section:

Before the Session

- Read chapter 7 of the book *Emotionally Healthy Spirituality.*
- Select a Daily Office from Week 7 of *Emotionally Healthy Spirituality Day by Day* to begin the session.

Starters

- (*Question 3*) Be aware this can lead to a lively discussion! The following are examples of possible answers: we often emphasize spiritual productivity and gifts, often overlooking troublesome character traits; we also equate the knowledge of Scripture to spiritual maturity and ignore emotional immaturity; loving well is much more difficult to measure than content and doing ministry for God. So be prepared to end this discussion in the time allotted and move on to the next section.

Bible Study

- (*Question 8*) It is important that we maintain the creative tension and healthy balance between self-care and self-giving. Living at either extreme leads us to eventually resent people or ignore those in need around us altogether. The Samaritan stopped to help the hurting man. At the same time, he had the self-awareness and self-respect to recognize his own limits and decided to resume his own journey the next day. A healthy balance of self-care and self-giving in our lives is necessary in order to live out an "I-Thou" relationship both toward ourselves and others.

Application

- (*Questions 10 and 11*) Advise participants beforehand to avoid examples of expectations around moral issues or responsibilities (*ex.*: domestic abuse, adultery, parent's role in nurturing children, financial integrity in the church). These issues go beyond the scope of this exercise.

SESSION 8: Go the Next Step to Develop a "Rule of Life"

In addition to the general guidelines, here are some other helpful items to note by section:

Before the Session

- Read chapter 8 of the book *Emotionally Healthy Spirituality.*
- Select a Daily Office from Week 8 of *Emotionally Healthy Spirituality Day by Day* to begin the session.

Bible Study

- Please note that this Bible Study section is intentionally only 15 minutes. We have placed the weight of this final meeting on the "Application" section, which requires about 45 minutes.
- (*Question 5*) Notice that there is no hint of legalism or "shoulds" in the description of the church in Acts. Jesus said, "Come to me, all you who are weary. . . . My yoke is easy and my burden is light" (Matthew 11:28–30). In the same way, any healthy Rule of Life we develop needs to fit how God made us at this particular season of our life.

Application

- This exercise is best done when participants are given physical space to be alone. If space allows, have the individual members find a personal spot where they can spend these 20 minutes in solitude contemplating the questions before God.

Notes

1. For a more complete understanding of what we mean by emotional health and contemplative spirituality, see the book *Emotionally Healthy Spirituality*, pages 212–213.
2. See *Emotionally Healthy Spirituality*, pages 212–213.
3. For a fuller discussion of Martin Buber's distinction between "I-It" and "I-Thou" relationships, see *Emotionally Healthy Spirituality*, 172–175.
4. This exercise is adapted from Pat Ennis, *The Third Option: An Ongoing Program to Build Better Marriages*, Teachers Manual, Topic #3, "Expectations," 1–9.
5. Remember, a Rule of Life is simply an intentional, conscious plan to keep God at the center of everything we do. It provides guidelines to help us continually remember God as the source of our lives. It includes our unique combination of spiritual practices that provide structure and direction for us to intentionally pay attention and remember God in everything we do.
6. Parker Palmer, *A Hidden Wholeness* (San Francisco: Jossey-Bass, 2009).
7. Adapted from James F. Nyquist and Jack Kuhatschek, *Leading Bible Discussions* (Downers Grove, Ill.: InterVarsity Press, 1985).

About the Authors

Geri Scazzero is the author of the bestselling *The Emotionally Healthy Woman*, *The Emotionally Healthy Woman Workbook*, and coauthor of *The Emotionally Healthy Relationships Course*. She is also, along with her husband Pete, the cofounder of Emotionally Healthy Spirituality, equipping the church in a discipleship that deeply changes lives.

Geri has served on staff at New Life Fellowship Church in New York City for the last twenty-nine years and is a popular speaker to pastors, church leaders, and at women's conferences—both in North America and internationally.

Connect with Geri on Facebook **(www.facebook.com/GeriScazzero)**.

Pete Scazzero is the founder of New Life Fellowship Church in Queens, New York, a large, multiracial church with more than seventy-three countries represented. After serving as senior pastor for twenty-six years, Pete now serves as a teaching pastor/pastor at large. He is the author of the recently released *The Emotionally Healthy Leader* and two bestselling books: *The Emotionally Healthy Church* and *Emotionally Healthy Spirituality*. He is also the coauthor of *The Emotionally Healthy Relationships Course*. Pete and Geri have four lovely daughters.

Connect with Pete on Twitter **@petescazzero** or Facebook.

For more information, visit emotionallyhealthy.org.

JOIN US

Make Disciples that Change the World

emotionallyhealthy.org

In this groundbreaking book, Peter Scazzero integrates a deep spirituality with Jesus to the crucial tasks of planning, creating healthy culture, team building, the healthy exercise of organizational power, transitions, and more. For good reason, this book has become a "must read" for leaders and teams around the world.

Chapter 1: The Problem of Emotionally Unhealthy Leadership

The Inner Life

Chapter 2: Face Your Shadow

Chapter 3: Lead Out of Your Marriage or Singleness

Chapter 4: Slow Down for Sabbath Delight

Chapter 5: Practice Sabbath Delight

The Outer Life

Chapter 6: Planning and Decision Making

Chapter 7: Culture and Team Building

Chapter 8: Power and Wise Boundaries

Chapter 9: Endings and New Beginnings

To download a free discussion guide, go to www.emotionallyhealthy.org

THE EMOTIONALLY HEALTHY LEADER

How Transforming Your Inner Life Will Deeply Transform Your Church, Team, And The World

9780310494577

ZONDERVAN®
.com

CHECKLIST | EMOTIONALLY HEALTHY **SPIRITUALITY** COURSE

SESSION #	**EHS BOOK**	**DAY-BY-DAY**	**WORKBOOK**	**DVD (or live)**
1. The Problem of Emotionally Unhealthy Spirituality	☐ Read Chapter 1	☐ Prayerfully read Intro & Week 1	☐ Read Intro and fill out Session 1	☐ Watch Session 1
2. Know Yourself That You May Know God	☐ Read Chapter 2	☐ Prayerfully read Week 2	☐ Fill out Session 2	☐ Watch Session 2
3. Going Back in Order to Go Forward	☐ Read Chapter 3	☐ Prayerfully read Week 3	☐ Fill out Session 3	☐ Watch Session 3
4. Journey through the Wall	☐ Read Chapter 4	☐ Prayerfully read Week 4	☐ Fill out Session 4	☐ Watch Session 4
5. Enlarge Your Soul through Grief and Loss	☐ Read Chapter 5	☐ Prayerfully read Week 5	☐ Fill out Session 5	☐ Watch Session 5
6. Discover the Rhythms of the Daily Office and Sabbath	☐ Read Chapter 6	☐ Prayerfully read Week 6	☐ Fill out Session 6	☐ Watch Session 6
7. Grow into an Emotionally Healthy Adult	☐ Read Chapter 7	☐ Prayerfully read Week 7	☐ Fill out Session 7	☐ Watch Session 7
8. Go the Next Step to Develop a "Rule of Life"	☐ Read Chapter 8	☐ Prayerfully read Week 8	☐ Fill out Session 8	☐ Watch Session 8

Congratulations on completing **The Emotionally Healthy (EH) Spirituality Course**, the first half of The EH Discipleship Courses.

Go to ***emotionallyhealthy.org*** to receive your **Certificate of Completion.**

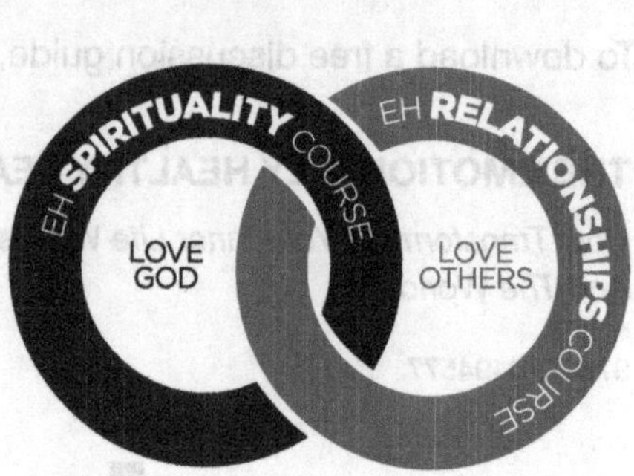